Contemporary Consumption Rituals:

A Research Anthology

MARKETING AND CONSUMER PSYCHOLOGY SERIES
Curtis P. Haugtvedt, Ohio State University
Series Editor

OTNES/LOWREY • Contemporary Consumption Rituals:
A Research Anthology

Contemporary Consumption Rituals:

A Research Anthology

Edited by

Cele C. Otnes
Tina M. Lowrey

Psychology Press
Taylor & Francis Group

New York   London

First published by Lawrence Erlbaum Associates, Inc., Publishers
10 Industrial Avenue
Mahwah, New Jersey 07430

Reprinted 2008 by Psychology Press

Psychology Press
Taylor & Francis Group
27 Church Road
Hove, East Sussex BN3 2FA

Cover design by Kathryn Houghtaling Lacey

Library of Congress Cataloging-in-Publication Data

Contemporary consumption rituals : a research anthology /
    edited by Cele C. Otnes, Tina M. Lowrey.
        p.   cm.
Includes bibliographical references and index.
ISBN 0-8058-4204-7 (cloth : alk. paper)
ISBN 0-8058-4779-0 (pbk. : alk. paper)
1. Consumption (Economics)   I. Otnes, Cele.
II. Lowrey, Tina M.
HC79.C6C678 2003
390—dc21   2003040770
                                                    CIP

Printed in the United States of America
10 9 8 7 6 5 4 3 2 1

To my family, near and far
—C.C.O.

To L. J.
—T.M.L.

Contents

Series Foreword

On a daily basis, people are exposed to thousands of marketing appeals (brand names, logos, advertisements, etc.). Attitudes toward products, brands, companies, and decisions to purchase, use, and dispose of products are common and important activities in our lives.

The Consumer Psychology and Marketing Series focuses on contemporary and long-standing issues relevant to psychology, sociology, anthropology and other social sciences as they relate to consumption activities, the multi-faceted influence of advertising, and the relationships between consumers, companies, and brands. The volumes are meant to serve as a bridge between basic and applied research, providing summaries of existing research findings, noting relevant theoretical frameworks, and identifying new areas of inquiry. The volumes in this series will appeal to advanced undergraduates, graduate students, and faculty in the social sciences interested in learning more about the relationship of their disciplines to the discipline of marketing. The volumes will also appeal to practitioners seeking to identify relevant theories and research methods to address practical problems.

For the first book in the series, Cele Otnes and Tina Lowrey have assembled an impressive list of experts to discuss perspectives on the roles of consumption rituals in the lives of consumers.

—*Curt Haugtvedt*
Series Editor

Contributor Biographies

Eric Arnould is Professor of Marketing at the University of Nebraska–Lincoln despite the fact that he holds a PhD degree in cultural anthropology from the University of Arizona (1982). He has also taught at Odense University, Denmark, the University of South Florida, California State University Long Beach, and the University of Colorado at Denver. From 1975 to 1990, he tried to do less harm than good working on economic development issues in more than a dozen West African nations for governmental and nongovernmental organizations. Since 1990, he has been a full-time academic. His research investigates consumer ritual (Thanksgiving, New Year's, football bowl games, Halloween, inheritance), service relationships (experiential services, commercial friendships, service betrayal), West African marketing channels, and the uses of qualitative data. To his enduring surprise, his work appears in the three major U.S. marketing journals, as well as many other social science periodicals and books. Dr. Arnould speaks French and Hausa and enjoys running, do-it-yourself projects, and being a parent. His dog Daisy loves him.

Carolyn Folkman Curasi is an Assistant Professor of Marketing at the J. Mack Robinson College of Business Administration at Georgia State University. She received her PhD in business administration with a specialization in marketing from the University of South Florida in 1998. She has published in scholarly outlets, including the *Journal of Consumer Research*, the *Journal of Services Marketing, Anthropology Newsletter, Advances in Consumer Research*, the *Quarterly Journal of Electronic Commerce*, the *International Journal of Market Research*, and in the *European Advances in Consumer Research*. Prior to joining the academic community, Dr. Curasi held several executive positions within corporate America.

Sameer Deshpande is a Doctoral Candidate in the School of Journalism and Mass Communication at the University of Wisconsin–Madison, where he also received his master's degree in 1999. He has taught courses in strategic communication, introduction to mass communication and advertising, and pop culture to high school and undergraduate students. His research interests include social marketing, cross-cultural issues, alliances between profit and nonprofit enterprises, and civic participation. A paper on cause-related marketing (coauthored with Jacqueline Hitchon) is forthcoming in *Journalism & Mass Communication Quarterly*. He received his MBA from the Narsee Monjee Institute of Management Studies, Bombay, in 1995 and has 3 years of industry experience in advertising agencies.

Ronald L. Grimes is Chair of the Department of Religion and Culture, Wilfrid Laurier University, Waterloo, Ontario, Canada. He was a founding editor of the *Journal of Ritual Studies* and has been a consultant on ritual for organizations such as the Sundance Institute Playwrights' Lab, the Cranbrook Institute of Science, the Irish World Music Centre, WordBridge, and the A&E Channel. He is author of several books on ritual, including *Ritual Criticism* (University of South Carolina Press, 1990), *Reading, Writing, and Ritualizing* (Pastoral Press, 1993), *Marrying & Burying: Rites of Passage in a Man's Life* (Westview, 1995), *Readings in Ritual Studies* (Prentice-Hall, 1996), and *Deeply into the Bone: Re-Inventing Rites of Passage* (University of California, 2000). In addition to his writing and research on ritual, he teaches courses on religion and the arts, the anthropology of religion, Zen in North America, and indigenous religions. Currently, he is working on a documentary film series on ritual as well as a book on ritual studies and performance theory.

B. Ece İlhan is a Doctoral Candidate in the Faculty of Business Administration at Bilkent University, Turkey. Her research interests include consumption rituals in transition, consumption of history, and the relation between identity, globalization, postmodernity, consumption, and marketing.

Robert V. Kozinets is an Assistant Professor of Marketing at Northwestern University's Kellogg School of Management. An anthropologist by training, he also has extensive consulting experience with over 500 corporations, including IBM, EDS, TV Guide, Mediacom, Interrep, Novartis, and Honda. His teaching and training skills include new product and service development, ethnographic consumer research, and entertainment marketing. His research interests include technology consumption, virtual communities, consumer activism, marketing to subcultures and communities, and media and entertainment marketing. He has written and published articles on *ESPN Zone*, Burning Man, *Star Trek*, the *X-Files*, coffee connoisseurs, Wal-Mart, and themed flagship brand stores for journals such as the *Journal of Consumer Research*, the *Journal of Marketing Research*, *Consumption, Markets and Culture*, the *European Management Journal*, the *Journal of Contemporary Ethnography* and the *Journal of Retailing*.

Tina M. Lowrey is Associate Professor in the Department of Marketing at the University of Texas at San Antonio. She has published articles in the *Journal of*

Consumer Research, Journal of Consumer Psychology, Journal of Advertising, and *Psychology & Marketing,* among others. She has chapters in *New Developments and Approaches in Consumer Behavior Research, Gift Giving: A Research Anthology, Marketing and Consumer Behavior Research in the Public Interest,* and *Gender Issues and Consumer Behavior.* Her main research interests include gift-giving behaviors, ritualistic consumption, and psycholinguistic analyses of advertising texts. She has presented numerous papers on these topics at conferences of the Association for Consumer Research, the Society for Consumer Psychology, the American Marketing Association, the American Academy of Advertising, the International Association for Research in Economic Psychology, the Midwestern Psychological Association, and the International Communication Association. She is a member of the *Psychology & Marketing* editorial board.

Jean-Sébastien Marcoux is Assistant Professor of Marketing at l'Ecole des Hautes Etudes Commerciales, which is affiliated to the University of Montreal. He trained as an anthropologist, and teaches consumer research and material culture studies. His current research interests are consumer support networks, informal economy, and the broader issue of the "second life" of things.

Mary Ann McGrath is Professor of Marketing and the Director of the Master of Science in Integrated Marketing Communication Program at Loyola University, Chicago. She earned her MBA and PhD degrees in marketing from Northwestern University. Her teaching and research special interests include consumer behavior and marketing communications. She has published numerous articles on shopping behavior, the retail setting, gender differences in consumer behavior, gift exchanges, children in the marketing context, and the application of a variety of qualitative methods to consumer research. She has also been a marketing consultant to several major firms and retailers.

Michelle R. Nelson is Assistant Professor in the School of Journalism and Mass Communication at the University of Wisconsin–Madison. Earlier in her career, Nelson taught in the Department of Communication at Emerson College (Boston, MA) and in the Marketing Group at Oxford Brookes University (Oxford, England). She teaches undergraduate courses in strategic communication and graduate courses in qualitative methods. Her research focuses on how culture and gender influence identity/values, communication, and consumer behavior. In addition to her current work on cross-cultural weddings, Nelson has investigated ritualistic consumption related to birthday parties, Christmas shopping, and Valentine's Day. She has published articles in the *Journal of Advertising, Journal of Advertising Research, Journal of Economic Psychology,* and *Journal of Cross-Cultural Psychology.* She received her PhD from the Institute of Communications Research at the University of Illinois in 1997, where she specialized in advertising.

Cele C. Otnes is Associate Professor in the department of Business Administration, the University of Illinois, Urbana–Champaign. She is also a member of the Campus Honors faculty, where she has taught a seminar on contemporary consumer rituals. She teaches courses in retailing, promotions, and consumer behavior at the undergraduate and MBA levels. She was previously a faculty member in the Department of Marketing at Rutgers University and the Department of Advertising at the University of Illinois. Her research focuses on understanding gift giving, as well as consumer behavior during holidays and other major rituals. She is coauthor with Elizabeth H. Pleck of *Cinderella Dreams: The Allure of the Lavish Wedding*, forthcoming from the University of California Press in 2003. She is also coeditor of *Gift Giving* with Richard F. Beltramini. She has published articles on ritualistic consumption in the *Journal of Consumer Research, Journal of Business Research, Journal of the Academy of Marketing Science, Journal of Retailing, Journal of Advertising, Journal of Ritual Studies*, and *Journal of Popular Culture*, among others. She serves on the editorial board of several journals, and is guest editor of a recent special issue of the *Journal of Advertising* that focuses on advertising and consumer culture. She received her PhD in communications from the University of Tennessee in 1990.

Elizabeth H. Pleck is Professor of History and Human Development and Family Studies at the University of Illinois, Urbana–Champaign. Her second historical monograph, *Domestic Tyranny: The Making of Social Policy Against Family Violence* will be reissued by the University of Illinois Press with a new introduction in 2003. She is coauthor with Cele C. Otnes of *Cinderella Dreams: The Allure of the Lavish Wedding*, to be published by the University of California Press in 2003.

Linda L. Price is E.J. Faulkner Professor of Agribusiness and Marketing at the University of Nebraska–Lincoln. She received her PhD in marketing from the University of Texas–Austin in 1983. She has also been on the faculty at the University of South Florida; the University of Colorado, Boulder; the University of California, Irvine; Odense University, Denmark; and the University of Pittsburgh. Dr. Price has published over 50 research papers in areas of marketing and consumer behavior, including leading journals such as *Journal of Consumer Research, Journal of Marketing, Journal of Public Policy and Marketing*, and *Organization Science*. Her research focuses on consumers as emotional, imaginative, and creative agents and on the relational dimensions of consumers' behaviors.

Dennis Rook is Professor of Marketing, Clinical, in the Marshall School of Business at the University of Southern California in Los Angeles. He received his PhD from Northwestern University (1983), where he studied consumer behavior analysis and qualitative research methods. His dissertation, *Consumer Products as Ritual Artifacts*, was chaired by Sidney J. Levy. Dr. Rook's research into impulse buying, ritualized consumption, and projective methods has appeared in various journals, books, and symposia proceedings. Since 1988, he has served on the editorial board of the *Journal of Consumer Research*. In between academic assignments, he worked as a strategic planner at DDB Needham Advertising in Chicago, and as director of qualitative research services at Conway/Milliken & Associates, a Chicago research and consulting firm. In 1999, he edited a compilation of Sidney J. Levy's writings, *Brands, Symbols, Consumers and Research*, and he is currently working on a research methods book, *Let's Pretend: A Handbook of Projective Consumer Research Techniques*. Dr. Rook recently served as program co-chairperson for the 2002 Association for Consumer Research annual conference.

Julie A. Ruth is Assistant Professor of Marketing at the Rutgers University School of Business, Camden. Her research focuses on affect-laden aspects of consumer behavior, including consumer emotions, gift exchange, consumers' relationships with significant others, and consumer response to co-branding marketing strategies such as brand alliances and joint sponsorships. She has published articles on these topics in the *Journal of Consumer Research, Journal of Marketing Research, Journal of Consumer Psychology, Journal of the Academy of Marketing Science,* and *Journal of Business Research*, among others. She serves on the editorial board of the *Journal of Advertising*. She teaches undergraduate and MBA courses in advertising, promotions, and marketing management, and has received numerous teaching awards, including the Rutgers University Provost's Award for Teaching Excellence. She received her PhD from the University of Michigan.

Özlem Sandıkcı is Assistant Professor of Marketing at Bilkent University in Turkey, where she teaches consumer behavior and advertising management courses to MBA and undergraduate business students. Her work addresses various culturally oriented issues in marketing. Her research interests include advertising reception, gender and advertising, consumption culture, and the relation between modernity, postmodernity, globalization, and consumption.

John F. Sherry, Jr. joined the Kellogg Marketing faculty at Northwestern University in 1984. He is an anthropologist (PhD, University of Illinois, 1983) who studies both the sociocultural and symbolic dimensions of consumption, and the cultural ecology of marketing. He has researched, taught, and lectured around the globe. He is a Fellow of the American Anthropological Association as well as the Society for Applied Anthropology. Sherry is a past president of the Association for Consumer Research, and a former associate editor of the *Journal of Consumer Research*. He sits on the editorial boards of four other journals, and is an ad hoc reviewer for a dozen journals in the fields of social science and management. He frequently serves the American Marketing Association as a Doctoral Consortium faculty member and Dissertation Competition Judge. He is an evaluator for the National Science Foundation, the Social Sciences and Humanities Research Council of Canada, and the Marketing Science Institute. He is also a consultant to Fortune 500 companies in foreign and domestic operations. Sherry's work appears in a score of journals (including the *Journal of Consumer Research,* the *Journal of Retailing,* the *Journal of Consumer Psychology,* and the *International Journal of Research in Marketing*), in numerous book chapters, in professional manuals, and proceedings. He has edited *Contemporary Marketing and Consumer Behavior: An Anthropological Sourcebook,* as well as *Servicescapes: The Concept of Place in Contemporary Markets;* he is coeditor of *Advances in Consumer Research,* (Vol. 19). He has won awards for his scholarly work and poetry. Time permitting, he is an avid flatwater paddler, and is still trying to perfect his 15-foot jumpshot.

Wesley Shrum is Professor of Sociology at Louisiana State University, where he has taught since 1982. His primary interests are the sociology of science and technology, with a particular focus on the globalizing effects of technology. He is currently engaged in a long-term study of the effects of the Internet on science in Kenya, Ghana, and India.

Debbie Treise is a Professor in the Department of Advertising at the University of Florida, and is an affiliate faculty member in the College of Natural Resources and Environment. She received her PhD from the University of Tennessee in Communications in 1992. At the University of Florida, she serves as graduate coordinator for the Health/Science Communication master's track. She teaches courses in advertising campaigns and graduate seminars in science/health communication and qualitative research methods. She was named as a University of Florida Research Faculty Fellow (3-year appointment) and has twice received the College Faculty Research Award. She has received over $1.5 million in grants from the National Aeronautics and Space Administration and the Henry J. Kaiser Family Foundation investigating her research area, science and health communication. She has contributed chapters in several books, and articles in *Journal of Advertising, Health Marketing Quarterly, Science Communication, AIDS Education and Prevention, Journal of Mass Media Ethics, Journal of Advertising Education* and *Journalism and Mass Communication Educator.* She serves on the editorial board of Journalism and Mass Communication Educator.

Joyce M. Wolburg is an Associate Professor in the Department of Advertising and Public Relations at Marquette University in Milwaukee, Wisconsin. She received her PhD at the University of Tennessee, Knoxville. Her research has been published in the *Journal of Advertising,* the *Journal of Advertising Research,* the *Journal of Communication, Journal of Consumer Marketing, Alcoholism Treatment Quarterly, Research in Marketing, Journalism and Mass Communication Quarterly,* and *World Communication.* Her research interests include ritual behavior, risk communication, public service announcements, and alcohol/tobacco issues.

Stacy L. Wood is Assistant Professor in the Department of Marketing, Moore School of Business, the University of South Carolina. Her research investigates how consumers change–specifically how consumers adopt innovations, learn about new products, and engage in emerging cultural trends. She has published articles in the *Journal of Consumer Research, Journal of Marketing Research, Journal of Marketing, Journal of Consumer Psychology,* and *Journal of Retailing,* among others. She and her coauthors were the recipients of the 1997 H. Paul Root Award given to the paper appearing in the *Journal of Marketing* that made the most significant contribution to the advancement of marketing practice. She serves as a reviewer for both the *Journal of Consumer Research* and *Journal of Marketing Research,* and as the conference track chair for the Emerging Business and Technology track of the 2003 American Marketing Association Winter Conference. She received her PhD in marketing from the University of Florida in 1998.

David B. Wooten is Assistant Professor of Marketing at the University of Michigan. He was previously on the faculties of the University of Florida and Columbia University. His research interests include consumption rituals, social influences on consumption, and impression management theory. He has published in the *Journal of Consumer Research, Journal of Consumer Psychology,* and *Advances in Consumer Research.* He earned a PhD in marketing from the University of Michigan.

Preface

Cele C. Otnes
University of Illinois, Urbana–Champaign

Tina M. Lowrey
University of Texas at San Antonio

How many consumption rituals have you found yourself engaged in, or have engaged you, in the past few months? As we were preparing this introduction, Cele was looking forward to attending the wedding of a colleague, and had bought a gift, made the necessary beautification appointments, and was following the reception plans with interest. Just 2 weeks before, she had hosted a "Hello Kitty" birthday party for her 8-year-old daughter, complete with the requisite cake and candles, party horns, gifts, birthday song, matching table settings, and goodie bags (which seem to get more elaborate every year). At around the same time, Tina was involved in the emotionally and physically arduous ritual of moving and reestablishing a household (see Marcoux, chap. 12) and in the upcoming months would be socialized with regard to the inner workings of gift giving and other workplace rituals at her new job (see Ruth, chap. 9).

Even during the relatively "down" time of summer (at least for academics), there is no escaping ritual participation. Nor do people necessarily (always) want to escape the family reunions (or even the ones created by commercial interests such as Saturn), birthdays, graduations, weddings, and seasonal holidays that give our lives structure, provide us with a sense of community, and even transform our lives with defining, memorable moments (Driver, 1991). As Rook (1985) demonstrated in his seminal article on ritualistic consumption–and as he echoes in the concluding chapter of this book–the use of products and services in activities that are expressive, symbolic, dramatically scripted, and performed with formality, seriousness, and inner intensity is an exciting and challenging topic through which to study the intersection of consumption, collectivity, and culture.

Rook's (1985) work and the countless others that have been published or presented in consumer behavior outlets notwithstanding, it is unfortunate that whereas marketing scholars have often chosen to integrate the literature on consumer rituals from other disciplines in their own work, for some reason the reverse is not always the case. A few years ago, Cele was compiling a readings packet for an undergraduate honors course on rituals in contemporary culture at the University of Illinois. Sifting through and selecting the material for this course was both gratifying and frustrating at the same time. It was gratifying because many of the best readings were recent articles from her home field of consumer behavior. Articles such as the classic piece on sacred and profane consumption by Belk, Wallendorf, and Sherry (1989), as well as those that explored aspects of more specific rituals (e.g., Sherry's, 1983, often-cited framework for studying gift exchange, and Wallendorf and Arnould's, 1991, piece on Thanksgiving) demonstrated the broad and dynamic nature of the topic of ritualistic consumption, and pointed the way to seminal readings in other areas.

Yet, creating a readings packet for this course was also frustrating because it brought home the point that scholars in other disciplines did not seem aware of the frenetic level of ritual scholarship that was helping to transform consumer behavior from a field traditionally focusing on the internal psychological aspects of search and purchase behavior, to one where understanding the symbolic function of goods and services was an equally legitimate approach. Ironically, many scholars who were hacking their way through this symbolic wilderness in marketing departments had received their original training in some of these more established social science disciplines. Yet it is fair to say that scholars in these other fields were not necessarily recognizing the contribution that this new generation was making, in terms of enhancing the understanding of ritualistic consumption.

It was the experience of compiling that readings packet, as well as our own interaction with scholars in other disciplines, that motivated the creation of this interdisciplinary anthology on consumption rituals. The scholars in this book reside in departments of communications, history, marketing or business administration, religious studies, and sociology. More of them do claim the field of consumer behavior as their home, but that is not surprising, given our own backgrounds and circles of scholarship in which we typically travel. Yet even within the marketing scholars, there is quite a bit of diversity. Some are anthropologists who teach in marketing programs. A few studied under the pioneer of the study of symbolic consumption in the marketing field, Sidney J. Levy, himself a psychologist. What they all have in common is the recognition that understanding why and how consumers imbue goods and services with meaning during rituals is a fascinating and seemingly never-ending research well from which to draw.

In short, perhaps no other area of study within the social sciences demonstrates the fuzziness of disciplinary boundaries like that of ritualistic consumption. In this volume, a religious studies scholar talks about the media representation of ritual, communication scholars discuss the transformational aspects of rituals surrounding alcohol consumption, a marketing scholar demonstrates the relevance of organizational behavior theory to understanding gift-giving rituals in the workplace, and an historian describes how the marketing of Kwanzaa was integral to its successful adoption. And so it goes.

This collection also follows on the heels of a fairly extensive stream of booklength treatments of ritual, all of which continue to demonstrate the interest that the topic holds for scholars in many disciplines. Recent contributions by historians include *The Battle for Christmas* (Nissenbaum, 1997), *Celebrating the Family* (Pleck, 2000), and *A World of Their Own Making* (Gillis, 1996). From anthropology, there is Yan's (1996) booklength treatment on gift exchange in rural China; from sociology, there is Carrier's (1995) discussion of the difference between gifts and commodities; and, as this book was being prepared for production, Lawrence Erlbaum Associates published *The Wedding as Text*, an examination of how cross-cultural weddings contribute to identity, by Leeds-Hurwitz (2002). Moreover, several edited volumes have been published that typically explore aspects of one ritual, such as the anthology on Christmas that was edited by Miller (1993) and one on gifts as well (Otnes & Beltramini, 1996). By both enhancing and supplementing these longer works, we hope to provide readers with a sourcebook that demonstrates the depth and diversity of scholarship in the area of contemporary ritual studies.

We have organized these submissions into five broad topics: consumer rituals and the media, holidays and consumption, wedding rituals across cultures, gift exchange, and "pushing boundaries" (e.g., new consumption rituals). These represent many of the areas that interest contemporary scholars of ritual. Part I, "Consumer Rituals and The Media," contains two chapters. The first is "Drinking Rituals Among the Heaviest Drinkers: College Student Binge Drinkers and Alcoholics" by Joyce Wolburg (Marquette University) and Deborah M. Treise (University of Florida). This chapter examines the commonalities of ritualized drinking behavior that appear in multiple published studies pertaining to two groups prone to alcohol abuse—college students who engage in binge drinking and alcoholics. The authors analyze these behaviors by applying both structural and functional frameworks for understanding ritual. They discuss strategies recommended for treatment that recognize the ritualistic nature of consuming this product.

In "Consuming Ritual: A&E's *Sacred Rites and Rituals*," Ronald L. Grimes (Wilfred Laurier University) reflects on his experience as a scholarly advisor in the creation of a program by the Arts and Entertainment network that continues to air. Grimes discusses both the rites depicted by the program and the ritualization processes surrounding its production. He examines the choices of rituals included, the criteria used by producers that result in an inaccurate representation of the potential scope of ritual behavior, the analysis of the meaning of ritual symbols in the program, and the tacit racism and sexism that pervade it. He concludes by comparing the "tourist aesthetic" (or television version) of ritual to the "contemplative aesthetic," or scholarly posture toward the subject.

Part II, "Holidays and Consumption," contains four chapters. Chapter 3, "Ceremonial Disrobement and Moral Choice: Consumption Rituals at Mardi Gras" by Wesley Shrum, Jr. (Louisiana State University), discusses the development and structure of a new deviant consumption ritual of public disrobement within the context of New Orleans' French Quarter at Mardi Gras. Shrum argues that deviance in a sacred context requires legitimating symbols that can be adapted from preexisting ritual practices and results in the innovation of new ritual paradigms. Public disrobement is examined in terms of cultural codes involving market relations, gender, and hierarchy.

Chapter 4, "Kwanzaa: The Making of a Black Nationalist Tradition 1966–1990," by Elizabeth H. Pleck (University of Illinois at Urbana–Champaign), explores the emergence of a new holiday estimated to now be celebrated by one in seven African Americans. She describes the ways Kwanzaa, which was originally designed to resemble the rituals of an African harvest festival, was transformed from a critique of capitalism to one that was successful because it was commercialized to include such elements as shopping, the sending of cards, gift giving, and home decorating.

While both Mardi Gras and Kwanzaa seem to involve expanding boundaries, Chapter 5, "The Evolution, Transformation, and Demise of a Ritual: The Case of May Day" by Mary Ann McGrath (Loyola University), traces the demise of the holiday in the United States. McGrath discusses the evolution of May Day from its roots as a pre-Christian celebration of spring and fertility to its more recent role as an international day honoring labor, but points out that the celebration of any part of this historical continuum on the first day of May has virtually disappeared within the United States. McGrath discusses the reasons for the disappearance of the holiday in this country.

Chapter 6, "Consumer Fairy Tales of the Perfect Christmas: Villains and Other *Dramatis Personae*" by Tina M. Lowrey (University of Texas at San Antonio) and Cele C. Otnes (University of Illinois at Urbana–Champaign), argues that consumers' experiences while shopping for Christmas gifts reveal the participation of most of the essential characters encountered in the literary genre of the fairy tale. Drawing on data collected with the same informants over a 7-year period, they describe how the *dramatis personae* that Propp (1928/1970) claimed are found in literary fairy tales also inhabit and influence their informants' gift-buying experiences.

Part III offers two chapters that focus on different aspects of one ritual–the wedding. Chapter 7, "Love Without Borders: An Examination of Cross-Cultural Wedding Rituals," by Michelle R. Nelson and Sameer Deshpande (both of the University of Wisconsin–Madison), argues that increased mobility and the globalization of world cultures have contributed to the growing number of interracial, interethnic, and interreligious marriages. Using introspection, participant observation, and in-depth interviews of a dozen couples, this chapter examines the wedding ritual from the perspective of bicultural couples. Processes of communication, negotiation, and compromise are explored as couples select and combine cultural and traditional artifacts and scripts for their weddings. Questions of identity as well as family influences are also considered.

Chapter 8, "Dowry: A Cherished Possession or an Old-Fashioned Tradition in a Modernizing Society?," by Özlem Sandıckı and B. Ece İlhan (Bilkent University), demonstrates that as an important rite of passage for many women, the wedding involves a rich palette of objects, roles, and behaviors. In Turkey, dowry is a very important part of the wedding ritual, representing the transition from childhood to adulthood as well as the parental support and confirmation of the wedding. The authors explore how the meanings and practices associated with dowry change over time and over social space, through life history analyses of women from two different sociocultural groups in Turkey.

Part IV includes chapters that explore gift exchange. In Chapter 9, "Gift Exchange Rituals in the Workplace: A Social Roles Interpretation," Julie A. Ruth (Rutgers University) argues that although research on gift exchange in the workplace has examined gifts between firms as a means of achieving business objectives, omitted from such inquiry has been gift giving among coworkers, marking work-related holidays such as Secretaries' or Bosses' Day. Gifts among coworkers can be distinguished from those among friends and family because of the additional pressure on givers and recipients in the workplace to carry out work roles. Ruth examines the social roles that emerge during coworker gifting, providing insight into the generalizability of consumer gift-exchange theories, as well as the dynamics of consumers-as-coworkers balancing rituals, relationships, and organizational culture and roles.

In Chapter 10, "In the Spotlight: The Drama of Gift Reception," David B. Wooten (University of Michigan) and Stacey L. Wood (University of South Carolina) employ dramaturgical analysis to illustrate the importance and difficulty of the recipient's role within the gift exchange process. The authors dissect the gift exchange ritual in accordance with the elements of a theatrical performance, from initial stage fright (i.e., recipients' anticipated anxiety) to the final encore (i.e., the role of thank-you cards). They discuss the routine verbal elements and the spontaneous nonverbal cues that make or break these performances. In addition, they contrast the performances of veteran actors (i.e., adults) with those of ingenues (i.e., children).

A different kind of gifting process is explored in Chapter 11, "Ritual Desire and Ritual Development: An Examination of Family Heirlooms in Contemporary North American Households," by Carolyn Folkman Curasi (Georgia Tech University), Eric J. Arnould, and Linda L. Price (both of the University of Nebraska). The authors focus especially on the intergenerational transfers of special and inherited possessions. They draw attention to consumers' longing for ritual, the behavioral latitude that ritual can absorb, and the characteristic *bricolage* through which people compose ritual activity. Contemporary family rituals are often an elective *bricolage* of new and borrowed rituals. The authors argue that inherited possession family rituals are performed in narrow and shallow, loosely structured groups that combine vertical and horizontal relationships.

Finally, Part V, "Pushing the Boundary of Ritual," contains discussions of new and emergent rituals in contemporary consumer culture. Chapter 12, "Moving on to Something Else: The Social Relations of Women During Separation," by Jean-Sebastien Marcoux (Haute Ecole Commerciale, Montreal) presents the results of an ethnography conducted in Montreal, Canada, between September 1997 and July 1999. By accompanying his informants throughout the entire process of moving, from preparation to resettling, Marcoux reveals that women often use the changes in residence and the sorting out processes tantamount to such changes to define their material environment and redefine themselves as subjects. As such, moving appears to be a critical ritual governed by a symbolic logic of order.

Chapter 13, "Sacred Iconography in Secular Space: Altars, Alters, and Alterity at the Burning Man Project," by John F. Sherry, Jr. and Robert V. Kozinets (both of Northwestern University), is a photo essay focusing on the transformational power of altars discovered through a consumer ethnography of the Burning Man project in 1999 and 2000. The Burning Man project is a utopian celebration and art festival, which began in 1985 in San Francisco, California. The resulting data reveal a rich and varied use of altars in consumption and anticonsumption contexts. With emphasis on its photographs, this chapter returns to the visual and attempts to address concerns raised in the important Crisis of Representation Critiques.

In the afterword of this book, Dennis Rook (University of Southern California), whose award-winning 1985 article in the *Journal of Consumer Research* brought the topic of ritualistic consumption to the attention of scholars in marketing and consumer behavior, reflects on the contents of these chapters, and on the current state of scholarship pertaining to ritualistic consumption.

ACKNOWLEDGMENTS

We would like to thank all of the contributors to this volume whose work is described here, whose dedication and diligence helped us compile and edit this book in a smooth and timely fashion. We would also like to thank Elizabeth Hirschman, L. J. Shrum, and the anonymous reviewers for their comments on the book prospectus, and our editor, Anne Duffy of Lawrence Erlbaum Associates, who has been helpful all through the process. Thanks also to Marianna Vertullo, Kristin Duch, and the rest of the production team at Lawrence Erlbaum Associates. We are also grateful to Kyoungmi Lee and Linda Tuncay, who served as research assistants on this book at the University of Illinois, and the faculty and staff at that university, Rider University, and the University of Texas at San Antonio, who provided support. We hope readers will find this book beneficial and stimulating, and that those who pursue scholarship in this area find it useful in considering ways to further broaden our understanding of ritualistic consumption.

REFERENCES

Belk, R., Wallendorf, M., & Sherry, J., Jr. (1989). The sacred and profane in consumer behavior: Theodicy on the Odyssey. *Journal of Consumer Research, 16*(June), 1–38.

Carrier, J. (1995). *Gifts and commodities: Exchange and Western capitalism since 1700*, London: Routledge.

Driver, T. (1991). *The magic of ritual.* New York: HarperCollins.

Gillis, J. (1996). *A world of their own making: Myth, ritual and the quest for family values.* New York: Basic Books.

Leeds-Hurwitz, W. (2002). *The wedding as text.* Hillsdale, NJ: Lawrence Erlbaum Associates.

Miller, D. (1993). *Unwrapping Christmas.* Oxford, England: Clarendon.

Nissenbaum, S. (1997). *The battle for Christmas.* New York: Knopf.

Otnes, C., & Beltramini, R. (Eds.). (1996). *Gift giving: A research anthology.* Bowling Green, OH: Popular Press.

Pleck, E. (2000). *Celebrating the family: Ethnicity, consumer culture, and family rituals.* Cambridge, MA: Harvard University Press.

Propp, V. (1970). *Morphology of the folktale* (L. Scott, Trans.). Austin, TX: University of Texas Press. (Original work published 1928)

Rook, D. (1985) The ritual dimension of consumer behavior. *Journal of Consumer Research, 12*(December), 252–264.

Sherry, J., Jr. (1983). Gift giving in anthropological perspective. *Journal of Consumer Research, 10*(September), 157–168.

Wallendorf, M., & Arnould, E. J. (1991, June), "We gather together:" Consumption rituals of Thanksgiving day. *Journal of Consumer Research, 18*, 13–31.

Yan, Y. (1996). *The flow of gifts: Reciprocity and social networks in a Chinese village.* Stanford, CA: Stanford University Press.

Part I

Consumer Rituals and the Media

1

Drinking Rituals Among the Heaviest Drinkers: College Student Binge Drinkers and Alcoholics

Joyce M. Wolburg
Marquette University

Debbie Treise
University of Florida

> I have watched the people I love most lose everything to drugs and alcohol, and yet I still drink in excess.... About a year ago, we were a family ravaged by addiction and on the brink of disaster.... So why, after all the suffering ... do I continue to drink in excess, often to the point of alcoholism myself? The answer: I'm young, I'll live forever, and it will never happen to me. (Wolburg, 2001, p. 29)

This quote reflects the questions that heavy drinkers ask themselves during moments of introspection, as well as the glib denial of the problem and its consequences. Considering the risks that drinkers take, the question—"Why do I continue to drink in excess?"—baffles not only the drinkers themselves, but also many university administrators, psychologists, and developers of public service announcements (PSAs).

To find some answers to the question of why people drink, this chapter examines the ritualized drinking behavior as reported across multiple published studies. In particular, it examines the behavior of two important groups, college student binge drinkers and alcoholics, who "literally keep the industry afloat" (Jacobson & Mazur, 1995). Jacobson and Mazur estimated that members of these two groups make up the 10% of the adult population who drink about 60% of all alcohol consumed (p. 165).

Defining the two groups presents a set of challenges in itself. Binge drinkers are traditionally defined by the amount of consumption, whereas alcoholics are defined by the amount of dependence on alcohol. A team of Harvard researchers defined binge drinkers as men who drink five or more drinks at a single sitting and women who drink four, regardless of dependence on alcohol or level of impairment (Wechsler, Moeykens, Davenport, Castillo, & Hansen, 1995). In contrast, the National Institute on Alcohol Abuse and Alcoholism uses the term *alcoholic* to specify alcohol dependence regardless of consumption level, although it is typically excessive (NIAAA Report, 2002). The person who is alcohol dependent experiences cravings for alcohol; loss of control over amount of consumption; physical dependence, which includes withdrawal symptoms when alcohol use is stopped; and greater tolerance for alcohol, which requires greater amounts of alcohol to "get high." The NIAAA distinguishes between those who are alcohol dependent and those who merely abuse alcohol. It defines alcohol abuse as a recurring pattern of heavy alcohol intake that results in one of the following situations within a 12-month period: failure to fulfill major responsibilities; drinking in situations that are physically dangerous, such as driving; having recurring alcohol-related legal problems, such as being arrested; and continued drinking despite relationship problems. For this chapter, the term *alcoholic* refers to those who are dependent on alcohol.

The chapter asks two research questions:

1. What insights are gained for understanding the meaning of drinking among the heaviest drinkers (binge drinkers and alcoholics) by examining alcohol consumption from a ritual behavior perspective?
2. How can these insights be incorporated into treatment strategies and PSAs?

The first research question is important because the ritual behavior perspective offers different insights into excessive alcohol consumption than other perspectives. It provides a way of making sense of this seemingly inexplicable behavior, which is important because many people, moderate drinkers and nondrinkers in particular, have difficulty understanding why drinkers put themselves and others at such risk. In the case of alcoholics, the repetitive, self-destructive behavior can be partially attributed to the addictive nature of alcohol. However, college students have had less time to become dependent on alcohol. Their abuse of alcohol is more likely to be by choice than addiction.

Excessive drinking among college students would be easier to understand if binge drinkers consisted only of students with the lowest GPAs. Although one of the consequences of excessive drinking is poor academic performance (Presley, Meilman, & Lyerla, 1993), many binge drinkers are intelligent students with high GPAs. Parents, school administrators, faculty members, and others who promote responsible drinking are often frustrated and dismayed by the behavior of intelligent students who should "know better." The ritual behavior perspective offers insights into the benefits and the meaning of drinking that go beyond the intoxicating effects of alcohol.

The second question addresses applications of the insights gained through the first question. Because PSA developers typically create messages aimed at the general population, they have not attempted to promote abstinence but instead encourage "responsible drinking." Most of these messages call for drinking in moderation or behavior modifications associated with drinking (e.g., designating a driver). In contrast, those who treat alcoholics typically set a goal of abstinence rather than drinking in moderation.

This question also addresses the need for message strategies that treatment providers and PSA developers can utilize. Past efforts often have tried to communicate risk through fear appeals in the logical hope that drinkers will take heed and modify their behavior (LaTour & Rotfeld, 1997). However, because not all drinkers are fearful, nor do they necessarily behave rationally, the strategy has been less effective than expected. This in turn has prompted a search for other approaches and message strategies to curb drinking. Because the ritual approach allows us to identify elements of drinking behavior that constitute ritual enactment and to understand the functional benefits of the drinking ritual, we can get past a superficial understanding of the behavior and look at what drinking means to the participants.

Before attempting to answer the research questions, we briefly examine the great toll alcohol takes on society.

SCOPE OF THE PROBLEM

The problems and costs that alcohol consumption present in the United States are overwhelming. Alcohol misuse has been associated with numerous behavior problems, including domestic violence, rapes, child abuse, fires, accidents, and falls, and alcohol consumption has been associated with diseases such as cancer, cirrhosis of the liver, and heart disease (U.S. Department of Health and Human Services, 2000). The estimated "cost of illness" of alcohol abuse in the United States was $185 billion in 1998, up from $148 billion in 1992 (Harwood, Fountain, & Livermore, 1998). Diminished productivity topped the list of losses from alcohol-related illnesses at $87.6 billion in 1998. The NIAAA (2002) estimated that nearly 14 million Americans abuse alcohol or are alcoholics, with several million more engaging in risky drinking that could lead to alcohol abuse or dependency.

The most sobering statistics are those obtained for motor vehicle accidents among young people. Although fatalities for youth alcohol-related accidents have fallen 5% since 1995, the figures remain quite alarming:

- In 1999, 2,238 youth (ages 15–20) died in alcohol-related crashes—or 35.1% of their total traffic fatalities.

18- 20-year-old group, 41.7% of traffic fatalities were alcohol re-
, as compared to 37.9% for the total population (National Highway
Traffic and Safety Administration, 1999).

In April 2002, the NIAAA released a report that outlined the problem of
high-risk drinking on U.S. college and university campuses. The institute made the
following claims:

- Nearly 1,400 students die from alcohol-related unintentional injuries including motor vehicle crashes.
- More than 500,000 students are unintentionally injured while under the
  influence.
- More than 600,000 students are assaulted by another student who has
  been drinking.
- More than 70,000 students are victims of alcohol-related sexual assault
  or date rape.
- More than 400,000 students had unprotected sex, and more than
  100,000 report they were too intoxicated to know if sex was consensual.
- Between 1.2% and 1.5% said they tried to commit suicide due to drinking or drug use (NIAAA Report, 2002).

Despite well-funded, comprehensive campaigns targeted to college-age
binge drinkers, the national percentage of students who binge drink has held
steady at 44% from 1993 to 1999 (Wechsler, Kelley, Weitzman, San Giovanni, &
Seibring, 2000). For example, a 5-year, $770,000 campaign to curb binge drinking
at the University of Delaware resulted in only a 3% drop (from 62% to 59%) in the
number of students who binge drink (O'Sullivan, 2001).

The Center for Science in the Public Interest reported that college students
spend $5.5 billion on alcohol—more than that spent on books, soft drinks, and
other nonalcoholic drinks combined—and more college students are expected to
die from alcohol-related causes than those who will later receive master's and doc-
torate degrees combined (Had Enough Campaign, 2001)

RITUAL MODELS

According to Rook (1985), ritual behavior involves four tangible components: ritual artifacts, a ritual script, ritual performance roles, and a ritual audience. Alcohol
consumption easily fits Rook's model of ritual behavior because the act requires an
artifact (the alcohol itself, as well as the proper clothes and accoutrements), a
script (rules that specify who can and cannot drink legally, when drinking can oc-

cur, where it should occur, transportation arrangements to and from places where drinking will occur), a performance role (how to drink, how much to drink, how to behave while drinking), and an audience (peers, bartenders, campus personnel).

While Rook (1985) focused on the structural elements of the ritual, Driver (1991) focused on the needs that are satisfied through ritual behavior and identified the functional elements. Driver's functional model names three "social gifts" of ritual that provide: order in society, a sense of community, and transformation. Order is achieved because routines are strongly established, which are not only comforting in themselves, but also give participants the security that their behavior is enacted correctly. Community is established because ritual not only brings people together in close physical proximity but also bonds them emotionally. Finally, transformation occurs because "social life in general ... requires ceremonies and rites, those quasi-dramatic enactments that define people's relationships and also make possible their transformation as part of the social dynamic.... These events change things, and do so by the technique of ritual—that is, by magic" (p. 169).

Clearly, when the drinking ritual is examined within Driver's functional model, evidence for the three social gifts easily emerges. The discussion returns here to the first research question (What insights are gained for understanding the meaning of drinking among the heaviest drinkers by examining alcohol consumption from a ritual behavior perspective?) and examines behavior guided by the functions of order, community, and transformation.

RITUAL BEHAVIOR AMONG COLLEGE STUDENT BINGE DRINKERS AND ALCOHOLICS

To consider the evidence for Driver's functionally based model, we examined five studies, all of which used qualitative research and directly or indirectly addressed ritual functions. (See the Appendix for a detailed account of methodology for each study.) Three studies focused on the drinking behavior of college students (Parker, 1998; Treise, Wolburg, & Otnes, 1999; Wolburg, 2001) and two addressed the drinking patterns of alcoholics (Treise, Taylor, & Wells, 1994; Wolburg, Hovland, & Hopson, 1999). To date, the most comprehensive investigation of college student drinking from a ritual perspective is by Treise et al. (1999). The researchers organized the data around Driver's (1991) functionally based model to provide an in-depth look at binge drinking at two large universities in the Southeast—one with 46,000 students and the other with 25,000. Both universities rank within the top 10 "party schools" in the United States in 2001 (Mansfield, 2001). The study first addressed order.

Order

Treise and her colleagues (1999) observed two primary ways that their participants found order in the drinking ritual. The first is temporal. For example, nearly all participants had specific days set aside for drinking—usually Friday nights and Saturdays—although many students also drank on Thursday nights because Friday class loads are usually light. Several participants also planned their day around drinking. Drinking decisions often dictated how to dress, what classes to attend, which ones to cut, what assignments to complete, and what to eat beforehand. Students who want to stay in control eat before drinking and those who want to "get drunk" choose not to eat.

In a study at a private university of 10,000 students in the Midwest, Wolburg (2001) found that the meaning of the drinking ritual can be significant enough to affect college students' perception of risk. The strength of the ordering function is evident in this participant's comment: "Some start to drink right after the last class on Friday. You go to lunch at noon and have about six beers, go back home, have some more from about 3 p.m. 'till 5 p.m. Then your friends come over and you keep drinking until 10 p.m. Then you go to a bar or party" (Student #35, p. 32).

Holidays—such as St. Patrick's Day, Halloween, and, more recently, Cinco de Mayo—have become heavy drinking occasions for students. Sporting events and fraternity parties are other drinking-related events that require careful planning. Students structure their drinking depending on the timing of the event. For example, one female student explained that on days when the university football games are scheduled at night, drinking starts by mid-afternoon, but when the game is in the afternoon, drinking starts by late morning. Drinking often continues throughout the game, despite the fact that it is prohibited (Treise et al., 1999).

Order was not only maintained by drinking on certain days and times, but also by drinking with the same people, even sitting in the same place in the same bar. For many, the nightly bar specials determined the time and place they drank. One participant from the study drank until midnight every Thursday at a bar that promoted "Ladies Night" with free admission until midnight. After midnight, she went to another bar to take advantage of a different special. Most students found enough specials from competing bars to plan where to drink every night of the week. The most frequent quitting time for the night was when the bar closed.

One last type of temporal ordering goes beyond the occasion, the time of day, and the day of the week. Instead, it reflects an attitude that the college years are the best time of life for drinking. Wolburg (2001) found that students reflect back on high school as a time when authority figures restricted their access to alcohol. After graduation from college, they expect the responsibilities of the job to get in the way of heavy drinking. Comparatively speaking, the college years are the best time in their lives to drink, and many are determined to make the most of the opportunity.

The second type of ordering function is spatial. Driver (1991, p. 79) observed that ritual places are very meaningful; they help individuals "construct alternative worlds ... different from ordinary life ... in the cracks between the mapped regions of what we like to call "the real world.'" This function was observed in the selection of different bars by different types of students. Some bars were for "geeks," whereas more alternative places drew the "artsy, eccentric" people. According to Treise et al. (1999), "People tend to go where they know their friends are going to be versus the places they don't know anyone. It is very much a pattern ... You see the same people every weekend and every night" (p. 23).

The choice of place is also somewhat determined by the age of the drinkers. The underage crowd often chooses bars that do not "card hard," but after turning 21, many prefer the more restrictive bars (Treise et al., 1999; Wolburg, 2001). Some underage students go to bars hoping that a legal drinker will order drinks for them.

Wolburg (2001) noted that drinking at house parties requires a different performance role than drinking at bars. Age is not monitored, which means that IDs are not required. Although it is illegal, most hosts charge admission and provide a cup that can be refilled an unlimited number of times. Compared to the bar scene, the party setting also facilitates a wider variety of drinking games, which orders the way alcohol is consumed. The games vary somewhat from group to group (e.g., doing keg stands, drinking Jell-O shots made with vodka), but they typically result in heavy consumption.

Parker (1998) applied a meaning-based, reader-response model of advertising and examined how life experiences and alcohol-related myths in beer ads influence the interpretation of ads among college students. Her data provided an interesting twist on the function of order and demonstrated that alcohol can both create and destroy order. One participant's life theme centered on her need to maintain control (order) over her life and her inability to tolerate lack of control. In theory the ordering function of the drinking ritual might have appealed to her, but this was not the case. She rejected the type of order that the drinking situation provided because it ultimately lead to loss of control, which is a type of ritual transformation that she found unacceptable. Her response to four Miller TV ads was that the advertiser was trying to convey an image of order and control—that beer makes the party and at parties everything is under control. However, she found the image of control to be false: "They wanted you to see the party. Everyone looks like they're having fun. When you go to a party, someone is out of control or doing something stupid. Everything here [in the ad] is under control" (Kim, p. 104).

Alcoholics, the second group of heavy drinkers, also experience order as part of the drinking ritual. Treise et al. and Wells (1994) sought to understand the meaning of alcoholic-beverage advertising to recovering alcoholics and found that advertising presents several triggers to further drinking, many of which tap into ritual functions.

For example, several recovering alcoholics referred to established drinking routines that they associated with certain times and activities, which advertising and media images helped them recall. One participant said, "When I see Crown Royal billboards, they bring back old memories, things I *always* did. I remember the times when I was fishing. I always took three gallons of that stuff" (P12, p. 24).

Similarly, other participants suggested that media images of certain activities brought back associations with previous routines. One said, "If I saw 15 inches of snow [in a commercial] I think that I'm normally skiing at that time of year, and I always did drink a lot with that." Another participant summed up the order dimension with the statement about certain commercials, "Sports equals beer," and that is the association that forever will be made for these participants between drinking and sports.

A study by Wolburg et al. (1999) adds indirect evidence for ritual meaning among alcoholics. The researchers examined the messages in beer ads for themes that appear particularly relevant to alcoholics, who are regarded as the heaviest of the heavy drinkers. These themes were identified through earlier research by Hopson (1993), who explicated four problematic modes of experience among recovering alcoholics. Hopson found that the addictive experience is characterized by intense feelings for which language is inadequate, a disruption in the experience of the passage of time, alienation from oneself and others, and lack of sense of agency, self-efficacy, or capacity for self-regulation. Wolburg et al. (1999) found strong support that beer ads are encoded with elements related to all of the experience modes of alcoholics.

The findings also support Driver's (1991) three "social gifts" in a number of ways. For example, the frequent references to time in ads, especially the implications that product usage can make time move at a more rapid pace or make the passage of time a pleasant experience, convey the need for order among the target market. This is relevant when considering that the disruption in the passage of time that alcoholics experience is usually characterized by the feeling that time drags or passes slowly. Examples of ads with time references include Coors Light ads, which used a slogan of "Keep on Movin," and Miller ads, which incorporated time in its long-standing "Miller Time" campaign. An ad from the sample tells viewers:

> Song: Time is on my side. Yes it is. Time is on my side. Yes it is.
>
> VO: The time is 5:01. The beer is Miller High Life. And the reason is clear. When the time is your own, it must be Miller Time ... (p. 190)

Michelob has also used a long-standing campaign with a variety of time-related slogans including "The night belongs to Michelob," "Weekends were made for Michelob," and "Some days are better than others." A sample ad with the "Some days" message asks viewers:

> VO: Did you ever have one of those days that starts off with a bang?
>
> When things take a turn for the best? When you practically walk on water?
>
> Michelob salutes the PGA golfers and golfers everywhere, and those special moments that make some days better than others. (p. 191)

Several ads use space metaphorically to suggest a spatial ordering function. Miller Genuine Draft ads told viewers, "The world is a very cool place; get out of the old and into the cold," and Busch beer used cowboy imagery in a series of ads encouraging users to go where "the land is pure, unchained and free, and there's no place that I'd rather be. Come on, come on head for the mountains of Busch Beer" (p. 191). The imagery used to signify the change in place can also help viewers feel transformed.

In summary, we find strong evidence for the function of order from the drinking ritual among both college students and alcoholics.

Community

Drinking together unites people emotionally and establishes a bond between them. As a "social lubricant," many people find that it puts them at ease, intensifies the relationship, and enhances the experience. Treise et al. (1999) found that even as high school students, their participants looked forward to the camaraderie that would come with being a college student in the drinking scene.

Wolburg's (2001) participants also spoke to the community function and the immediate benefits of fitting in. One student said, "When you go to college, you realize that alcohol is the one thing that you probably have in common with all these strangers around you. It almost makes sense to drink—aside from the fact that it is illegal … and dangerous" (Student #42, p. 32).

Wolburg's participants noted that the need for bonding is especially true of freshmen, many of whom have just left a high school environment where they feel accepted by friends, only to come to a new city where they are among strangers and feel isolated. Drinking provides such a strong opportunity for bonding that it is difficult to resist, particularly when saying no to drinking risks social alienation. One of Parker's (1998) participants reflected this feeling with the comment that "I feel like an outsider if I don't drink" (Chas, p. 108).

Certain performance roles (Rook, 1985) are natural outcomes of the community function. One is the designated driver or caretaker, which has been promoted through years of public service announcements. In theory it establishes a role for the nondrinker, but in practice many are reluctant to deprive themselves of the meaning that the ritual provides. Some designated drivers do not abstain; they merely drink less than they would otherwise.

Because many bars and parties are within walking distance from campus residence halls, many students entirely avoid the drinking and driving dilemma. The caretaker, or "babysitter," is the logical evolution of the designated driver role for occasions when driving is not required. Typically, this role requires overseeing the safety of members of the group—making sure that individuals do not leave the party with a stranger, or walking them home at the end of the night. On the surface, the tactic of designating a caretaker is a logical way to decrease the risks involved; however, the benefits are mixed. Growing concerns exist that students in groups with caretakers drink more than they would have otherwise because they know that someone else is responsible for their safety (Wolburg, 2001).

Treise et al. (1999) found that some students did not participate in either the designated driver or caretaker role because they simply did not care or did not want to think about it. Often these students had no recollection of how they got home; instead of being concerned for their safety, they bragged about their accomplishment. One female participant who showed no concern for danger explained, "There have been several times when I blacked out and I don't remember a whole lot. There were days when I asked someone how I got home. When I woke up the next day, I never felt like I was in danger—even with the influence of a lot of alcohol" (p. 24).

To maintain the sense of community, participants found it important to drink according to the rules established by the drinking ritual. Not only did they feel compelled to drink in the prescribed way and in the prescribed amount, they appeared to exert pressure on others to do so as well. None of the participants felt they would be openly criticized for not drinking, yet they could not bring themselves to risk being different, standing out, missing their turn to buy drinks, or missing out in general (Treise et al., 1999). The ritual seemed to offer very little latitude for deviating from what constitutes acceptable drinking behavior. Certainly, not drinking was not an option. One female participant explained:

> I've tried several times not to drink, but it's really hard out in the social crowd not to. It doesn't really make sense.... No one I know really enjoys the taste.... So if I'm not wanting to get drunk, there is no purpose to drink. But there is that pressure to drink. I mean if you're out on a Friday night, I guess I'm going to drink. I mean, when you're surrounded by it, it's just the thing to do. (p. 26)

The community function was also quite apparent for the recovering alcoholics in the Treise et al. (1994) study, because not only did "sports equal beer" as mentioned in the previous section, but sports were also associated with good times and friends. Several participants cited the long-running Miller beer commercials and slogan: "It doesn't get any better than this." They believed that the typical male-bonding activities being depicted (fishing, hunting, etc.) in the commercials "give the feeling that the beer is what's making it happen." Many of these participants were troubled by the qualities of commercials that most closely mirrored their own drinking situations with their friends, and clearly they missed these activities:

> Stroh's beer has the people playing volleyball on the beach and everyone's having a good time. (P9, p. 133)

> Everything and everyone revolves around the food and alcohol. (P4, p. 133)

> It (advertising) makes me miss the activities surrounding it ... yeah, the good times ... the drinking ... the unity, so to speak, of the activities of the group ... the energy you get from that. (P8, p. 134)

Advertising sometimes reminds alcoholics of their own alienation from others. One participant said, "I've always wanted to fit in so bad, the commercials remind me of that sometimes.... The camaraderie looked so inviting" (P14, p. 134).

Interestingly, for the alcoholic in recovery, alcoholic beverage advertising oftentimes can make the loss of community acute. For example, one participant said, "It [advertising] bothers me. I feel uncomfortable. I feel like I've lost something and that I can't be like that" (P16, p. 134). Another recovering alcoholic echoed that belief and said, "That's what the [alcoholic beverage] ads make me feel—lonely—that I want the good times again" (P10, p. 134). Thus, the drinking ritual both creates and destroys community for the drinker who becomes an alcoholic.

The community function is also supported by Wolburg et al. (1999) in their investigation of elements in ads related to the alcoholic's sense of interpersonal alienation. In particular, the researchers observed that the majority of beer ads presented the drinker in social settings and utilized strong appeals to affiliation. Although this may be somewhat appealing to all drinkers, it may hold special promise to the person who feels alienated or isolated from others and still holds to the belief that alcohol can make their life different.

The two most common types of interaction involved friendship and sexual attraction. A humorous "buddy" ad featuring two anthropomorphic bears ends with a recommendation to drink "Molson—of Canada. Because good friends deserve a great beer" (p. 192).

Other evidence of the community function in beer advertising comes from a Budweiser ad:

> Beer is about friendship. It's about making friends. It's about relationships. It's about going out and meeting new people, and I don't believe there is a better beverage to do this with than a Bud. It's part of the good life. It's part of a life with friends. It's part of enjoyment, relaxation, sporting events, and ball games. It's part of America. (Treise et al., 1999, p. 23)

Transformation

Transformation, the third ritual function, allows people to release inhibitions, induce relaxation, and assume a different identity. Because alcohol is a drug, it offers its users more forms of transformation than most ritual artifacts. However, the drinking ritual offers opportunities for transformation that transcend the drug effects. Most drinkers find welcome relief from stress because the ritual encourages them to escape the harsh realities of their lives. The drinking ritual also takes away the fear of rejection in social settings. Outside the drinking environment, many people feel too ill at ease to socialize with a stranger; however, in a bar or a party setting, many are magically transformed into outgoing, fun-loving types who become the life of the party.

Treise et al. (1999) found two main transformative themes: escape and coming of age. Students often described highly stressful lives that held coursework, social activities, and other pressures in a precarious balance. Some students simply live by a "party hard" ethic, whereas others live by a "work hard, party hard" ethic. The latter group feels that partying hard is the reward for dealing with heavy academic pressures. Regardless of the source of the pressure, they often drank with a mission: "to forget, to become more comfortable, to relieve stress, to cheer up, to forget about people and to be part of the social scene" (p. 25). One female explained, "We call it our mission.... we're in the mood to drink. We're sick of everything ... and then there's the night when it's our mission to meet guys. Then there's the night when we hate guys and it's our mission to go out and drink and forget them" (p. 25).

Sometimes the drinking missions were more positive: "to have a good time, to meet someone of the opposite sex, to be with friends, to celebrate passing an exam or a difficult class, to get a buzz, or to 'get good and drunk'" (p. 25). The mission determined the performance roles, and regardless of the mission, some form of transformation occurred.

The second transformation occurred with age. Many participants reported a change in attitude when they reached age 21. One female participant explained that "the attraction to alcohol is so much more when you're younger.... The joke is once you turn 21, it's not exciting anymore. The thrill of getting through that door and trying to get served is gone because you're legal" (p. 26).

From the participants' perspective, it was as though the drinking ritual offered an artificial passage into adulthood. They could behave as an adult without fulfilling the necessary requirement of turning 21. Once they actually became legal drinkers, they did not need the drinking ritual to accomplish the transformation. Not all students consume less alcohol with age but, nevertheless, the ritual meaning changes.

Wolburg's (2001) participants also spoke to the transformation function of the ritual. In addition to the age themes already identified, they found that alcohol allowed them to change from people governed by strong moral codes that forbid immoral or "bad behavior" into those who are unencumbered by codes. Most felt they can get away with "bad behavior" while intoxicated and are not held responsible for acts performed while drinking. Thus, they used the common excuse, "I was so wasted."

One of Parker's (1998) participants experienced a similar need for transformation. Tom's primary life theme involved a struggle between his need to break free of societal barriers and his need to obey the rules imposed by society and "do the right thing." When he interpreted a Miller Lite Ice print ad that used the headline, "New rules!," he commented that it means it's a "different, different game now. They make it different," (p. 106). However, he continued, "New rules doesn't go with beer very well. Breakin' the rules would be a cooler thing! Beer and rules don't go together. You think of rules as not a laid-back thing" (Tom, p. 106).

On the surface, his response to the ad seems to reflect the function of order, and in one sense it does. However, the deeper function is transformation. The ad implies that there are rules that go with drinking, but they are not the rules that impose restrictions on people. The rules that apply to drinking allow "bad behavior," which in turn allows people to be who they want to be.

Sensation seeking and the desire for thrills also emerged as transformation themes in Wolburg's (2001) study. Students believed that drinking brings a rush of adrenalin that cannot be achieved by other activities. One participant explained:

> In a setting with friends and no parents, it is exciting and thrilling to try to do things you shouldn't be doing. When an underage person gets into a bar for the first time, the feeling is a rush—you can get unlimited drinks, there are older people around, and there are other sorts of entertainment that you just don't get from hanging out at a friend's dorm room on a Saturday night. (p. 33)

Treise et al.'s (1994) data also showed strong evidence for the need for transformation among alcoholics. Many participants discussed alcoholic beverage advertising as containing blatant suggestions that "you too can become this fun-loving partier." For example, one participant said, "They have billboards everywhere for Colt 45 and the like, the way the characters dressed and posed ... all very up front about wanting you to buy the product so you will look and feel like the models.... it's the whole ambience of the situation" (P12, p. 132).

Wolburg et al. (1999) discovered a fantasy world in beer ads, which offers rich opportunities for transformation on many levels. The researchers specifically examined beer ads for elements related to efficacy through skill, power, and accomplishments for a possible connection to alcoholics' feelings of low self-worth and lack of self-efficacy. What they discovered were ads filled with fun-loving people, who are successful in relationships and able to perform superhuman stunts. Through the use of fantasy and "limit violations," a term that denoted the stretching of reality beyond its limits, people in billboards came to life while others performed daredevil acts of skill that defied gravity. This happened in a magical world where beer cans forged through mountains, snowstorms came out of beer bottles, frogs and bears talked, and monsters walked through cities while women watched in amusement.

Other transformations included the cowboy figure, who is called a "modern-day hero," and the "mountain man," who draws a number of attractive women to his side. Each male viewer is challenged to be a "mountain man," and beer makes the transformation complete, as in the following ad: "Have you got what it takes to be a mountain man? All it really takes are the two cool beers of the mountain man. Smooth Busch Beer and easy drinking Busch Light. So, be a mountain man. All you gotta do is head for the mountains" (p. 194).

The transformations in beer ads probably have wide appeal to audience members; however, the alcoholic who struggles to feel capable of meeting the demands of life may find these ads particularly appealing. Regardless of whether or not advertisers have knowingly tried to tweak the needs and feelings of their "best" customers, Wolburg et al. (1999) concluded that advertisers know this audience well. Advertisers may not formally speak the language of ritual function, yet they are adept at appealing to human emotions and needs.

Finally, it is worth noting that the evidence of ritual functions in ads can lead to multiple interpretations. First, the presence of ritual functions in ads may be a reflection of behavior that already exists within the culture in an effort to make the advertising more relevant. Second, Pollay's (1986) "distorted mirror" perspective suggests that the inclusion of ritual functions in advertising not only reflects existing behavior, but also helps construct, maintain, and perpetuate the ritual. Following these lines of thought, advertisers who are aware of the ritualized behavior among alcoholics and other heavy drinkers have perhaps incorporated ritual functions in the ads to make the ads resonate better and make the product more appealing. However, when advertisers incorporate ritual functions in ads, with or without conscious knowledge of ritual behavior, they are able to strengthen the ritual itself, help maintain it, and so forth.

IMPLICATIONS OF A RITUAL-BASED PERSPECTIVE FOR DRINKING MODIFICATION STRATEGIES

We now address the second question (How can these insights be incorporated into treatment strategies and PSAs?) and offer suggestions for applying the ritual insights. The three ritual functions clearly provide meaningful rewards to alcoholics and college student binge drinkers, despite the fact that the cost and availability of alcohol, the strength of the drinking culture among peers, and the stigma of drinking all affect the specifics of ritual enactment. Order fills the need for security, community fills the need for intimacy at best and connectedness at the very least, and transformation fills the need for escape and thrill while also offering a rite of passage.

On the surface, asking students and alcoholics to modify their drinking behavior appears to be a logical, commonsense request to avoid the negative consequences; however, modifying their drinking presents them with a different set of risks: the loss of order and security, the loss of a community of friends, and the loss of escapism and other forms of transformation. To effectively ask people to curb their drinking or abstain from drinking, it is essential to find ways to resolve the loss of ritual functions.

Treise et al. (1999) offered three themes for PSA development aimed at college students that take into consideration the "social gifts." The first has the overall objective of imposing order on drinking habits with a social norm that suggests the right number of drinks. The PSA uses the theme, "Make three your limit." The second theme addresses the need for community and offers a new social role while using a term familiar to students, "Be a real drinking buddy." Instead of using the term "drinking buddy" in the usual sense, which implies being someone to share the experience of heavy consumption, the PSA uses the term to imply a higher order of friendship that requires taking charge if drinking gets out of control. The third PSA theme promises transformation and plays off the language of the drinking ritual. Students on a mission to "drink to forget" are now encouraged to "drink to remember."

The communication challenge is different for alcoholics than for students. There are no current PSAs in mainstream media outlets that ask for abstinence. Instead, recent announcements have tried to undermine the "cool" image of alcohol, have asked drinkers not to drive drunk, or have asked adults not to buy alcohol for minors (Andsager, Austin, & Pinkleton, 2001). Most likely the recovery process for alcoholics requires a more aggressive commitment to abstain from drinking than what most PSAs generate.

Treise et al. (1994) found that some alcoholics, particularly those who have been in recovery for a long period of time, are not affected by the alcohol advertising they see. Others, however, find that the alcohol advertising triggers the desire to drink. They in turn develop a variety of strategies to deal with ads—including avoiding the ads they encounter, reinterpreting the messages, and adding their own cognitions to the ads. Adding their cognitions often requires recalling the negative aspects of alcohol dependency that do not appear in the advertising. One participant in the study explained that "Beer commercials don't show it when the ambulance gets there. Those commercials don't show the families that are broken or the pain that the drinking starts … when you would do anything for a drink" (P14, p. 135).

The researchers suggest that counselors in treatment programs should incorporate instructions on how to deal with advertising as part of the overall therapy. They also note that proposals to limit alcoholic beverage advertising to "tombstone" approaches have merit when the rights of alcoholics to recover are considered paramount.

Similarly, Wolburg et al. (1999) proposed that alcoholics in treatment should learn to "talk back to beer ads" as a relapse prevention strategy. By talking back, they are counterarguing the messages in ads and giving the ads a new interpretation. If advertising were easy to avoid, alcoholics could simply remove themselves from the persuasive message that encourages drinking; however, the ubiquity of alcohol advertising makes avoidance an inefficient, ineffective strategy. The reinterpretation of ads and the insertion of one's own cognitions are forms of oppositional decoding that allow alcoholics to cognitively restructure their world. The researchers recommended that key areas for decoding should focus on the four experience modes, which also include the three ritual functions.

Treatment of alcoholism can impose a new ritual that has the potential for replacing the drinking ritual. Instead of the community of drinkers who are united by their consumption of alcohol, they become part of a community of recovering alcoholics, particularly as members of Alcoholics Anonymous or other self-help groups. Recovering alcoholics may also regain emotional bonds with family members that were broken as a result of drinking.

Treatment programs also impose a certain order or structure, whether it comes with a complete change in routine through hospitalization, or simply through attendance of meetings for self-help groups. Twelve-step programs often emphasize the need to take "one day at a time," which addresses the need for temporal ordering.

When alcoholics become recovering alcoholics, they also experience a type of transformation. Key to their success is finding meaning in their new transformation so that they do not revert back to the drinking ritual. This may be the most challenging part of recovery for many because the transformation that alcohol produces is so meaningful to them. By recognizing the social gifts of the drinking ritual, caregivers in treatment programs may help recovering alcoholics replace those functions by creating new rituals based on abstinence.

The research we examined offers strong support that drinking is a meaningful ritual that offers order, community, and transformation to college students and alcoholics. It validates and is validated by Rook's structural framework and Driver's "social gifts" of ritual. Furthermore, we demonstrate that a theoretical framework of drinking-as-ritual can be used to improve the efficacy of persuasive messages targeted toward each group. For college students, we show that the ritual framework can be used to create PSAs that can both incorporate aspects of that ritual and invert those aspects to encourage moderation. For alcoholics, we recommend ways that those in recovery can cognitively restructure their world when the impulse to drink is triggered by advertising. Ultimately, we believe that strategies from the ritual perspective can successfully contribute to social change.

APPENDIX:
SUMMARY OF METHODOLOGIES
FOR THE FIVE STUDIES

1. Treise, Taylor, and Wells (1994)

Depth interviews with 20 recovering alcoholics were conducted at an alcohol-dependence treatment program in a midsize city in the southeast. Participants included 15 men and 5 women between ages 25 and 64. Transcriptions were analyzed using analytic induction to determine common themes.

2. Parker (1998)

Seven student informants (3 female, and 4 male) from a large midwestern university participated in life story interviews and gave in-depth descriptions of a series of ads for alcohol. Interpretive analysis was used to demonstrate how ad interpretations are a function of individual cognitions and alcohol advertising.

3. Treise, Wolburg, and Otnes (1999)

Participants were students at two large southeastern universities. A series of qualitative techniques were used, including interviews with key informants to provide grounding—one campus police officer, four bartenders, and one resident assistant;

systematic observations in bars near campus; eight focus groups ranging in size between 8 and 11 students, with a total of 25 female and 30 male students between ages 21 and 25; and 20 in-depth interviews with 10 male and 10 female binge drinkers across both campuses. Focus groups and individual interviews began with "grand-tour" questions in four topic areas: typical drinking occasions, drinking amounts, decisions about when to quit drinking, and typical driving decisions. Transcriptions of data were analyzed for common themes.

4. Wolburg, Hovland, and Hopson (1999)

Document analysis was applied to television ads for two product categories: beer and automotive parts. Forty-one hours of sports programming produced 50 unduplicated ads in each category. The three authors used a team approach similar to that used in phenomenological research and examined ads for evidence of four experiential modes, use of transformational or informational strategy, use of standard advertising appeals, and depictions of time. Themes were noted and recommendations for treatment strategies were given.

5. Wolburg (2001)

Research was conducted at a private, midwestern university. A series of qualitative techniques were used, including interviews with key informants—four campus administrators, two campus security officers, and one counselor from student health; four focus groups of five students each among binge drinkers, moderate drinkers, abstainers, and residence hall personnel; written essays from 51 students who earned extra credit in an introductory advertising class; and in-depth interviews among 10 students who met the definition of binge drinkers. Interview questions focused on the meaning of drinking, the potential risks and consequences of drinking, and risk management strategies. Analytic induction was used to generate common themes.

REFERENCES

Andsager, J., Austin, E., & Pinkleton, B. (2001). Questioning the value of realism: Young adults' processing of messages in alcohol-related public service announcements and advertising. *Journal of Communication, 51*(1), 121–142.

Driver, T. (1991). *The magic of ritual.* New York: HarperCollins.

Had enough campaign (2001). Sobering statistics. Center for Science in the Public Interest. Accessed April 19, 2001, from www.cspinet.org/booze/hadenouch/campuslife/studentstories.html

Hopson, R. (1993). A thematic analysis of the addictive experience: Implications for psychotherapy. *Psychotherapy, 30*(fall), 481–494.

ι Mazur, L. (1995). *Marketing madness: A survival guide for a consumer so-*
ʃoulder, CO: Westview Press.

& Rotfeld, H. (1997). There are threats and (maybe) fear-caused arousal: The-
.nd confusions of appeals to fear and fear arousal itself. *Journal of Advertising,*
ʑʋ(ɜ), 45–60.

Mansfield, D. (2001). Survey shows University of Tennessee rates as No. 1 U.S. "party
school;" Louisiana State 2nd. Accessed August 22, 2001, from www.hecnews@
phoenix.edc.org

National Highway Traffic and Safety Administration (1999). 1999 youth fatal crashes and
alcohol facts. Accessed August 22, 2001, from www.nhtsa.gov/

National Institute on Alcohol Abuse and Alcoholism College Drinking Report (2002). A
call to action: Changing the culture of drinking at U.S. colleges. Accessed May 14,
2002, from www.edc.org/hec/niaaa/report.html

O'Sullivan, S. (2001) Drinking habits die hard at University of Delaware. Accessed 10,
2001, from www.edc.org/hec/news/necnews/1041.html

Parker, B. (1998). Exploring life themes and myths in alcohol advertisements through a meaning-based model of advertising experiences. *Journal of Advertising, 27*(1), 97–112.

Pollay, R. (1986). The distorted mirror: Reflections on the unintended consequences of advertising. *Journal of Marketing, 50*(2), 18–36.

Presley, C., Meilman, P., & Lyerla, R. (1993). *Alcohol and drugs on American college campuses: Use, consequence and perceptions of the campus environment: Volume 1.
1989–1991.* Carbondale, IL: Core Institute.

Rook, D. (1985). The ritual dimension of consumer behavior. *Journal of Consumer Research, 12*(December), 252–264.

Treise, D., Taylor, R., & Wells, L. (1994). How recovering alcoholics interpret alcoholic-
beverage advertising. *Health Marketing Quarterly, 12*(2), 125–139.

Treise, D., Wolburg, J., & Otnes, C. (1999). Understanding the "social gifts" of drinking rituals:
An alternative framework for PSA developers. *Journal of Advertising, 28*(2), 17–31.

U.S. Department of Health and Human Services (2000). Special report to the U.S. Congress on Alcohol and Health. Accessed from http://www.niaaa.nih.gov/publica-
tions/aa51.htm

Wechsler, H. Kelley, K., Weitzman, E., San Giovanni, J., & Seibring, M. (2000). What colleges are doing about student binge drinking: A survey of college administrators.
Journal of American College Health, 48, 219–226.

Wechsler, H., Moeykens, B., Davenport, A., Castillo, S., & Hansen, J. (1995). The adverse
impact of episodic drinkers on the other college students. *Journal of Studies on Alcohol, 56*(6), 628–634.

Wolburg, J. (2001). The "risky business" of binge drinking among college students: Using risk
models for PSAs and anti-drinking campaigns. *Journal of Advertising, 30*(4), 23–39.

Wolburg, J., Hovland, R., & Hopson, R. (1999). Cognitive restructuring as a relapse prevention strategy: Teaching alcoholics to talk back to beer ads. *Alcoholism Treatment
Quarterly, 17*(4), 29–51.

2

Consuming Ritual:
A&E's *Sacred Rites and Rituals*

Ronald L. Grimes
Wilfrid Laurier University

The popular understanding of ritual is shaped less by scholarly debate than by media presentation. The media package rites into saleable, consumable products. Documentaries and other programs aired on television market not only the paraphernalia and performances of rites but also the idea of ritual. Because it attends to the full range of ritual, ritual studies must attend not only to scholarly definitions of ritual but to popular depictions as well, because they help form the attitudes participants carry into the enactment of rites. The trouble is that media renditions of rites (as enacted) and ritual (as thought about) are seldom studied critically even by ritual studies scholars, because they are often preoccupied with physically and socially embodied rites, rather than virtual ritualizing. But media renditions of ritualized activity persist, for example, in *Survivor* and other so-called "reality" shows. So it is worth attending to the details of a specific example.

Sacred Rites and Rituals, produced by FilmRoos for A&E's Ancient Mysteries series,[1] was released in December 1996, and it continues to be aired and re-aired. It helps shape public attitudes toward the rites of others. In 50 or so minutes, the film tries to introduce viewers to ritual, and its tenor and attitude are now echoed by other media presentations of ritual.

As one of the scholarly consultants for the film, I know something about the process that lies behind the production. I kept drafts of the interviewers' questions and my responses to them. I also had the interview independently videotaped by a student so I could later reflect on the final film's editing and construction. Having subsequently worked with two other documentary series on ritual, one of which proposed to take the A&E production as a worthy model, I have arrived at a critical and comparative perspective on *Sacred Rites and Rituals*.

---

[1]The Web site for Arts and Entertainment's *Ancient Mysteries* is: http://www.aande.com/tv/shows/ancientmystery.html

After agreeing to an interview by the FilmRoos producer, I received a list of 19 questions that were to form its basis. There were three kinds of questions: about the nature and definition of ritual (e.g., Is ritual an inherent need? Are we by nature ritual beings?); about contemporary North American ritualized activities (e.g., Are mundane, secular events such as Super Bowl Sunday rituals? Can you comment on the lack of ritualized passage, particularly puberty rites, in contemporary Western societies?); and about rites from ancient or non-North American cultures (e.g., Could you discuss some of the oldest examples of ritual? Do you know what the origin of circumcision is and why it is such a widespread rite of passage?).[2]

I suggested deleting a few, adding one or two, and rewording others. All the suggestions were accepted. On the whole, the questions, as negotiated prior to the interview, were not naive; they were the work of inquiring minds. But a few of them were tendentious or leading: Why are these ritual passages so critical, in your view, to a healthy society/individual? Do you feel there is a condescending, almost puritanical attitude toward the more physical, ecstatic, or theatrical rituals found in more primal traditions? The answers were implied in the rhetoric and tone.

The actual interview, conducted long distance with the interviewers in Los Angeles and the camera in Waterloo, Canada, was noticeably different from the e-mail questions. The interviewers posed many more leading questions. The interviewers clearly had an agenda to portray ritual in a particular light and to draft me into saying what they would like said. The questions, as actually posed in the filmed interview, had a distinctly psychological bias. The producer-interviewers were largely uninterested in the political, economic, or ecological dimensions of ritual. They displayed intense curiosity about the ways rites heal and showed little interest in the ways that they abuse or exploit.[3]

To access the film's ritual dimensions, then, consideration must be given not only to the *rites* depicted by the film but also to the *ritualization processes* in and around it. Because *Sacred Rites* was part of the Ancient Mysteries series, there was considerable pressure to chant a kind of mystery mantra, not only to use the word "mystery" but also to cloak the idea of ritual in an ancient and impenetrable aura. Even though I protested that my field was contemporary North American religions, I was repeatedly pressed by the two interviewers to comment on ancient rites. I resisted, insisting that the producers find scholars with expertise in ancient ritual texts. They resisted my resistance, wanting to attribute a kind of expertise to me that I did not have. And the reason for doing so was not so much because they

---

[2]After several media interviews on ritual (with NPR, PRI, and BBC), it is easy to anticipate the questions, since they are remarkably similar. The queries, desires, and fantasies bearing on ritual are clearly culture and time bound.

[3]An interest in the negative sides of ritual did, however, show up in the final version of the film.

thought that I, in fact, possessed knowledge about ancient rites, but because they did not want to spend time locating yet another expert.

The result is a film that glosses contemporary rites with unexamined claims about their longevity (made by the narrator, not by me, nor by one of the other consultants). By implication, "ancient" includes not only things done a long time ago but also things that viewers would readily accept as having been done for a long time. For instance, there is tendency in the series to count as ancient or mysterious things from non-Euroamerican cultures. Thus, exotic implies ancient, and ancient implies exotic.

The implied definition of "mystery" in this film and most of the series is twofold: (a) A mystery is any problem that filmmakers cannot quickly summarize for viewers. Even problems for which there are good data become mysteries if scholars have differing interpretations, if the data are incomplete, or if explanations are complex. And (b) a mystery is also anything that evokes a sense of great depth— anything uncanny or eerie. Both connotations are evoked regularly and indiscriminately in Ancient Mysteries programs. Asked to comment on the mystery of ritual, I replied that a mystery in the philosophical and religious sense has little to do with lack of information or human inability to explain a phenomenon. Birth, I said, is a mystery. A mystery is a mystery even when one can explain it genetically and biologically. A mystery is not something exotic but an event that implicates one's very being so profoundly that it evokes awe. The editors did not use the comment, probably because it questioned a key premise of the program. A noticeable difference between the 2 ½-hour interview and the final product was that the interviewers repeatedly sought explanations, especially popular psychological ones, of ritual behavior. I offered social or political ones not much to their liking, so the film itself chooses mystification over explanation.

Because the film was called *Sacred Rites and Rituals*, I inquired whether there was a meaningful difference between "rites" and "rituals." The question was ignored. The aired version only uses the phrase once, and makes no meaningful distinction between the two terms. My suggestion that producers delete the redundancy by calling it either *Sacred Rites* or *Sacred Rituals* was also ignored. I have since encountered the phrase in the mouths of three other potential documentary makers. My guess is that its only function is to echo "death and dying," a phrase that sold, and continues to sell, books and courses. The qualifier "sacred" adds nothing substantive to the title or the film. It does not determine, for instance, that the focus will be on, say, worship rites rather than rites of passage or secular rites as distinct from those associated with religious institutions. The notion of sacredness is not explored or used in the film itself, even though the interview questions submitted to me had distinguished sacred from mundane rites. My inference is that the term "sacred" is rhetorical, calculated to claim importance for the film itself.

Sacred Rites and Rituals is divided into five, explicitly named parts: Passages, Journey of Faith, Flesh and Blood, Beyond Death, The Quest Continues. Although these sections are called theatrical "acts," their real function is clearly that of providing commercial breaks. Acts 1, 2, and 4 are largely organized around ritual types: rites of passage, pilgrimage, and ancestor veneration, respectively. No explanation is offered for choosing these kinds of ritual rather than other kinds to represent the whole of ritual.

Act 1, Passages, focuses on Jewish circumcision and an African women's initiation rite, but it also includes the Hindu Agnicayana, which is not a rite of passage. Act 2, Journey of Faith, is largely about two pilgrimage rites, the Kumbha Mela of India and the Hajj of Saudi Arabia. In Act 3, all pretext of the film's being a treatment of ritual types breaks down. Subtitled "Flesh and Blood," the section is also referred to by Leonard Nimoy, the narrator, as "Rites that Stagger the Imagination." The section is blatantly voyeuristic. Clips appear because they depict bizarre, bloody, or painful acts. Act 4, Beyond Death, features an attempt in 1986 by Chinese actors to reenact Confucius' birthday ceremony. It is not so much a rite as an instance of "restored," or "re-behaved" behavior, that is, people pretending to be engaged in ritual (Schechner, 1996). This example is followed by an account of a South Korean businessman who venerates an ancestor and relates to his employees as if he were their patriarch. Act 5, called both Rituals that Shape Our Lives and The Quest Continues, is a miscellany. It is vague in intent, and the film had not had an earlier quest that this quest purports to continue. The largest portion of the final act contrasts constructive and destructive, as well as religious and nonreligious, rites.

The choice of rites depicted in the film is driven almost exclusively by visual interest and the availability of footage and archival materials, not by the pervasiveness or importance of the rites, nor how well they illustrate a category, nor by how much is known about the rites. The implied criteria for visual interest are how much movement and color there is, the recording quality of the clip, and the projected ability to attract and hold viewers' interest. Among the aesthetic preferences exhibited by *Sacred Rites and Rituals* are largeness of scale (big crowds and wide vistas are preferred), scenes involving blood or pain, actions with no obvious explanations, culturally unfamiliar sites, and ornate or minimal clothing.

Besides movement through five phases, the film alternates between the voices of Leonard Nimoy (who is seen on screen only at the beginning and end) and the talking heads of experts (whose authorizing biographical blurbs are superimposed on the screen). Scholars rarely speak for more than 20 seconds at a time. They do not interact with the narrator, much less the participants, and participants are never asked about the meanings of their own rites. Although it is never said, the film implies that one class of people acts, whereas another class understands. There is neither discussion nor debate over interpretation, because observers and participants do not interact, nor do the experts interact with one another.

Contradictions abound, but they are rarely commented on. For instance, Philip Novak, one of the experts, speaks of ritual as action "which intends a transformation of state," whereas Nimoy describes a situation in which ritualists are "transported," that is, not transformed but elevated then returned to where they started (Schechner, 1977). In another example, the audience is shown the very concrete act of burning a ritual site, while Nimoy refers to it as an instance of "abstract mystical belief." The dissonance between things shown and things said, as well as between one claim and another, is considerable.

One of the most striking features of the narrator's script is its barrage of rhetorical questions: How original are these rites? Does pilgrimage change people? Which rites endure? Are all these rites related to one another? How did these rituals originate? Some of these questions are good ones, but others are nonsensical or unanswerable because of the way they are framed. Rarely is a question posed, pursued, and then debated or answered. When answers are given, there is never more than one. Thus, ambiguity and conflict are edited out. Answers either are singular, authoritative, and implicitly absolute, or they are "mysteries."

As for the meanings of ritual symbols, there seem to be three possibilities in the film: (a) what they mean is obvious; (b) what they mean is a mystery; or (c) what they mean can be summarized in two or three sentences, usually concerning their imagined origin or supposed psychological function. Much of what is offered as interpretation is at the level of truism or supposed common sense, having little to do with either participants' or scholars' ways of speaking about the meanings of rites. "This simple ritual [Muslim circumcision]," according to the narrator, is not threatened (as is the Agnicayana). Why? His answer to his own question is: Because it relates "so directly to the idea of a people's survival." How or why circumcision means survival is not at all obvious, but the comment is offered as if it were.

After a series of clips on weddings, births, and funerals, the narrator claims there is "no doubt as to the meaning of these symbolic gestures," even though viewers may have not the faintest idea what they have seen. For instance, John Kennedy, Jr., as a boy, is shown saluting the flag. It would be hard to imagine a more familiar but more thoroughly equivocal gesture. How old would a viewer have to be to recognize the scene as that of a presidential funeral? Does the boy realize what is going on? Is this his declaration that he, the son, will carry on in the absence of the father? Is he playing soldier? Who taught him to salute? What does saluting mean to him? At the very point when a series of interesting but hard-to-answer questions might be expected, the film claims the meaning is obvious. But, the power of the famous photograph is due, in part, to its ambiguity.

Sacred Rites and Rituals is littered with tacit racism and sexism:

- Viewers are shown African women dancing bare-breasted. Judith Gleason, the expert who is credited with having shot the film, is shown saying that some of the dancers are Western-educated and embarrassed. Despite that, the camera continues to follow their breasts. White, American breasts would not be shown in such a manner on an A&E documentary. I overheard a woman watching *Sacred Rites and Rituals* mutter, "Wanna take bets on how many dicks we see!" She was right: The only naked male in the film is shot discreetly and momentarily from the side.

- Viewers are shown some old drawings of the Lakota Sun Dance. The narrator speaks about it as a dead rite no longer performed. There is no awareness that the Sun Dance is, in fact, still enacted. In the final analysis, the film's producers do not use scholars to check the accuracy of their data, offer nuanced interpretations, or elicit undiscovered meanings from participants. Instead, the producers use the scholars as legitimizing agents, coopting their names, institutional affiliations, and demeanor to enhance the saleability of the film.
- The film includes some old black and white footage of the Hajj, as a newsreel commentator refers to pilgrims as "Mohammedens," and Allah as "*their* god." The insensitivity and inaccuracy are blatant and dated. Viewers who hope the film will pull back out of this time warp and comment on the offensive, Orientalist ways Westerners used to speak of such rites are disappointed. The only revision of the picture painted by the old clip is that of pushing up the number of those attending from 200,000 to 2 million.
- Bathing in the Ganges during the Kumbha Mela is described as purification of "past sin," a blatantly Christian way of explaining a Hindu practice.
- Although the narrator never directly accuses ritualists of being primitive or irrational, he implies as much by his rhetoric. He refers to rites as performance that "challenge logic." He asks his audience, "What belief is so strong that it has convinced these people to undertake this daring ritual?"

Some of the film's basic assumptions are contradictory. On the one hand, it assumes an easy universalism. "Every culture fears disaster, disease, and death," claims the narrator, implying that people are the same everywhere. He suggests that *we* can understand *them*, even if they are "Stone Age mystics of 40,000 years ago." The universalist premise allows the narrator to offer commonsense interpretations when no participant or observer interpretations support his interpretation. On the other hand, the film assumes a kind of evolutionary superiority: *We* can explain what *they* do (but not vice versa), so we are superior to them. Our rites, unlike theirs, are not logically challenged. This tendency to "other" is obvious in another way. When *Sacred Rites* wants to offer examples of destructive ritual, it shows Hitler's Nuremberg rallies, not initiatory hazing in American Marine boot camps. Implied critiques are usually aimed elsewhere, not at the heart of American cultural ceremony.

Ritual is made strange by *Sacred Rites and Rituals*. Its connection with ordinary life is severed; both religion and ritual are reduced to one dimension: mystery. "Rituals obscure and mysterious," says Nimoy, "seem" to fulfill human needs. He, of course, does not pause to reflect: Do they, in fact, do so? Or do they only appear to? Ritual is rendered odd, in need of an explanation but one that participants cannot, or do not, provide.

If this television presentation of ritual is compared with ice skating, for example, some of the peculiarities of *Sacred Rites and Rituals* appear more clearly. One of the primary aims of sports interviewers is to engage, not avoid, athletes such as figure skaters. Performers are consulted, as if their responses are more important than those of observers. Skaters are not asked *why* they engage in such odd behavior. Instead, the beauty or importance of ice skating is assumed. Skaters are asked how they felt during the event, how they prepared, where they are going to skate next. Ritualists, on the other hand, are rendered absent from the ritual event. We do not learn their names or hear their voices. We gaze at their bodies, but their bodies are not real persons. We do not know or care what they think they are doing. The A&E narrator assures us, "The lives of billions on the planet are still affected by ancient rites," as if this were an amazing rather than an ordinary fact, and as if these rites had not changed across history.

At the end of the film, a pun is used to force the final transition. From a reference to ritual within "*family* space," we cut to Leonard Nimoy and a reference to "*outer* space," the place that many viewers associate with his most popular role, Spock. Nimoy looks up at the stars as he links space with the future, implicitly consigning ritual to the past. In the film, ritual space, like outer space, is necessary to the health of the planet, but because ritual is not quite here in this world, not fully inhabiting the present, it is a mystery. By being rendered other, ritual—like Spock—is not quite human. By being portrayed as either more than human or less than human, ritual is made alien. We viewers are led to watch ritualists the way we watch animals in a zoo—with fascination, occasionally seeing our behavior aped, but comfortable in the knowledge that we inhabit a different plane of being from the animals.

RITES, RITUALIZING, AND THE MEDIA

It is helpful to distinguish and relate four terms:[4]

Rite: sequences of action rendered special by virtue of their condensation, elevation, or stylization. Rites are distinct, socially recognized sets of procedures. Often they are named, as well as enacted, in set-aside times and specially chosen places.

Ritual: the general idea of actions characterized by a certain "family" of qualities, for instance, that they are performed, formalized, patterned, con-

---

[4]The terms are more fully explained in Grimes (1990, 1994).

densed, and so on. No one or two of these qualifies is definitive. Therefore, ritual is not "digital," that is, either on or off (Grimes, 1990). Rather, all behavior is ritualized—some of it more, some of it less. The degree of ritualization increases as the number and intensity of these and other behavioral qualities increase.

Ritualization: (1) Activities not normally viewed as rites but treated as if they were or might be (e.g., giving birth, house cleaning, canoeing, TV watching, all have been regarded as ritual;) (2) In ethology, ritual insofar as animals engage in it, actions usually associated with aggression or mating.

Ritualizing: The act of deliberately cultivating or constructing a new rite.

Strictly speaking, A&E's 1-hour production was not a rite, because the genre of action is not culturally recognized as such by either its producers or consumers. However, the film contains both semblances and representations of rites, and its production and consumption were marked by ritualized behavior.

The layers separating the viewers from the ritualists are several. From the "inside" to the "outside" they are: (a) the rites as performed by ritualists themselves; (b) the observed, filmed, and edited rendition of those rites; (c) the film clips as selected for showing by producers and series editors; (d) the clips, films, or rites as written about by the script writer and commented on by the narrator and scholarly consultants; and (e) the film as seen, heard, and remembered by viewers. In short, the transformations effected by the rites are overshadowed by the media transformation of the rites. Rites as such appear in level one, but the multiple transformations and distortions that occur between the first and final level are examples of what I call *ritualization*, which is to say, they display qualities that are ritual-like without ever becoming rites per se. Viewers undergo a process that resembles pilgrimage or tourism: We are transported around the globe and returned home again (without leaving our seats). In this respect, the film is an instance of what might be tagged as "subjunctive," or "as-if," ritualization.

What leads viewers forward through the film is the repeated promise of revealed secret knowledge. In this respect, the film is a quasi-initiation. Viewers are shown or told about mysteries, events, which if they will but wait for their arrival, will reveal something important. In the end, however, viewers return with mere souvenirs, the trinkets of pilgrimage, and not the transforming knowledge imparted in an initiation.

Ordinarily, most viewers—and even some scholars—do not think of rites as products that compete on a market with other products. But on television and stage, rites become not only aesthetic objects but commodities. When rendered as such, producers give primary attention to product recognition: What will audiences-as-buyers immediately recognize as ritual? Often the first answers are predictable: masks, drumming, dancing, costumes, and, of course, "mystery."

The A&E production *Sacred Rites and Rituals* illustrates much of what I do not care for in media treatments of ritual. Besides the obvious fact that it co-opts scholarship, it neither increases human knowledge of ritual nor enhances viewers' sense of it. If one wanted to conduct in-depth research and write a book-length ethnography, it would be essential to interview and observe both producers and consumers themselves. This chapter has done neither. The aim was more modest: to provide a peculiar kind of outsider–participant perspective. Asked subsequently by other film companies to consult in the production of two different series of films on ritual, I am now being forced to think like a visual artist as well as a critic and scholar. Given the resources, how would I present ritual differently? What would it take to make me proud of the production rather than critical of it?

Table 2.1 summarizes the A&E aesthetic and an alternative one. The chart contrasts what I call the "tourist," or "quasi-pilgrimage," style of *Sacred Rites and Rituals* with a style that I call "contemplative." (One could use other terms. These are imperfect, and my investment in them is not high.) The aesthetic of a film series I would like to make is in the right-hand column.

The tourist treatment of a rite is partly determined by subject matter. Like the tourist, the A&E film seeks out eye-catching phenomena. To warrant inclusion on the ritual tour, a certain size, scale, or grandeur are essential. Rites that are domestic, local, or improvised are unworthy of sustained media attention. In the tourist aesthetic, grandeur of scale is augmented with intensity of color and rapidity of motion. The filtered colors and accelerated pace are not meant to enhance a viewer's comprehension of the rite but to increase the capacity of the film to hold viewers' attention.

The tourist filmmaker assumes short attention spans, holding them by the rapid pace of its short clips. Rhythm is one of the most basic mechanisms of a rite. Rites do not merely use rhythms to convey messages; rhythms are messages. Rhythms are part of the content and effect of a rite. To overwhelm those rhythms is to engage in a counterritualizing move or, in some instances, even to show a fundamental disrespect for them. Like the tourist's eye, the A&E camera is busy, sometimes intrusive, sometimes distant. It seldom takes the time to dwell or participate, even momentarily. Often, the most arresting movement in the A&E film is that of the camera, soaring over a crowd or zooming in on a face but not seriously attending to the actions of participants.

The contemplative camera is less prone to express its distance from or power over what it shoots. It offers longer, fewer segments, and attempts to honor at least some of the rite's subdivisions and rhythms. It follows rather than drives the action. It meanders and dwells. It is attentive to detail or color but does not artificially enhance or amplify it.

All film de- and recontextualizes its subject matter, but the contemplative camera is wider, more circular in its attentiveness. It helps viewers grasp context, what surrounds or is behind a rite. However visually arresting a rite may be,

TABLE 2.1
Tourist Versus Contemplative Style

	A Tourist Aesthetic	A Contemplative Aesthetic
Subject matter	Exotic dimensions of large-scale celebration or worship. Bigger is better.	Domestic dimensions of small-scale or marginal rites of passage. The small and local are worthy of attention.
Subdivisions	Many, very short clips of the most visually arresting portions. The whole is broken into pseudo-dramatic "acts."	Longer, fewer segments of preparation, crucial portions of rite, and aftermath. Subdivisions, if any, follow those of the rite.
Color, costume	Major emphasis on intense color and unusual costume.	Attention to color and costume is incidental, not a major emphasis. Color is "natural" rather than enhanced. Costume is seen in relation to everyday wear.
Camera, movement	Camera is busy, peers in, then moves away rapidly. Camera is a tourist.	Camera is slower, more contemplative; sometimes dwells on small details. Camera is a participant.
Music, sound	Music drives the action.	Music creates a space for contemplation or reflection.
Narrator	Cinematic celebrity-actor-narrator who provides continuity and vocal emphasis but is not in the ritual space. Shot in an exotic space, the desert, the narrator raises a host of unanswered, or unanswerable questions, to create a sense of "mystery." Narrator takes up considerable auditory air space but neither challenges nor interacts with participants or experts.	Narrator who reflects, converses, and sometimes participates. Narrator is seen in ritual space, as well as in other places, for instance, in domestic space. Sometimes challenges participants' claims or views. Raises questions that challenge both participants and viewers. Attempts are made to answer some of them, or to show why there is no easy answer to them.
Narration, explanation	Explanations tend to be abstract and general—not about specific symbols or moments in the ritual process, but about the whole rite or even ritual in general.	Meanings tend to be local, if not idiosyncratic—very rooted in time and space. Explanations are negotiated among participants or between participants and the narrator.

(continued)

TABLE 2.1
(continued)

	A Tourist Aesthetic	*A Contemplative Aesthetic*
Participants	Ritual participants unnamed and uninterviewed. Pronounced tendency toward exoticism: the "others" are "over there" or "back" in time, and viewers need experts and narrators to make them intelligible.	Participants are named and interviewed. Emphasis on the here and now. Some actions are allowed "to speak for themselves." They do not always need explanation or interpretation.
Experts	Imported experts who engage in brief monologues. Those who ritualize are not the ones who know what the ritual means: Those who enact don't know; those who know don't perform.	Participants are consultants: Those who perform also know. Scholars are inquirers, sources of a different kind of knowledge: Those who study rites have a different perspective, but they don't know all.
Viewers	Viewer feels, "I wouldn't perform such things, and I couldn't possibly understand them without expert help."	Viewer asks, "Why not do it that way?" Viewer feels, "I am like that too" or "I'd never do that, but it makes sense that they do."

much of its impact arises from the preparation that leads to it and the wake created in its aftermath. Ritual is ensconced in a social matrix that needs to be understood. A rite, even more than a play, is seriously distorted by excision and dismemberment.

Rites do not typically have narrators, although there are exceptions such as celebrations and festivals in which public orators have a legitimate part. It is possible, of course, to present a rite as if it were an aesthetic object capable of speaking for itself. But if one grants the necessity of narration when viewing rites from unfamiliar cultures, there are differing styles of interaction. The tourist style is "dramatic," whereas the proposed alternative is more "ethnographic." (Neither term should be taken literally.) The former is authoritative, imposing, and articulately declaratory. The latter is more interrogative—sometimes more sure, sometimes less sure—about what one witnesses. The "dramatic" narrator does not take risks either with viewers or with ritual participants by asking real questions. The questions are empty, merely rhetorical; they are not the questions of a serious inquirer but those of a tourist.

Tourist-type narration, although often delivered with passion, tends to be generalized and abstract, not about this rite enacted by these persons in this place but about ritual in general as enacted by "mankind." By contrast, contemplative narration is local and situational, an expression of this narrator's encounter with these people at this time.

Any filming can make participants seem other. We can "other" ourselves by shooting family videos, for instance, so a certain exoticism is inevitable. But it is possible to choose whether to heighten or dampen it. In the tourist aesthetic, participants are exoticised. Anonymous people are generalized into "others" "over there." There is local color but not local knowledge. On the rare occasion when local knowledge is presented, it is held by no one in particular. The participants, although they have faces, do not have names. They are cultural representatives but not persons.

An alternative would be named, interviewed participants who, by virtue of their participation, are experts of a kind different from the scholarly experts. They are allowed considerable headway in speaking for themselves. Their words do not always require interpretation.

The A&E film's experts are imported into the film and then carefully controlled. They are unable to question the rite, the participants, each other, or the narrator's interpretation of the rite. They speak in short monologues, not in dialogue. So, in effect, they authorize the film itself. Worse, they do so with little or no knowledge of the film's claims, and sometimes even with little or no knowledge of the rites presented or the ritualists who performed them. The questions to which they may have responded in preceding interviews are edited out, so that original dialogues are presented as monologues.

Experts of the contemplative school would emphasize the dialogical and tentative nature of their interpretations. They become inquirers, that is, people who do not know but are interested in learning. Experts, they nevertheless hold their expertise lightly. When they challenge or question, their challenges are open to question. They invite either dialogue or debate.

In the final analysis, viewers of a "touristic" documentary are rendered dependent on the film. They could not possibly understand performances so exotic and impenetrable without experts, narrators, and filmmakers. Viewers would not perform such rites, because they are too "mysterious," and viewers could not make intellectual sense of the rites without assistance. In contrast, the viewer of a contemplative documentary thinks, "Well, that makes more sense than I would have imagined. Why not do it the way these folks do it?" Or muses, "I would never do that, but now it makes sense why they do it that way."

I have summarized two possibilities, and, for the sake of making the differences obvious, drawn a sharp line between them. There are other ways of constructing portraits of ritual for widespread media consumption. The point of this comparison is not to claim that one aesthetic is superior to another—although my own preference is obvious—but that we should reflect more fully on the ways that media transpose ritual enactments.

I have explored, and worse, helped produce, a mediocre, if not poor, instance of a film about ritual. There are better examples. *Gathering up Again: Fiesta in Santa Fe,* another film for which I worked as an advisor, tracks real, named people both on and off the ritual stage. It captures performative failure as well as ritual success.[5] *If Only I Were an Indian,* by the National Film Board of Canada,[6] contemplates the problems of ceremonial appropriation with great patience, humanity, and insight. And *Kosher Valley*[7] achieves the doggedly local and deeply humane qualities that ought to characterize films about ritual life. So I am not advocating a style that is impossible, only one not always considered commercially lucrative.

Better documentaries should evoke better theories, and better theories should lead to better media productions. The connections, although not necessary, are both possible and desirable. Since the 1980s, the term *ritual* has shown up with considerable regularity in writings about performance and media. James Carey's few remarks on ritual in *Media, Myths, and Narratives* (Carey, 1989), for instance, are widely cited. But his use of the notion of ritual is so underdeveloped that it has little theoretical utility. Phrases such as "ritual view of communication" leave it unclear whether ritual is an activity in its own right or merely a point of view taken in studying something else.

In addition to theoretically underpowered uses of "ritual," there are incantatory and ecstatic uses. Quentin Schultze, for instance, declares, "Television is ritual" (Schultze, 1990a, 1990b, 1990c). Not only is it ritual, it is also "religion," "theology," "sacred text," "mythopoesis," "storytelling," "liturgy," "morality play," "soap opera," and "drama." Others want us to know that TV watching is ritual (Goethals, 1981), negotiating cyberspace on the Internet is ritual (O'Leary, 1996), and attending genre films is ritual (Sobchack, 1982). The equating strategy, at first tantalizing, soon goes flat if the metaphoric differences are traded in for a metaphoric identity.

As an object of scholarly attention, ritual can be tantalizing, and stretching definitions can sometimes be provocative. In the end, however, equations and incantations are not enough. Ritual studies needs richly interpreted case studies, ex-

---

[5]Contact information: Jeanette DeBouzek, 413 10th St SW, Albuquerque, NM 87102. Phone: 505-242-6198. E-mail: jd@alphavillevideo.com.

[6]Available from the National Film Board of Canada at: http://cmm.onf.ca/E/titleinfo/index.epl?id=33029

[7]Available from Throughline Productions, 2080 Josyln Place, Boulder, CO, 80304, (303) 443-7588.

tended theoretical reflections on key ideas, and scholarly terminology that is more discerning than popular usage. In examining dances of the Concheros of Mexico, Susanna Rostas (1998), for example, does not merely "apply" a well-worn theory. Instead, she recasts the theory of Humphrey and Laidlaw (1994), producing a more nuanced dialectic between ritualization and perfomativity. Her data enable her to advance, rather than merely replicate, the theorists' generalizations. And Edward Schieffelin (1976, 1985, 1996), in wrestling with the idea of performance itself, has authored some of the most nuanced reflections on ritual produced by a contemporary writer. But Schieffelin and Rostas are exceptions. Unfortunately, the rule, too often illustrated by articles in journals and edited collections, is uncritically to appropriate and apply one of Turner's ideas (usually liminality or communitas) or one of Schechner's distinctions (ritual as efficacious/performance as entertaining). The more sustained theorizing about ritual of in Rappaport (1999), for instance, is rarely brought into critical dialogue with data that might expose its strengths and limitations.

The mediated versions of rites are in some ways more difficult to study than the nonmediated ones. Mediated ritualization transposes the human body and human society in extraordinarily complex ways. Because I have summarized some of these ways, as well as critiqued writing on ritual and media elsewhere (Grimes, 2002),[8] I do not repeat the summary and critique here. Suffice it to say that no matter how sensitively used, film and television, by transposing ritual enactments into aesthetic performances shown for entertainment and education, enhance certain ritual activities more than others. On the one hand, festivals show and play well. On the other, meditation rites do not. Rites are among the most common occasions on which humans reach for cameras, but they are also one of the occasions during which cameras are most often forbidden. This double impulse, to display and to sequester, has long marked ritual events, and the introduction of media produces additional complexity and interpretive torque into this impulse.

We will only begin to understand the effect of media transpositions if we invest time in studying media renditions of rites as well as rites themselves, and if we resist the easy equations and reductionistic formulas that typify much contemporary scholarship. Claims that the media *are* ritual, that ritual is *really* a kind of performance, that social interaction *is* ritual, or that ritual is *really* social interaction will not get us very far. There is truth in all these equations, but if the tensions between domains are relaxed by making the one equal the other or by rendering one thing a mere subcategory of the other, then the dialogue among performance studies, ritual studies, and media studies scholars will become monologue.

---

[8]See also Hoover (1988) and Hughes-Freeland (1998).

REFERENCES

Carey, J. (1989). *Media, myths and narratives: Television and the press.* Newbury Park, CA: Sage.

Goethals, G. (1981). *The TV ritual: Worship at the video altar.* Boston: Beacon.

Grimes, R. (1990). *Ritual criticism.* Columbia, SC: University of South Carolina Press.

Grimes, R. (1994). *Beginnings in ritual studies* (rev. ed.). Columbia, SC: University of South Carolina Press.

Grimes, R. (2002). Ritual and the media. In S. Hoover (Ed.), *Practicing religion in the age of the media: Explorations in media, religion and culture* (pp. 219–234). New York: Columbia University Press.

Hoover, S. (1988). Television myth and ritual: The role of substantive meaning and spatiality. In J. Carey (Ed.), *Media, myths and narratives: Television and the press* (pp. 161–178). Newbury Park, CA: Sage.

Hughes-Freeland, F. (1998). *Ritual, performance, media.* London: Routledge & Kegan Paul.

Humphrey, C., & Laidlaw J. (1994). *The archetypal actions of ritual: A theory of ritual illustrated by the Jain rite of worship.* Oxford, England: Clarendon.

O'Leary, S. (1996). Cyberspace as sacred space: Communicating religion on computer networks. Unpublished manuscript, University of Southern California.

Rappaport, R. (1999). *Ritual and religion in the making of humanity.* Cambridge, England: Cambridge University Press.

Rostas, S. (1998). From ritualization to performativity: The Concheros of Mexico. In F. Hughes-Freeland (Ed.), *Ritual, performance, media* (pp. 85–103). London: Routledge & Kegan Paul.

Schechner, R. (1977). *Essays on performance theory, 1970–1976.* New York: Drama Books.

Schechner, R. (1996). Restoration of behaviour. In R. Grimes (Ed.), *Readings in ritual studies* (pp. 441–458). Upper Saddle River, NJ: Prentice-Hall.

Schieffelin, E. (1976). *The sorrow of the lonely and the burning of the dancers.* New York: St. Martin's.

Schieffelin, E. (1985). Performance and the cultural construction of reality. *American Ethnologist, 12*(4), 707–724.

Schieffelin, E. (1996). On failure and performance: Throwing the medium out of the seance. In C. Laderman & M. Roseman (Eds.), *The performance of healing* (pp. 59–89). New York: Routledge & Kegan Paul.

Schultze, Q. (1990a). The place of television in the church's communication. In T. Inbody (Ed.), *Changing channels: The church and the television revolution* (pp. 23–42). Dayton, OH: Whaleprints.

Schultze, Q. (1990b). Secular television as popular religion. In S. Hoover & R. Abelman (Eds.), *Religious television: Controversies and conclusions* (pp. 239–248). Norwood, NJ: Ablex.

Schultze, Q. (1990c). Television drama as sacred text. In J. Ferre (Ed.), *Channels of belief: Religion and American commercial television* (pp. 3–27). Ames: Iowa State University Press.

Sobchack, V. (1982). Genre film: Myth, ritual, and sociodrama. In S. Thomas (Ed.), *Film/culture: Explorations of cinema in its social context* (pp. 147–165). Metuchen, NJ: Scarecrow.

Part II

Holidays and Consumption

3

Ceremonial Disrobement and Moral Choice: Consumption Rituals at Mardi Gras

Wesley Shrum
Louisiana State University

In the mid-1970s, a new phenomenon began to occur in New Orleans' French Quarter during Mardi Gras. That phenomenon may be described simply as an exchange of beads for nudity. Nudity, of course, has always been a common sight in the area, from the old brothels of Storyville, to the strip clubs of Bourbon Street, to the occasional concomitant of extreme intoxication. Beads are the primary currency of Mardi Gras, thrown from parade floats and balconies. The exchange of beads for nudity is a new kind of ritual, a ceremonial interaction involving negotiation and reciprocity among strangers. Its popularity derives from the modeling of the ritual on the free exchange of goods and services for a generalized medium that is characteristic of capitalism.

The linkage of deviance and market behavior is a subject of both public interest and striking theoretical importance. When I began to study ritual disrobement in 1983,[1] the practice was circumscribed roughly by the temporary boundaries of Mardi Gras and the spatial boundaries of the French Quarter. Nearly 20 years later, it has diffused beyond both of these boundaries, and may be witnessed the entire year on Bourbon Street, in some Southern locations during Mardi Gras, and even at social gatherings by fraternities and sororities in other areas of the country. Part of the reason for the interest in nudity is that American society, compared with many others, remains relatively modest with respect to such public displays (Weinberg, 1965). But the reason for the diffusion of ritual disrobement is more fundamental: It models the core values of market societies.

First consider a definition. "Disrobement" is an action (a) performed by nonprofessionals; (b) that is relatively brief, leaving most of the body clothed; and (c) directed to strangers. It is also, strictly speaking, illegal. One can say without exaggeration that its relational and behavioral topography are identical to exhibi-

---

[1]Primary data for this study are described in Shrum and Kilburn (1996), which provided quantitative evidence for the claims in this chapter.

...m, or "flashing," a category of action that is highly deviant and often thought to warrant punishment or therapy (Cox & Daitzmann, 1980). Intimate body parts, which are not voluntarily exhibited even to close friends, are exposed for the acclaim of strangers, often numbering in the hundreds. What is perhaps most fascinating about the practice is that a behavior that is so clearly deviant is also, in one sense, so easy to understand. People disrobe for beads. Of course, in another sense such understanding is partial, at best, and begs the important question: *Why* do people disrobe for beads? To the extent that it exists, that understanding is a primary signal of position in the social system. Insiders, or those fully conversant with the interpretive apparatus of a culture, have that kind of understanding. And everyone is an insider here.

Public disrobement is a consumption ritual, based on a paradigm that expresses and reveals the moral order of contemporary society through its invocation of important cultural codes. The first section of this chapter is devoted to the argument that the *existence* of such a paradigm is predicted by a theory of moral order with Wuthnovian roots. Whereas everyday interactions have often been viewed as a kind of ritual performance, classical theories of exchange regard the difference between everyday and ceremonial interaction as central. Wuthnow's theory of moral commitment to the market is used to introduce a distinction between inherent and distinctive enactment. The development of trust between strangers and moral commitment to the market leads to the expectation of the existence of a type of consumption ritual that symbolizes and affirms market relations in modern society, a type that receives its fullest expression in the paradigm of disrobement. Next, the dependence of the origin and development of the practice on the prior symbolic traditions of Mardi Gras is described, as are the ways performance variations reflect cultural codes of gender and hierarchy that coexist with the fundamental commitment to market values expressed in ritual disrobement.

INHERENT AND DISTINCTIVE ENACTMENT

A fundamental difference in social relations between premodern and modern society is the presence of strangers. Contemporary life involves frequent and consequential contact with individuals who are completely unknown to one another.[2] Lofland (1973) suggested such interactions have the potential for "a chaotic unpredictability that no human would find tolerable": The central problem of urban social relations is "making strangers routine" (pp. x, 176). The analysis of forms of behavior that make such episodes possible has largely focused on the diagnosis of trust, its management

---

[2]Levy (1972) stated the proposition baldly: "The vast majority of all peoples who have ever lived have had a very simple attitude toward strangers: 'You either fete 'em or eat 'em.'" (p. 57).

and consequences. Both Goffman's pioneering work (1967) and Collins' (1988) more systematic development of the theory emphasized the everyday rituals of encounters as a means of producing, maintaining, and repairing this trust.

Goffman and Collins were far from alone in extending the concept of "ritual" to phenomena remote from its traditional meaning. Wuthnow (1987) stressed that ritual is not a "special or sacred event set off from everyday reality" (p. 102).[3] To be sure, some insights have been gained by examining everyday interactions from the standpoint of ritual behavior. Yet these extensions are largely diversionary with respect to the analysis of sacred and ceremonial forms of behavior. The microstructures of daily interaction have seemed to substitute for the solidarity-producing "gathering" in the Durkheimian sense: Behaviors that were paradigmatically "profane" have undergone an analytic transformation. The distinction between everyday life and sacred times has been blurred.

If pressed, most scholars would admit that routinized daily interactions are distinct from ritualized performances. Durkheim (1912/1965) was at pains to point out that everyday life is different in important ways from ceremonial and sacred times, as in his discussion of the alternation between "dispersed" and "concentrated" phases in the life of Australian societies. Ritual helped to define the sacred realm and set it apart from the defiling elements of the profane. The discovery that many, if not all routine, instrumental behaviors of everyday life have "ritual elements," or symbolic-expressive dimensions, does not in itself entail expanding the denotation of ritual indefinitely. Why should everyday interactions, if not all symbolic life, be characterized as ritualistic? Some warrant might be found if the exchange of greetings, civil inattention, markers of self, and other "interaction rituals" that establish trustworthiness in routine interactions have *replaced* the collective occasions that sacralize the institutional order in premodern societies. Yet festivals and religious rites, the prototypes of ritual performances, have not diminished in importance. At best, "interaction ritual" theories simply require developing a typology of rituals, where before it was necessary to distinguish between "ritualized" and "routinized" action.

One of the best contemporary accounts to locate the ritualistic dimensions of behavior in everyday exchange activities is Wuthnow's theory of moral commitment to the market (1987).[4] Wuthnow argued that the market is not simply a mechanism for the exchange of goods and services, but a system to which people are morally committed, an integral aspect of both basic values and assumptions about

---

[3]However, Wuthnow (1987) defined ritual as "a symbolic-expressive aspect of behavior that communicates something about social relations, *often in a relatively dramatic or formal manner*" (p. 109, emphasis added). The issue is whether to take this latter property as conceptually or empirically linked to ritual.

[4]The idea of the market is consistent with multiple moral models, as indicated in Carrier (1997).

reality (p. 79). Market activities are the single most important form of public participation, permitting social actors to discharge moral obligations to society by exercising self-interested choice. One's behavior as a consumer is more than an instrumental economic calculation. It is a symbolic-expressive way of acting responsibly toward the larger society, fostering a sense of self-worth.

Buying, selling, working, and consuming are actions that link people to each other and to a social whole, which simultaneously organizes and permits the market to exist. With the advent of capitalism, the market has come to be defined as a "natural" economic form. The right to choose and the parallel right to provide goods and services in exchange for financial capital has largely eclipsed earlier concepts of freedom (pp. 85–88). Inevitably, the market was held to be a crucial reason that the morally virtuous Western nations "defeated" the corrupt socialist nations. By artificially limiting the freedom to engage in market activities, socialist regimes subverted the "normal" or "natural" exchange proclivities of autonomous individuals, frustrating the prosperity of people and the economic growth of nations. The essence of the marketplace, imbued with moral significance, is the exchange of goods and services for some generalized medium.

The difficulty with this approach is that ritual inheres in the behavior it symbolizes. That market behavior has an expressive dimension is not at issue, because this is a property of all behavior. Is the idea of moral commitment to the market simply a question of how to fully interpret or clarify this symbolic aspect? If so, then no specific empirical consequences can be expected. The weakness in this account is the absence of any indication of how commitment to the market is symbolized apart from participation in market activities themselves. Individuals' opportunities to fulfill ritual obligations are none other than the instrumental actions that, in the aggregate, are the market for goods and services. If moral commitment to a course of action is expressed simply through what may be called its "inherent enactment," then the concept is vacuous: People are morally committed to all of their actions. If moral commitment to the market is as important as this argument suggests, then it should be ritualized–*enacted distinctively*–in sacred settings as well as routinized in profane ones.

Inherent enactment, symbolizing moral commitment to the market through the exchange of goods and services, contrasts with classical theories of "distinctive enactment." Without questioning the expressive dimension of everyday activities, Malinowski (1922), Boas (1966), Mauss (1925/1967), and Lévi-Strauss (1949/1969) pioneered the concept of ceremonial exchange as a way of describing transactions that occur for symbolic and, ultimately, social ends rather than utilitarian value. The most famous and influential example, reviewed and reinterpreted countless times, was Malinowski's Kula Ring involving the exchange of necklaces for armlets around a chain of islands. But the Kula was a dyadic encounter with ritualistic qualities. It was not a "sacred gathering" or religious occasion producing the kind of collective effervescence Durkheim described, but an interaction between trading partners. The function of the periodic prestations was symbolic rather than instrumental, and it was understood as such by the Trobrianders. These reciprocal gifts maintained relations of trust and harmony between traders who did not often meet. In contemporary terms, the Kula might be described as a ritual revival of weak ties.

But the importance of relations with strangers and moral commitment to the market imply that exchange rituals should, if anything, be more important in the modern world.[5] The necessity of frequent and consequential interaction with strangers and the establishment of routine choices in the market for goods and services suggests strongly the existence of symbolic rites that distinctively enact these dominant new social relationships. Further, the Durkheimian roots of both Wuthnow's theory of moral order and Collins' theory of interaction rituals lead to the suspicion that microrituals of trust are not functionally equivalent to the consecrated gatherings characterizing premodern peoples. Where are the sacred exchange rituals in modern society?

The consumption ritual first developed at Mardi Gras is configured precisely in conformity with this expectation. Symbolic resources are assembled in ways that dramatize regions of consensus constituting the contemporary moral order. Evidence for the claims to be made is based on observations since 1983; documents; interviews with participants and French Quarter residents, merchants, tourists, and police officers; and an analysis of videotapes (Shrum & Kilburn, 1996). I begin with the question of why is there public nudity at Mardi Gras at all, discuss the general form of the ritual, and then examine observed differences in the ritual performance itself.[6]

---

[5]Wuthnow (1987) noted that Goffman's work on rituals seems compelling because evidence is in the domain of shared experience, whereas anthropological work succeeds even with sketchy evidence because it deals with societies about which little is known (p. 377, note 2). Studies of exchange rituals are a "tangle of categories pulled from widely different thinkers" (Grimes, 1985). In sociology, there are studies of political and legal ceremony, life-cycle rituals, and crowd behavior studies of games and spectacles (Gusfield & Michalowicz, 1984) Most other works on rituals are by theologians, anthropologists on rites in preindustrial cultures, or historians of religion.

[6]Shrum and Kilburn (1996) identified three main "ritual paradigms" based on the social and spatial relation between participants and the direction of transfer of symbolic goods. This analysis was based on approximately 40 hours of videotaped crowd interaction in 1991. We filmed at least five times in locations on the 300, 500, and 700 blocks of Bourbon Street and at one comparison site on Royal Street on Mardi Gras day. These represented several alternative socio-spatial configurations (including both street to street and balcony to street interactions). Analysis of 1,205 interactions showed that (a) both males and females participate in ritual disrobement in exchange for ceremonial beads, (b) gender patterning in the character of the ritual is shaped strongly by spatial configuration, and (c) the ritual order of exchange is a function of the hierarchical symbolism inherent in the relation between balcony and street.

HOW IT BEGAN

When I began lecturing on the subject in 1987, few outside New Orleans were aware of the phenomenon discussed here. In 2001, nearly all tourists know that disrobement is a prominent part of Mardi Gras. For many, it is the main attraction. They know there is much to be seen that is out of the ordinary, but their knowledge is limited. One particular limitation involves gender. Discussions of the ritual typically focus on performances by females, indicating both that cultural attitudes toward women are shaping popular understanding in important ways, and little awareness of performances by males. As indicated later, this is produced in part by the spatial patterning of disrobement ritual. It is important to note that historically, as well as contemporaneously, both women and men were involved in solicitation and display. In its overt display of body parts, this ritual performance seems sexual in its motivation and practice.[7] Again, popular understanding is produced by systematic neglect of certain exchanges that are extremely common.

When I first asked Louisianians about the origin of disrobement in 1983, there was no "origin myth." What I heard was simply that it was "traditional" at Mardi Gras, or that it has "gone on forever." I believed my interlocutors, for no other reason than I was new and I figured they should know. For an outsider, it seemed no different than being told that parades traditionally roll down St. Charles Avenue, and that if you stand on the street and yell, float riders will throw you beads. However, as I began to ask more people, and then to study the subject systematically, one thing became clear: No one had credible memories of disrobement earlier than the 1970s, not even in the free wheeling 1960s movie *Easy Rider*, which features both nudity and New Orleans. My belief is that the practice of disrobement for beads originated in the mid-1970s, probably in 1974 or 1975, not long before I first began asking! I have no quarrel with the statement that it was "traditional" even then. It was simply a practice that was invented and probably repeated multiple times at the same Carnival and thereby became, almost immediately, a tradition. I doubt seriously that an unambiguous origin for disrobement will ever be revealed, although future studies might well push the origin back several years. The reason it is so difficult to pinpoint a time and place is because the diffusion of the practice was so rapid. It was an "instant tradition" because it was an incremental twist on older symbolic traditions, an idea whose time had come.[8]

---

[7]The popularity of commercial establishments featuring female and male seminude dancing attests to the fact that both men and women are willing to exchange "real" currency for such displays. As the doorman for a Bourbon Street burlesque club professed: "The show is outside on the street. I can't get anybody in during Mardi Gras. An' I got strippers in here."

[8]One early photo of an individual exposing her breasts from a Bourbon Street balcony was published in *Figaro* in 1978. The photo is most likely from the 1977 festival. The absence of corresponding text may indicate the expectation that the practice was already understood by the New Orleans audience.

In order to understand this twist, it is important to ignore the persistent notions that New Orleans' Mardi Gras is a colonial, a Catholic, or a "pagan" festival. These ideas are based on a charming impetus: the desire to legitimate public intemperance through association with ancestors, religion, and ancient tradition. Yet, there is no compelling reason for it, apart from the date of Mardi Gras, which is set by the Catholic calendar to precede a Lenten period of abstinence, itself observed more in breach than practice. The Catholic symbolism of Mardi Gras is minimal or nonexistent. The idea that Mardi Gras is a pagan festival derives mainly from the cessation of work, relaxation of behavioral norms, and widespread consumption of alcohol, all of which are trivially widespread festival practices, as is nudity itself.

The Anglo-Americans who formed the first parading societies ("krewes") in the 19th century were the first to initiate the practice of a "reverse quete," casting tokens or small gifts into a crowd of onlookers (Kinser, 1990). Even in the early 1900s, the city of New Orleans was swarmed by upwards of 100,000 tourists, who came to view elaborate processions of floats, horses, flambeaux carriers, and maskers dressed as nobles and royalty. Those who rode in the parades were rewarded, more and more, for casting objects down into the multitudes who watched and yelled, at the top of their lungs, for the attention that might lead to a throw of beads. Once the practice began, it was self-reinforcing: The more the clamor, the more the throws; numerous throws led to greater tumult.

The membership of these oldest krewes (e.g., Comus & Rex) was White, male, and secretive, such that identities were concealed by masks. The symbolism—originally, at least—was not far from the truth of the matter: A small elite, raised on moving platforms, cast gifts of beads down into the begging multitudes. It does not take much of a semiotician to do the decoding. The riders simply pretend to be the historical antecedent of who they are: an upper class—the hereditary elite of an agrarian social order that offers its benefactions to peasants and beggars. Until recently, the consumption ritual that dominated Mardi Gras was that of masked aristocrats, riding through thousands of people on raised platforms, casting beads, "doubloons," and other tokens into the crowd. I have described this ritual as a "command paradigm" because largesse is an expression of the command economies that characterize agrarian societies, and because of the posture of arrogance that frequently characterizes the throwers.[9] The command paradigm persisted throughout the 20th century as the number of krewes increased and the cost of membership was reduced. The rich were not the only riders or the only throwers. Most middle-class people could join a krewe if they had a mind to. As Huey Long put it, "Every Man a King."

---

[9]Some years later I rode in my first parade down St. Charles Avenue masked as Elvis atop a float in the Krewe of Tucks. I found to my astonishment that by the end of the parade route, I had adopted this attitude myself, tired by the din of the beggars below, making fools of themselves for a string of beads, notwithstanding the fact that I had done it myself countless times.

In practice, however, most people played the role of beggars on the streets. The innovation of a *market* paradigm expresses, in ritual time and space, the desire for control over one's fortune, the promise and myth of capitalism. In its most basic form, the difference between the command and market paradigms is the changed relationship between a giver and recipient of beads. The command paradigm involves a pure gift, or favor by the giver. Nothing merits the gift on the part of the recipient. Begging is not a symbolic nothing, of course. But, ultimately, the recipient is begging. The potential receiver of beads has few options for gaining the attention of the gifter and motivating the gift. Anyone who has watched parades at Mardi Gras will have noted the great variety of behavior involved in accomplishing these two tasks: lifting one's arms, waving, screaming, positioning oneself with respect to others, arriving early for an ideal location, constructing symbolic exclusion zones with blankets and plastic tape, raising oneself on a stilted chair, holding a child or adult on one's shoulders to be closer to the floats, wearing colorful or revealing clothing or costumes, extending one's reach with a pole and a basket.

These strategies are child's play compared to undressing in public. More important, they are merely *strategies*, or attempts to curry favor. There is no obligation involved. Throwers cannot contrive to satisfy all the desires of the masses, any more than money grows on trees. Jumping and jiving are mannerisms of distinction, but they do not guarantee a throw, and they most certainly do not guarantee any particular *kind* of throw. As a solicitor you can always ask, but it is unlikely the riders can hear you above the bedlam. You are lucky to get any beads at all. Only a frenzied episode will indicate to a float rider that you have a special need for a particular object. Beggars, as you know, can't be choosers.

Beginning with these components, what has evolved over the past quarter century is a market in which recipients offer a specific service in exchange for a ceremonial currency. This market grew alongside those ritual encounters in which recipients are dependent on chance, or the arbitrary favor of the thrower. In the new "market paradigm," an action (public disrobement) is performed either before or after the receipt of beads. Moreover, whereas the command paradigm always involves a raised thrower, in the market paradigm the thrower may stand in any of several spatial relation to the recipient, and engage in a variety of bargaining practices that result in a diverse array of ritual practices, variations on a theme. But all this was yet to come. As with any new social practice, someone had to make a start.

Let me emphasize, since the point has been subject to misunderstanding, the following story is not to be viewed as the definitive origin of disrobement. The case of the "nudist's bargain" is important because it could be the origin, but especially because it reveals something important about the adoption and diffusion of social forms. The French Quarter area, and particularly Bourbon Street, has always been associated with nudity in one form or another—brothels, burlesque clubs, and a sexually open gay community. The "open door" policy for some clubs meant, literally, that establishments operated so that passersby could view a bit of the show. Routinized, commercial voyeurism may have provided the structural conduciveness needed for innovation, but urban districts elsewhere in the United States developed no such practice. What made the French Quarter different was the presence of a ceremonial currency—although no one viewed beads in this way at the time.

Where performers receive dollars from customers for stripping, a standard market relation exists. Performers take payment for services rendered. "Disrobement," as referred to herein, is exhibitionistic exposure by nonprofessionals, that is, a brief, alfresco display of private bodily regions to strangers. What may be viewed as a theoretical issue here was also a very practical problem for a group of practicing nudists at their annual gathering. Their approach to the problem involved two innovations, one highly successful and the other an utter failure. With parades now banned in the French Quarter, and most tourists on their way to Bourbon Street, a group of revelers engaged in innovative exhibitionism. This group on Royal Street determined, sometime during the 1975 festival, to stop passersby and try to prolong the interaction. Many in the group were nudists, so the "nudist's bargain" was not a stretch of the imagination. They sought to offer a motivation based on nakedness. One woman held up a sign, "SHOW YOUR PENIS," on the balcony, while a male friend below bargained with passing men. The idea was simple: The woman would raise her shirt and expose her breasts when the man below lowered his trousers and exposed his penis. It seems like nothing so much as a replication of the game often played by young children exploring their bodies: "You show me yours and I'll show you mine."

The nakedness was not complete. It exhibited precisely the brief, partial exposures by nonprofessionals to strangers that may be observed today. The topography of exhibitionism was in place, but not the motivation. What the nudists valued most deeply was the adoption, however brief, of an alternative behavioral code by non-nudists. What they found, to their amazement, was that reciprocal nudity was not required. Beads, in fact, worked just as well.

The evolution of parade throws has been more dramatic in recent years, but by the mid-1970s, a variety of beads were already available. Instead of offering the passersby a performance in kind, another motivator was quickly discovered. The nudists would offer beads for nudity—or offer to expose themselves for beads. For parade goers who had a bad night of it—well, it might have been a bit unusual, but it worked. Variation in the *quality* of beads seems to have been important even in the early stages of the development of the ritual, owing to the opportunities it offers for bargaining and collection. If all beads were the same, in length or color or characteristics, social interaction that affected the terms of the exchange would not be important. That interaction (i.e., what will be exchanged for what) is one of the main features of the ritual today. By the late 1970s, ritual disrobement was common, but the "nudist's bargain" of a reciprocal, exhibitionistic exchange is rarely seen today.

Reciprocal nudity was proposed and rejected at the same period as the consumption ritual that is now widespread. As a ritual, it is much easier than the exchange of beads for nudity. It can be spontaneously performed, without advance planning. It requires nothing more than mutual consent. Most importantly, it requires no gear. This phenomenon of multiple innovation and social selection is clear evidence that simultaneous nudity has no particular resonance outside the carnival context. This means that it does not remind people, through its basic form, of anything important in their daily lives. Those inclined to think of Mardi Gras nudity as debauchery should consider that: neither exhibitionism nor voyeurism require beads. Those that view the goings-on here in the French Quarter as a shameless perpetuation of bacchic indecency have no answer to the question of why a ritual of reciprocal nudity is not widespread. The theory of moral commitment to the market, by contrast, suggests that such a practice invoked no deeper social meaning, whereas the disrobement ritual that diffused connected precisely with the values of accumulation and consumption that permeate modern society.

The transformation of beads into a symbolic currency and the linkage of beads with nudity made disrobement quite understandable: Beads justify disrobement as a motivated action within the ritual system. The resourceful acquisition of a generalized medium of a exchange, whether beads or hard cash, is widely understood and accepted not only in the United States, but globally. Whether or not individuals wish to participate is a matter of choice, just as it is a matter of choice whether to purchase a television or have a garage sale. The action required, disrobement, is deviant from the standpoint of most external contexts, but that does not mean it should be performed for money—quite the opposite. What is taken over from the profane context of daily life is the structural isomorphism of service for currency, and that is all the more reason that money should not be involved, lest there be some flavor of prostitution or erotic dancing. Disrobement is legitimized by the resourceful acquisition of a generalized medium that is clearly a currency, but only in this symbolic universe. Ritual disrobement is an action widely understood and accepted as self-explanatory (which means it is largely self-legitimating) by observers and coparticipants. In American society, it is understood that wealth is a good thing. And free speech is not the same as free beer.

By the early 1990s, ritual disrobement had become extremely common. Using cameras positioned on both balcony and street, Shrum and Kilburn (1996) videotaped approximately 700 instances of disrobement (visible or probable), a rate of over 23 episodes per hour for the three main camera locations. Casual ethnographers, tourists, and participants notice that beads are still thrown without nudity and nudity does occur without gifts of beads. Consumption rituals at Mardi Gras are not cut from a single cloth. The following three points are important in understanding most of the patterns that may be observed in contemporary, turn of the millennium Carnival.

Market Ritual Differs from Command Ritual by Mutualizing Choice

As in the 1960s and 1970s, before the market paradigm developed, it is still possible to accumulate vast quantities of beads without disrobing. Most people do not take their clothes off at Mardi Gras, and most people still get beads. So if it is true that beads can be acquired without disrobement, why is the latter necessary for the accumulation of wealth? What has happened is, quite simply, inflation, owing to an uncontrolled increase in the supply of currency. There are many more beads in the system and there is a much greater difference now between beads that are worth very little and beads that are worth a lot. As a result, if individuals want simply a short string of cheap plastic beads, then it is no problem to get them. It is increasingly the case that such beads, eagerly sought 30 years ago as part of one's Carnival treasure trove, go unnoticed on the street. People feel they are not worth the trouble to bend down. By the 1990s, manufacturers produced strings of increasing length, larger beads, and more elaborate, painted designs. Rather than a uniform commodity distinguished mainly by color, beads are currency with a great range of values, like various denominations of bank notes.

These are now the "high end" of the market. It is quite difficult to acquire these valued strings. Not being a participant in ritual disrobement, it was approximately 15 years before I was thrown any long beads. It is not impossible to get these beads at Mardi Gras, but very few of the best and most attractive beads are thrown randomly. So the question becomes, how can individuals come into possession, not of one, but many beautiful strings of beads? In general, there are three possibilities: (a) to buy them, which is how many beads come into circulation before they begin to change hands; (b) to be (or have) a child—children, who are not participants in disrobement, receive many good beads; (c) to engage in ritual disrobement. In the latter case, not only can people accumulate significant quantities of good beads—more than they can carry—but they can select the ones they want. In effect, what was strictly a unilateral exchange in which choice resided with the gifter has become a moment of mutual choice, in which the gifter decides whether a performance is worth giving up something of value, while a performer decides whether the gift is worth the display of private regions to strangers. Participants gain control over the conditions of the exchange, making the ritual of disrobement structurally isomorphic to the exercise of personal choice in negotiated transactions.

Ritual Privilege Is Conferred by Spatial Symbolism

An important feature of the French Quarter is the zoning law that prohibits buildings above a certain height. The picturesque, wrought-iron balconies, two and three stories above the street, are an ideal location for revelers. Many times, but especially on Mardi Gras day, throngs of people clog the street, and interact across the spatial boundary that separates balcony and street. The ceremonial significance of elevation was incorporated early into the command paradigm, where the riders in the grand parades practiced gifting, where their symbolic gratuities were distributed from higher to lower spatial positions. This spatial relation is an important element to the ritual because occupancy of high social positions is often symbolized by elevation. Put simply, the ritual redistribution of wealth from higher to lower *social* positions occurs from higher to lower physical positions. The spatial configuration that characterized the development of throwing from floats at parades expressed both the hierarchy of class relations and its associated resource differentials. This relation was imported directly into the ritual practices of the French Quarter, such that celebrants on balconies typically cast beads downward to the symbolic beggars below. The "ritual inversion" of street-to-balcony gifts is much less common: Peasants do not provide wealth to the elite. Again, this command paradigm typically involves low value currency, but it is crucial for the understanding of subsequent status orderings.

Market Rituals Reinforce Gender Differences Through the Legitimation Conferred by Moral Choice

It is not and has never been true that disrobement is restricted to women. Not only were men involved in the earliest days, as suggested in the case of the nudist's bargain, but men have been significantly involved in disrobement throughout the 1990s and their participation is still growing. Although women were dominant in the early days, there has been a conscious movement by women (a mild form of "affirmative action," if you will) to provide men with the opportunity, and include men more directly in the act of disrobement. The balance depends heavily on time and place, but men sometimes participate more actively in daylight street disrobements than women. However, the fluid nature of individual market transactions between thousands of individual participants means that the "personal choice" characteristic of reciprocal exchange may aggregate into patterns that display strong gender differences.

Gender differences have been incorporated into the consumption rituals of Mardi Gras and exist as a function of the importation of traditional role stereotypes and relations into these new social forms. Men, but typically not women, engage in the display of buttocks ("mooning"), as a substitute for genitalia. Whereas I once speculated that this was due to the association of the exposed genitals with "deviant" exhibitionism, now I think it is more likely due to cultural sensitivity regarding genital size. The display of genitals was once predominantly an activity of men, but is increasingly practiced by women as well. How, then, are gender differences expressed? Women are more likely than men to disrobe dramatically, from positions of elevation, and to disrobe without receiving beads.

By the late 1980s, it was clear that more was happening at Mardi Gras than a simple exchange of beads for nudity. Large crowds, consisting dominantly of men, would orient toward a woman, or group, on a balcony and chant, "Show Your Tits." The command and market paradigms were synthesized and reversed. Although the command paradigm involves a unilateral gift of beads, and the market paradigm involves an exchange of beads and disrobement, "veneration" involves a unilateral performance of disrobement. Spatial configuration remains key to understanding the emergence of this "third" ritual form. This form is exclusively the province of women, except in the gay sector of Bourbon Street, where it is also practiced by men. "Veneration" has been called a third ritual paradigm (Shrum & Kilburn, 1996), but I admit to reluctance in providing a distinctive label for the practice. Veneration is indeed marked by an extremely gendered character in elevated action, impression management, and ritual ordering, but is in many ways a simple extension of the market paradigm, following from its distinctive logic of negotiated choice.

As mentioned earlier, discussions of disrobement focus on performances by women. Now it is easy to understand why this is so. Performances by men, with the exception of gays, always occur on the street, whereas performances by women often occur from the highly visible balconies. Even if it were true that equal numbers of men and women populated the street, it would appear that women were more actively involved in the ritual.[10] In fact, disrobement by women is more noticeable, it more often occurs in elevated locations, and is accompanied by different characteristics and mannerisms. Most important are the pattern of refusals, the performance of disrobement in the absence of exchange, and ritual sequencing.

So it is possible to get certain kinds of beads without disrobement, as part of the command paradigm. But, what happens when individuals *refuse* to disrobe? Refusals may be accompanied by begging (a command practice), but they occur in the context of market practice as well. Refusal involves solicitation and visible rejection, either because some one does not participate in disrobement at all, or because that person is not willing to disrobe for a particular offer. Hence, refusals to disrobe are never associated with the receipt of beads. What is interesting about the phenomenon of refusal is that within the several days that lead up to Fat Tuesday, it tends to occur earlier rather than later, which implies a process of learning or ritual socialization. Moreover, refusals from women on balconies are extremely rare. It is not that all or even most women on balconies participate in disrobement—far from it. On balcony and street, most participants at Mardi Gras do not engage in disrobement. What occurs is a process of *ritual identification* in which the voyeuristic audience is matched with willing participants. Audience members correctly identify potential targets, and do not often solicit nonparticipants. Participants engage in a process of impression management through cues based on attire and demeanor that indicate their willingness to engage in negotiation. Because much of this interaction occurs across the boundary of balcony and street, these indicators are largely visual. Ornamentation with valuable beads functions as the foremost indicator of willingness to disrobe—just as it is common to signal status as an entrepreneur through symbols of past success (e.g., expensive suits).

Disrobement in the absence of exchange occurs from balconies and is generally practiced by women. The gendered patterning of the practice and the behavior

---

[10]Men outnumber women on both street and balcony, which makes it even more likely that the focus will be on female nudity.

of men on the street below is a form of *veneration* that accompanies a metamorphosis of identity transforming women into ritual objects. Because ritual privilege is conferred by spatial positioning, it might seem as if women on balconies were in the best position to acquire large quantities of valued currency. Yet, they are observed to disrobe without beads, for the veneration of the crowd, an act of "pure performance." Does this undermine the argument for the ritual privilege conferred by spatial symbolism?

This question may be addressed through observations of ritual sequencing. Detailed examination of the negotiation process in relation to throws of beads and disrobement reveals that balcony participants compel reciprocity where they choose. This is so not only because of the logic of market ritual, in which beads must accompany performance, but because of the public nature of balcony performances. This publicity means that although "free riding" is possible, one or more persons in a large crowd is always willing to bear the cost. Hence, tokens are more readily available for balcony performers than for street performers whose audience is small. It is not the availability of currency or the motivation of throwers that affects pure performance, but the moral choice of performers.

Two observations reinforce this point, and lead to the notion that veneration expresses moral codes of gender rather than economic structure. First, unilateral disrobement occurs only if each act or throw is considered to be a discrete unit rather than part of a sequence. This is not the case, especially where the spatial position of participants is fixed on a balcony. What typically occurs is a series of negotiations, accompanied by repetitive disrobement and throwing by various members of the audience. Invariably, the first instance of disrobement is accompanied by beads. The characteristic sequence involves beads, disrobement, further negotiation, and sometimes disrobement without beads. A single disrobement may also be accompanied by multiple throws from the audience. So it is not the case that disrobement occurs without beads, when the entire pattern of interaction is analyzed.

Second, there is a sequence or ordering involved in consumption rituals at Mardi Gras. The ordering in the exchange of beads and disrobement is significant because the temporal relation between actions has ritual meaning, expressing power and deference in social relations. Disrobement rituals that take place on Bourbon Street involve the following sequence: identification of participants, selection, bargaining, disrobement, and a gift of beads, often (although not necessarily) followed by a brief kiss. This sequence applies to disrobement by men and women. When disrobement occurs on the balcony, identification, selection, and bargaining occur as usual, but the sequence of events may take a different turn. Instead of disrobement followed by beads, the performer chooses whether the performance shall occur before or after the throw. There can be no clearer evidence of ritual privilege. Not only do balcony performers choose the terms of the exchange, but they also determine its sequencing. Attention to these matters of temporal duration and sequencing show that gender is strongly embedded in the market structure of the ritual.

CONCLUSIONS

In the late 1970s, the ceremonial exchange of nudity for beads was practiced by a small number of innovators and early adopters. By the new millennium, disrobement had become one of the principal rites of Mardi Gras, practiced by large numbers of celebrants, many of whom have never removed their clothes in public and will never do so again. Exhibitionistic display is difficult to imagine in the abstract—in the United States because nudity is rare, and elsewhere because it is common. At Carnival in Brazil, nudity is far more prevalent than at Mardi Gras, representing a simple extension of the lack of bodily covering characterizing ordinary sunbathing. Nudity at Carnival is not a consumption ritual in the Brazilian context. The key realization is that disrobement is more than nudity. Certain forms of nudity are legal if not widely accepted. Nudists and strippers of both genders are likely to be viewed as peculiar or financially motivated. Exhibitionism involves brief displays of sexual organs to strangers and is widely seen as perverted. Mental health professionals seek to understand why people expose themselves to others and alter the underlying personality disorder that causes it.

I have no way of assessing, in any realistic fashion, the motivations of those who disrobe. But much of the audience appeal clearly derives from the fact that participants are viewed *as and only as* "ordinary, normal folks," rather than prostitutes, strippers, or dirty old men in greatcoats. For tourists and locals who have heard about the "goings on"—even for those who heartily disapprove[11]—there is a childlike amazement in seeing for oneself one of the earliest and most fundamental social inhibitions in American society violated publicly by ordinary people.

Participant understanding begins to take shape when it is explained or noticed that exhibitors are not "just flashing" but are rewarded with strings of beads. Anyone who does not know the value of long beads has yet to be properly socialized. During Mardi Gras, the value of beads is not a matter of pretense. People do not "make believe" in their value any more than they make believe in the value of money. True, beads will not buy dinner at Galatoire's. But it is equally true that money lacks ritual value and cannot be exchanged for disrobement. The duality of beads resides in their character as display currency. Beads are money people can wear and also visible symbols of status. When children first discover sex, they look at people differently. Likewise, newcomers to the French Quarter notice those with massive amounts of beads.

---

[11]Significant numbers of Christian evangelists converge on the French Quarter during Mardi Gras. Leafleting and singing, they form their own street processions, often carrying a large wooden cross. Their presence constitutes a contrastive symbolic idiom and an important source of interaction for festival participants.

Small Groups

After two or three days, this sense of strangeness declines. The symbolic universe of Carnival is the only relevant system of action. The contextual framework is negotiated and often adopted by local groups of friends. Participation in disrobement takes several forms but is rarely practiced by singles. Small groups of people stand or travel together. As they travel, they are frequently separated by strangers in the crowd. At minimum, these dyads involve same-sex friends, spouses, or partners, but they often combine in pairs. A pair of couples is often conducive to ritual participation because it readily leads to active encouragement,[12] passive support, or at least "permission" by both same-sex and opposite-sex partners. For some, disrobement is defined as a matter of "bravery." Those who disrobe are themselves unsure whether they will, in the end, have the nerve. Their associates anxiously await the verdict—before themselves disrobing. For others, all this is a simple matter of maximizing wealth. Disrobement is not deviant in this context, so they participate without reservation. But we should keep in mind that the majority of participants at Mardi Gras elect not to disrobe. They follow the original Mardi Gras paradigm, simply begging and catching. They also serve as the audience for the smaller number of performers.

Gender and Interpretation

Other approaches to disrobement form part of the microstructure of the ritual largely neglected here. Onlookers in the crowd discuss the behavior of women and men negotiating for beads in terms of widely used cultural categories. The existence of these situational variations, as well as the larger patterns already described, make possible patterned differences in interpretation. The most prominent divergence is based on differential involvement by gender in the configuration of balcony and street rituals. Because the likelihood of witnessing these variations depends on spatial position and time of day, most observers differentially witness one form or another. Many observers say they have never seen a man disrobe. But they are not looking.

"Types," whether archetypal or stereotypical, are formed by a focus on the uniformity underlying the diversity of strangers. In this case, the potential for bystander generalization is increased by the prevalence of disrobement and the immense range in the social and physical characteristics of actors who disrobe. The denominator of disrobement is nothing more than the display of sexual parts. Female participants represent Woman, males represent Man. For many of the men who crowd the street, exposure by women from balconies reinforces sexist atti-

---

[12]Disrobements often occur simultaneously, with up to seven people performing together.

tudes concerning what women "really are" or "really want." The most common mundane account asks simply, "Why would they do it unless they enjoyed it?" These are not strippers or paid performers. They are girls-next-door, middle-aged women and elderly matrons, attractive and unattractive, flirtatious and reluctant. They disrobe for male strangers to be photographed and cheered. They do it for a string of beads.[13]

Women, in turn, often see an undifferentiated, inebriated audience character-ized by stereotypically masculine, pack behaviors, such as chanting, aggressive-ness, and voyeurism. Yet women have been quick to support equality in the form of male disrobement and if the nudists' account is accurate, women were among the key innovators. During certain daylight periods, the frequency of male disrobe-ment is higher than the frequency of female disrobements. Women on balconies with long beads to throw are active and insistent solicitors. Further, from the per-spective of some active feminists, public disrobement by women is a sign of libera-tion rather than exploitation. If anything is clear, there is no generalized "meaning" of the disrobement ritual.

Markets and Strangers

The foregoing argument highlights the dependence of ritual origin and evolution on prior symbolic traditions, the difference between command and market rituals, and the importance of structural variations to the multivocality of ritual. Exhibitionistic nudity is the central component of a contemporary consumption ritual that originated as an effective and appealing use of existing symbolic re-sources. Its ritual significance is an isomorphic expression of market behavior in a capitalist economy. Without assuming any psychoanalytic causation, it might well be the case that a proportion of the population at risk has a deep-seated desire to flaunt convention or overcome personally experienced repression by appearing unclothed in public. But it seems more likely that the explanation for the diffusion, popularity, and structure of the practice is its symbolic resonance as an expression of moral commitment to the market.

Structural conduciveness is provided by a capitalistic economic system. Rit-ual recruits are drawn from a context wherein the price for goods and services is regulated–ideologically at any rate—only by the "law of supply and demand," the basic economic mechanism. Psychological factors alone do not explain the ob-served level of public exhibitionism. Ritual disrobement is the empirical instantiation of the theory of moral commitment to the market. One might ask if

---

[13]In American society there is a good deal of pressure to show only the "body beautiful." At Mardi Gras, a wide range of body types is on display. Part of the popularity of disrobement ritual is due to the relaxation of these restrictions on the kinds of bodies that may be dis-played.

disrobement is primarily a strategy for the accumulation of wealth or a form of deviance that requires legitimation. If it is a strategy for accumulation, then what seems most significant are the many revelers, the problematic nature of success through begging, and search for symbolic currency. If it is mainly a form of deviance, with a concomitant need for legitimation, then what seems significant is the public nature of nudity and the strangers in the audience that lead to a desire to avoid the deviant label. But the account provided here suggests that neither view is complete by itself. Instead, disrobement is a ritualized expression of moral commitment to the market. The distinction between accumulation and legitimation fails to express the nature of market ritual as a special kind of ritual, a paradigm with variations. Sheer accumulation behavior does not characterize many women on balconies and does not explain the observed ritual ordering. If beads simply serve a legitimating function, then multiple disrobements would only require one legitimating throw. Yet this is not the case. From a balcony, disrobement can be a "pure performance," only when installed in a sequence of negotiations that makes clear the relations of privilege implied by spatial hierarchy. Street disrobement by both men and women reflects, sometimes in a boringly routine manner, the transactions of commercial life.

Ritual Choice

The practices described in this chapter are obviously different from the highly structured, even invariant, sequences that are oftentimes understood as ritual. But the ordering of actions in disrobement varies and has meaning. Participation in the market involves buying and selling goods and services through the exercise of self-interested choice. It should now be clear that where social forms express the market, no rigid mechanism could be expected. It would violate the structures of negotiation and decision that are dramatically in evidence here. The freedom to decide whether and how to participate is arguably the most important value expressed at Mardi Gras.

Meanings, likewise, are tied to the many variations in types of performance, although they are also matters of interpretation. Owing to the importance of choice, variations are more likely to occur in the context of market rituals. Neither inevitable sequence nor fixed interpretation would be predicted of a naturally developing structural form based on the idea of a market. Market rituals are nonetheless effective because variability occurs within an architectural framework expressing "mutual intentionality." This feature leads to its effectiveness in perpetuating social patterns based on gender and hierarchy as well. Market relations do not exist in a vacuum but in a context of many existing social forms and relations, gender and class among them.

Some scholars have argued that ritual emerges during periods of uncertainty or conflict regarding basic social relations (Wuthnow, 1987, p. 120). Ritual articulates the character of moral obligations, so its dramatizations are in greater demand whenever the character of these obligations becomes uncertain. From the mid-1970s until the present, with the breakdown of traditional gender roles, the relations between men and women have become more complex and ambiguous. Read as a ritual script for changes in the contemporary social order, the practices of street and balcony disrobement indicate that women may enter the economic marketplace and compete for wealth, but remain on a pedestal for men to worship and solicit as sexual objects.

In 1947, Tennessee Williams published *A Streetcar Named Desire*, the drama that would soon become New Orleans' most celebrated work of art. Blanche Dubois, a southern belle with a suspect past, flirts with her new beau, Mitch. "I'm not properly dressed," she says. Mitch, completely unprepared for a woman such as Blanche, rejoins: "Well, that don't make no difference in the Quarter." As we have seen, it most certainly does.

REFERENCES

Boas, F. (1966). *Kwakiutl ethnography*. Chicago: University of Chicago Press.

Carrier, J. (1997). *Meanings of the market: The free market in Western culture*. Oxford: Berg.

Collins, R. (1988). *Theoretical sociology*. San Diego: Harcourt Brace Jovanovich.

Cox, D., & Daitzmann, R. (1980). *Exhibitionism: Description, assessment, and treatment*. New York: Garland.

Durkheim, E. (1965). *The elementary forms of religious life*. New York: The Free Press. (Original work published 1912)

Goffman, E. (1967). *Interaction ritual*. New York: Doubleday.

Grimes, R. (1985). *Research in ritual studies: A programmatic essay and bibliography*. Metuchen, NJ: Scarecrow.

Gusfield, J., & Michalowicz, J. (1984). Secular symbolism: Studies of ritual, ceremony, and the symbolic order in modern life. *Annual Review of Sociology, 10*, 417–435.

Kinser, S. (1990). *Carnival, American style: Mardi Gras at New Orleans and Mobile*. Chicago: University of Chicago Press.

Lévi-Strauss, C. (1969). *The elementary structures of kinship*. Boston: Beacon Press. (Original work published 1949)

Levy, M., Jr. (1972). *Modernization: Latecomers and survivors*. New York: Basic Books.

Lofland, L. (1973). *A world of strangers: Order and action in urban public space*. New York: Basic Books.

Malinowski, B. (1922). *Argonauts of the Western Pacific*. London: Routledge & Kegan Paul.

Mauss, M. (1967). *The gift: Forms and functions of exchange in archaic societies*. New York: Norton. (Original work published 1925)

Kilburn, J. (1996). Ritual disrobement at Mardi Gras. *Social Forces, 75,*

Weinberg, M. (1965). Sexual modesty, social meanings, and the nudist camp. *Social Problems, 12,* 311–318.

Wuthnow, R. (1987). *Meaning and moral order: Explorations in cultural analysis.* Berkeley: University of California Press.

4

Kwanzaa: The Making of a Black Nationalist Tradition, 1966–1990

Elizabeth H. Pleck[1]

University of Illinois, Urbana–Champaign

Kwanzaa, a 7-day festival beginning on December 26, was created in 1966, and is one of the most lasting innovations of U.S. Black nationalism of the 1960s. Although it is becoming more popular in Canada, the Caribbean, and elsewhere, Kwanzaa is still chiefly celebrated in the United States. Designed to resemble the ritual at an African harvest festival, Kwanzaa consists of a number of activities, including feasting, lighting candles, recitations, and the giving of small gifts to children. A marketing survey in 1997 estimated that Kwanzaa is celebrated by one out of seven U.S. Blacks.[2] Two successive acts of national imprimatur demonstrate the growing acceptance of Kwanzaa. The postal service offered a Kwanzaa stamp in 1997. The same year, President Clinton became the first U.S. president to issue a proclamation sending good wishes to Americans who celebrate Kwanzaa. Kwanzaa is significant both because of its popularity and because it retells the African American story, with the distant African rural past elevated to the point of origin. It is even more significant as a cultural event where African American racial identity is formed and refashioned in the post-civil rights era.

As a flexible ritual that changed, grew, and flourished over the years, the history of Kwanzaa is replete with ironies. Born in part out of a critique of capitalism

---

[1]Reprinted by permission of Transaction Publishers. "Kwanzaa: The Making of a Black Nationalist Tradition, 1966–1990," *Journal of American Ethnic History,* By Elizabeth H. Pleck, v. 20, no. 4, Summer, 2001. Copyright 2001 by Transaction Publishers.

[2]Maritz Marketing Research polled a nationally representative sample of 907 adults in 1977. Tibbett L. Spear, "Stretching the Holiday season," *American Demographics,* 19 (November, 1997): 42~9. The article did not report whether the interviewers asked about the type of Kwanzaa celebrations the respondents participated in. For a bibliography about Kwanzaa, see Itibari M. Zulu, *Kwanzaa 1969–1989: A Selected Bibliography* (Los Angeles, 1994).

in the United States, the holiday owed much of its growing acceptance to refurbishing through consumerism. Originating among a Black nationalist scornful of Black "matriarchy," Kwanzaa found its most eager enthusiasts among Black women, who usually organized the feast in the home. Seen as an accessible ritual bound to appeal to the Black masses, Kwanzaa was taken up mainly by the Black middle class. A ceremony intended to replicate a simple harvest festival, most Kwanzaa celebrations occurred among residents of large cities or suburbs. Created by an intellectual hostile to Christianity, Kwanzaa proved dynamic enough to be redefined as religious, secular, or both, and as fully compatible with Christianity. Stemming from a rejection of racial integration, the holiday time Kwanzaa celebration at many public schools functioned as a sign of toleration for cultural difference. Seen as a ritual to develop a diasporic African identity, Kwanzaa became more appealing as it came to include many more elements of African American history and culture. This chapter details this ironic transformation in the meaning, practice, and discourse of Kwanzaa between its founding in 1966 and an artificial end point, 1990. Like all rituals, Kwanzaa is both a reflection of changing discourses as well as a ritual that helps to shape them.

The typical way of explaining the popularity of a nationalist ritual is to begin by classifying it as an "invented tradition," using Eric Hobsbawm's phrase. Hobsbawm defined an invented tradition as a custom of relatively recent origin deliberately designed to resemble an ancient tradition. Hobsbawm found that many invented traditions, from kilt-wearing to Bastille Day, were inspired by various forms of nationalism.[3] These rituals were intended to celebrate a glorious national

---

[3]Eric Hobsbawm. "Introduction: Inventing Traditions," in *The Invention of Tradition*, eds. Eric Hobsbawm and Terence Ranger (Cambridge, 1983), pp. 1–14; Richard Handler and Jocelyn Linnekin, "Tradition, Genuine or Spurious," *Journal of American Folklore*, 97 (1984): 273–290; John R. Gillis, ed., *Commemorations: The Politics of National Identity* (Princeton, N.J., 1994). Every history of an American festival, holiday, and domestic occasion is a study of an invented tradition. The stories vary in how explicitly they embrace the phrase and Hobsbawm's conceptualization. For examples of his influence on U.S. historiography on this subject, see April Schultz, "The Pride of the Race Had Been Touched: The 1925 Norse-American Immigration Centennial and Ethnic Identity," *Journal of American History*, 77 (March, 1991): 1265–1295; John Bodnar, "Symbols and Servants and the Limits of Public History," *Journal of American History*, 73 (June, 1986): 137–151; Rudolph Vecoli, "'Primo Maggio' in the U.S.: An Invented Tradition of the Italian Anarchists," in *May Day Celebration*, ed. Andrea Panaccione (Venezia, 1988), pp. 55–83; Kathleen Conzen, "Ethnicity as Festive Culture: German-America in Parade," in *The Invention of Ethnicity*, ed. Werner Sollors (New York, 1989), 44–76; Stephen Nissenbaum, *The Battle for Christmas* (New York, 1996); Penne L. Restad, *Christmas in America: A History* (New York, 1995); Leigh Eric Schmidt, *Consumer Rites: The Buying and Selling of Holidays* (Princeton, N.J., 1995); S. W. Pope, *Patriotic Games: Sporting Traditions in the American Imagination, 1876–1926* (New York, 1977), pp. 85–119; Michael Kazin and Steven J. Ross, "America's Labor Day: The Dilemma of a Worker's Celebration," *Journal of American History*, 78 (March, 1992): 1294–1323; Larry Danielson, "St. Lucia in Lindsborg, Kansas," in *Creative Ethnicity: Symbols and Strategies of Contemporary Ethnic Life*, ed.   (continued on next page)

past. Hobsbawm thought the late 19th century was a stretch of time particularly significant in the development of nationalist ritual because many European countries and the United States confronted the difficulty of forging bonds of national loyalty among large, often urban immigrant populations. In the United States, newcomers and the native-born lower classes were made into patriots by pledging allegiance to the flag and celebrating Thanksgiving and Christmas in school pageants and at home.[4]

The ability of a small group of adherents to invent new myths and traditions is one sign of the strength of nationalism. Yet, not all the rituals proposed by nationalists succeed. A sure indication of success is the public's willingness to regard the new ritual as authentic. Thus, there are similarities between Gilded Age U.S. and European nationalist rituals and Kwanzaa. Nonetheless, the differences are more striking than the similarities. Kwanzaa was not merely a new nationalist ritual, but also an alternative to the dominant one of the season. Black nationalists were U.S. citizens assigning their national identity a far lower priority than their racial identity. In fact, they were hostile to the country of their birth and patriotic display, decidedly opposed to serving in the Vietnam War, and critical of the nation's values and institutions. Black nationalists did not control the government or seek to secure the allegiance of the masses to the government. Instead, they were radicals, engaged in frequent armed confrontations with the police and shootouts with other Black nationalist groups. Kwanzaa became widely adopted in schools and homes only when it shed its oppositional character and came to be redefined as a more familial event. It was especially appealing to the Black middle class—and the main holiday makers, Black women—who were seeking a child-oriented, highly sentimental Christmastime holiday with racial self-definition.

By the 1990s, Kwanzaa had become established enough to inspire critique from Black intellectuals writing in mainstream journals and in Black magazines. Anna Wilde, a journalist, whose article appeared in the *Public Interest* in 1995, and Gerald Early, a professor of African American literature at Washington University

---

Stephen Stern and John Allan Cicala (Logan, Utah, 1991), pp. 187–203; Len Travers, *Celebrating the Fourth: Independence Day and the Rites of Nationalism in the Early Republic* (Amherst, Mass., 1997); Shane White, "'It was a Proud Day': African Americans, Festivals, and Parades in the North, 1741–1834," *Journal of American History,* 81 (June, 1994): 13–50; Timothy Meagher, "'Why Should We Care for a Little Trouble on a Walk through the Mid': St. Patrick's and the Columbus Day Parades in Worcester, Massachusetts, 1845–1915," *New England Quarterly,* 58 (March, 1985): 5–26; Kenneth Moss, "St. Patrick's Day Celebrations and the Formation of Irish-American Identity, 1845–1875," *Journal of Social History,* 29 (Fall, 1995): 125–148; William H. Wiggins, Jr., *0 Freedom! Afro-American Emancipation Celebrations* (Nashville, Tenn., 1990); David Waldstreicher, *Perpetual Fetes: The Making of American Nationalism, 1776–1820* (Chapel Hill, N.C., 1997).

[4]Elizabeth H. Pleck, "The Making of the Domestic Occasion: The History of Thanksgiving in the United States," *Journal of Social History,* 32 (Summer, 1999): 773–789.

in a *Harper's* article in 1997 have offered assessments of the festival. Both articles combined sociological analysis and a bit of contemporary history with largely negative views of Kwanzaa. Wilde, who described celebrations in the Roxbury section of Boston and in Cambridge, Massachusetts, briefly traced the commercialization of the holiday through expositions of consumer goods, adoption in the public schools, museums, and at Black churches. To Wilde, Kwanzaa helped to develop Black middle-class racial identity but was marred by antagonism toward whites. She noted the exclusion of Whites—even a White mother of an interracial child—from some Kwanzaa celebrations. Wilde concluded that "Kwanzaa is essentially an effort on the part of African Americans to create community cohesiveness, though still unfortunately coupled in some ways with anti-white feeling."[5]

Early offered a second negative appraisal in *Harper's* in 1997 as he pondered his own ambivalence about attending student-initiated Kwanzaa celebrations at his university. He examined the ritual of Kwanzaa and the seven principles (called the Nguso Saba) affirmed each night of the festival. He wrote, "For in creating a cultural orthodoxy designed to combat racism, urban disorder, and a legacy of oppression, we subject ourselves to delusional dogma, the tyranny of conformity, and language that rings of fascist imagery."[6] Like Wilde, Early argued that the holiday appealed mainly to the black middle class who found the ritual a kind of therapy to heal the wounds inflicted from racial slights and insults. Along with other influential Black scholars, Early was concerned that in creating a mythic African heritage, Black nationalists were rejecting the creativity of U.S. Black culture from jazz to the blues to dance to southern cooking.

Early's essay is longer and more comprehensive than Wilde's. He perceptively noted how Kwanzaa was able to capitalize on Black hostility toward the whiteness and commercialism of Christmas. Both authors sensed that the Kwanzaa of the 1990s differs from the ritual of the 1960s, but, not being historians, do not attempt to date the transformation or explain why it occurred. Both authors understood that the holiday became popular mainly among the Black bourgeoisie, without providing a complete explanation of the appeal of the holiday to the middle class. To historicize Kwanzaa is to place the holiday within the dual contexts of Black nationalism of the 1960s and the development of the Black middle class in the 1980s. In this dual context, this chapter examines the dynamic and protean character of Black nationalism and the ways that the ritual of Kwanzaa could address the needs and anxieties of the burgeoning Black mid-

---

[5]Anna Day Wilde, "Mainstreaming Kwanzaa," *The Public Interest*, 119 (Spring, 1995): 68–79.

[6]Gerald Early. "Dreaming of a Black Christmas: Kwanzaa bestows the gifts of therapy," *Harper's*, 294 (January, 1995): 55–61; Adolph Reed, Jr., "Marxism and Nationalism in Afro-America," *Social Theory and Practice*, I (Fall, 1971): 16; "Do We Need Kwanzaa?" *Essence*, 29 (December, 1997): 68, 70.

dle class in the post-civil rights era. There is a gender as well as class dimension to the history of Kwanzaa, in that Black women put the familial version of Kwanzaa into practice as they sought a holiday of family gathering and instruction for children.

The origins of Kwanzaa lie in Black nationalist responses to the Watts riot of 1966. Because Kwanzaa had a single creator, Maulana Ronald Karenga, Kwanzaa emerged from Karenga's distinct brand of cultural Black nationalism and from the aesthetic decisions he made. The early history of Kwanzaa from 1966 to the end of the 1970s is the story of the rise of Black cultural nationalism from the urban riots of the 1960s and its floundering amidst government infiltration and internecine warfare between Black nationalist groups, including the arrest, murder, or exile of some Black nationalists. In a cultural renaissance, Black artists and intellectuals were allied. Kwanzaa rose, fell, and floundered in relation to Karenga's alliances and schisms. His personality, role, and ideas, although crucial to the origins of Kwanzaa, also tended to keep Kwanzaa confined within a limited circle of Black cultural nationalists.

Black cultural nationalists believed that the United States was an imperial nation, which had both external colonies (e.g., the Philippines or Puerto Rico) and colonies situated on the U.S. mainland. U.S. Blacks, they held, were an internal colony. Just as peoples around the world, but especially in Africa, were struggling to end colonialism, so, too, U.S. Blacks needed to overthrow what they regarded as colonialism in favor of a "struggle for liberation." These ideas appealed most to Blacks living in large northern and western cities. As Komozi Woodard noted, Black cultural nationalism formed in relation to the urban crisis of the 1960s. He wrote, "The cultural nationalist strategy of African American radicals was to develop *parallel* black institutions in the void left by the urban crisis, emphasizing the failure of the American government and mainstream economy in providing basic services and offering black nationalism and cooperative economics as rational alternatives."[7] Karenga favored the formation of a Black independent political power in municipal government. He also believed that cultural liberation was both a necessity and the first stage in the longer process of establishing a separate Black nation.

As 1960s cultural politics, organizational affirmation, and imagined historical memory of Africa (with gender assumptions close to the surface), Kwanzaa was entirely Karenga's. At age 25, he was a student, an intellectual, and a revolutionary Black nationalist. At the time he created Kwanzaa, Karenga had not visited Africa. He was born Ronald Everett in 1941, one of 14 children of a Baptist minister from Parsonsburg, Maryland, and a homemaker mother. He moved to Los Angeles in 1959 because he had an older brother, employed as a teacher, living there. Everett attended Los Angeles City College, where he became the first Black elected student

---

[7]Komozi Woodard, *A nation within a nation: Amiri Baraka (LeRoi Jones) and Black power politics* (Chapel Hill, N.C., 1999), p. 8.

body president. He was active in campus civil rights activities supporting the work of SNCC and CORE in the South.[8] Karenga transferred to UCLA and received a BA in political science with an emphasis on African Studies in 1963. The same year, a Bay area Black activist, Donald Warren, founded a small local organization, the Afro-American Association. The group rejected racial integration and called for Black self-help and greater economic development within black neighborhoods. Members of the organization lectured (using "street language") in Black neighborhoods. Warren asked Karenga to head a Los Angeles branch of the association. The association fell apart within a year because of personality conflicts and struggles for power. But Karenga was on his way toward not only self-definition as a nationalist, but toward the idea of heading his own organization. In 1964, Karenga received an MA in political science from UCLA. His personal transformation into a Black nationalist is reflected in two stages of re-naming: In 1963, he became Ron Karenga (Swahili for tradition) and in 1965, he became Maulana Karenga (master teacher of tradition).[9] (He also began to shave his head, adopt his trademark Genghis Kahn-type mustache, and wear sunglasses during this period.)

Although Karenga was a Black nationalist before the Watts riot in August 1965, the riot helped Black nationalism gain ground in Los Angeles and other large cities. The rioting and destruction of property by Black residents of a mainly Black section of Los Angeles was at the time the largest single urban rebellion of the 1960s, born out of frustration with police brutality and continued inequality amidst the surface prosperity and civil rights legislative advances of the 1960s. The Watts riot lasted 5 days in August 1965; it left 34 known dead and about 900 injured.[10] Karenga actually tried to quell the violence because he believed that Black residents of Watts were destroying their own neighborhood.[11]

Less than a month after the Watts riot, Karenga founded a Black nationalist organization in Los Angeles, "US" (as opposed to them). The main task of US under the leadership of Karenga was to create a cultural revolution among US blacks as the basis for a revitalization of African American life and the eventual formation of an independent Black political party—or a violent revolution.[12] (Karenga's

---

[8]Interview with Ron Karenga by Komozi Woodard, 27 December 1985, in the possession of Dr. Komozi Woodard.

[9]Victor S. Alexander, "Interview: Dr. Maulana Ron Karenga," *African Commentary*, I (October, 1989): 61–64. In 1968 he was also calling himself Ron Ndabeszitha Everett-Karenga, "Militant Negro Leader," *New York Times* (2 September 1968), p. 13.

[10]Gerald Horne, *Fire This Time: The Watts Uprising and the 1960s* (Charlottesville, VA., 1965).

[11]"Black Enigma," *Wall Street Journal* (26 July 1968), p. 15.

[12]Maulana Karenga, *The Quotable Karenga* (Los Angeles, 1967), p. 11.

statement about his ultimate goal varied, depending on his audience and/or his interviewer.) Karenga, employed as a Los Angeles County social worker and teaching Swahili at the Fremont Adult School, seems to have recruited many members of US from East Los Angeles gangs. Some former gang members became armed bodyguards of Karenga, his Simba Wachukas (young lions). A few of the Simbas even lived next door to Karenga in a Los Angeles apartment house complex.[13]

Karenga's nationalism led him to create a "vanguard" organization, insist on the learning of a national language, Swahili, and fashion a philosophy that elaborated black nationalism more in cultural than political terms. A vanguard organization was by definition a small one, with about 500 members at its peak.[14] Karenga looked to Marcus Garvey and W.E.B. DuBois, as well as several African intellectuals for inspiration. As to the national language, Swahili was a nontribal language of the east African coast. Because of the impact of Julius Nyerere's Tanzanian socialism on militant U.S. Blacks in the l960s, Swahili became the *lingua franca* of American Black nationalism.[15] Karenga's Kawaida philosophy was the Swahili name (translated as reason and tradition) for Karenga's fusion of Black nationalism, pan-Africanism, and anti-capitalism. Karenga seems to have drafted his Nguso Saba, his seven principles, in September 1965 as a form of pledge of allegiance to the organization and a statement of the "basic values" fundamental to Kawaida. His followers were supposed to memorize the seven principles in English and Swahili. The seven principles (in English) were unity, self-determination, collective work and responsibility, cooperative economics, purpose, creativity, and faith. Cooperative economics was an ideological tenet of Julius Nyerere's form of African socialism; unity was important to Nyerere and to Leopold Senghor, the president of Senegal, whose concept of Pan-Africanism through Negritude depended on it.[16] At each of the seven days of Kwanzaa, participants af-

---

[13]Imamu Amiri Baraka, *The Autobiography of 'LeRoiJones/Amiri Baraka* (New York, 1984), p. 254.

[14]"Black Enigma," p. 15.

[15]Interview with Ron Karenga by Komozi Woodard, 17 December 1985. Nonetheless, even in the use of Swahili, Karenga made significant alterations to adapt to holiday circumstances. First in Swahili is usually spelled Kwanza, with one "a" at the end. Karenga wanted a group of seven children to participate in the festival by spelling out the letters of the holiday, so he added an extra a. M. Ron Karenga, *Kwanzaa: Origins, Concepts, Practice* (Inglewood, Calif, 1977), p. 16. Maulana Ron Karenga, "The Black Community and the University: A Community Organizer's Perspective," in *Black Studies in the University: A Symposium*, ed. Armstead L. Robinson, Craig C. Foster, and Donald H. Ogilvie (New Haven, CT., 1969), p. 54.

[16]Imamu Halisi, *Kitabu: Beginning Concepts in Kawaida* (Los Angeles, 1971), p. 2; Maulana Karenga, *Kawaida Theory: An Introductory Outline* (Inglewool CA, 1980).

firmed one of seven principles. The origin of Karenga's interest in numerology—seven principles, seven candles, seven days—is not clear.[17]

A little more than a year after establishing his organization and drafting the Nguso Saba, Karenga held the first Kwanzaa. The first Karamu (last-night feast of Kwanzaa, occurring on New Year's Eve) took place at the Los Angeles apartment of a supporter of US in December 1966.[18] About 50 people participated in a feast that included African dancing and telling of African folk tales. The apartment was decorated with black, red, and green candles, the Black nationalist colors Garvey had chosen. A woman member of US living in one of their communes (called a House) both explained the elements of Kwanzaa and described a Karamu in a 1972 Black nationalist publication. She mentioned the same elements as those at the event in 1966. She also described the candle lighting ceremony each night of Kwanzaa, and the importance of having children try to explain one of the seven principles emphasized that night, "since it is for them that this is done." She added that at the karamu everyone present drank from a unity cup and said, "Harambee." The karamu, she wrote, was an all-night New Year's Eve party for adults. She added, "After the African part of Karamu we move to a position of Afro-American expressions and gig all night long."[19]

In the late 1960s and early 1970s, Kwanzaa spread to other cities where cultural Black nationalism flourished—at a branch of US in San Diego, and in San Francisco, Brooklyn, New Orleans, Newark, Chicago, Durham, and Atlanta. The diffusion was far more ideological than organizational. US remained a small group and even briefly disbanded in the mid-1970s. Instead, cultural nationalists, who agreed with Karenga about the necessity for a revolution in cultural values, began to adopt Kwanzaa. Those most influenced by Karenga and his seven principles were two Black poets and writers, Amiri Baraka (formerly LeRoi Jones) in Newark, New Jersey, and Haki Madhubuti (formerly Don L. Lee) in Chicago. These two men were leading figures in the cultural renaissance of the 1960s, called the Black arts movement. Karenga had been particularly supportive of the effort to "make warriors out of poets and writers." He flattered these writers, because he assigned culture such a revolutionary role in his philosophy. In turn, Black artists added poetry and performances of African dance to Kwanzaa celebrations at Black theaters, museums, and cultural institutions.[20]

---

[17]Halisi, ed., *Kitabu,* p. 8. The number seven does appear frequently in the Bible.

[18]Karenga, *Kwanzaa,* p. 20; Elizabeth Softky, "A Kwanzaa Memory: Growing Up With Dr. Karenga." *Washington Post* (20 December 1995), E1, D4; Scot D. Brown, "The US Organization African-American Cultural Nationalism in the Era of Black Power" (PhD dissertation, Cornell University, 1999), pp. 130–132.

[19]Kasisi Washao, "Marriage Ceremony," in *African Congress: A Documentary of the first Modern Pan-African Congress,* ed. Imamu Baraka (LeRoi Jones) (New York, 1972), p. 186.

[20]Komozi Woodard, *A Nation within a Nation,* pp. xi–xiii, 43.

Nonetheless, the pattern of adoption of Kwanzaa was quite checkered. Black Muslims, although Black nationalists, did not generally celebrate Kwanzaa initially because they considered it incompatible with their faith. Moreover, outside of a few southern cities, Kwanzaa was slow to catch on in the urban South. For example, the first article on Kwanzaa did not appear in Baltimore's Black newspaper, *The Afro American*, until 1978. Kwanzaa was virtually nonexistent in the rural South because of the continuing hold of Black Christianity and the appeal of Christmas rituals of feasting and visiting neighbors.

Internal divisions within the Black nationalist movement also hampered the adoption of Kwanzaa in the late 1960s and 1970s. Kwanzaa was a divisive Black nationalist ritual, because it symbolized the differences between the "revolutionary nationalism" of the Black Panthers and the cultural nationalism of Karenga.[21] At first glance, the Panthers and US appear remarkably similar. They were relatively small groups, founded about the same time in California cities by charismatic men. Karenga even participated in Panther meetings in the early years. Like Karenga, two founders of the Panthers, Bobby Seale and Huey P. Newton, had belonged to the Afro-American Association. Both groups were heavily armed; both groups opposed the war in Vietnam. As the Panthers grew, however, they developed strong ties with White leaders of the New Left and embraced their own version of Marxism and support for wars of national liberation on many continents, not just the African one.

The Panthers castigated cultural nationalist ritual and Karenga's community activities. In 1969, the Black Panther newspaper began publishing a series of articles attacking Karenga as a "bald headed pig" and his organization as a group of "sissies and acid heads in yellow sunglasses and African robes." (The Black Panther paper claimed Karenga was using LSD. Charging opponents with lack of manliness—or even homosexuality—was a standard feature of much Black nationalist rhetoric in this period).[22] Bobby Seale of the Black Panthers made fun of Karenga's "weird rituals" and "strange fashions," referring to the sunglasses, buta (toga-like olive green garment), and the carved tiki doll hanging from Karenga's

---

[21]Bobby Seale of the Panthers criticized Karenga's sexism, but the main differences between the Panthers and US were about ideological matters other than gender. Tracye Matthews, "'No One Ever Asks, What a Man's Place in the Revolution Is': Gender and the Politics of the Black Panther Party, 1966–1971," in *The Black Panther Party Reconsidered*, ed. Charles E. Jones (Baltimore, 1998), pp. 272–273.

[22]E. Frances White. "Africa on My Mind: Gender, Counter Discourse and African-American Nationalism," *Journal of Women's History*, 2, 1 (Spring, 1990), 75; Cheryl Clarke, "The Failure to Transform: Homophobia in the Black Community," in *Home Girls: A Black Feminist Anthology*, ed. Barbara Smith (New York, 1983), pp. 197–208; Isaac Julien, "Black Is, Black Ain't: Notes on De-Essentializing Black Identities," in *Black Popular Culture*, ed. Gina Dent (Seattle, 1992), pp. 255–263; Isaac Julien and Koben Mercer, "True Confessions: A Discourse on Images of Black Male Sexuality," in *Brother to Brother: New Writings by Black Gay Men* ed. Essex Hemphill (Boston, 1991), pp. 161–173.

neck. Elaine Brown of the Panthers dubbed the post-riot Watts Summer Festival (which US helped to sponsor) a "Darkey Carnival" or "Darkey Parade." Panthers further argued that the desire to invent African traditions was at best apolitical, and at worst a form of escapism, deterring a focus on contemporary social and economic problems.

Karenga's feud with the Black Panthers, especially between 1969 and 1971, if not instigated by the FBI, then certainly fueled by them, led to permanent enmity between the two organizations.[23] The Panthers believed that Karenga was a spy (perhaps for the Los Angeles police department or the Los Angeles County Commission on Human Rights) or an FBI informer. These charges have never been proven.[24] The Panthers were suspicious for several reasons. Suddenly, in 1968, US had money to buy new vans and cars. Panthers were frequently stopped by Los Angeles and San Diego police for carrying weapons, but the Panthers believed that the police did not stop gun-toting US members. After Dr. King's assassination, Karenga attended a meeting with the Los Angeles police chief designed to discuss how to quell rioting. Moreover, Governor Ronald Reagan called Karenga immediately after King's murder. Karenga attended a private meeting with Reagan, where, he claimed, he tried to persuade the governor to release some US members from prison.[25]

Of the many specific incidents of violence between the two groups, the most significant was the murder of two Black Panthers at UCLA in January 1969 by four members of US. The Panthers and US were fighting for control over the power to choose the administrators for UCLA's newly developing Black studies program. Although Karenga was not present when the murders occurred, the Panthers believed he ordered the killings.[26] There were several factors contributing to the murders. The FBI's efforts

---

[23]Kenneth O'Reilly, "Racial Matters": The FBI's Secret File on Black America, 1960–1972 (New York, 1989), pp. 304–309.

[24]Historian Clayborne Carson argues that he has seen nothing in FBI Cointelpro files to indicate that Karenga was a government informer. *AP Online* (April 22 1998), no page.

[25]"Black Enigma," p. 1; Elaine Brown, *A Taste of Power: A Black Women's Story* (New York, 1992), pp. 176–177.

[26]U.S. Congress, Senate, *Supplementary Detailed Staff Reports on Intelligence Activities and the Rights of Americans, Book III*, S.R. No. 94–755, 94th Congress, second session (Washington, D.C., 1976), p. 194. For a defense of these charges against Karenga, see Scot Ngozi-Brown, "The US organization: Maulana Karenga, and conflict with the Black Panther Party: A Critique of Sectarian Influences on Historical Discourse," *Journal of Black Studies*, 28, 2 (November, 1997):157–171. Gail Sheehy provides an account of the deaths of two Black Panthers, Bunchey Carter and John Huggins, in *Panthermania: The Case of Black Against Black in One American City* (New York, 1971), pp. 16–21. She was sympathetic to the Panther point of view. *Muhammad Speaks* repeated the charges against Karenga. See 19 November 1971, pp. 4–5. For a Panther recollection of the shootout, see Brown, *A Taste of Power*, pp. 156–170.

under its counterintelligence program, COINTELPRO, between 1969 and 1971 served to exacerbate Panther–US rivalry and to curtail the sporadic efforts of nationalist leaders to effect a truce between the two warring organizations. FBI informers seem to have exploited the enmity between Panthers and US by relaying inflammatory statements about the one group to the other in the context of a situation where both groups were armed and already held antagonistic views about the other. In addition, the fact that the Panthers and US recruited members from the Gladiators and the Sawsons, two rival youth gangs, added combustion to the mix.[27] After the murders, Karenga, who liked to call the Panthers "kamikaze niggers," believed that the Panthers intended to retaliate for the deaths of their two members and were plotting to kill him.[28] In addition, members of US, their weapons hidden in briefcases they carried, threatened the Black nationalist organization headed by Amiri Baraka in Newark because Baraka had refused Karenga's orders to cancel a major conference.[29]

Kwanzaa grew slowly in the early years; the preoccupation of Karenga and US with physical survival probably retarded its growth. Government infiltration may have contributed to a decline in US membership and to imprisonment of several US leaders and members.[30] Undoubtedly, Karenga's imprisonment at the medium security California Men's Colony at San Luis Obispo between 1971 and 1975 impeded the growth of Kwanzaa, because the major leader of the organization was unavailable to tour the country and speak on behalf of the holiday.

Moreover, the incident that led to Karenga's imprisonment increased his unsavory reputation in some Black circles and probably deterred interest in Kwanzaa among mainstream Black publications such as *Ebony* and *Jet* or adoption of Kwanzaa at Black churches. Karenga was sentenced to prison in 1971 on multiple charges of conspiracy and felonious assault in the beatings of two 20 year old women, both former members of US. The two women, held in a garage, were burned with cigarettes and a hot soldering iron was placed in the mouth of one woman. They were tortured in order to make them confess that they had tried to poison Karenga. Amiri Baraka, who broke with Karenga in 1974 over political differences in their mutual path toward a nationalist form of Marxist-Leninism, claimed that Karenga was at this time dependent on "diet pills" (the Panthers said LSD) which led him to slur his words, stagger about, and become incoherent.[31] Karenga's first wife, Brenda, already separated from him, was a witness against

---

[27]Brown, *A Taste of Power*, p. 176.

[28]Baraka, *Autobiography*, p. 279.

[29]Woodard, *A Nation within a Nation*, p. 166.

[30]Scott Ngozi-Brown, "The US Organization," pp. 157–171.

[31]Baraka, *Autobiography*, pp. 280, 289; *Los Angeles Herald Dispatch* (13 May 1971), p. 1.

him at his trial in Los Angeles. She testified that Karenga had sat on the stomach of one of the girls, while water was forced into the girl's mouth through a hose.[32] Karenga, convicted by a majority Black and Hispanic jury, maintained he was innocent of the charges.[33]

The holiday thus carried the weight of this specific incident, as well as of Karenga's fairly well-known attitudes toward Black women and toward Christianity. In the 1960s, Karenga believed that the proper role of Black women was to be submissive to Black men: he opposed equality between the sexes. In speeches between 1965 and 1967, he argued that "equality is false, it is the devil's concept." He said that the black husband had "any right that does not destroy the collective needs of the family."[34] The *Quotable Karenga* (1967) reproduced quotations from Karenga's speeches, hostile to Christianity. Patterned after little red books of quotations of Chairman Mao, popular in leftist circles, the *Quotable Karenga* was a compilation of short excerpts from Karenga's speeches, intended to be deliberately provocative. Karenga is quoted as saying, "Christianity is a white religion. It has a white God, and any 'Negro' who believes in [sic] it is a sick 'Negro.' How can you pray to a white man? If you believe in him, no wonder you catch so much hell." He also described Jesus as "psychotic. He said if you didn't believe what he did you would burn forever."[35]

---

[32]Brenda Karenga also used the first name Haiba. *Jet,* xl (3 June 1971): 54.

[33]The jury consisted of six African Americans, one Hispanic, and five whites. Imamu Clyde Halisi, "Maulana Ron Karenga: Black Leader in Captivity," *The Black Scholar,* 3 (May, 1972): pp. 27–31; *Los Angeles Sentinel* (20 May 1971), pp. A1, A4; *Los Angeles Herald Dispatch* (3 June 1971), p. 1.

[34]Halisi and Mtume, ed.., *The Quotable Karenga,* p. 20. US members in San Diego took submissiveness to mean that Black women should not play any leadership role in the organization. When Angela Davis, then a graduate student living in San Diego, sought to organize local activities, US members criticized her and told her that the proper place for women was to give their men "'strength and inspiration' so that the men could carry on the struggle."

Karenga believed that women in his organization should dress so as to make themselves sexually attractive to men. Karenga told the poet Amiri Baraka that "they [women in US] should show flesh to intrigue men and not be covered so much." As Baraka (who later broke with Karenga) recalled, "he was always making 'sexy' remarks to women, calling them 'freaks' and commenting loudly on their physical attributes. In Los Angeles, Karenga even sanctioned 'polygamy' and was rumored himself to have pulled many of the women in the LA organization." Ritual greetings of US mirrored Karenga's beliefs. When he walked by, Baraka recalled, "the women were supposed to 'salimu' or 'submit,' crossing their arms on their breasts and bowing slowly." Angela Davis, *Angela Davis: An Autobiography* (New York, 1974), p. 161; Baraka, *Autobiography,* pp. 200, 208, 275.

[35]Halisi and Mtume, *The Quotable Karenga,* p. 25.

It seems possible that dislike or distrust of Karenga deterred celebration of Kwanzaa among a small group of intellectuals and devout Christians. There were occasional denunciations of Karenga for being hostile to Christianity.[36] As a result of the growth of the women's movement and Black feminism, Black women intellectuals were keenly aware of Karenga's sexist attitudes and practices. In 1997, the feminist social critic bell hooks was interviewed in *Essence* and offered several reasons why she did not celebrate Kwanzaa. She began by noting her dislike for what she considered the rigid format of Kwanzaa and the Ngusa Saba. She also told the interviewer, "Another troubling thing about Kwanzaa is that you're talking about patriarchal Black Nationalist men who decided they had to reinvent [these principles]. As if they didn't already exist."[37]

After having survived in the doldrums through Karenga's imprisonment and the second half of the 1970s, Kwanzaa was discovered by the Black mainstream. The first article on Kwanzaa in *Essence,* which appeared in 1979, appears to have been an act of self-promotion by a Bay Area nationalist, who had written a Kwanzaa manual. In 1979, Black power was a fading slogan. *Essence* took little risk in publishing an article about it. The more significant date is 1983, when *Ebony* and *Jet* first published articles about Kwanzaa.[38] Black sororities began to invite speakers to show their members how to celebrate Kwanzaa. Cedric McClester's handbook on the holiday, written in a more accessible style than Karenga's or Madhubuti's pamphlets, appeared in 1985. He developed a lengthier script for the Karamu. He also created the folk figure of Nia Umoja, a Kwanzaa "Santa" and teller of African tales, who brought gifts to children.[39]

---

[36]"Karenga's Contradictions." updated 17 December 1997, http://ourworld.CompuServe.com/homespagcs/CMoiTOW/contrdct.html This condemnation is quite recent. Black churches did not initially hold Kwanzaa celebrations, either in their basements or in the main part of the church. There is an absence of evidence as to whether black churches were ignorant of Kwanzaa or actively opposed to it. I suspect that there were more ministers and church leaders in the latter than the former category because Black nationalists, like Karenga, were known to be hostile to Christianity.

[37]"Do We Need Kwanzaa?" *Essence*, 28, 8 (December, 1997): 68. E. Frances White wrote, "Karenga has significantly modified his sexist ideas about gender relations, but the ideology of complementarity and collective family needs continues to work against the liberation of black women." E. Frances White, "Africa on My Mind," p. 75.

[38]Omonike Weusi-Puryear, "How I Came to Celebrate Kwanzaa," *Essence*, 10 (December, 1979), pp. 112, 115, 117.

[39]Cedric McClester, *Kwanzaa: Everything You Always Wanted to Know But Didn't Know Where to Ask* (New York, 1985); David A. Anderson, *Kwanzaa: A Everyday Resource and Instructional Guide* (New York, 1992).

Large national museums, such as New York City's American Museum of Natural History (beginning in 1985) and the Smithsonian (beginning in 1988), staged Kwanzaa celebrations. These large institutions, located near Black ghetto populations, sought to add programming that showed interest and demonstrated good will toward African Americans. Celebrations of Kwanzaa at many college campuses date from this period. Increased publicity about Kwanzaa on television, radio, and in mainstream newspapers encouraged the celebration, although many first learned about it from a friend.[40] Some of those who celebrated Kwanzaa in public school or at a community center later came to practice it at home.

Writers other than Karenga became more important in the diffusion of Kwanzaa because they wrote in a popular style and thought of Kwanzaa in decorative and culinary rather than revolutionary terms. To some extent, Karenga became an elder statesman, Kwanzaa's founding father. Black magazines interviewed him, using the format of the celebrity profile. But some Kwanzaa manuals did not even mention him. Black newspapers regularly described Kwanzaa as an "authentic harvest festival, first celebrated by the ancient Egyptians."[41] In so doing, Karenga did not receive proper credit for authorship. He wrote a small book about Kwanzaa in 1977, in part to set the record straight.[42]

The rediscovered Kwanzaa was no longer hostile toward Christianity and Christmas. As a holiday that could be defined as religious, secular, or both, Kwanzaa came to be celebrated at a Black church—initially not at the actual service, but as a separate program. Kwanzaa became more successful as it was seen as a supplement to Christmas rather than as an alternative to it. The 1983 articles in Black magazines made clear that Kwanzaa was compatible with Christmas. The headline of the first article about Kwanzaa in *Ebony* in 1983 read, "The New Soul Christmas" and the photograph of a family accompanying the article showed a Christmas tree in the background.[43] Kwanzaa could also be redefined as a less

---

[40]Ysamu Flores-Pena and Robin Evanchuk, "Kwanzaa: The Emergence of African-American holiday," *Western Folklore*, 56 (Summer, 1997): 281–294.

[41]*Atlanta Daily World* (24 December 1978). p. 7; *Chicago Defender* (31 January 1983), p. 5; Lesley Crosson, "A New Leaf," *New York Amsterdam News* (5 January 1974), D-7, *The First Book of Kwanza* (Brooklyn, NY, 1977) ; *St. Louis Argus* (22 December 1977), p. 2. A widely adopted U.S. history textbook described permanent changes wrought by black cultural nationalism of the 1960s. Among the changes was that "the traditional African holiday Kwanzaa began to replace Christmas as a seasonal family celebration." John Mack Faragher, Mari Jo Buhle, Daniel Czitrom, and Susan H. Armitage, *Out of Many: A History of the American People*, 2nd. ed. (Upper Saddle River, NJ, 1997), p. 29.

[42]For an example of a Kwanzaa manual that fails to credit Karenga with the creation of Kwanzaa, see The Kwanza Celebrants, *The Kwanza Handbook* (Palo Alto, Calif., 1977).

[43]Frank White III, "The New Soul Christmas," *Ebony*, xxxix (December 1983): 29–32.

commercial Christmas, and therefore, a holiday less sullied by the marketplace.[44] Black writers in women's magazines wrote that Kwanzaa was a Christmas holiday from which one need not feel alienated.[45]

As part of becoming more mainstream, and more compatible with Christianity and Christmas, Kwanzaa also became more American Black, more celebrated at home, and more choral (in that participants often sang "Lift Every Voice and Sing"). Writers in magazines and authors of Kwanzaa manuals now claimed that southern Black cooking—along with cosmopolitan borrowing from West African, Ethiopian, and Caribbean cuisine—was suitable for Kwanzaa feasts. (Karenga had advocated West African cooking.) Cookbooks for Kwanzaa and celebration manuals for a mass audience, rather than a nationalist select few, appeared as it became clear to publishers that there was a market for such books. Because Kwanzaa was most often celebrated in the home, it was usually women who organized the event and did the necessary shopping and cooking.[46]

Writers in Black popular magazines of the 1980s transformed the seven principles into statements of middle-class belief, along with the newly popular therapeutic idea of "healing." More importantly, magazine writers in *Ebony* and *Essence* combined Black nationalism with Black middle-class allegiance to individual achievement. Thus, even racial unity was individualized. A writer for *Essence* thought that "if we embrace unity and believe in ourselves, our families and our leaders, we will be victorious in our struggles as individuals and as a race."[47] Other celebrants saw in the seven principles affirmations of upward mobility. As part of the feast on New Year's Eve in 1984, a Detroit schoolteacher recalled her conversation with her four children about the Nguso Saba. She made sure that "the children committed themselves to going to college, so that they could be useful and helpful to themselves." A Black schoolchild in Rochester, New York, translated the principle of "purpose" into wanting "a good home and a good school and a good community. I will make a plan every day so I will know what to do to make the good things happen."[48] Occurring between Christmas and

---

[44]*Atlanta Daily World* (24 December 1978), p. 7.

[45]Desda Moss, "A special celebration," *Ladies' Home Journal*, 111 (December, 1994), p. 95.

[46]When two folklorists handed out a questionnaire to about fifty blacks in Los Angeles in 1997, they found that 69 percent of those who filled it out were women. They inferred that women were the major organizers of Kwanzaa, and those most interested in it as a form of family celebration. Flores-Pena and Evanchuk, "Kwanzaa," pp. 293–294.

[47]"Celebrate in Holiday Style" *Essence*, 20 (December, 1989): 50–58.

[48]Anderson, *Kwanzaa*, p. 56.

and New Year's, Kwanzaa could function as both the Black Christmas and the Black New Year's Eve. Thus, Kwanzaa became the time when adults made New Year's resolutions.[49]

Writers in the 1980s also helped create a nationalism that used the rhetoric of nationhood (not diaspora or exile), valorized Malcolm X and Muhammad Ali, and incorporated more recognition of African American history. U.S. Blacks were now portrayed as having their own heroes within the United States, not just in Africa. (After having been released from prison, Karenga himself had included mention of black American heroes in a newly written libation statement for Kwanzaa.) As one instance of this new way of thinking, in 1985 a Baltimore black newspaper claimed that as Kwanzaa became more popular, it would hopefully "come to symbolize each year another step toward the goal of full citizenship into American society."[50]

More than anything else, Kwanzaa became more widespread because it served the important function of affirming racial and familial identity within the Black middle class. There are no social surveys to prove definitively that most celebrants were middle class. Newspaper and magazine articles invariably describe events attended by the wide swath of the Black middle class—beauticians, postal clerks, administrators and managers, nurses, teachers, caterers, writers, lawyers, doctors, and students at universities. It seems likely that such articles accurately reflected the class composition of the celebrants, although there were certainly some working-class celebrants as well.

The ideological needs and interests of the Black middle class are central to understanding the growth in the popularity of Kwanzaa. Since the 1960s, the black middle class had become larger than ever before and less dependent on racial segregation for its livelihood. It had been expanding since the 1950s and grew even more during the 1960s. One reason for the growth was the general economic boom of the 1960s. The other was affirmative action in the public schools, at colleges and universities, and in private and government employment. One result of affirmative action was an increase in the number of Blacks in professions such as law and medicine. The Black middle class has been defined in terms of education, occupation, income, net worth, self label, or as a way of viewing the world. Whatever the definition, it was burgeoning. The proportion of Black households with incomes of $50,000 or more in 1977 was 9.9%; a decade later, the percentage was 13.5%. There were comparable in-

---

[49]Marilyn Bailey, "Kwanzaa: Afro-American Holiday Evolves," *Oakland Trihune* (26 December 1982), pp. El, E5.

[50]"Kwanzaa," *Afro-American* (28 December 1985), p. 4. See also Eric V. Copage, *Kwanzaa: An African American Celebration of Culture and Cooking* (New York, 1991), p. xxii.

creases in the $35,000 to $50,000 income range.[51] Between 1976 and 1978, 28% of Blacks defined themselves as middle class; the percentage of Blacks defining themselves as middle class rose eight points by the next decade, according to social science surveys.[52]

If the Black middle class was rising since the 1950s, and growing rapidly by 1966, why did Kwanzaa not gain popularity until 1983? One possibility is that Black society, like the rest of America, had become more conservative and had embraced rhetoric about "family values." Jimmy Carter had first introduced this term in his 1976 presidential campaign. The Black public in the 1980s often defended the holiday as a way to strengthen and affirm the family. Kwanzaa was declared "a celebration of black family life," a time for family gathering. A Berkeley high school counselor explained her interest in Kwanzaa in precisely those terms. She remarked in 1984, "I had attended a Kwanzaa festival the previous year and it seemed like a good way of bringing the family together and [for] the adults [to learn] about their historical beginnings."[53]

The Black version of the idea of family values was to teach children their racial heritage. Middle-class Black mothers upheld the ideal of a sentimental view of the child and of the mother–child bond. The child, in this view, was seen both as an innocent being and a malleable one, to be properly instructed in a racial or religious heri-

---

[51]Bart Landry's definition of the middle class is very spacious, and includes blacks in sales and clerical work as well as small business owners, administrators, and professionals. He even rejects the notion that there is a black upper class. Bart Landry, *The New Black Middle Class* (Berkeley, Calif., 1987), pp. 185, 221. Income figures are from U.S. Bureau of the Census, *Money Income of Households, Families, and Persons in the United States: 1987*, P60–162 (Washington, D.C., 1993), B–3, B–4. For a cultural and social history of the black middle class, see Charles Pete T. Banner-Haley, *The Fruits of Integration: Black Middle-Class Ideology and Culture, 1960–1990* (Oxford, MS, 1994); Judith Waldrop, "Happy Kwanzaa," *American Demographics*, 16 (December, 1994): 4. Journalist Leon Dash interviewed Rosa Lee Cunningham, an African American grandmother living in Washington. D.C. beginning in 1987. She and her family were members of the "underclass," drug dependent, unemployed, and on welfare. No member of her family celebrated Kwanzaa. Her son, Alvin, had escaped from the family's poverty and become a bus driver. He had heard of Kwanzaa but did not celebrate it. Interview with Leon Dash, 9 May 1999. Leon Dash, *Rosa Lee: A Mother and Her Family in Urban America* (New York, 1997).

[52]Stephan Thernstrom and Abigail Thernstrom, *America in Black and White: One Nation, Indivisible* (New York, 1977), p. 200. The Thernstroms review occupational, educational, and economic progress of the black middle class in chapter seven of their book, pp. 183–202.

[53]Skye Dent, "Kwanzaa: A Black Holiday of Unity," *The Oakland Tribune* (27 December 1984), B 1.

tage. Because of the history of racial discrimination and American racial definitions of who was Black, the complex heritage of African Americans was traced to African ancestry.[54] The waning of Black radicalism, the aging of the generation influenced by the civil rights movement, and the raising of children in racially integrated settings seemed to require additional efforts. In turn, the desire to develop the child's racial identity fed the demand for Kwanzaa children's books, children's programs at museums during the Christmas season, and programs about Kwanzaa in the public schools.

Kwanzaa was not only a family holiday, but also a ritual of African American identity, arising out of the changing racial attitudes of the Black middle class. In the 1960s, pollsters found that the Blacks most distrustful of Whites had low incomes. By the 1980s, higher income African Americans exhibited the most distrust. In the 1960s, the Black middle class, when polled, was optimistic about the opportunities opening up for all Blacks, but especially for professionals. By the 1980s the optimism was gone. To political scientist Jennifer Hochschild, middle-class Blacks in the 1980s were "succeeding more but enjoying it less."[55]

There are several reasons why middle-class Blacks did not enjoy the success they had fought to achieve. One reason is that they were beginning to measure their situation not by the standards of where they had come from, but by the standards of their White peers. Compared to Whites, the Black middle class had lower net worth and more responsibilities for kin and neighbors who had not fared well. The rise of the Black middle class thrust more Blacks than ever before into situations where they functioned as tokens in a largely White environment. The Black middle class was chafing at the racial slights and discrimination encountered in taxis, offices, hotels, businesses, neighborhoods, shopping centers, restaurants, and at universities. They also felt their economic and social progress was threatened. The resurgence of interest in Kwanzaa began a few years after the growth of the attack on affirmative action. The Supreme Court decision in *Regents of University of California v. Bakke* (1978) restricted the range of affirmative action remedies.[56] In his presidential campaign in 1980, Ronald Reagan called for an end to such programs. This attack on affirmative action contributed to the growth in pessimism among the Black middle class. Finally, the middle class felt responsibility toward the black poor and recognized that social conditions for them were worsening.[57]

---

[54]For an example of a black father who rediscovers Kwanzaa as a means of imparting racial heritage to a child, see Eric V. Copage, *Kwanzaa*, p. xiv.

[55]Jennifer L. Hochschild, *Facing Up to the American Dream: Race, Class, and the Soul of the Nation* (Princeton, NJ, 1995), pp. 72–90, 267–270; Luke S. Tripp, *Black Student Activists: Transition to Middle Class Professionals* (Lanham, MD, 1987), pp. 58–61.

[56]*Regents of University of California v. Bakke*, 483 U.S. 265, 311–313 (1978).

[57]Joe R. Feagin and Melvin Sikes, *Living with Racism: The Black Middle-Class Experience* (Boston, 1994), pp. 326–327.

Crack cocaine was beginning to devastate the family and personal life of the Black poor.

Even so, the significant mass movements of Black nationalism in the 20th century, Garveyism, Black Communism, and the Black Muslims, drew support from the poor or the working class. Even though nationalism is a discourse about race, not class, Black nationalists have usually regarded the Black middle class with a certain skepticism. After his release from prison in 1975, Karenga declared himself a Marxist. He favored an alliance between the White and Black working class and considered the Black middle class too wedded to capitalism and individualism to be capable of revolutionary change.[58] Garvey, Muhammad, and Malcolm X, like Karenga, viewed the Black bourgeoisie as potential traitors (in Malcolm X's words, "house niggers") because of their class interests and lack of proper racial consciousness. Up to the 1960s, the Black middle class formed the backbone of support for the NAACP and its program of racial integration.

Still, intellectuals and the educated middle class usually lead the effort to commemorate holidays, establish museums, and collect folklore. Usually, a college-educated urban elite initiates an interest in the arts, history, folklore, and ritual. Most of the writers in the Black Arts movement of the 1960s had graduated from college. New myths, folklore, and ritual initially appeal to the educated Black middle class because of their reading, taste for abstraction, and greater opportunities for foreign travel. Moreover, as Early noted, it is the middle class that wants to make holidays more decorative and aesthetically pleasing through purchases of consumer items, including gifts and the serving of family feasts. They could display their status and racial identity by purchasing a kinara (a seven-pronged candleholder), wearing West African garb, and for women, a headwrap, and by photographing the family feast.[59]

This display of status and racial identity is a variant form of Gans' concept of "symbolic ethnicity," the desire to maintain an ethnic identity while still living a middle-class style of life. In this form of ethnicity, it was possible to "feel Black" while residing in a largely White suburb and/or attending a largely White university. Indeed, the desire to "feel Black" was actually increased by such circumstances. However, Gans argued that symbolic ethnicity could exist and flourish without consciousness of persecution, whereas the Black middle class combined middle-class status with rising indignation at being discriminated against on racial grounds.[60]

---

[58]Maulana Ron Karenga, "Which Road: Nationalism, Pan-African Socialism?" *The Black Scholar*, 5 (October, 1974): 25.

[59]Helen Bradley Griebel, "The West African Origin of the African-American Headwrap" in *Dress and Ethnicity: Change Across Space and Time*, ed. Joanne B. Eicher (Oxford. 1995), pp. 207–224.

[60]Herbert J. Gans, "Symbolic Ethnicity: The Future of Ethnic Groups and Cultures in America," *Ethnic and Racial Studies*, 2(1979): 1–20.

Solving these crises of Black middle-class identity in the 1980s was part of the appeal of Kwanzaa: the holiday also gained adherents from increasing publicity as it became more commercial. Consumer culture commodifies identity; it allows people to use purchased material objects as statements of racial identity, even as they participate in American consumer culture.[61] Still, some of the appeal of Kwanzaa was that it was less commercial than Christmas. (Madhubuti and Karenga had adopted various stances toward gift giving, from insisting that there should be none at all, to arguing that gifts were acceptable, if they were small and only given to children.)

By the 1980s, the balance had decidedly swung in favor of combining Kwanzaa with shopping, sending of cards, giving gifts, and home decorating. The leaders in the commercialization of Kwanzaa were Black entrepreneurs. Two of them, Jose Ferrer and Ahmed Malik, held a small exhibit of goods for Kwanzaa in a high school gymnasium in Harlem in 1981; by 1989, 60 vendors were exhibiting Black dolls, African imports, books, sculpture, paintings, and Kwanzaa greeting cards at a Kwanzaa exposition.[62] Another Kwanzaa Expo began in Saint Louis in 1983. These trade fairs subsequently expanded into huge several day-long shows of Kwanzaa items held in larger and more centrally located quarters.[63] In the 1980s, most of the business owners at the exhibits were Black, some former nationalist radicals, who had opened bookstores, African import stores, toy companies, greeting card, or book publishing businesses.

Because of the growing success of Kwanzaa and the subsequent redefinition of it as a supplement rather than alternative to Christmas, public schools began to recognize the holiday. Black nationalist teachers, most of whom were women, introduced Kwanzaa in their classrooms as early as 1969, in part as a means to remedy student ignorance about Africa.[64] The first published school district manuals

---

[61]For the embrace of consumer culture among Jewish immigrants in the early twentieth century, see Andrew R. Heinze, *Adapting to Abundance: Jewish Immigrants. Mass Consumption, and the Search for American identity* (New York, 1990); Jenna Weissman Joselit, *The Wonders of America: Reinventing Jewish Culture, 1880–1950* (New York, 1994).

[62]Waldrop, "Happy Kwanzaa," p. 4.

[63]"Expo Celebrates Better Living Through Kwanzaa," *St. Louis Post Dispatch* (5 December 1977), E3; *The Philadelphia Tribune* (9 December 1994), p. 16; Waldrop, "Happy Kwanzaa," p. 4.

[64]Sister (J. Smith) Makingya, *Kwanza* (Berkeley. Calif. 1969); *New York Times* (20 December 1971), p. 47; Jacyann Mcintosh and Patricia Monroe, "Exploring Afrikan Studies through a Contemporary Cultural Event," (MA thesis, Banks Street College of Education, 1974).

date from 1979.[65] The major growth in public school celebrations came in the middle to late 1980s, that is, a few years after the rediscovery of Kwanzaa by *Jet* and *Ebony*. Public school teachers, White as well as Black, organized Kwanzaa events. The holiday appears to have been celebrated both in school districts in university towns and in large urban systems with significant Black populations.

Although individual teachers created their own activities, school departments in some large cities began to issue curriculum guides. A manual published in the Portland public schools in 1987 showed the pattern of diffusion. A Black woman librarian in a Portland public school encouraged Black women teachers in the newly created "Multicultural/Multiethnic Office" to prepare an instructional guide for the school district on activities for Kwanzaa (e.g., a yam race, making a kinara).[66] The goal was to increase the understanding of students of the history, culture, and contribution to the United States of African Americans. Teachers came to believe that by recognizing the "culture" of Black students, they were showing them respect.[67] A Kwanzaa celebration was thus a symbolic way for the school and the teacher to acknowledge the African heritage of Black students, even though the vast majority of the Black students did not celebrate Kwanzaa.

In the 20th century, public school celebrations at Christmastime reflected prevailing ideas about the American cultural mosaic. The initial purpose of incorporating invented traditions into the classroom was the one Hobsbawm suggested, the goal of developing emotional ties to the nation. Thus, in the Progressive era, teachers used classroom celebrations of president's birthdays, holidays, and the pledge of allegiance to the flag as a means of encouraging national identity and reinforcing Christian hegemony. By the 1950s, the balance began to shift in favor of acknowledging religious differences. Teachers in majority-Christian classrooms made some token attempts to acknowledge Chanukah.[68] Kwanzaa, in the 1970s, was a ritual created by Black teachers for Black students. By the late 1980s, teachers in an integrated or even mainly White classroom celebrated Kwanzaa as a way of affirming multiculturalism, the belief that all cultures were equally valued and no single one was dominant. Other holidays,—including Diwali, Buddha's birth-

---

[65]Community School District Twelve, *Community School District Twelve Celebrates Kwanza and our African Heritage* (Bronx, NY, 1979); Milwaukee Public Schools, Department of Elementary and Secondary Education, *Kwanzaa: An Afro-American Celebration* (Milwaukee, WI, 1979).

[66]Mariam Baradar, Brenda Jackson, and Khasoa Waskhangu, *Kwanzaa* (Portland, OR, 1988); Sali Sicraa and Sandra Jackson-Opohu, *Kwanzaa, a New Afro-American Holiday* (Chicago, 1986).

[67]Vivian Gussin Paley, *Kwanzaa and Me: A Teacher's Story* (Cambridge, MA, 1995).

[68]Irving Cantor, *Christmas in the Life of a Jewish Teenager* (Washington, DC, 1960).

day, Chinese New Year, and sometimes even Winter Solstice—were added to the celebration.

Black nationalism of the 1960s created Kwanzaa, but Kwanzaa as it developed and grew helped to shape Black identity, specifically, the racial identity of the Black middle class. Originating at the nexus of Black nationalism and black alienation from Christmas, Kwanzaa expanded both because of the needs for racial self-definition of the Black middle class and from consumerism intended to provide a satisfying substitute for and addition to Christmas. Most of the influential authors of Kwanzaa manuals were men; women took on most of the work of organizing the Kwanzaa festival in the home. As more Black women created feasts at home, they fused ideas of race with those of family sentiment. In so doing, they erased entirely Karenga's initial ideas about the submissiveness of women.

The history of Kwanzaa shows considerable change as it became transformed from an organizational celebration to a family one, and from a ritual celebrating Black nationalist unity to one also embracing and affirming family history, feasting, homecoming, and cultural difference.[69] Consumer culture, far from creating a mass society, helped to create an ethnically segmented one. The Black middle class made relatively simple ceremonies more elaborate with the purchase of wine cups, straw mats, candleholders, black, red, and green candles, kente cloth, and the wearing of West African garb. But Kwanzaa also drew much of its appeal from appearing to be the less commercial alternative to Christmas. As both a small nationalist ritual and a larger one in the 1980s, Kwanzaa had been mainly practiced by the middle class. Kwanzaa helped to allay the anxieties, fears, and ongoing rejection and discrimination middle-class Blacks encountered in their interactions with individual Whites and the larger American society.

The traditional view is that Black nationalism and acculturation to the dominant society are diametrically opposed. The effect of practicing Kwanzaa was to fuse the two, just as successful ritual is always said to bridge opposing values. This could only be done, however, as Kwanzaa was redefined to uphold a more middle-class conception of Black nationalism. The Black middle class has usually been noted for its adherence to entrepreneurship, and the values of individuality, self help, and upward mobility. The seven principles were redefined to affirm these values. As Gerald Early argued, Kwanzaa allowed upwardly mobile middle-class Blacks to feel comfortable with belonging to the middle class by reassuring them that they remained true to their racial identity. Kwanzaa was meeting the needs for racial self definition that the celebration of Christmas alone could not. It seems likely that the blackening of Christmas and the growth of Kwanzaa proceeded

[69]Geoff Eley and Ronald Grifor Suny, "Introduction," in *Becoming National: A Reader* (New York, 1996), p. 32.

[70]Beverly Seawright Taliaferro, "Celebrating Kwanzaa: One Family's Story," *Essence*, 14 (December. 1983): 106.

apace, the one reinforcing the other. Thus, the work of racial self-definition probably went on at Christmas as well as at Kwanzaa.[70]

Some interpretive questions about the impact of Kwanzaa are the most difficult to answer. Did the creation of a mythic African past substitute for engagement with contemporary African nations and the need for assistance in trade, development, and peacekeeping? The anti-apartheid movement blossomed in the United States in the 1980s at the same time as Kwanzaa grew. There is at least a positive correlation among African Americans between rising interest in Kwanzaa and the struggle to end apartheid in South Africa. Similarly, did the cultural ritual substitute for political engagement among the Black middle class? Was Kwanzaa an emblem of the growing class division within Black America? The decline of Black power, and of specific organizations, such as the Black Panthers, occurred by the early 1970s. Would there have been more political activism if Kwanzaa had not been invented? That seems unlikely.

The one pertinent negative assessment is that Kwanzaa creates a mythic version of Africa, which embodies Western assumptions about the nation, civilization, and about Africa. In taking up Kwanzaa, African Americans were creating their own highly eclectic image of Africa. Europeans as much as Africans, black intellectuals along with European travelers and journalists, Velentin Mudimbe (1988) argued, helped to create the idea of the continent of Africa as a single coherent identity, a super-nation.[71] The creation of Kwanzaa reflected this decidedly Western gaze—making "Africa" the exotic other—in which a composite harvest festival was interpreted as the changeless essence of Africanness. In exoticizing the African continent, American Blacks, far from revealing a pan-Africanist solidarity based on familiarity, instead showed how Western their views were. In the decades since the 1960s, educated Africans saw American Blacks constructing Africans in this manner. Africans who had migrated to the United States since 1965 were sometimes aware of Kwanzaa. Those who identified themselves as African Americans tended to celebrate it; those who saw themselves as African nationals rarely did so.[72]

Although Black Americans viewed the African continent with rose-colored glasses, they removed them to perceive clearly the Whiteness of Santa and commercialism of the American Christmas.[73] Because Christmas is such a command-

---

[71]See his *The Invention of Africa: Gnosis, Philosophy, and the Order of Knowledge* (Bloomington, IN, 1988). For an even stronger critique of Afrocentrism, see Steven Howe, *Afrocentrism: Mythical Pasts and Imagined Homes* (London, 1998),

[72]Interview with Ribka Berhanu, 5 August 1998; Interview with Stephanie Tankou, 30 May 1999.

[73] *New York Amsterdam News* (6 January 1973). B-5; *The First Book of Kwanzaa* (Brooklyn, 1977).

ing, indeed, overwhelming presence in American culture, attempts to create alternatives to it inevitably stand in its shadow. Kwanzaa, as it developed, took on many features of the Christmas season—parades, greeting cards, a Santa, charitable giving, shopping at after Christmas sales, New Year's Eve parties, New Year's resolutions, and greetings of "Merry Kwanzaa."[74] Eventually Kwanzaa, like Christmas, became so successful that it was capable of generating nostalgia for one's childhood, festive excess, popular songs, criticism from Black intellectuals, and discontent with excessive commercialism.

ACKNOWLEDGMENT

I want to thank Wileescha Taylor for research assistance. I have made use of some of the research by undergraduate students in History 298, fall 1998. As a class project they examined reports about Kwanzaa in Black newspapers. Juliet Walker first suggested that I research Kwanzaa in Black newspapers. Komozi Woodard furnished me a copy of his 1985 interview with Maulana Karenga. I have benefitted from the comments and suggestions of Scot Brown, Laurence Glasco, Fred Hoxie, James R. Barrett, Diane Koenker, Clare Crowston, Orville Vernon Burton, Joseph Pleck, and Komozi Woodard. Nancy Hafkin answered many questions I posed about African history.

---

[74]On the Kwanzaa parade in Los Angeles, see "Highlights of Kwanzaa Gwaride" (Parade) in Los Angeles, *Los Angeles Sentinel* (31 December 1981), Sec. A, p. l; "Kwanzaa Gwaride (Parade) Held in Los Angeles," *Los Angeles Sentinel* (30 December 1982), Sec. A, p. 3.

5

The Evolution, Transformation, and Demise of a Ritual: The Case of May Day

Mary Ann McGrath
Loyola University Chicago

> Upon reflection, is it not odd that human beings, everywhere and in all ages, have engaged in the making and performing of rituals? Why have they done this, when life is full of dangers and challenges that would seem to require more practical kinds of activity? Contrary to common-sense expectation, rituals are not, in most cases, the product of affluence and leisure. (Driver, 1993, p. 8)

Rituals are part of everyday life in all cultures. They can serve as automatic decision-makers in everyday existence. They guide people in deciding when to work and when to set their work aside; what, when, and with whom to eat; how to dress appropriately in various settings; who to include and exclude in various occasions; and, generally, how to engage in full and varied social and personal lives without agonizing over each detail. Calendrical celebrations and holidays are replete with rituals that cue accompanying appropriate behaviors. Rituals present an overlay or skeletal outline for living life, and the flexibility and dynamism of this outline allows for individuality, adaptation, and evolution.

Family and community life are replete with rituals that function to provide a gratifying form of stability and structure to daily life. Any parent will concur that children love routine. In fact, many would say that children need this combination of predictability and specialness, and "ritual is routine with sprinkles and extra sauce" (Cox, 1998, p. 4).

Adults, as well, find rituals vital. Rook (1985) explored meanings given to grooming rituals by young adults, whereas Fulghum (1995) described in detail one woman's regular morning routine, which includes wearing a different bathrobe for each season and sitting quietly with her dog, Elvis. He concludes that an anthropologist analyzing this woman "would see ritual behavior of the most classic kind—the kind that gives structure and meaning to daily life. It is behavior that is regularly repeated because it serves a profound purpose" (Fulghum, 1995, p. 213).

It is the attention to a calendrical, rather than a daily, ritual that gives rise to this chapter. In addition to repeated stability, rituals also are dynamic and evolutionary. Rather than analyze an existing ritual context, this chapter investigates how and why an annual holiday and its accompanying rituals have been altered and in the end, has virtually disappeared from contemporary American culture. The occasion is May Day, traditionally celebrated on the first day of May. Currently, the date is given scant attention in the United States, but it continues to remain a loosely celebrated holiday in other parts of the world. An early accretion of the day, the May basket, once handmade and hung on doorknobs as a surprise for loved ones, has for all purposes disappeared. The evolution and demise of this ritual context is the subject of this chapter.

May Day exhibits a striking example of dynamic change and adaptation as a holiday and ritual context. Its long history is replete with polar opposites involving both ritual behaviors and accompanying emotions. Over the course of two millennia, May Day has evolved from a popular holiday set aside for carefree indulgence (and forgivable overindulgence) to a sedate (and staid) demonstration of purity, to the serious business of examining and demonstrating the role and power of labor in society, to a political demonstration of military might designed to intimidate the capitalist cultural system. This chapter traces the historical path of this holiday and its accompanying rituals, and, based on this exploration, poses three hypotheses as explanatory reasons for these changes and the subsequent rejection of the holiday in the current U.S. culture. In addition, several insights into the role of rituals in modern society in general are posed.

The transformation and subsequent demise of this holiday and its accompanying rituals in the United States is tied to the long and varied history of the holiday. As a nation of immigrants, the population of the United States has amalgamated, transplanted, and morphed rituals and sacred occasions from many ethnicities and all reaches of the globe. Thus, to understand its virtual disappearance in the United States, it is helpful to review in an abbreviated format the history of the holiday as it has been celebrated in various contexts of Western civilization.

A BRIEF AND VARIED HISTORY OF MAY DAY

Ancient Roman Traditions

Earliest recorded May Day traditions appear to stem from a 5-day-long Roman celebration honoring Flora, the Roman goddess of flowers. This festival of Floralia or Florifertum, the Festival of Flowers, took place annually between April 28 and May 3. Offerings of milk and honey were made to the goddess, and flowers were used to decorate both cities and individuals, who wore floral wreath necklaces and adorned their hair with flowers. Dances and games would take place during the month, because it was considered a time to welcome joyfully the onset of spring (Walsh, 1987).

Although during the Middle Ages, sexual license was associated with the day, the Roman culture was not concerned with monogamous relationships, and the formation of multiple sexual liaisons was neither unusual nor shocking. Whereas the season afforded the Romans an occasion to rejoice at the end of their mild winter season and make offerings to ensure a fertile growing season, the onset of May for them had a serious side. The month of May, named after the goddess Maia who was the wife of Mars and mother of Mercury, was considered a month of purification and religious ceremony in honor of the dead. The first of May was a particularly sacred day at temples. Although sexual liaisons were the norm, May was generally thought to be an unlucky month for marriage, and thus permanent wedding ceremonies generally did not take place during the month (Ingpen & Wilkinson, 1994).

May Day in the Middle Ages

Medieval celebrations followed the Roman precedent, although the duration was shortened. The first day of May become a time for frolic, revelry, and a day of pleasure in the open air. Labeled May Day, its origin was related to pre-Christian (tied to the paganism of the Romans) agricultural rituals and involved a variety of ritual options, including a procession of people carrying trees, branches, or garlands; the appointment of a May king and queen; and the setting up of a May tree or Maypole in a town square. An original Roman motivation to ensure the fertility of crops, domesticated animals, and people gradually evolved from superstition to a rare occasion for personal indulgence, and finally to a widely accepted and anticipated popular festival. Since the remaining days of May would be filled with the hard work of planting crops that would feed the community for the entire year, such a busy month appropriately began with a single day of communal fun. Offerings and other ritual artifacts and behaviors were not considered magic or related to superstitions, but rather appropriate to the day's celebration, which comprised a community outpouring of hope and joy. Emphasis was on social solidarity, rather than on the supernatural or metaphysical. The community would play together on May 1, and then work together through the harvest season (Forest, Morris, & Matachin, 1984).

The celebration began on the eve of the holiday. Young unmarried men paraded around the village and fastened garlands and boughs of evergreen on the windows and doors of the houses where there were unmarried young women. A vocabulary of plants evolved that allowed young people to convey their sentiments without words. For example, a bush with thorns denoted scorn, whereas mountain ash leaves meant love. Before dawn, all the young people of a village went into the woods to gather leafy branches and to help bring in the maypole, a downed tree dragged by oxen into the town square. Each pole served as a gathering place for community dances and activities.

Although similar celebrations took place throughout Europe, the best-documented versions of the holiday were predominantly Saxon and Celtic, where it was entitled "Beltane," or the day of fire (after Bel, the Celtic god of the sun). Fire was used to celebrate the start of summer. The Celts rolled flaming wheels down hills, lit bonfires, and drove cattle through flames in ceremonial purification, a throwback to Roman celebrations. Circle dances were performed as a salute to the circling sun (Ingpen & Wilkinson, 1994).

As European peasant societies evolved from hunting and gathering to agrarian, medieval villagers adapted the rituals by revising their meanings. The hunting gods Diana and Herne became fertility deities of crops and fields. Diana was queen of the May, and Herne became Robin Goodfellow, or "Green George," a predecessor of Robin Hood. As the characters, legends and folklore evolved, focal entertainment for the day involved dancing and masquerade; people dressed to represent Robin Hood, Maid Marion, Friar Tuck, Little John, and Robin's other merry men. Another common disguise was that of Jack-in-the-Green, a young man enshrouded in fresh greenery (Judge, 1978). Along a similar vein, various other European countries developed May Day customs, often related to courtship rituals, but always involving the flora of spring, including flowers and the planting or draping of trees, shrubs, and greenery.

Christian Influences

In the 15th century, the Catholic church attempted to bless and absorb the pagan festival by repositioning it as a time to be thankful to God. Part of the May Day ritual celebration was planned to include the villagers assembling in church for a liturgical ceremony. Frustrated in its attempt to truly Christianize the occasion, the church eventually outlawed the feast, although it was still celebrated by peasants until the late 1700s. Those less intimidated by papal authority continued to celebrate, donning animal masks and costumes akin to those associated with modern-day Halloween festivities in some cultures. Once the church banned the feast, the celebration took on a focused anti-Catholic, pagan bent. Known as Walpurgisnacht, or the night of the witches, the celebration's symbolic leader was the goddess of the hunt, sometimes a pagan priest wearing women's clothing (Plawiuk, 1995).

Since the Christian church could not eliminate many of the traditional feasts and sacred days of the pagans, it attempted to transform them into Saint's Days. The French were the first to Christianize the feast by dedicating the month of May to the Virgin Mary. The virginal young May Queens led processions to honor Mary around the villages and into churches.

Despite attempts to incorporate a religious dimension, the associations of the day with love and fertility remained resilient. The phallic maypole was still raised in many villages. Young men and women would dance around it, holding onto ribbons and hoping to become entwined with those to whom they were attracted and held affection. In addition to the sexual connotations, the celebration also involved an inversion of authority and hierarchical status. Robin Goodfellow, Jack-in-the-Green, and eventually Robin Hood, were essentially anti-establishment characters, essentially Lords of Misrule. May Day became a holiday for the common people, and the players of Robin and Jack became the satirical rulers of this special day. They had the power, to the delight of the observing crowds, to mock priests, nobles, and anyone else who on the other days of the year were in positions of absolute authority over the common people (Plawiuk, 1995).

The Puritan Influence on May Day

Sober-minded Puritans bitterly attacked the traditional celebration of May Day. A petition in 1579 called for an end to "fairs, markets bear-baits, ales, May-games, piping and dancing, hunting and all manner of unlawful gaming" (Bennett, 1946, p. 136). The objection raised was that such gatherings were apt "to generate into orgies of wasteful eating, woeful drinking, rioting and wantonness and were the centers of attraction for idle vagabonds and all lewd fellows of the beset sort" (p. 158).

The sexual license attributed to the day both shocked and outraged Puritans. The Puritans especially objected to the setting aside of the accepted social hierarchy on that day. They preferred strict and clear gradations in society. Their dissatisfaction led to the banning of all May Day celebrations by the English Parliament in 1644. This Puritan influence remained permanent. Even after Charles II reinstated the celebration of May Day in 1660, the elements of sexual license and social reversal remained permanently eradicated (Berger, 1996).

Victorian Influence

A sedate and innocent Victorian version of the holiday reemerged in the 19th century. This new version of May Day excluded any adult revelry, but rather became the domain of well-behaved children. The Victorian image of May Day is that of young girls wearing white dresses and holding flowers. Victorians overlaid a moral tone on the festival. Rather than a celebration of fertility, it was positioned as a throwback to Merry England in the time of Robin Hood. The revisionist historical focus was on purity, innocence, and an earlier time of some adventure, appropriately tempered with propriety and simplicity (Berger, 1996).

The traditional May Basket dates to the Victorian era. A basket of posies decorated with a perfectly tied silk ribbon, ostensibly grasped in a gloved hand, came to represent the ritual celebration of the holiday during this period. Children gave and received these baskets, which were frequently hung on doorknobs. The deliverer would attempt anonymity by ringing the doorbell and quickly disappearing from view. It was during this period that the maypole was reintroduced into country or church "fetes" as an anachronistic representation of civility and days of yore.

Contemporary May Day

Despite the attempts of the Catholic church, the Puritans, and the Victorians to Christianize, moralize, and sanitize the celebration of the first of May, it remained a strong but virtually invisible secular festival among working people in Europe. Immigrants brought this interpretation with them to the United States. In both Europe and the United States, despite efforts to the contrary, this date retained its character as the single festival for which there was no significant church service. Its secular roots and the propensity of celebrants to take a clandestine holiday from work made it a covert Everyman's day. Nineteenth-century analysis of medieval celebrations pointed out that the taking of a tree for a maypole reasserted the serf's right to take wood for building and fuel from forests, which ostensibly belonged to the Lord (or the establishment). These and other similar connections made May Day ripe to become the natural choice for a connection with the labor and socialist movements (Foner, 1986). Labor organization has traditionally been viewed as threatening and adversarial to business in general, with this period being one of even greater conflict.

The modern celebration of May Day as a working-class holiday evolved from the worker's desire for an 8-hour workday in North America. In the United States and elsewhere, May 1 was the date consistently chosen as the occasion for important political demonstrations. In a historic move to support this shorter workday, the Knights of Labor, a group in the process of evolving from a guild to a union, called for a national strike in the United States and Canada on May 1, 1886.

On that same day in Chicago, police attacked a gathering of striking workers and killed six of them. Three days later, workers demonstrated in the city's Haymarket Square to protest this action as an incident of police brutality. Just as the meeting was breaking up, a bomb exploded in the midst of a crowd of police officers, killing one officer and wounding several. The police began shooting into the crowd, and in the end eight police officers died. To this day, the details of the attack remain unclear and controversial. The question remains as to whether the bomb was thrown by workers at the police, or whether the police (either in uniform or dressed as workers) dropped it in their haste to retreat from what they perceived to be charging workers. In any event, the police arrested eight trade unionists thought to be leaders of the initial demonstration and charged them with conspiracy. Labor unions were deemed illegal under the conspiracy laws and membership in a union was considered criminal activity (Cobban, 1995).

The workers who were on trial were labeled anarchists, agitators, and troublemakers, although most were educated men who held white-collar jobs. The state of Illinois tried and convicted the workers on the charge of conspiracy and sentenced them to death by hanging. Depending on the source of the report, both the eight dead police officers and the eight convicted labor leaders were dubbed the Haymarket Martyrs. Most accounts characterize the result of the trial as predictable, and vindictive. During this period, the labor movement in the United States was viewed with suspicion and was seen as a threat to those in power. Whether the workers were guilty or innocent of involvement in the bombing was irrelevant. They were perceived as agitators, instrumental in organizing what was akin to a revolution and stirring up the working class. They were the objects of a public lesson, not directly related to themselves, but toward all workers, so that they would understand the futility of trying to organize. The trial of the eight men was characterized as a sham and as emotionally charged as the incident that gave rise to it. According to Foner (1986):

> The judge cooperated with the prosecutors to make sure that a biased jury was selected. The usual method of picking the trial jurors by lot was dispensed with. Instead the judge appointed Henry L. Rice as a special bailiff.... Rice placed on the juror list only persons of obvious prejudice against the defendants.... One of the jurors was a relative of a police officer who had died as a result of the Haymarket bomb. (pp. 34–35)

Labor Day in May

The Haymarket debacle postponed, but did not eliminate, dissatisfaction with the plight of workers and the quest for an 8-hour workday. The first of May, May Day, was designated as an international day honoring labor by the International Socialist congress in 1889. This World Congress, held in Paris, chose May 1, 1890 (4 years after the Haymarket incident), as another day for demonstrations in favor of the 8-hour workday supported by the U.S. labor movement. Subsequent to this galvanizing and emotional event that now emphasized the plight of workers, May 1 became a holiday called Labor Day in many nations, resembling the existing September 1 holiday in the United States. The September date for Labor Day in the United States had been initiated 8 years earlier in September 1882 and made the celebration of labor on May Day redundant. The U.S. holiday was deemed a time to celebrate the contributions of American workers to the United States and its economy. Discussions took place concerning whether Labor Day in September should be changed to the May 1 date on which much of the globe was honoring labor. In the end, it was felt that the May date was too acutely associated with the Haymarket tragedy and the negative image of unions to be an occasion for a positive celebration (Cobban, 1995).

In 1947 the discussion was resurrected amid hysteria related to the anti-Communist cold war. The U.S. Veterans of Foreign Wars renamed May 1 "Loyalty Day" and a joint session of Congress made this pronouncement official. The rationale was that citizens were to reaffirm their commitment to the State as a weapon against the perceived threat of leftist labor tendencies and specifically the American Communist Party. Loyalty Day parades were held in major cities in the 1950s, New York's being the largest. Their purpose was to distract from former Union-

Square rallies and the Communist Party marches that took place on the same day. By 1960, the celebration of Loyalty Day and accompanying parades became associated with support for the unpopular war in Vietnam. Thus, the holiday disappeared from both practice and memory in the United States by the early 1960s (Thomas, 2002).

Over time the May date became aligned with a radical leftist ideology, first in connection with the international class struggle and more recently as a celebration of the Marxist, socialist, and communist labor perspectives. Particularly during the cold war period, the United States wanted to separate its own celebrations of the labor force at home from the political and economic ideology that was perceived as contrary to the capitalist system.

It was during the 1900s that May 1 became a particularly notable holiday in socialist and Communist countries. The rituals related to this day involve not only political demonstrations, but also military parades. Still secular, the day lost any sense of its earlier carefree indulgence as it evolved into a major holiday in the Soviet Union and other communist countries. With the access and availability of mass media, the day became an occasion for Eastern bloc nations to showcase their military troops and hardware to the West.

Since the dissolution of the Soviet Union and the emergence of many Eastern European republics in the early 1990s, celebrations on May 1 have taken on a newly subdued character. The date remains an official paid day off from work in most European countries. Parades and demonstrations, however, have given way to the simple enjoyment of a quiet day at home. Similar to the practice common in the United States, the date is sometimes adjusted to provide a 3-day weekend for workers. Even in Moscow and St. Petersburg (formerly Leningrad), once the site of massive outdoor gatherings on May 1, of late the day has been relatively quiet. Russians are most likely to celebrate by taking advantage of the long weekend to visit their dachas in the country. A review of May 1, 2000, through May 1, 2002, issues of the Russian newspaper *Pravda* indicated no mention of any official celebratory activities for the day. In addition, the world political and labor situation does not appear ripe for the resurgence of a "Labor Day" with historic roots in Chicago.

Modern May Day in the United States

Today the celebration of May Day in the United States is optional and flexible. Overall, it is ignored by most adults, although it can be part of a quaint and educational springtime ritual for children. Cox (1998) suggested school activities that acquaint children with the history of the holiday. Using the traditional ritual elements, flowers, strands of ivy, spring greenery, and ribbons, Cox suggested weaving crowns and raising a maypole. Children are taught songs and dances that encourage them to weave the ribbons together and, in what may be revealed to be a surprise, a May Queen (perhaps a teacher) is crowned. In order to infuse the day with meaning and a lasting lesson, Cox (1998) asked that the day be used to teach children how to honor other people. Other appropriate activities take the form of simple spring crafts appropriate for children. These involve pressing flowers and using the dried flowers to decorate candles, picture frames, stationery, or other items that can be given as gifts to parents, teachers, or friends.

EXPLANATION FOR CHANGES AND DEMISE
OF THE RITUAL

As detailed in the previous account, the formal celebration of May Day in contemporary North America and in much of the rest of the world has virtually ceased. The dynamism of rituals and celebrations in general predicts that there would be alternations and adaptations over time in any festivity. Such changes are borne out in the history of this particular case in point, but the disappearance of a holiday and accompanying rituals requires further examination and explanation. Three major factors are hypothesized as contributors to the dramatic change that resulted in the virtual elimination of the May Day rituals from North American culture: transference, ideological rejection, and individualization.

Transference

Although May Day as a holiday has become institutionalized in numerous places around the globe, actual celebrations of the day have become generally subdued. The holiday and its accompanying rituals in the United States have both evolved and been transferred to other calendrical occasions. Analysis of this transference will utilize the four elements that Rook (1985) identified in all rituals.

The first element involves the *ritual artifacts,* those consumer products "that accompany or are consumed in a ritual setting" (Rook, 1985, p. 253). When related to the early history of the holiday, the artifacts take the form of flowers and, more recently, cards. These have been redirected and transferred to several springtime holidays in the United States. They are the artifacts used to honoring mothers on the second Sunday of May, a date that is relatively proximate to the traditional occurrence of May Day. In addition, spring flowers are also part of other celebrations, most notably Easter (a moveable springtime fertility feast formally embraced by Christianity) and the courtship feast of Valentine's Day occurring in mid-February. The more recent connotation as a labor holiday appears to be devoid of artifacts, although a paid day off from work may be the single accretion of the day. Perhaps if labor leaders had developed a recognizable logo that could be visually repeated on flags, pins, or decals, the movement would be more concrete and subsequently more memorable and powerful.

The second element, *ritual scripts*, dictates the use of these ritual artifacts. For this case in point the flowers and cards are given as gifts (and may become part of more elaborate gifts) to demonstrate honor and love and to accompany courtship rituals. Once again, Mother's Day and Valentine's Day have subsumed this script. Fertility and the onset of spring have been transferred to Easter, a time for coloring, hiding, finding, and consuming eggs, a symbol of fertility and new life. The absence of artifacts related to the labor movement context also leaves a void in this category. The engagement in parades, demonstrations, and shows of force during the early labor movement was neither popular nor patriotic at the time. In addition, the Haymarket roots of this movement illustrate the dark side of spontaneous demonstrations. Because several people were killed as a result of the "script," these actions could not be considered a laudable circumstance to emulate and repeat.

Ritual performance roles are detailed norms of behavior taking place during the ritual. In this case, lovers and children are to present significant others and mothers with these gifts, celebrating fertility in a less explicit manner, and the recipients have an obligation to respond appropriately. The second more contemporary performance role relates to honoring the contribution of workers in society, most appropriately with an official paid holiday from their labor. This modern script has been transferred to the U.S. national holiday of Labor Day on the first Monday of September. It is a secular day of leisure planned to give workers a mini-vacation in the form of a 3-day weekend. Thus, the major ritual elements originally related to May Day have been transferred to Mother's Day and Labor Day in the U.S. culture and, to a lesser extent, to Valentine's Day and Easter.

The fourth of Rook's elements is *the ritual audience*. In the case of the original May Day revelry, the entire community both watched and concurred with the ritual scripts and performance roles. In its later labor orientation, the mainstream society watched, but did not approve of or side with, the demonstrators. Although U.S. culture tends to sympathize with humanitarian causes, it remains predominantly capitalist and entrepreneurial. The perceived movement of labor toward socialism, especially during the era of the cold war and the threat of Communism, evoked a negative reaction in the U.S. population. Thus it was the ritual audience, the U.S. population, that in the end rejected the May Day labor connotation.

Easier to accept and embrace by the U.S. ritual audience was the concept and practice of Mother's Day, traditionally paired with apple pie as quintessentially American. The day originated in the early 1900s in West Virginia by a woman named Anna Jarvis. She at first sought to erect a memorial plaque honoring her own deceased mother in their church, but later launched a more expansive plan to create a national holiday through which all mothers would be remembered. In 1914, the U.S. Congress adopted a resolution that a May date be designated Mother's Day. Upon its passage, President Woodrow Wilson proclaimed "the second Sunday in May as a public expression of our love and reverence for the mothers of our country." Thus the holiday was not created by marketers as a "Hallmark Holiday," as is the popular belief, but rather grasped on quickly as an opportunity by the floral and greeting card industries. The creator of the day, Anna Jarvis, strongly resented this commercial intrusion, as she characterized greeting cards as "a poor excuse for the letter you are too lazy to write" (Schmidt, 1995, p. 197). It may be these ritual artifacts, however, that have helped perpetuate the celebration of this day.

After World War II, there was a spirited but unsuccessful attempt to refocus Mother's Day as a well-spring movement toward world peace. This was orchestrated by a group of mothers who had lost sons in the World Wars. The group wrote a charter insisting that the day be installed to remember mothers in mourning and to make a forceful political and isolationist statement against war in general. Their laudable goal was that sons and their mothers would never again participate in such an atrocity and suffer the pain related to the loss of a child in war. This attempt provides another example of how difficult it is to add or alter a holiday. Despite the noble cause, there was not enough public support (in the form of acceptance by the ritual audience) to create and sustain this new meaning in the institutional memory of a nation.

Thus, in the 20th century, the focal celebratory day in May had been redirected toward mothers (and in a subtler way their fertility) and away from labor, wars, the rites of spring, fertility of the crops, and courtship. The Mother's Day celebration continues to utilize the accretions of the early Roman celebrations of spring in the form of flowers. There remains the strong emotional tie with love, but maternal love has replaced courtship rituals and sexual license. This sanitized version of love reflects the purity ideal of the Victorian influence, as does the ritual performance role of children honoring their mothers. Mother's Day has developed a modified symbolic language of fauna, similar to the May Day practice in medieval times. The carnation initially become a symbol of Mother's Day, based simply on that fact that it was the favorite flower of the woman who originated the day, Mrs. Reece (Anna) Jarvis. The very first Mother's Day involved two memorial church services, one in Grafton, West Virginia, and one in Philadelphia, held at Mrs. Jarvis' request upon her death. She asked that white carnations grace the altars, and the flowers be distributed to participants at the end of the service to honor all mothers present. Roses have also become popular on this day to communicate rarity and status, while flowering spring bulbs, theoretically from the garden of the recipient and closer to the spirit and practice of the original May Day, are also viewed as appropriate as the offerings of young children.

Ideological Conflict and Rejection

Thus a crowded calendar and the availability of myriad springtime holidays for floral celebrations may have served as an incentive to transfer the ritual elements of May Day to other celebrations. A stronger stimulus, however, may have come from an outright conflict of ideology. The honoring of the U.S. labor force had been preempted in 1882 by its assignment to another date, the first Monday in September. As pointed out earlier, labor groups were viewed with suspicion during the early period of organization and unionization. More importantly, Labor Day associations with the May date became affiliated with Marxist, and later Communist and Leninist, ideologies. These political ideologies were the antithesis of the capitalist system as it functioned in the United States.

This conflicting political environment gave rise to the strongest motivation to separate the celebration of labor with the May 1 date. During the post–World War II cold war era, relationships were particularly strained between the United States and the Soviet Union. Communist bloc countries embraced May 1, mainly due to its secular appeal, after discarding or banning various other holidays with overt religious connotations, practices, and affiliations. Individual citizens of the countries that made up the Soviet Union continued to celebrate religious occasions privately and covertly, but it was the historically nonreligious character of May Day and its more recent connection with the plight of the common worker that deemed the date appropriate for a high profile, public celebration. The famous quote of Karl Marx that labeled religion as "the opiate of the people" reinforced the importance of such secular celebrations. Even though the United States has traditionally consciously worked to separate church and state, there was an aversion to having major celebrations shared with political entities holding the socialist, Marxist and later Leninist and communist perspectives. In addition, because the United States had a previously agreed-on alternative date in September devoted to honor working people (utilizing the transference of the ritual elements), there were neither historical reasons nor popular support for maintaining the May date.

Individualization

A third factor that contributed to the demise of various forms of the May Day celebration is the tendency of the North Americans toward individualization. This is a cultural bias that values the importance of the individual and generally diminishes the power and cooperation of a group. Such a preference toward individualization was instrumental in the transference and rejection of several May Day rituals and of the holiday itself. The roots of the May Day ritual behavior involved group cooperation and communal behaviors. The participation in the raising of and ritual dancing around the Maypole, for example, cannot take place without the engagement of a community of revelers. This type of communal celebration has been cast aside in favor of celebratory ritual behaviors between individuals. As a group, North Americans feel more comfortable and thus prefer to honor individual mothers, lovers, and other special interpersonal relationships. In that same vein, the parades and demonstrations that characterized the labor protests that comprise the roots of the May Labor Day are often rebellious, and involve people who are disenfranchised, out of the mainstream, and countercultural. Although Americans have demonstrated solidarity when a short-term cause or threat is evident, they tend not to be a communal culture. It is difficult in such a heterogeneous group to gain a

consensus on any specific issue. Thus basic values held by individuals (e.g., moth-
erhood, family, and love, and until recently Christianity) rise to the level of a national celebration and holiday status. In the current U.S. environment, the 40-hour
work week is a fact rather than a cause. The U.S. working population is an amal-
gamation of union labor, nonunion labor, management, and the self-employed. As
with most demographic differences among members of the American culture, the
only common aspect of the workforce that may merit celebration may be the diversity of the working public.

IMPLICATIONS FOR RITUALS IN GENERAL

An interpretive summary of the historical evolution of May Day reveals some abstract aspects that may be generalized to all rituals. The level of analysis in this
case is cultural, rather than personal. In such a cultural system, the decisions and
actions of individuals do matter, but these individuals realize that they are expected
to play a part in the larger society (Douglas, 1996). The rituals associated with May
Day over its diverse history can be modified with a variety of opposing adjectives.
May Day rituals have at various times been indulgent and repressed, pleasurable
and painful, blissful and angry, anticipated and ominous, coquettish and predictable, nostalgic and novel, repetitive and revolutionary.

These are be discussed in terms of into two superordinate categories. The
first focuses attention on the emotional significance of the ritual, and the second
emphasizes the cognitive or socially constructed meanings of the event. Clearly,
each layer of meaning, both affective and cognitive, is multifaceted and together
the two perspectives attempt to capture the multidimensionality of ritual behavior.
The discussion of each superordinate category explores theoretical issues concerning its impact on the participation of the individual as well as the social significance of rituals.

Ritual Ambivalence: The Emotionality of Ritual Events

Even though rituals assume repetitive actions, they are far from emotion-free. The
actions associated with ritual behaviors have emotional overlays and can express
love, longing, and loss. Fused with behaviors, the emotional themes convey the basic
ambivalence of the ritual event (Otnes, Lowrey, & Shrum, 1997). There is joy and
satisfaction in the annual repetition of ritual behaviors, and yet anxiety and frustration related to the social pressure to fulfill a predetermined script, as was found to be
the case in holiday gift giving (Sherry, McGrath, & Levy, 1993, 1995). As may be
true of most rituals, there are mixed emotions that comprise ritual participation and
these emotions may at times conflict with each other and with the manifest meaning
of the ritual itself. In this case, hope and fear, the past and future, the young and the

elderly, dignity and fun, and communion and obligation are dichotomies that contribute to the emotional ambivalence of a celebratory ritual event. The idealized status of the Victorian May Day ritual (a perfect May Basket constructed in Martha Stewart fashion with a hand-woven basket and filled with flowers from a personally tended garden) is difficult to reconcile with the increased proportion of working women who have less time at home to garden or to construct such celebrations. The alternative May Day worldview, that of a day devoted to the struggle of the worker, is also difficult to resolve with the demise of labor unions in the United States and the convention of a 35- to 40-hour work week. Both beauty and justice are admirable causes in the abstract, but the reality of the time and effort to make the cause into reality contribute to this emotional ambiguity.

The bundled celebration itself, not knowing what exactly is being feted and what is an appropriate celebration, has contributed to ambiguity, confusion, and finally abandonment. Here there is a divergence between an individual participant's affective experience and what is socially dictated an "appropriate emotion." Reconciliation of this disparity is no mean task.

Cognitive Significance: Learning and Constructing Identity Through Ritual Events

To learn the ritual behaviors expected on various occasions is part of the socialization process that accompanies maturity within a culture. Observing and mirroring behaviors, even though the learner may not understand their significance, allows social participants to join a group by sharing in activities before they actually feel comfortable with the ethos or mores of a situation.

A ritual occasion is at once both social and cognitive. The social context of the ritual provides a setting imbued with deep meaning for participants in the here and now, but it also provides a rich set of cognitive cues that provoke reminiscence. The reminiscences elicited can be idiosyncratic and reflect personal history and relationships with the people present (and remembrance of those absent) or they can be communal and aligned with the mainstream culture. These reminiscences can also serve to reconnect participants to elements of their own identity (e.g., by recalling one's own childhood or by recalling events associated with another time, date, or place similar to that of the present). Finally, the ritual can serve to reinforce identification with a cultural group. Indeed, for some participants, ritual (and other social) enactment has links to cultural and subcultural identity. In the United States, as elsewhere, people honor the contribution and plight of labor in society, but the celebration is on a day different from the celebration in other cultures. Among a diverse U.S. population, however, members of various subcultures may choose to celebrate with the country of their origin. Thus, the ritual exhibition acts as a salient social-cognitive stimulus that can potentially influence identity construction of the self and of the group.

CONCLUSIONS

Rook's (1985) seminal work on rituals has precipitated a wellspring of creative thought and research. Relating this important topic to contemporary consumer behavior has motivated the cross-disciplinary movement that has enriched the body of literature as well as enlightened its researchers. Linking the construct, which has strong roots in anthropology, to the examination of consumer lifestyles has lessoned the bias toward the psychological and opened the field to a wider range of theories, paradigms, and research methodologies.

Rituals are one of the subtleties of consumer culture that are easily overlooked and understudied. Consumers lean and depend on their relative stability, yet their ability to adapt and change makes them both useful and ephemeral. This overview of a changing ritual occasion over time demonstrates the importance, flexibility, and durability of such occasions and their accompanying artifacts. Hopefully, it contributes to the illumination of the query that defies a complete solution and serves as the engine that drives this discipline forward: What is it that people do and why do they do it?

REFERENCES

Bennett, W. (1946). *History of Burnley*, (Vol. 2, 1400–1650). Burnley, England: Burnley Corporation.

Berger, J. (1996). The pagan origins of May Day. *About time*. London: BBC.

Cobban, M. (1995). May Day: What happened to the radical worker's holiday? *Labour News, 12*.

Cox, M. (1998). *The heart of a family: Searching America for new traditions that fulfill us*. New York: Random House.

Driver, T. (1993). *The magic of ritual*. San Francisco: HarperCollins.

Douglas, M. (1996). *Thought styles*. London: Sage.

Foner, P. (1986). *May Day*. New York: International Publishers.

Forest, J., Morris, M., & Matachin, M. (1984). *A study in comparative choreography*. Sheffield, England: Sage.

Fulghum, R. (1995). *From beginning to end: The rituals of our lives*. New York: Villard Books.

Ingpen, R., & Wilkinson, P. (1994). *A celebration of customs and rituals of the world*. New York: Facts on File.

Judge, R. (1978). *The Jack-in-the-Green: A May Day custom*. Ipswich, England: Sage.

Otnes, C., Lowrey, T. M., & Shrum, L. J. (1997, June). Toward an understanding of consumer ambivalence. *Journal of Consumer Research, 24*, 80–93.

Plawiuk, E. (1995). The origins and traditions of Mayday. *Labor News, 12*.

Rook, D. (1985). The ritual dimension of consumer behavior. *Journal of Consumer Research, 12*, 251–264.

Schmidt, L. (1995). *Consumer rites: The buying and selling of American holidays.* Princeton, NJ: Princeton University Press.

Sherry, J., Jr., McGrath, M., & Levy, S. (1993). The dark side of the gift. *Journal of Business Research, 28*(3), 225–244.

Sherry, J., Jr., McGrath, M., & Levy, S. (1995). Monadic giving: Anatomy of gifts given to the self. In J. Sherry, Jr. (Ed.), *Contemporary marketing and consumer behavior: An anthropological sourcebook* (pp. 141–166). New York: Sage.

Thomas, M. (2002). May Day in the USA: A forgotten history. Accessed on http://www.mayweek.ab.ca/index.html . *The Union Ring,* Edmontor, Canada.

Walsh, W. (1987). *Curiosities of popular customs.* Philadelphia: Lippincott.

6

Consumer Fairy Tales of the Perfect Christmas: Villains and Other *Dramatis Personae*

Tina M. Lowrey
University of Texas at San Antonio

Cele C. Otnes
University of Illinois, Urbana–Champaign

Research on the modern-day Christmas—describing fractured families and decreased leisure time—indicates that ideal celebrations, although mythologized in literature and film, are hard to achieve (Otnes, Zolner, & Lowrey, 1994; Sherry, McGrath, & Levy, 1992). But as Christmas has taken on a more secular meaning (Belk, 1989, 1993), it has become *the* occasion for acknowledging important social bonds. In fact, for increasingly mobile and malleable families, it may be the only significant recognition of kinship ties to occur all year (Cheal, 1987, 1988). Thus, the risk of not "doing Christmas right" seems to outweigh any inconveniences or ill tempers that result from the holiday.

Many orchestrators of Christmas celebrations (typically women; Fischer & Arnold, 1990; Laird, 1996) are not content with having merely tolerable holidays. Instead, they often aspire to creating a Christmas more memorable than the previous one. In fact, we argue that our informants strive to create a "fairy tale" Christmas. Although this term is typically associated with weddings, our data demonstrate it is just as relevant to this similarly complex consumption ritual. In the vernacular, a "fairy tale" Christmas would seem to mean that consumers seek happy endings for their celebrations, like those fairy tales that end with a joyous family reunion (*Hansel and Gretel*), the acquisition of precious goods (*Jack and the Beanstalk*), or recognition for creativity and cleverness (*Puss 'N Boots*). Moreover, not only do our informants strive toward fairy tale endings, our data reveal that their experiences actually involve the characters (or *dramatis personae*) found in fairy tales. In short, our informants' tales are filled with valiant heroines, evil villains, daring deeds, and dastardly deceptions, or what Tatar (1987) called the "hard facts" of these tales.

Our informants' tales reaffirm the power of narratives in everyday consumption experience. Richardson (1990) argued narratives organize people's lives into "temporally meaningful episodes ... the narrative mode looks for particular connections between events [and] is contextually embedded" (p. 118). One's life is understood, in part, through the stories told about it. According to Berger (1997), "narratives furnish us with both a method for learning about the world and a way to tell others what we have learned" (p. 10). In fact, life and story are not separate, "they are part of the same fabric, in that life informs and is informed by stories" (Widdershoven, 1993, p. 2).

Creating and analyzing consumer-based text is a mainstay of interpretive and postmodern consumer research (Brown, 1998; Hirschman & Holbrook, 1992). A few studies have applied existing literary narrative structures to examine consumer-based text. These include Levy's (1981) study of the mythic dimensions of consumer experience, his use of familiar fairy tales as projective stimuli in a study of women's self-concepts (Levy, 1985), Durgee's (1988) exploration of the Consumer Behavior Odyssey, and Stern's (1995) explanation of how Frye's taxonomy applies to Wallendorf and Arnould's (1991) Thanksgiving-based text.

Although the narrative form of the fairy tale might seem too "juvenile" to pertain to adult consumer behavior, Berger (1997) argued that it is a "proto-narrative, or ur-narrative, from which other popular genre narratives have evolved" (p. 83). Moreover, he argued the fundamental conflicts found in fairy tales are highly relevant to people's everyday lives. And because consumption is now often touted as one of the defining aspects of the postmodern condition (Firat & Dholakia, 1998; Firat & Venkatesh, 1995), it is reasonable to assume these narrative structures might play themselves out in consumption contexts.

The most compelling evidence that consumers' experiences can be understood as fairy tales stems from consumers themselves. When the study was begun a decade ago, neither of us expected the Christmas-as-fairy-tale metaphor to emerge as the most persistent and persuasive in the text. But the more we understood our data, the more this metaphor imposed itself on us. By building our interpretation around this genre, we have cast consumers' Christmas experiences in a new light, and a greater understanding of them is offered in this ritual context. The complexity and liminality of Christmas make it a natural context for the emergence of multifaceted narratives (Rook, 1985; Turner, 1969). We heed Brown's (1998) call to examine consumption as narrative, as we interpret our informants' lives in the context of planning their Christmas holidays.

We provide a brief history of the fairy tale genre, and expand our discussion of its relevance to consumer behavior. After presenting our methodology, we offer our informants' stories as evidence that *dramatis personae* greatly impact their Christmas fairy tales.

ONCE UPON A TIME,
THERE WAS A LITERARY GENRE ...

the origins of which, like many narrative forms, remain obscure. It has been hypothesized that the fairy (or folk) tale originated in the Pre-Indo-European Megalithic culture (Eliade, 1963), that it dates back to stories written on papyrus in Egypt (von Franz, 1982), and it spread from Asia and the Middle East to Spain and North Africa (Eliade, 1963). Early fairy tales—with their bawdy themes and ribald humor—were definitely not for children. Tatar (1992) recounted an early version of *Little Red Riding Hood* where the heroine undresses "while provocatively asking the wolf what to do with her bodice, her petticoat, and her stockings, and who then tricks the wolf by asking if she can go outside to relieve herself" (p. 3). Fairy tales began as orally transmitted stories, and this pattern was reinforced during the 17th century, when modifying them was a popular parlor game among the French nobility. During this time, the standard plots and characters became fixed in what Zipes (1994) termed the "literary fairy tale."

The transformation of fairy tales to a genre for children accompanied the development of the market for children's literature. Zipes (1994) observed that most literary historians attribute Charles Perrault with developing the genre of the children's literary fairy tale, with the publication of *Contes du temps passe* in 1697." Although originally designed to entertain (Brewer & Lichtenstein, 1982), fairy tales were also used as tools of moral and spiritual instruction, and were "harnessed into service as stories for children, so long as [the tales were] divested … of their earthy humor, burlesque twists, and bawdy turns of phrase" (Tatar, 1992, p. 8).

One of the most significant events in the history of the genre was the publication in 1812 and 1815 of *Children and Household Tales* by the Brothers Grimm. Reinforcing the fact that, at the time, fairy tales were considered bourgeois art forms, their collection was based on tales told by middle-class or aristocratic young women. Although they whitewashed the more sexual aspects of the tales and added Christian lessons, they maintained and even enhanced violent images to help the stories' harsh lessons hit home with children. In their version of *Cinderella (Aschenputtel)*, the stepsisters cut off their toes and heels in order to try to fit their feet into the glass slipper. And on the day of Aschenputtel's wedding to the prince, doves peck out the stepsisters' eyes. This focus on revenge contrasts sharply with Perrault's earlier *Cinderella*, which contained a final message of forgiveness (Andersen & Perrault, n.d.). By the early 20th century, the Grimms' volumes were outsold only by the Bible in Germany, and remain one of the most popular collections in the world (Zipes, 1988).

More recently, disseminating fairy tales has largely been the work of the Walt Disney Company. Starting with *Snow White* in 1937, the company adapted several tales in a string of successful films. Although earlier versions follow the traditional format, Zipes (1994) observed: "One of the qualitatively distinguishing features of the [recent] fairy tales [sic] in America … has been the manner in which it has questioned gender roles and critiqued the patriarchal code … so dominant in both folk and fairy tales until the 1960s" (p. 142). Thus, the postmodernist questioning of existing narrative structures has affected fairy tales as well.

The psychological depths of fairy tales have been plumbed from both Freudian (e.g., Bettelheim, 1976) and Jungian (e.g., Birkhauser-Oeri, 1988; von Franz, 1982) perspectives. Bettelheim (1976) believed the ultimate lesson children learn from fairy tales is that despite the inevitability of conflict, they can triumph. Danilewitz (1991) stated, "The message of fairy tales to children is that a struggle against severe difficulties in life is unavoidable, it is part of one's existence, but one can master the obstacles and emerge victorious in the end" (p. 89).

Studies of commonalities across tales are prevalent in fairy tale research. In addition, life histories of single tales, over time and across cultures, have been conducted (Utley, 1976). Structural analyses are also common, with one of the earliest undertaken by the Finnish Structuralist School in the early 1920s. This school classified folk tales by geographic origin, then organized the tales into three basic themes: animal tales, tales proper, and anecdotes (Propp, 1928/1970). Propp, in *Morphology of the Folktale*, argued that all Russian folk tales classified by the Finnish School contained the same basic structure. More importantly for the purposes of this discussion, Propp outlined seven possible *dramatis personae* in a fairy tale:

1. the *villain*, who deliberately attempts to thwart the progress of the hero(ine) on his/her quest
2. the *donor/provider*, who offers magical agents to the hero(ine)
3. the *helper*, whose direct deeds assists the hero(ine)
4. the *princess/sought-after person and his/her father*
5. the *dispatcher*, who sends forth the hero(ine) into the world
6. the *hero(ine)*, whose deeds lead to a satisfactory resolution of the plot
7. the *false hero(ine)*, who poses as the hero(ine) in an attempt to gain fame

To date, only one scholar has drawn an analogy between fairy tales and consumer behavior. Specifically, Heilbrunn (1998, 1999) showed that four narrative elements posited by Greimas (1966) can explain consumers' relationships to brands, and these elements can be found at the core of the narrative structure of some advertisements. We extend this work by asking: What exactly are consumer fairy tales? We begin with this definition:

> *Consumer fairy tales (CFTs)* are narratives that are partially enacted in the marketplace, in which consumers employ magical agents, donors,

and helpers to overcome villains and obstacles, as they seek out goods
and services in their quest for happy endings.

In comparing CFTs and literary fairy tales (LFTs), we used Propp's *dramatis personae* as a benchmark for analysis. Specifically, once the salience of the fairy tale narrative in our text emerged, we based our analysis on the following research questions: (a) How are the *dramatis personae* in LFTs discussed by Propp similar to and different from those in CFTs? And, (b) How do the *dramatis personae* in CFTs influence our informants' Christmas gift-giving activies?

Similarities Between CFTs and LFTs

Although CFTs are based on real life and LFTs follow a strict structure, our CFTs contain most of the *dramatis personae* specified by Propp. Indeed, only the false hero(ine) and the dispatcher are absent. Also, although these tales typically do not feature quests for princesses and/or their fathers, they do feature a reasonable substitute in materialistic cultures—highly sought-after goods and services.

Differences Between CFTs and LFTs

There are qualitative differences in the ways the *dramatis personae* are enacted in the CFT. As one obvious example, LFTs are replete with magical animals, phantasms, and a host of other-worldly beings. In contrast, CFTs are primarily populated by people. Moreover, in real life villains can sometimes (but not often) redeem themselves, and previous helpers can become villains. Table 6.1 compares LFTs and CFTs.

METHODOLOGY

We interacted with four informants during four Christmas seasons from 1990 to 1997. Our data collection included in-depth interviews and shopping trips (see Otnes, Lowrey, & Kim, 1993, for both informant and procedural details). To analyze the text, the constant comparative method was used (Lincoln & Guba, 1985). Briefly, the researcher unitizes the data, then continually compares each unit to all others. Distinct categories emerge that the interpreters then analyze for their overall importance. The first author engaged in the initial analysis. The second author audited this interpretation. After we agreed that the *dramatis personae* were highly emergent in the data, we chose to write our interpretations in the form of fairy tales. We believed doing so would capture the presence and power of the *dramatis personae* in our informants' CFTs. By opting for this form, we embrace Richardson's (1994) argument that experimental forms of writing provide evocative representations and alternative ways of

TABLE 6.1
Consumer Fairy Tales Versus Literary Fairy Tales

Elements	Literary Fairy Tales	Consumer Fairy Tales
Hero(ine)s	Both male and female; children, adults, animals	Typically female adults
Qualities of Hero(ine)	Compassionate, clever, creative, persistent	Compassionate, clever, creative, persistent, cost-conscious
Villains	Typically one; typically not blood relative; typically invariant over time	Typically multiple; family members or friends or condition (e.g., Death); can vary by year
Nature of Villainy	Physical	Psychological
Helpers and Donors	Animals, enchanted beings	Relatives, friends, strangers, retailers
Nature of Quest	Simple (e.g., one or a few deeds)	Complex—multiple deeds
Object of Quest	Person	Commodity or commodity-laden experience
Nature of Narrative	Linear, singular plotline	Circular (repeats over time), multiple plotlines
Nature of Character	Invariant (e.g., once a villain, always a villain)	Variant (e.g., can change roles over time)

knowing that conventional techniques may not permit. Each author was initially responsible for creating two fairy tales, which were revised and refined by the other.

As we spent time with our informants, we became "case researchers as biographers" (Stake, 1995), where, "the chronology of life is explored against a thematic network ... writing more for the illustration of an idea than for understanding the individual's life" (pp. 96–97). Rather than complete biographies, our informants' "Christmas lives" were the focus. The longitudinal design is critical to the depth of understanding achieved with respect to CFTs, particularly regarding the ability to verify our interpretation. As we strove to uncover the underlying themes of our informants' stories, we saw similar plots emerging—involving quests for perfection and villains engaging in dastardly deeds. Our informants' stories were so similar to fairy tales, it was imperative to understand them as such. This led us to the literature on fairy tales to further explore the meaning of our informants' stories. We now offer the CFTs from our data, as our informants engaged in their "infinitely serious and responsible adventure[s]" of planning the perfect Christmas (a phrase used by Eliade, 1963, to describe fairy tales).

FOUR CONSUMER FAIRY TALES

Anne

Once upon a time, a young woman named Anne lived with her parents in a cottage. Anne's generosity and love of Christmas were evident in the many compassionate deeds she performed every year, such as bringing hot chocolate to the Salvation Army workers as they rang their bells in the cold and snow. Anne's quest was always twofold: First, to create a Christmas that was singular, special, and filled with warmth; and, second (and most importantly), to create Christmas within a limited budget, while receiving recognition for selecting unique gifts: "I like getting stuff for people that they really like so that they look at it and go, 'Oh, wow ...' and that they remember me. You know, 'Anne got that,' instead of 'Oh God, I can't remember who gave me that' (INT92).

One of the most consistent elements of Anne's tale every year was her creation of "themes" for her recipients, allowing her to gain praise for her cleverness and thoughtfulness at the same time: "I think I'll do a theme this year [for her fiancé]. He started coaching part-time.... I thought about getting him a briefcase and getting him some leather binders and a calculator and a pen set and a desk set and stuff to organize himself" (INT90).

Anne's Villains.   Each year, Anne faced villains whose treachery was not always obvious at first. Over and over again, Anne's first fiancé Chuck kept her from realizing her ideal Christmas. In 1990, Anne had to return Chuck's main gift and forego buying other presents, because he had gotten a job in a nearby town and needed "cash to get down there." At the same time, 21-year-old Anne paid for gifts for Chuck's daughters even though "he can't get me anything for Christmas because he's a month behind on his child support right now." In 1992, Anne overcame obstacles such as a big truck payment and her own hectic schedule to outfit Chuck with a new desk and accessories for his coaching job. Again, Chuck gave Anne nothing. Anne did not view Chuck as a villain at the time. But by 1994, after he stole thousands of dollars from her and made threatening calls to her office, Chuck's villainy was finally revealed.

Anne's other villains were more sporadic throughout the years. In 1990, her "old and mean" grandmother insisted Anne pay back a loan, although she was not requiring Anne's brother to do so. Anne relied on her own wily ways to punish her grandmother, withholding her usual generous spirit while shopping for her gift: "She looked at thermal blankets and wondered if that would make a good gift. Then she found one smaller lap blanket which was the price she wanted to pay. She mentioned that would be 'good enough'" (FN90).

Other times, Anne was cryptic as to why a particular family member achieved "villain" status. One painful memory was of giving a beautiful airplane book she thought would make her father happy. But alas, he "flipped through it on Christmas Day and never read it. So, you know, something that I thought was perfect, wasn't" (INT92). In 1990, Anne became upset with her father, who had "been a bad boy" and "wasn't getting shit." But after that year, her father's "villainous" status was downgraded, as he actually became a "donor." Simply put, by buying a computer, he "gave" Anne a theme enabling her to buy him satisfactory gifts: "I'll just get him software. He'll like anything if it's computer related," (INT92). Later, Anne said that since he had bought a home computer, it 'made him so easy' (FN92). Anne had given him the computer games early (a common tendency with her), and he was "thrilled to pieces, thrilled beyond belief." In fact, two out of the five games dealt with airplanes, which he loved (FN92), allowing Anne to finally "score" with that idea.

Another year, Anne became angry with her sister, with whom she had never gotten along particularly well. Anne punished her by sending flowers from "Guess Who" to try to make her sister's husband jealous and get her sister into trouble.

Prince Charming Arrives: The Ultimate Helper. Over the years, Anne relied on a variety of men in marketplace settings to act as helpers and donors, often playing the "helpless female" to acquire desired items. But in 1994, after her ill-fated years with Chuck, Anne had found her "Prince Charming" in the form of Gerry, who literally delivered himself to her office ("I bagged the UPS man!"). Although Anne and Gerry had just started dating that year, Anne recounted many ways Gerry helped her in her quest for Christmas, including shopping with her and decorating the tree. By 1997, they had bought a house together and were planning to elope the next summer. Anne literally glowed when she described how Gerry shared her tendency toward generosity and tenderheartedness, "That's the one thing that I like most about him, is that, the effort that I put in, he gives back just as much" (INT94).

Much to Anne's delight, Gerry proved to be the helper she had always wanted, insisting they split the Christmas expenses, allowing her to shower her family and friends generously. He also encouraged her creative efforts in decorating, suggested gift ideas for his relatives, wrapped and mailed packages, and— perhaps most importantly—helped her achieve more harmonious Christmases, because her parents "adored" him. It was clear by 1997 that Gerry had become Anne's primary helper in achieving her ideal Christmas.

Happy Endings. When asked to describe her perfect Christmas, Anne described how wonderful it would be if the entire family could be together (something that had not happened in over 5 years), and said, "the older I get, the more important people are." At the same time, not surprisingly, Anne's vision of the perfect Christmas includes lots of "goodies"—special and singular gifts both for and from her. By the 1997 season, Anne seemed well on her way to achieving her vision of Christmas: owning her own home that she could decorate, being able to afford more generous gifts, and having a helpful, loving companion.

The Moral of Anne's Story.   Of all our heroines, Anne underwent the most dramatic transition during the course of the study. She unmasked one significant villain (her ex-fiancé) and replaced him with Gerry, who reciprocates her thoughtful, romantic gifts at Christmas and helps her shower gifts on friends and family. Yet beneath Anne's goodwill at Christmas lurks a more ruthless side, where "good" recipients are rewarded with gifts early, but those who have angered Anne are targeted with weapons in the guise of gifts. Both actions reflect Anne's use of gifts as control mechanisms (McGrath, 2000). And, of course, Anne's elimination of a recipient from her gift list—or her expression of the "Avoider" role (Otnes et al. 1993)—is the ultimate expression of the "dark side" of her gift giving (Sherry et al., 1993). So whereas part of Anne's story resembles *Cinderella*—as she meets a Prince who helps in her quest for an abundant Christmas—it is the Grimms' version (featuring a vengeful heroine), rather than Perrault's more forgiving portrayal, that is the more accurate analogy.

Betsy

(Not) long ago, a woman named Betsy lived in a cozy house with her husband and children. Betsy took on many obligations for her family. Betsy had cared for her mother every day while she was dying, and often visited her elderly grandparents. Each year, Betsy's quest was to create a special Christmas that helped recapture the spirit of long-lost family members, while selecting unique gifts for many difficult recipients: "I look forward to when I find something right, I say 'Good job—you did it, Betsy!' (INT90).

The Grim Reaper: Betsy's Main Villain.   Almost every year, Betsy fought the same villain while planning Christmas: Death. In 1990, she had four grandparents still living. But by 1997, only one grandmother remained. No doubt, the first blow of the Grim Reaper, which resulted in the death of Betsy's mother in 1987, was the cruelest. Although these losses may have lightened Betsy's Christmas load, they actually made it harder to get through the season because she was constantly reminded how she no longer needed to buy particular items: "Each year somebody gets taken away from me that I usually shop for. It kind of reduces some of my joy and I feel a lot of sadness sometimes when I'm shopping and I see something and I go, 'God, that's Granny.' I used to have to shop real hard to find Mallow Cups but now I don't have to buy them this year.... And that hurts" (INT90).

It might be assumed Death would triumph over her Christmas, but Betsy relied on many magical agents to keep pain and grief at bay. One way she found to keep the spirit of her lost loved ones alive was to take up the gauntlet of maintaining their traditions: "My husband's thing is ketchup. My mom used to buy [him] ketchup every year.... And she'd wrap it in boxes with bricks to disguise it. Or she'd tape [a toilet paper] tube on ... I mean, we spent hours disguising ketchup.... The first year [after she died] I put Mom's name on it, because that's what she did" (INT90).

Keeping traditions alive while battling Death also helped Betsy protect her family's precious Christmas celebration: "One year I got crazy busy at Christmas and my Mom was dying of cancer and I didn't really have time to bake cookies.... What I did is I ended up buying a five lb. bag of sugar and a five lb. bag of flour and chocolate chips—and wrapping them and saying 'Here are your chocolate chip cookies.' One way or another you'll get your cookies!" (INT90).

In 1994, Betsy's father-in-law was battling cancer. True to form, Betsy wanted to give her father-in-law an unforgettable Christmas gift—the Purple Heart he had earned in World War II but had never received. During this battle, Betsy encountered many obstacles, including the bureaucracy of the U.S. Army and a fire that had destroyed her father-in-law's service records. Betsy began this battle in 1994, and was still waging it determinedly in 1997.

The Stepmother Effect.   A few years after Betsy's mother passed away, her father remarried. Betsy and her sister were in their thirties and had their own families, so his new wife was not their stepmother in any real sense. And although her father's new wife wanted to become part of the family and was not evil, her presence caused Betsy's most surprising villain to emerge—her sister Jane. In 1990, Betsy had worked hard to buy gifts she knew Jane would enjoy: "We're totally opposite, and I end up buying things that I'm not particularly fond of ... you [pause] *learn* to do that." But by 1992, the relationship between Betsy and her sister "the bitch" was strained, because Jane refused to accept this new addition to the family, even going so far as to boycott holiday occasions if her stepmother was present. Needless to say, Betsy was upset by this: "If you want to come and be there for my kids, then you come and be there for my kids. And it doesn't make any difference if Atilla the Hun is going to be there, or the Devil himself. If you love my kids enough, you'll be here" (INT92).

In 1992, Betsy expressed newfound apathy toward selecting her sister Jane's gift: "It's almost like I want to get it over with. Be done with it ... " Clearly, this was Betsy's way of punishing Jane for her actions and the resulting family tension. In 1994, she said she was having trouble finding something for her sister's Christmas present. But by 1997, Betsy had defeated her sister. She "put her foot down ... and told her to come to all of [the family functions] or none of them, but that Jane couldn't hurt her kids' feelings by coming to the ones Jane felt like coming to." Jane acquiesced, and the sisters settled into an uneasy truce.

No Helpers For Betsy.   As far as we could tell, Betsy did not have any true helpers. Indeed, she took on so many holiday-related activities herself that this became a "sore subject" with her husband. Although he did not deliberately undermine her efforts (as a villain would), he did present an obstacle for Betsy to overcome, objecting to the energy and effort she devoted to these activities. However, he also revealed "Despite the fact that he pays for it [in loss of time], this is part of the reason why he loves me—because of my generous nature ..." (INT90).

Happily Ever After.   In 1997, Betsy said that in her fantasy Christmas her mother would be alive to see her daughter's school play, her son's concert, and how much her children had grown. But when pressed to describe an attainable perfect Christmas, Betsy said it would involve everyone being together for the holidays. Although she had certainly known her share of tragedies, Betsy said "the reality is that I will have the perfect Christmas this year—I have the perfect Christmas every year" (INT97). Because her husband and children are all healthy and happy, and because they live a comfortable life, Betsy feels very blessed.

The Moral of Betsy's Story.   Betsy's CFT is the most heavily laden with Christmas duties. Having lost her mother, she handles many of the logistical details of Christmas that her mother had shouldered. Although Betsy has an older sister, she has become the "ritual" matriarch of the family, ensuring that Christmas is kept properly, and filling the emotional void left by the loss of relatives year after year. As a result, Betsy's biggest challenge is keeping herself balanced during the holiday season, as she is a "juggler" (Thompson, 1996) who moves from commitments at her children's schools, to those in the community, to those in her own family.

Betsy and her villainous sister have reached an uneasy truce, one that enables our heroine to continue her quest for a family-filled Christmas. And throughout the journey, Betsy also displays craftiness and persistence in her attempt to commemorate relationships through gifts. In that way, Betsy resembles a Princess Valiant in her success at optimistically perceiving that the holidays are still joyous. Although the Grim Reaper takes away members of her extended family almost every year, Betsy feels blessed that her nuclear family is healthy and content.

Hannah

Long ago, a young girl named Hannah lived with her family in a happy home. But one day her wealthy father went away and took her sister, leaving Hannah and her mother to fend for themselves. Over the years, Hannah's life revolved around selling decorative stamps, babysitting, going to church, and devoting herself to her ailing mother. Every year, Hannah's quest at Christmas was the same—to have a low-key, harmonious holiday with her family.

Hannah's Villains.   Even though her father lived across the country, he was her main villain during the holidays. Almost every year, Hannah referred to the story of her father's cruelty toward her one Christmas:

> My mom and dad were divorced that year and Dad came up with Angela [her sister] for Christmas ... so he walks into the house with these gifts that are, I mean, humongous and they didn't have any tags on them.... I'm like, "Who are these for?" Well, they are *not* for me. My sister got ... a new robe ... new jogging shoes ... a set of cookware.... I got an Andy Gibb album and a picture of my father and if I wasn't going to put it up, he took the frame back. So I got this 8 x 10 picture of my dad. When you're 13, that doesn't do it.... I went into my bedroom.... I just cried and cried and cried. (INT92)

Over the years, her father was very inconsistent in his gift giving. One year, he would get Hannah "a sweatshirt, and we'd all have the same sweatshirt" (INT92); another time he mailed her a big book on Hollywood that was just Hannah's taste. And although Hannah thought in 1992 her father was "getting a little better ... becoming nicer," in 1993 he dealt another disastrous blow to her harmonious Christmas fantasy. That year, Hannah and her sister's family decided to visit her father and uncle in Florida. The trouble started when Hannah made her uncle "a nice calendar ... from Kinko's.... I had a picture of him and Dad when they were younger, and then for each month I had the person in the family [whose birthday] it went with ... and my Dad liked it better [than the lamp she gave him]" (INT94). Hannah also had to convince him to get a tree for his grandchildren. And on Christmas Day, "my Dad went out to work in the garage, and I was supposed to sit all alone ... and I called my Mom ... just sobbing ... and she said, 'If I could get you on a plane I would have you home in a minute.'" That year, Hannah's gift from her father was a T-shirt that was a "man's XL ... that's the way he perceives me. And always has.... I got this thing that was down to my knees" (INT94). Even 4 years after this disaster, Hannah recalled how church on "Christmas Sunday was important ... and he ... Dad turned to me and said, 'I'm not taking you, so if you want to go you've got to find another way to get there'" (INT97). Given Hannah's strong faith, this was a severe blow.

Because Hannah saw her father so infrequently, she did not punish his thoughtlessness directly. Instead, she used her wiles to try and secure the kinds of gifts she wanted from him: "If it's something ... he feels he's an expert on then you can get it. And I wanted a knife set, and he thinks he's an expert, so I said, 'Daddy, I'd really like a kitchen knife'—it's his ego ... get you the best. So I got a real nice set of knives" (INT94). She also punished him by buying items in 1994 for that year and the next: "If he dies [before 1995], I can just give the other gift to his brother.... Isn't that terrible?" (FN94).

By 1997, Hannah realized their problems were deeply rooted in the differences they had over religion: "It boils down to the fact that her faith is important to her and he's an atheist" (FN97). Thus, Hannah felt they could never have a truly close relationship.

For a while, Hannah had another villain in the form of her brother-in-law. She was vague about the cause of the tension, but things were especially strained in 1992. Hannah said that before he entered the military, "she used to get him great presents like Billy Joel albums and rock posters. But not now" (FN92). Instead, that year she bought him a portable tension relief massager: "It was real cheap, plus ... I had a coupon for ten percent off.... I thought, 'Hmmm, I wonder if this would be a good enough gift.... So I got it for five bucks.... To tell you the truth, I don't care if he really likes it" (INT92).

Interestingly, this villain redeemed himself in Hannah's eyes by being one of the few people who tried to make her disastrous "Florida family Christmas" in 1993 bearable. In 1994, Hannah's gratitude was evident when she described how she got him "the funniest thing ... big animal slippers ... coyotes ... that when you squeeze their ears, they howl."

Hannah's Helpers and Donors.   The most constant helper in Hannah's quest for a peaceful Christmas was her mother. Through the years, she helped Hannah cope with the father's disappointing behavior, and she was the one person with whom Hannah felt comfortable celebrating the holidays. A later helper was Hannah's brother-in-law, who, as previously noted, had earlier been cast as a villain. Finally, one year, Hannah had a special donor that she truly believed was magic. In 1997, Hannah discovered that a minor TV star in the 1960s, "Dirk Grayson" (not his real name), had written a Christmas book and was signing it at a local store. She decided to get the book for her sister. She recounted this magical encounter as follows:

> Later that night I called Angela.... I said, "Are you ready for this?" ..."I was hugged by Dirk Grayson ..." She said, "This is pretty good, Hannah, we've known him 20 years and watched him on TV."... I said "This is what you're getting ... an autographed copy of his book.... It ruins your surprise, but this is part of the present, the excitement I have of telling you about it tonight." And she was ... just so excited.... I said "You would have missed out a lot if you hadn't heard me screaming and giddy tonight ..." She said "I'm glad that you shared it

with me. It means so much more to me when I open it up to know that
you actually talked with him and he wrote this for me." (INT97)

Not So Happy Endings.   Although Hannah loved her mother deeply and
seemed content overall, at times she seemed lonely. In 1994, she bought a
sleeveless black cocktail dress: "'I'll probably never have occasion to wear it
… but I still wanted it.' She said every once in a while she'll try it on and look at
herself in the mirror" (FN94). Hannah's best friend is married with children,
and her sister lives in Colorado with her family, so Hannah is not their top priority. Clearly, the most important person in Hannah's life is her mother, with
whom she enjoys a mutually supportive and loving relationship. Given that
Hannah never mentioned a romantic relationship in 7 years, it seems likely that
she will continue to live with her mother. Hannah's life is made meaningful
through her Christian faith and her strong bonds with her sister, mother, and
friend. And in terms of fulfilling her quest for a harmonious family Christmas,
experience has taught Hannah simpler is better. She prefers a quiet holiday with
her mother over an unpredictable roller coaster ride with her father.

Hannah's Moral.   Of all the CFTs, Hannah's contains the most obvious un-
dercurrents of tragedy. Abandoned by her father at an early age, for many years
Hannah seemed hopeful that their relationship would improve, and her father's
gifts to her would reveal that he finally understood her interests and desires, including how important the religious aspect of the holiday was to her
(Hirschman & La Barbera, 1989). By 1997, Hannah had realized that because
of these differences in religious faith, there would always be a chasm between
them.

   With limited resources, Hannah does her best when creating Christmas—
seeking out avenues for singularity through such sources as TV celebrities from
the 1960s who could "contaminate" gifts with sacredness (Belk, Wallendorf, &
Sherry, 1989). Perhaps Hannah's faith and close relationships are enough to fulfill
her. Yet Hannah also tells of the cocktail dress she bought but knew she would
never wear. The fairy tale image that seems to most resemble Hannah is that of a
lonely Rapunzel in her tower, waiting for a life filled with more harmonious family
relationships, and perhaps even more excitement and adventure.

Laura

In her happy home nestled among the pines, a woman named Laura sat in front of
the fire, tying ribbons on Barbies for the Salvation Army Christmas tree. Laura did
so every year, as her quest was to create a Christmas filled with the fellowship of
family and friends, the joy of helping others, and a generous outpouring of gifts for
her loved ones. This last goal was so important, it even penetrated her subcon-
scious: Every year, Laura would dream, "it was Christmas Eve, and I'm just stand-

ing in front of the store, and it's closed, and I don't have any presents" (INT92). In earlier years, Laura had tried to "do" Christmas economically. But as her husband's job became more secure and her daughter became more involved in school activities, Laura said, "her time was worth more" than shopping around for the absolute best buy (INT97).

Laura's Villains.   Laura's mother died when Laura was in her twenties. Since then, her father has had several girlfriends. Laura loved her dad and tried to make sure he was provided for, but he was also her most consistent villain. He often frustrated Laura's attempt to create a family-filled Christmas. Over the years, Laura's complaints about her father were remarkably consistent: He would rather spend his time (and money) with the current woman in his life than with his grandchildren. Laura seemed especially disappointed, considering she had helped him get out of debt (after he bought a girlfriend $12,000 worth of gifts), sold her house to him, and made sure that "since Mom's gone ... [he] has plenty to open [on Christmas] too, so he doesn't feel left out" (INT90). In short, Laura felt her father did not reciprocate her generosity during the holidays. When asked about her father's fiancée in 1994, Laura said they liked her, "but don't get a chance to know her.... He just isn't much into doing family things ... you know, he has her and does stuff with her" (INT94). In 1997, Laura reported her father had a new "lady friend" who probably wanted to see her grandchildren on Christmas, and as far as her dad coming to her house that day, "if he does he does, and if he doesn't he doesn't" (INT97).

Laura's father also interfered with her quest to find cherished gifts for her daughter, Kara. In 1988, Laura bought Kara the first Happy Holidays Barbie issued, and wanted to continue the tradition. This gift was meaningful to Laura, because Kara was "like her father—real practical," rarely asking for specific gifts. In 1990 and 1992, Laura proudly reported she had found the Happy Holidays Barbie for Kara. But in 1994, Laura had a different tale to tell:

> *I:* How about the collector Barbie (for Kara?)
>
> *L:* Well, *Dad* got that (displeased)...I won't be able to set that out from Santa.
>
> *I:* Are you disappointed about that?
>
> *L:* We-ll, I just kinda always did that, but I don't think she thinks about it (laughs). (INT94)

Laura's means of punishing her father were subtle; she just expressed displeasure at his deeds, but did not seek revenge on him by acting vindictively.

Not All in the Family (or the Tale of the Ex-Neighbors). For many years, Laura and her family lived in a modest neighborhood. In addition to having many friends in the area, Laura babysat some of the neighborhood children after school. In 1992, Laura noted: "The neighbors are always over, and we always do things together, and we've talked about caroling and ... a progressive type dinner. And so we're trying to spend more time with the meaning of Christmas, you know, being together and sharing time together. *But it's more ... with friends and neighbors than with family*" (INT92, emphasis added). In 1994, her in-laws decided their house was too big, so they sold it to Laura and her husband. Although happy with the move, Laura said it was "hard to change from the neighbors.... I think that's why I haven't been in the Christmas spirit and stuff" (INT94).

Unfortunately for Laura, the move to her new home revealed a villainous side to her old neighbors. They no longer made an effort to include Laura, and even shunned activities she had planned. Whatever their reasons, Laura felt betrayed by her neighbors' apathy, and it clearly affected her ability to create her perfect Christmas:

> I was pretty bummed out because I ... asked the others to come out, and they were going to come out with the kids ... [but] when I talk to the Moms later on they were like: "Oh, we have so much to do, and we have to work full-time ..." And then finally I decided that it was better just to, rather than meet them here at home and worry about it, just bow out and say, "You know, that's fine, you guys do what you have to do." (INT94)

Later during that same interview, Laura observed: "It'll never be the same because I don't live down the street and watch their kids.... I'm not convenient.... It's like they would call me up and say, 'Can you go down and shut the windows in the house ... and can you do this ...?' So now ... I'm starting to see it." While Laura was hurt by her ex-neighbors' behavior, she chose to move on with her life rather than using her energy to settle scores (and in 1994, for the first time in years, she did NOT have her annual dream of not having presents on Christmas Eve).

Laura's Helpers? Although Laura did rely on coupons, flyers, and salespeople (to find scarce products and reward her store loyalty) in the early years, she found less of a personal need for these later on. However, she could not resist helping out strangers herself (McGrath & Otnes, 1995). She would show up at stores with a bag of coupons and flyers, ready to help others save money, "I got a bag in the car that has them in it.... I think about that and laugh ... because I think people think I'm the bag lady" (INT94). This tendency became an obstacle for her when her efforts failed, as helping others was an important aspect of the holiday for her.

Happy Ever After, at Last.   Over the years, many of Laura's dreams had come true. Her daughter was happy and healthy, her husband had a successful job, her marriage was stable, and her money worries were minimal. And although Laura had paid a price for her good fortune (i.e., losing the friendship of her old neighbors), she was philosophical about it: "You can't stop your life and stay in a neighborhood because all your neighbors are your friends and that's what you want. You have to go on" (INT94). By 1997, she had even realized the hustle and bustle of Christmas that she'd created for her daughter wasn't necessary: "I used to think, 'Well, gosh, Kara is an only child so you know it's like you needed more people to make it more important,' but it doesn't have to be that way.... I was trying to make it big for her, but she's like her Dad.... She's perfectly content being at home, and having her things and having quiet" (INT97). Laura even came to accept her father's behavior: "[She] had gotten used to the fact that when her Dad has a girlfriend, he would not be around much" (INT97). Laura also seemed to have forgiven her father for the fact that he was still buying Kara the Happy Holidays Barbie—a tradition she had started and cherished. So as Laura decorated her new home, she was at peace.

Laura's Moral.   Laura no longer celebrates the communal Christmas that had been the norm in her old neighborhood. In those days, Laura had been one of the main orchestrators of social activities, taking charge of everything from caroling nights to progressive dinners. But Laura's move isolated her from her old friends and neighbors, leaving her feeling lonely and a little used. As a result of her move away from a more communal celebration, Laura has changed her vision of what Christmas should be, and now focuses on her husband and daughter. As she has simplified her life, her anxieties that had manifested themselves in the form of a nightmare where she forgot to go Christmas shopping have dissipated. Laura, like Sleeping Beauty, has awakened from her slumber to realize who is really central to her celebration.

CROSS-CASE ANALYSIS
AND INTERPRETATION

Because our heroines have unique personalities and life circumstances, each tale naturally contains idiosyncratic elements. However, the narratives also greatly resemble each other, particularly with respect to *dramatis personae*, which are compared in Table 6.2. We compare both across the CFTs presented in this chapter, and with elements of LFTs. We also interpret our CFTs in light of how Christmas is constructed in contemporary American culture.

TABLE 6.2
Key *Dramatis Personae* of Informants' CFTS

Heroine	Major Villian	Minor Villains	Helpers	Donors/Providers
Anne	ex-Fiancé	Father (recast as donor) Sister Grandmother	new Fiancé	Father (later in CFT)
Betsy	Death	Sister	None	None
Hannah	Father	Brother-in-Law (recast as helper)	Mother Brother-in-Law (later in CFT)	Celebrity
Laura	Father	ex-Neighbors	None	Salespeople

Stereotypical Nature of Villains

Central to all the narratives is the struggle between what Hirschman (1999) termed "binary archetypal oppositions" or, in this case, between villains and heroines. Obviously, these CFTs take place in the real world—a contemporary urbanized setting in a capitalist country. So it is significant that the villains in these tales are strikingly similar to those found in LFTs, which originated in feudally based cultures (Eliade, 1963). Of course, the acts of villainy are somewhat different. Few of our heroines' villains kidnapped, robbed (with the exception of Anne's ex-fiancé), or hijacked to cause Christmas imperfections. Rather, acts of betrayal and other forms of emotional damage are the common abuses in CFTs. Moreover, the types of villains who emerge across the CFTs are remarkably consistent: namely, fathers, other family and friends, and death.

Evil Fathers.   All of the heroines' fathers interfered with the ability to create Christmas. Anne's father was such a "bad boy" one year she would not even explain what he had done, but crossed him off her Christmas list. Caplow (1984) explained removing relatives upon whom one relies for emotional support from the gift network can lead to "consequences ... too serious to contemplate, and few are willing to run the risk" (p. 1321).

Hannah's relationship with her father is clearly tragic (Stern, 1995). Year after year, she articulated all too well her father's cruelty. First, he consistently disregarded the Christmas "gift selection rule" (Caplow, 1984), which suggests gifts should be geared toward the recipient's preferences, and should surprise the giver "either by expressing more affection ... than the recipient might anticipate or more knowledge than the giver might reasonably be expected to have" (p. 1313). Moreover, when Hannah was an emotionally vulnerable teenager, he violated the unwritten rule of "equipollence," which says that one's children should be gifted equally (Lowrey, Otnes, & Robbins 1996). Even worse, his gifts often reinforce the wide gulf between how Hannah views herself and how her father sees her (e.g., as a "man's XL"). And although the misdeeds of both Laura's and Betsy's fathers are not as obvious, in both cases their replacement of their deceased wives resulted in disharmony and disruption of the family unit.

Why do fathers consistently emerge as villains across these CFTs? Consider the cultural milieu in which these stories are created. As Christmas evolved in the United States, its meaning changed from one that centered around the drunken and bawdy behavior of men to one that valorized home and hearth (Nissenbaum, 1997). At the same time, men have become more and more removed from the ritual (Fischer & Arnold, 1990). It has become a cultural truism that "kin work ... is like housework and child care; men in the aggregate do not do it" (Di Leonardo, 1987, p. 443). Still, fathers' lack of effort during the holidays may be met with resentment, because they are "only" expected to spend time with the family—not engage in holiday planning *per se*—yet few of the fathers in our tales seem able to do so to these informants' satisfaction.

Di Leonardo (1987) also observed that for women, ritual is a "realm in which one may attempt to gain human satisfactions—and power—not available in the labor market" (p. 445). Yet when daughters attempt to construct Christmas, they not only have to fill their mothers' shoes, but to direct, and have expectations of, fathers who may have been the authoritarian figure within the family. Given such role inversions, it seems almost inevitable tensions will result.

Other Wicked Family Members and Friends.   While fathers are clearly the most consistent villains, they are not the only kin who cause trouble. Both Anne's and Betsy's sisters thwart their quests for a harmonious family Christmas. Other villainous relatives include Anne's "old and mean" grandmother and Hannah's brother-in-law. Yet villains need not always be family members, as Laura's ex-neighbors and Anne's duplicitous (first) fiancée, demonstrate.

The labeling of these characters as villains can be explained by their violations of ritual (Rook, 1985) and familial norms. Anne's grandmother is villainous because she expected Anne to pay back a loan, but did not require Anne's brother to do so, violating the norm of equipollence (Lowrey et al., 1996). Hannah's brother-in-law underwent a change in the Air Force that made him less interested in the kinds of fun gifts that Hannah had always given him and he therefore violated previously negotiated gift norms. Betsy's conflict with her sister was based on her unwillingness to participate in family ritual occasions in the presence of her father's new wife. This same opting out of traditional ritual activities was what lead Laura to see her ex-neighbors as villains.

Our heroines' strategies for punishing these villains are consistent. One of the most prevalent is the withholding of time, effort, and thought during the purchase of gifts. This enables givers to express their psychological reactance about being "forced" to give a gift in the context of this holiday (Brehm, 1966). Moreover, they seem relatively unconcerned that recipients may be aware of this lack of effort, and that the relationship may decline as a result (Ruth, Otnes, & Brunel, 1999). For example, Laura canceled an event she had been planning for her ex-neighbors and eventually removed them from her list entirely. In other cases, givers demote the social role expressed through a gift. Betsy moved from being a Pleaser (Otnes et al., 1993) for her sister (buying unique items) to an Acknowledger (buying a "ho-hum" sweatshirt). Likewise, Anne moved from trying to be a Pleaser (buying a beautiful book on airplanes) to an Avoider for her father (not giving him anything).

Yet in contrast to villains in LFTs, in CFTs villains may actually redeem themselves over the course of time. In cases where this has happened, a giver who has expressed a less recipient-centered social role indicates forgiveness by reverting to one of these roles. Consider Hannah and her brother-in-law. In 1992, she bought him a gift that "she didn't really care if he liked...." But after he helped her during the unhappy Christmas visit with her father, Hannah gave him coyote slippers in 1994 that she thought were "cute," and hoped he would find hilarious.

Death—The Permanent Villain.   Whereas the other villains could potentially redeem themselves, the permanent nature of this particular villain, and its impact on this family-oriented holiday, makes it one of the most difficult to combat. Yet, interestingly, Betsy and Laura both fight Death with Life, keeping alive the traditions created by or shared with lost loved ones. Gillis (1996) observed how these traditions can literally make time stand still at Christmas: "The ritualized nature of the day, with its emphasis on doing things just as they had always been done, gives it the unique feeling of being time out of time, the opposite of linear time in that it is 'recoverable time'—what Mircea Eliade would call a 'succession of eternities'" (p. 102). In a very real sense, these traditions function like heirlooms, tangibilizing lost love ones (Arnould, Price, & Curasi, 1999).

THE END ...

In summary, the complexity of Christmas means that gender roles, social obligations, and marketplace variables all influence the fairy tales that emerged from our heroines over 7 years' time. No doubt it is the importance of this holiday as a celebration of the stability and harmony implied by idealized families, and portrayed through multiple cultural venues, that motivates our heroines to fight so valiantly in the creation of their desired Christmases. Our heroines display vast amounts of craftiness and even courage as they battle their various villains and obstacles in their creation of Christmas.

Our chapter heeds Levy's (1996) call to be receptive to "fresh areas of inquiry, novel theoretical foundations and variations in methodology" (p. 164). By so doing, we contribute to the understanding of consumer experience in the following ways. First, our research demonstrates the value of a longitudinal approach. Specifically, this study enhances the explanatory power of Otnes et al.'s (1993) study of social roles by demonstrating the potential fluidity of the roles expressed to recipients over time. Moreover, the fairy tale metaphor, and the *dramatis personae* that it implies, provides the theoretical underpinning that explains why these social roles are fluid (e.g., a recipient is perceived as a helper one year, as a villain the next).

This chapter also demonstrates that within a ritualistic consumption context, individuals' lives often mirror ancient narrative forms, and contain archetypal characters that have existed in the human psyche for thousands of years (Hirschman, 1999). Indeed, the villains, kind strangers, and valiant heroines seeking to fulfill sometimes seemingly impossible quests are as real in these Christmas tales as they are in *Snow White* and *Sleeping Beauty*. This work extends the existing research that examines the narrative nature of consumer text, employing Propp's typology of *dramatis personae* that had previously not been utilized. Although a perfect one-to-one correspondence cannot be expected between consumer text and the frameworks of literary theory, the discussion demonstrates that nevertheless applying such frameworks is enlightening.

Certainly, limitations exist in this study. Informants were self-selected participants, who clearly enjoy Christmas. Thus, there was no interaction with those who do not enjoy the holidays. Further, no claim is made that everyone's Christmas rituals will resemble fairy tales. Only those who pursue the quest for the "perfect" Christmas will likely emulate these tales, because their concern will cause them to devote time and energy to the adversities encountered along the way. Second, as White females living in a small urban area, who are relatively the same age and class, our informants are quite similar demographically. However, they differ psychographically. Moreover, the themes we have uncovered do not seem related to race, religion, or social class. Admittedly, our inability to interact with more than a few informants in such an in-depth manner has its drawbacks. However, we believe our longitudinal approach compensates for the size of our sample.

As findings inevitably do, ours lead to additional questions that would be fruitful to address. Christmas is a fairly high-involvement, ritualized consumption context. Would CFTs emerge in lower involvement consumption situations? Would CFTs be evident in other high involvement consumption contexts that are not as ritualistic in nature (e.g., buying a car)? Are there inherent gender differences in CFTs, and how might CFTs change if men were the heroes?

In the end, the similarity of characters in LFTs and CFTs was so overwhelming, we were compelled to make this comparison. Like fairy tales of old, our heroines demonstrate courage, cleverness, and—especially interesting in a longitudinal study—a high degree of consistency when pursuing their quests. And like LFTs, their tales illustrate that Christmas is hard work, often involving the kind of agapic sacrifices in the marketplace recently discussed by Belk (1996) and Miller (1998).

Whether penned by the Brothers Grimm or still unfolding in the lives of consumers, triumph over hardships is the stuff of fairy tales. The heroic figures in both types of stories would agree that their ultimate victories are worth the struggles and sacrifices. For if Anne, Betsy, Hannah, and Laura teach us anything, it is that a Christmas laden with material and emotional abundance is the reward for those who possess hope, perseverance, and creativity.

REFERENCES

Andersen, H. C., & Perrault, C. (n.d.). *The fairy tales of Hans Christian Andersen and Charles Perrault.* New York: Illustrated Editions Company.

Arnould, E. , Price, L., & Curasi, C. (1999, October). *The afterlife of things: consumer legacies in narrative perspective.* Paper presented at the conference of the Association for Consumer Research, Columbus, OH.

Belk, R. (1989). Materialism and the modern U.S. Christmas. In E. Hirschman (Ed.), *Interpretive consumer research* (pp. 115–135). Provo, UT: Association for Consumer Research.

Belk, R. (1993). Materialism and the making of the modern American Christmas. In D. Miller (Ed.), *Unwrapping Christmas* (pp. 75–104). Oxford: Clarendon.

Belk, R. (1996). The perfect gift. In C. Otnes & R. Beltramini (Eds.), *Gift giving: A research anthology* (pp. 59–84). Bowling Green, OH: Popular Press.

Belk, R., Wallendorf, M., & Sherry, J. (1989). The sacred and profane in consumer behavior: Theodicy on the Odyssey. *Journal of Consumer Research, 16*(June), 1–38.

Berger, A. (1997). *Narratives in popular culture, media, and everyday life.* Thousand Oaks, CA: Sage.

Bettelheim, B. (1976). *The uses of enchantment: The meaning and importance of fairy tales.* New York: Knopf.

Birkhauser-Oeri, S. (1988). *The mother: Archetypal image in fairy tales.* Toronto: Inner City Books.

Brehm, J. (1966). *A theory of psychological reactance.* New York: Academic Press.

Brewer, W., & Lichtenstein, E. (1982). Stories are to entertain: A structural-affect theory of stories. *Journal of Pragmatics, 6,* 473–486.

Brown, S. (1998). *Postmodern marketing II: Telling tales.* London: International Thomson Business Press.

Caplow, T. (1984). Rule enforcement without visible means: Christmas gift giving in Middletown. *American Journal of Sociology, 89*(May), 1306–1323.

Cheal, D. (1987). Showing them you love them: Gift-giving and the dialectic of intimacy. *Sociological Review, 35*(1), 150–169.

Cheal, D. (1988). *The gift economy.* London: Routledge & Kegan Paul.

Danilewitz, D. (1991). Once upon a time … the meaning and importance of fairy tales. *Early Child Development and Care, 75,* 87–98.

Di Leonardo, M. (1987). The female world of cards and holidays: Women, families and the work of kinship. *Signs: Journal of Women and Culture in Society, 12*(3), 440–453.

Durgee, J. (1988). Interpreting consumer mythology: A literary criticism approach to Odyssey informant stories. In M. Houston (Ed.), *Advances in consumer research* (Vol. 15, pp. 531–536). Provo, UT: Association for Consumer Research.

Eliade, M. (1963). *Myth and reality.* New York: Harper & Row.

Firat, A. F., & Dholakia, N. (1998). *Consuming people.* London: Routledge & Kegan Paul.

Firat, A. F., & Venkatesh, A. (1995). Liberatory postmodernism and the reenchantment of consumption. *Journal of Consumer Research, 22*(December), 239–267.

Fischer, E., & Arnold, S. (1990). More than a labor of love: Gender roles and Christmas gift shopping. *Journal of Consumer Research, 17*(December), 333–345.

Gillis, J. (1996). *A world of their own making: Myth, ritual and the quest for family values.* New York: Basic Books.

Greimas, A.-J. (1966). *Semantique structurale: Recherche de methode.* trans: [Structural Semanties: Research of Method] Paris: Larousse.

Heilbrunn, B. (1998). My brand the hero? A semiotic analysis of the consumer brand relationship. In M. Lambkin et al. (Eds.), *European perspectives in consumer behavior* (pp. 370–401). London: Prentice-Hall.

Heilbrunn, B. (1999, June). *When Snow White dates Mr. Clean!! A narrative approach to advertising discourse.* Paper presented at the Association for Consumer Research European Conference, Jouy-en-Josas, France.

Hirschman, E. (1999). *Consumers' use of intertextuality and archetypes.* Paper presented at the Association for Consumer Research Conference, Columbus, OH.

Hirschman, E., & Holbrook, M. (1992). *Postmodern consumer research: The study of consumption as text.* Newbury Park, CA: Sage.

Hirschman, T., & La Barbera, P. (1989). The meaning of Christmas. In E. Hirschman (Ed.), *Interpretive consumer research,* (pp. 136–147). Provo, UT: Association for Consumer Research.

Laird, J. (1996). Women and ritual in family therapy. In R. Grimes (Ed.), *Readings in ritual studies* (pp. 353–367). Upper Saddle River, NJ: Prentice-Hall.

Levy, S. (1981). Interpreting consumer mythology: A structural approach to consumer behavior. *Journal of Marketing, 45*(Summer), 49–61.

Levy, S. (1985). Dreams, fairy tales, animals, and cars. *Psychology and Marketing, 2*(Summer), 67–81.

Levy, S. (1996). Stalking the Amphisbaena. *Journal of Consumer Research, 23*(December), 163–176.

Lincoln, Y., & Guba, E. (1985). *Naturalistic inquiry.* Newbury Park, CA: Sage.

Lowrey, T. M., Otnes, C., & Robbins, K. (1996). Values influencing Christmas gift selection: An interpretive study. In C. Otnes & R. Beltramini (Eds.), *Gift giving: A research anthology* (pp. 37–56). Bowling Green, OH: Popular Press.

McGrath, M. (2000). Giving until it hurts: Two case studies of compulsive gift giving behavior. In A. Bensen (Ed.), *I shop, therefore I am: Compulsive spending and the search for self* (pp. 169–188). New York: Aronson.

McGrath, M., & Otnes, C. (1995). Unacquainted influencers: When strangers interact in the retail setting. *Journal of Business Research, 32*(March), 261–272.

Miller, D. (1998). *A theory of shopping.* London: Routledge & Kegan Paul.

Nissenbaum, S. (1997). *The battle for Christmas.* New York: Knopf.

Otnes, C., Lowrey, T. M., & Kim, Y. (1993). Gift selection for easy and difficult recipients: A social roles interpretation. *Journal of Consumer Research, 20*(September), 229–244.

Otnes, C., Zolner, K., & Lowrey, T. M. (1994). In-laws and outlaws: The impact of divorce and remarriage upon Christmas gift exchange. In C. Allen & D. John (Eds.), *Advances in consumer research* (Vol. 21, pp. 25–29). Provo, UT: Association for Consumer Research.

Propp, V. (1970). *Morphology of the folktale.* Trans. Laurence Scott, Austin, TX: University of Texas Press. (Original work published 1928)

Richardson, L. (1990). Narrative and sociology. *Journal of Contemporary Ethnography, 19,* 116–135.

Richardson, L. (1994). Writing: A method of inquiry. In N. Denzin & Y. Lincoln (Eds.), *Handbook of Qualitative Research* (pp. 516–529). Thousand Oaks, CA: Sage.

Rook, D. (1985). The ritual dimension of consumer behavior. *Journal of Consumer Research, 12*(December), 251–264.

Ruth, J., Otnes, C., & Brunel, F. (1999). Gift receipt and the reformulation of interpersonal Relationships. *Journal of Consumer Research, 25*(March), 385–402.

Sherry, J., Jr., McGrath, M., & Levy, S. (1992). The disposition of the gift and many unhappy returns. *Journal of Retailing, 68*(Spring), 40–65.

Sherry, J., Jr., McGrath, M., & Levy, S. (1993). The dark side of the gift. *Journal of Business Research, 28*(3), 225–244.

Stake, R. (1995). *The art of case study research.* Thousand Oaks, CA: Sage.

Stern, B. (1995). Consumer myths: Frye's taxonomy and the structural analysis of consumption as text. *Journal of Consumer Research, 22*(September), 165–185.

Tatar, M. (1987). *The hard facts of the Grimms' Fairy Tales.* Princeton, NJ: Princeton University Press.

Tatar, M. (1992). *Off with their heads!* Princeton, NJ: Princeton University Press.

Thompson, C. (1996). Caring consumers: Gendered consumption meanings and the juggling lifestyle. *Journal of Consumer Research, 22*(March), 388–407.

Turner, V. (1969). *The ritual process: Structure and anti-structure.* Chicago: Aldine.

Utley, F. (1976). Introduction. In M. Luthi (L. Chadeayne & P. Gottwald, Trans.) *Once upon a time: On the nature of fairy tales* (pp. 1–20). Bloomington, IN: Indiana University Press.

von Franz, M. (1982). *An introduction to the interpretation of fairy tales.* Dallas, TX: Spring Publications.

Wallendorf, M., & Arnould, E. (1991). We gather together: Consumption rituals of Thanksgiving day. *Journal of Consumer Research, 18*(June), 13–31.

Widdershoven, G. (1993). The story of life: Hermeneutic perspectives on the relationship between narrative and life history. In R. Josselson & A. Lieblich (Eds.), *The narrative study of lives* (Vol. 1, pp. 1–20). Newbury Park, CA: Sage.

Zipes, J. (1988). *The Brothers Grimm.* New York: Routledge & Kegan Paul.

Zipes, J. (1994). *Fairy tale as myth: Myth as fairy tale.* Lexington, KY: University Press of Kentucky.

Part III

Wedding Rituals Across Cultures

7

Love Without Borders: An Examination of Cross-Cultural Wedding Rituals

Michelle R. Nelson and Sameer Deshpande
University of Wisconsin–Madison

Marriage occurs in the majority of world cultures (Rosenblatt & Anderson, 1981), and the wedding itself is considered a special ritual event. It is a rite of passage that culturally marks a person's transition from one life stage to another and redefines social and personal identity (Bell, 1997). This vital ritualistic event, long dictated by cultural values and processes, offers an opportunity for couples to declare their new identity publicly and to bring together families and friends through a prescribed collection of artifacts, roles, and scripts (Rook, 1985). Such ritual elements were historically dictated by local communities (K. Bulcroft, R. Bulcroft, Smeins, & Cranage, 1997): So what happens to the ritual when the community becomes a *global* village? Whose cultural values and customs are used? How are divergent personal and cultural values of the couple and their extended families negotiated when planning the cross-cultural wedding?

Past research has shown that the selection and negotiation of cultural values and ritual decisions can create conflicts (Nelson & Otnes, forthcoming) and lead to "heated arguments ... over finding religious services that won't offend either culture, planning receptions that honor both sides equally and accommodating an array of guests" (Nguyen, 1996, p. B01). These conflicts, often caused by clashes between cultural values and customs or norms, may reflect a special type of mixed emotions or ambivalence called cultural ambivalence (Merton & Barber, 1976). We define *cross-cultural ambivalence* as the emergence of a mixed emotional state, or multiple emotional states, that arise from conflict between norms, traditions, and practices of different cultures not found within the same society. This research was conducted to examine cross-cultural wedding rituals; the chapter focuses on emergent findings related to cross-cultural ambivalence as we identify antecedents and strategies for coping with these conflicts.

GLOBALIZATION AND THE WEDDING RITUAL

Globalization has challenged the notion that wedding rituals are unchanging traditions where people see themselves as transmitting or responding to local customs
(Bell, 1997). Indeed, the influence of the mass media in promoting and packaging
the Western "white wedding" has obliterated many traditional ethnic customs
(Otnes & Pleck, 2003). Ironically, the white wedding, aptly named for the appropriate color of the bride's dress, shoes, and veil, as well as the frosting on the cake
(Pleck, 2000), was largely invented in the early 19th century after the much-publi-
cized cross-cultural wedding of England's Queen Victoria to her German cousin Al-
bert. The Westernized ritual of today has evolved from this event, adding traditions
and customs along the way such as the engagement, the bouquet toss, and the honeymoon. Through newspapers, magazines, films, and more recently Web sites, the
white wedding has spread throughout the world. White dresses are featured on such
global wedding Web sites as www.latinabride.com and www.asianbrideonline.com.
In the last century, the white wedding has been "heralded as the proper way to marry
… filtering down from the well-to-do to the working poor, from Yankees to immigrants and people of color, and from British and Americans to couples in virtually
every part of the globe" (Pleck, 2000, p. 208). This trend suggests a homogenization
of the wedding ritual and a growing influence of media over local customs.

Globalization has also resulted in a growing number of mixed marriages
worldwide. In the last 50 years, sweeping demographic shifts, greater mobility,
and increased educational opportunities have caused profound lifestyle changes
worldwide (Stanton, 1995). These changes include exposure to alternative cultures, values, and people, which has resulted in a larger marriage market that is not
always defined by geographic boundaries or social norms (Breger & Hill, 1998,
pp. 13–14; Bulcroft et al., 1997). Religion and ethnicity have become less important in delineating the pool of eligible partners as the custom of endogamy (requiring individuals to marry within their own racial, religious, and social groups) has
declined among some, but not all, ethnic groups. Indeed, spreading Westernization
and increased individualism have contributed to racial, religious, and ethnic tolerance, which also results in diversity in marital relationships (Triandis, 1995) and
the spread of "romantic love" cross-culturally (Pleck, 2000).

EXAMINING WEDDING RITUAL
EXPERIENCES

Rituals have received a great deal of attention in consumer behavior (e.g., Belk,
1989; Rook, 1985), including a growing body of literature on weddings (e.g.,
Dobscha & Foxman, 1998; Kates, 1998; Lowrey & Otnes, 1994; Nelson & Otnes,
forthcoming; Otnes, 1998; Otnes & Lowrey, 1993). Past U.S. research has offered

important insight into emotions associated with wedding planning (Otnes, Lowrey, & Shrum, 1997) and has illuminated differences in the priorities of brides and grooms (Lowrey & Otnes, 1994). Work on non-U.S. cultures has also examined weddings (e.g., Barker, 1978; Kendall, 1989). However, the special circumstances surrounding cross-cultural weddings have not yet been fully considered.

Because local customs have historically dictated wedding rituals, wedding party and ritual audience members learn the scripts, roles, and artifacts through exposure to mass media (Otnes & Pleck, 2003) or by attendance at family or friends' weddings. But when the couple hails from two different cultures or religions, the wedding ritual can offer uncertainty to all involved. Instead of relying on well-defined practices, couples must co-create, invent, or discard ritual experiences. Apart from online information (Nelson & Otnes, forthcoming) or hiring a cross-cultural wedding planner, very little guidance exists for couples planning cross-cultural weddings.

Ethnographic research conducted among cross-cultural brides on wedding message boards suggests that couples use negotiation and compromise processes to cope with potential conflicts related to issues of language, ceremony place, and invitations (Nelson & Otnes, forthcoming). Many comments made by brides-to-be reflected a cultural ambivalence or values conflict during the planning process (e.g., "One doesn't realise how different cultures can be until you start planning a wedding" Swedish bride-to-be, March 15, 2001). Indeed, in previous research, Otnes et al. (1997) showed some evidence for the existence of custom and value conflicts in same-culture or cross-cultural weddings. These conflicts were resolved through coping strategies related to resignation, modification, and defiant nonpurchase.

In our analysis, we explore how and when cross-cultural ambivalence occurs in wedding planning and focus on the antecedents and strategies employed by cross-cultural couples. In so doing, we respond to the call for future research by Otnes et al. (1997) to examine the issue of "how subcultural and cultural factors may conflict with internal values, and thus, lead to consumer ambivalence" (p. 93) in the context of wedding ritual creation.

METHOD

This research consisted of three stages that examined the experiences of 26 cross-cultural couples from 23 national cultures. More than 650 pages of text were generated and analyzed.

Stage 1: Lived Experience and Participant Observation

Personal experience (Ellis & Flaherty, 1992) related by one of the authors, who recently married a person from a different national culture, offers the inspiration for this research and an insider's view. Participant observation, performed according to principles prescribed by Spradley (1980), followed the courtship, planning, and attendance of the weddings of three additional cross-cultural couples. Conversations between the researcher and couples were numerous, informal, and often involved advice seeking. These couples were not interviewed due to the emotional closeness of their relationship to one of the authors.

Observations were also conducted virtually by participating in and observing conversations among cross-cultural brides in public computer-mediated environments on three wedding Web sites (www.ultimatewedding.com, www.theknot.com, www.weddingchannel.com) (see Nelson & Otnes, forthcoming). These conversations helped researchers to understand the issues involved in planning a cross-cultural wedding, which proved useful in creating the interview questions.

Stage 2: In-depth Face-to-Face Interviews of Brides and Grooms

Twelve engaged or married couples were interviewed in person over a 6-month period (October 2000 through March 2001). Participants were recruited from posters placed across the university campus and ads in a newspaper. Couples were also recruited through the snowball technique. The face-to-face interviews conducted by three interviewers (two coauthors plus a trained undergraduate) were semistructured and conducted according to the stages advanced by Lincoln and Guba (1985). This approach resulted in a fairly consistent format across interviews, while allowing researchers enough freedom to probe into matters unique to the participants. The questions focused on the planning process, activities, and emotions surrounding the engagement, wedding, and honeymoon. For the most part, two different researchers interviewed each member of the couple, with a male researcher interviewing the husband and a female researcher interviewing the wife to help eliminate possible gender bias. Although each partner was essentially discussing the same wedding event, recall and interpretation of the rituals sometimes differed. Most interviews were conducted separately at a coffee shop or at the informant's home and were tape-recorded and transcribed. One couple was interviewed together and only 60% of the interview was taped due to equipment malfunctions. A compensation of $20 was offered for interviews that lasted, on average, 90 minutes.

Description of Informants.   Couples hailed from two different nations, irrespective of religion, color, creed, beliefs, or worldviews. The sample was similar to other studies that have found cross-cultural couples to be highly educated middle-class professionals (Blau, 1977; Whyte, 1990). In addition, because informants were recruited from an academic community, many were connected to the university as students or professors. Only one woman and one man had been married previously. Most of the couples were in their late twenties and thirties, which suggests that they might also be more economically independent than is typical of younger couples. Names of the informants were changed to protect their identity. See Table 7.1 for complete informant profiles.

Stage 3: E-mail Surveys

Informants were recruited from wedding-related Web sites (www.ultimate-wedding.com, www.weddings.co.uk) and web rings such as "international couples" via e-mail. They were asked the same general questions as were asked in Stage 2; however, the online interviews lacked the probes and nonverbal information gained through face-to-face interviews. Interestingly, only women responded to e-mail queries; however, given that the bride is still the primary wedding planner (Lowrey & Otnes, 1994), their responses were deemed of primary interest.

Description of Informants.   The sample was similar to couples interviewed in Stage 2, except that fewer informants were in academia and none currently lived in the midwestern United States; indeed, only one couple lived in the United States. Profiles are also included in Table 7.1.

Analysis of Text

This research takes both a top-down, theory-driven approach in its examination of cross-cultural ambivalence and a bottom-up approach to seek out strategies devised by couples when facing these mixed emotions and values. We explored the relevance of antecedents and strategies identified in Otnes et al.'s (1997) discussion of consumer ambivalence (e.g., resignation, modification, nonpurchase) and we examined and reexamined our data to build our own categories by using the constant comparative method (Glaser & Strauss, 1967). With this method, the researchers independently read through the text several times, moving from the specific to the general, and devising categories, based on an examination of strategies or processes prevalent in cross-cultural weddings. Common themes were identified independently by the two authors and then final interpretations were discussed and negotiated (see Belk, Wallendorf, & Sherry, 1989; Otnes, Lowrey, & Kim, 1993). The resulting analysis yielded themes that helped identify antecedents and strategies related to cross-cultural weddings. Like Otnes et al. (1997), "critical incidents" from the text (Lincoln & Guba, 1985) are shown to illustrate where conflicts related to values/traditions occurred. Table 7.2 summarizes key themes found in the text and provides an outline of the following interpretation section.

TABLE 7.1
Description of Informant Couples

Names/National Culture	Age (Data Collection/ Wedding)	Education/Occupation
Ellen (Russia)	21/21	5 years university, Chef
Javed (Turkey)	32/32	Graduate school, PhD student
Gretchen (U.S.)	21/21	BA Undergraduate student
Wenxiang (Hmong-American)	23/23	BS, Undergraduate student
Cheng (China)	37/36	PhD, Professor
Robert (U.S.)	52/51	MS, Psychotherapist
Kiyomi (Japan)	36/24	2 years university, Homemaker
John (U.S.)	36/24	PhD, Professor
Kathy (U.S.).	33/27	MS, Naturalist/homemaker
Kumar (India)	35/28	MS, Student, Writer
Noriko (Japan)	52/33	BS, Teacher
Ben (U.S.)	50/31	PhD, Professor
Yuki (Japan)	37/36	PhD, Professor
Gerald (U.S.)	59/58	ABD, Lecturer
Elizabeth (U.S.)	33/23	BS, Manager, museum store
Javier (Cuba, Puerto Rico)	33/23	BS, Owner of travel agency
Tamara (U.S.)	25/24	MA, Case coordinator
Ruben (Puerto Rico)	26/25	PhD student
Alician (U.S.)	33/33	PhD, Professor
Ibrahim (Tanzania)	38/38	BS, Accountant
**Sandra (U.S.)	21/21	Some university, Part-time positions
**Markus (Germany)	21/21	Some university, Waiting for visa status
*Martha (U.S.)	33/33	PhD, Professor
*Jeremy (UK)	29/29	PhD, Software consultant
* Florence (France)	30/30	BS, Manager
* Michael (UK)	39/39	BS, Computer technician
*** Deborah (Canada)	30/30	BA, Educational assistant
Sven (Norway)	30/30	BS, Unknown
*** Christina (Canada/Wales)	22/22	MD, Medical student
Edward (U.S.)		Business owner
***Jenny (Canada)	26/25	BS, Social worker
Sang-Moon (S. Korea)	24/23	BS, Law student
*** Helen (UK)	24/23	Undergraduate degree
Camilo (Mexico)	24/23	Data analyst
*** Janelle (New Zealand)	31/24	MA, Researcher
Hiromi (Japan)	31/24	Completing MA, Student

(continued)

TABLE 7.1

(continued)

Names/National Culture	Age (Data Collection/ Wedding)	Education/Occupation
***Dorothy (U.S.)	31/32	Some university, Transportation worker
Helge (Germany)	32/32	Business owner
***Cheryl (Jamaica)	26/25	Some university, Student
Ahmed (Bangladesh)	——	Unknown
***Nancy (Philippines/Hawaii)	32/27	EdD, Professor
Justin (Canada)	42/37	MS, Engineer
***Kim (U.S.)	23/23	BA, Development officer
Aleksander (Poland)	41/41	MD, Photographer
***Andrea (Russia)	21/21	Veterinary doctor
Daniel (Wales)	——	Unknown
***Joan (U.S.)	20/20	Attending university
Francisco (Uruguay)		Attending university
*Jackie (Ireland)	34/34	MS, Information technology
Hans (German)	38/38	PhD, Professor
*Jessica (U.S.)	29/29	MS, Engineer
Bill (Ireland)	33/33	PhD, Lecturer

*indicates participant observation
**indicates engaged to be married
***indicates e-mail interview with bride

TABLE 7.2

Summary of Antecedents and Coping Strategies for Cross-Cultural
Ambivalence in Cross-Cultural Weddings

Antecedents	Coping Strategies
Otnes, Lowrey, & Shrum (1997):	
Resistance to custom	Resignation
Desire for self-expression	Modification
Inability to provide customary items	Defiant nonpurchase
Nelson & Deshpande:	
Realization of differences	Nonpurchase and modification
Rejection of "American/Western" materialism	Embrace simplicity and creativity
Worry about different ritual audiences	Organize one balanced hybrid ritual (accommodation, instruction, deceit)
	Plan separate ritual events
	Select neutral location

131

ANTECEDENTS AND COPING STRATEGIES PERTAINING TO CROSS-CULTURAL AMBIVALENCE AMONG CROSS-CULTURAL COUPLES

Realization of Differences

Several of the cross-cultural couples expressed a realization that they were different from same-culture couples. In this capacity, couples discussed difficulties related to discrimination or immigration but also expressed the hope and belief that they were breaking new ground and even building a "better, multicultural world." Emphasis here was on retaining and combining each individual's cultural heritage, often referred to as additive multiculturism (Triandis, 1995) or integration (Berry, 1980), where people add new skills and perspectives rather than subtract cultural elements. These views contrast sharply with the assimilation view of mixed marriages by Chicago School sociologists who proposed a melting pot model of immigration (Park, 1950; Gordon, 1964) where mixed marriages were viewed as a "convincing sign of social integration by immigrant groups to the United States" (Breger & Hill, 1998, p. 16). Assimilation occurred when individuals passively adopted American attitudes and behaviors. A converse view by social psychologists in the 1940s and 1950s viewed mixed marriages as signs of community disintegration and often labeled individuals who married "out" as social deviants (Spickard, 1989).

Deviance in this study was expressed consciously by individuals selecting a partner different from their own national culture. Attraction to an exotic *Other* has been studied in previous research (e.g., Kohn, 1998) and was referred to in this study in various ways. For example, Elizabeth explained her cross-cultural relationship: "Opposites attract! We like the companionship and we enjoy learning about each other's cultures. Our intercultural and interfaith lifestyle is very exciting and we would probably find a non-mixed couple marriage quite boring!" In fact, many of the individuals and couples within the study were self-described nonconformists in one capacity or another. Further, cultural theorists have argued that it is "those people who were the most emancipated from their ethnic heritage chose to intermarry" (Spickard, 1989, p. 348).

Emancipation in the study was shown in part by the number of years individuals lived outside their own culture and the perceived geographic and emotional distance from extended families. Economic emancipation was also likely due to the older age and higher education of most informants. In some cases, individuals themselves felt a cultural ambivalence in the form of a bi-cultural identity and expressed feelings of displacement no matter where they lived.

Interestingly, 12 of the 26 couples did not have one or more set of parents present at the wedding ritual, and many parents had not met their son/daughter's partner before they were married. Financial reasons limited travel for some of the couples and their parents; however, most of the informants hailed from middle to upper-middle class families who had previously traveled abroad. The limited parental involvement for spousal selection might be indicative of individualistic cultural values (Triandis, 1995). Indeed, all 26 couples in this study married according to their own choice, and for "romantic" (rather than matched) reasons. Triandis (1995) noted, "Romantic love is treasured where kinship ties are weak and becomes diluted when kinship ties are strong" (p. 119). Among individualistic couples, "it is the individuals who marry" as opposed to collectivist marriages where "the whole extended family 'marries' the other extended family" (Triandis, 1994, p. 135). Based on the couples studied in this research, it would appear that individualistic values afforded cross-cultural informants the freedom to move away from local villages and eventually date individuals from outside their own cultures, marry them, and create their own wedding rituals.

Strategies for Coping with Differences: Nonpurchase and Modification. Individualistic values and deviation as a cross-cultural couple allowed individuals or couples to actively reject or modify traditional cultural practices. Such *nonpurchase* or *modification* strategies have been noted as coping strategies for dealing with cultural ambivalence in past research (Otnes et al., 1997). How individuals or couples chose to modify practices, however, often conformed to their own personal wishes with regard to artifacts and scripts not directly involving a ritual audience. For example, Cheng described how she was able to easily discard the cultural norms related to Chinese attire by hosting her wedding in the United States: "At the Chinese wedding, people would wear red, but I actually don't like red (laughs), so it's good for me." Sandra (U.S.) and Marcus (Germany) admitted they were having a nontypical Wisconsin wedding and discussed how they selected leather trousers with a "European look" over traditional tuxedos or suits for the men; instead of Wisconsin polkas, they opted for European techno music. In these cases, the cultural ambivalence was noted between the bride's or groom's different cultural values and "expected" ritual artifacts and scripts, which resulted in nonpurchase or modification. The cross-cultural wedding allowed informants to "gracefully" resist cultural practices and follow their own preferences instead.

Rejection of "American/Western" Materialism

One of the most common value clashes witnessed in this study occurred in relation to the materialism values associated with the white wedding. Due to the prevalence of the white wedding globally and to the primarily Western influence of the sample (19 couples contained one North American partner), the white wedding was typically held up as a "norm" for ritual elements. However, this norm offers a multitude of artifacts and scripts with rising costs averaging $20,000 to achieve a perfect wedding and magical transformation (Otnes & Pleck, 2003). Several of the cross-cultural couples in this study, regardless of their countries of origin, rejected the materialism values and norms that often coincide with white weddings. Although previous research noted that U.S. brides tend to emphasize material artifacts more than their male counterparts (Lowrey & Otnes, 1994), this study did not reveal any inherent gender differences with regard to materialistic elements of the wedding.

Strategies for Coping with Rejection of "American/Western" Materialism: Embrace Simplicity and Creativity. Strategies arising from this value–norm conflict related to various ways to modify the ritual elements with an emphasis on creativity and/or simplicity. Three areas where these strategies were employed most often were selection of rings, wedding dresses, and the wedding registry.

The selection of engagement and/or wedding rings was typically shared by both partners (but did not usually extend to other ritual role players). Thus, the personal wishes and the cultural customs of the couple came under consideration leading to more discussions and negotiations. Historically, the ring has changed from rushes, hemp, or braided grass to iron and then gold. Today in many cultures, due to Western influence and to DeBeers' ubiquitous advertising campaigns, the diamond engagement ring (and the bigger the better) has come to symbolize romantic love on a worldwide scale (Otnes & Scott, 1996). According to *The Knot's Complete Guide to Weddings in the Real World*, "The most universal of engagement traditions, by far, is the groom-to-be presenting his bride-to-be with a ring. Customarily, there's a luscious diamond involved, perched atop a band of pretty damn expensive metal" (Roney, 1998, p. 7).

In our study, most couples deviated from the aforementioned script. Eight of the 26 couples did not exchange the cultural artifact of a diamond engagement ring, two couples gave engagement rings to the groom as well as the bride, and four couples were given rings from relatives or designed their own rings. In the majority of cases, emphasis was placed on obtaining simple rings rather than luxurious diamonds reminiscent of the white wedding script. In this way, couples accepted the visual symbol of a ring, but rejected the materialist values associated with dominant white wedding cultures (see Table 7.3A).

Occasionally, new scripts were created (e.g., wedding rings were exchanged and worn prior to the wedding), perhaps in part as a compromise for the lack of an engagement ring. Jenny, a Dutch-Canadian now married to a Korean, explained, "I did not receive an engagement ring. It is not in their culture for the female to get a ring! We did pick out rings about eight months before our wedding and chose to wear them to symbolize that we were together." Yuki explained, "my American fiancé brought a wedding ring (but no engagement ring) before the wedding and

TABLE 7.3
Rejection Of American/Western Materialism Values:
Embrace Simplicity And Creativity
(Excerpts from Data)

A) Ring Selection

I don't believe that a woman should be "branded" as "taken off the singles market" with an engagement ring when a man has nothing to show his engaged status. I told my fiancée that he can put his "2-months' salary" into our wedding expenses. (Nancy, age 32, Polynesian-Filipina married to a Canadian, e-mail interview)

I wasn't really caught up in the whole "I need to have a ring before I get married" thing, but I accepted it for his pride, I think he felt he needed to get me something. The ring was just simple, he knows I like simple things, and it's just a simple band with the smallest single-cut diamond you can get because I didn't want anything frivolous. (Tamara, age 25, American married to a Puerto Rican, interview)

My ring was emerald platinum ... very different to the "in vogue" diamond solitaire that Japanese girls usually demand.... I love the color green and like to have something different. (Janelle, age 31, New Zealander married to a Japanese, e-mail interview)

B) Wedding Dress

I wanted to wear not a white gown, and I didn't even know at that time that in traditional Indian society that red is an auspicious color, but I had wanted a red, very simple red gown.... And I just wanted a very simple, you know, kind of short-sleeved, scooped neck dress that became full at the bottom that was a full length. That's really all I wanted. But I couldn't get that material, of course, in Ghana. It was just nowhere to be found. I found some Indian women. And one in particular saved basically the whole wedding. She had a silk brocade sari that was cream-colored with a really hot pink border, which of course, we cut off. She made the dress in that same style of cut that I wanted out of the sari cloth. (Kathy, age 33, American married to an Indian, interview)

I couldn't decide on a design, so we decided to "go ethnic" and copied my mom's wedding gown. My other godmother, a Filipina designer, took my measurements and surprised me with the gown on my wedding day! I also wore a white grass skirt and headdress at the reception. (Nancy, age 32, Polynesia-Filipina married to a Canadian, e-mail interview)

I had a dress which I got probably fifteen years before when I was in college.... It's kind of a whitish pink and it's got lace and it's kind of frilly, and I had never worn it that much because I wanted to look kind of not too fancy. I thought this would be just perfect so I pulled it out of the closet and had it altered so that it sort of reduced the puff. (Alician, age 33, American married to a Tanzanian, interview)

C) Wedding Registry

I find that [wedding registry] vulgar—telling people what you want them to buy you.... I prefer that people buy you what they want to buy you. (Janelle, age 31, New Zealander married to a Japanese, e-mail interview)

We felt a bit odd about saying this is our wedding list—you're kind of saying you're expecting a gift and we didn't expect anything. (Jeremy, age 29, British married to an American, interview) we started wearing the rings before the wedding and then on the way to the wedding ceremony we took off the rings and then we exchanged the rings officially." Deborah chose to adhere to both Canadian and Norwegian customs: "In Norway both men and women wear gold bands on their right hand to show they are engaged (no diamond engagement ring for the bride). Sven chose this custom, so we both wear the gold bands, although I also wear a North American diamond engagement ring from my mother on my left hand." In each of these cases, the groom's cultural traditions were adhered to, but the couple achieved compromise by forming new scripts (wearing rings before the wedding) or wearing two rings—one from each culture and on each hand.

The selection of the dress was typically left solely up to the bride or to the bride and her mother. Only 11 brides hailed from the United States, yet the global white wedding influence was witnessed in this study. Twenty-one of the 26 brides selected white dresses for at least part of their wedding ceremonies. In recent years, white has been a symbol of romance and modernity and the white wedding dress is a sacred artifact that should be worn only once (Otnes & Pleck, 2003). Interestingly, those brides selecting a white dress did not comment on the color of the dress; rather, it was assumed. Presumably the influence of mass culture and/or the desire to be "bridelike" influenced decisions. However, the presumed sacredness or whiteness of the artifact did not necessarily lead to the same highly involved search and monetary allocation dictated by Westernized norms and noted in previous research among U.S. brides (Lowrey & Otnes, 1994). Regardless of the color of the dress, cross-cultural brides often relied instead on their own economy or creativity over material consumption (for examples, see Table 7.3B). In addition, two other brides (an American and a Japanese bride) bought dresses from secondhand shops. Generally, the brides in the study witnessed little conflict over decisions related to the choice of dress because it was deemed their decision. The fact that most of the brides were in their thirties and economically independent from their parents may have contributed to the perceived power over decision making for this artifact.

Similar to modification strategies employed for rings and dresses, couples in the study also exhibited variations in gift giving, particularly related to the wedding registry. The wedding registry (or wedding list) is a common ritual script in gift giving among Western nations. According to *Bride's* magazine (2000), in the United States, over 91% of all to-be-weds register for gifts. Such practices are also becoming common across Europe as major department stores (e.g., Marks and Spencer in London and Printemps in Paris) are offering such services. Compared to the high rate of participation for Americans (91%), only about one half of the couples in this study indicated that they were registering (or had registered), and did not otherwise instruct guests on gift-giving procedures. Instead, couples received either gifts of money or simply accepted the gifts provided by ritual audience members. Reasons varied from functional concerns (moving, international retail difficulties) to symbolic reasons (nonmaterialistic tendencies, cultural concerns about the practice); for examples, see Table 7.3C.

Worry About Different Ritual Audiences

Although partners in the study hailed from different national cultures, they were usually very similar in education, socioeconomic status, and worldview values. However, even when partners within a cross-cultural couple did not experience vast cultural value differences, they recognized how families and external audiences might differ.

Couples expressed resignation or fears about the meeting of their diverse audiences due to language issues, cultural differences, or apprehension over diversity (for examples, see Table 7.4). These fears factored into decisions made about where and how to host the wedding. Indeed, virtual discussions on cross-cultural wedding message boards (Nelson & Otnes, forthcoming) and explanations given by brides and grooms in our study showed that the determination about where to hold the wedding ceremony and/or how many ceremonies/celebrations to have was probably the most important decision couples (and sometimes, their families) faced. Typically, functional factors related to economics and logistics, and symbolic reasons, all played a role in the decision. Upper-class and upper-middle-class couples tend to host two complete ceremonies (one in each culture), according to a cross-cultural wedding planner (Elaine Parker, interview, July 2001). However, most couples in our study planned one ceremony/reception in one culture followed by a celebration dinner or party in the second culture, or they selected a third location away from both cultures. Also unlike upper-middle-class couples, the couples did not use wedding consultants or planners who could negotiate or arbitrate between partners or extended families.

The factors and strategies employed regarding the decision of "where to host the wedding" highlighted issues of power and control because where the event is held likely impacts who is able to attend, whose culture is dominant and, possibly,

TABLE 7.4
Worry About Different Ritual Audiences (Culture Clash)
(Excerpts from Data)

I think both of us were a little unclear about how it was going to be having my family from India and from around America who are very different in background from her family all together in this tiny town in South Dakota ... (Kumar, age 35, Indian married to an American)

Two cultures coming together, two ways of being and two families ... within our parents, they get along just great, but as you get into the extended family—for example my grandma you know feels a little uncomfortable and they don't have much experience dealing with diversity. (Ruben, age 33, Puerto Rican married to an American)

Even though Americans and English speak the same language, I was kind of stressed out.... I had a couple of friends coming over—I was worried that they wouldn't know anyone or wouldn't mingle or wouldn't have a good time. (Martha, age 33, American married to an Englishman)

who pays for the wedding. In North American mainstream culture it is traditional for the bride's family to host and pay for the wedding and many brides and their mothers take control of the planning (Lowrey & Otnes, 1994). However, in other cultures (e.g., Hmong,[1], Korean), it is traditional for the groom's family to host and pay for the wedding. What happens when cultural traditions directly clash is largely left up to negotiation. The following sections illuminate considerations and strategies related to place and ritual audience.

Strategies for Coping with Worry About Different Ritual Audiences: Organize One "Balanced" Hybrid Ritual Through Accommodation, Instruction, or Deceit. Couples in the study typically chose to hold one wedding ceremony but tried to integrate cultural elements. Modification occurred, therefore, by selecting and combining cultural elements into one wedding ritual. Breger and Hill (1998) noted these opportunities in cross-cultural marriages in general: "Coping with the alternative customs, roles, norms, and ideologies offered to those in a mixed marriage can enable creative incorporation and choice" (p. 20). Couples in this study were generally conscious of the "mixing" or balancing of ritual elements across cultures to reflect their identities. In this way, couples actively "reconstructed a micro-identity through negotiating what customs and rituals from both parental cultures to include in the new family, an ongoing process of what might be called 'cultural bricolage'" (Breger & Hill, 1998, p. 20).

Importantly, couples often referred to the goal of achieving a cultural balance or equality across cultural customs in the wedding. A *bricolage*, or dual-culture, wedding, according to informants in the study, must be balanced so that audience members could understand and participate equally. Balance was also closely linked to an equality of power related to the couple's new identity. In this capacity, language during the ritual ceremony was an important consideration for many couples. Twenty-one of the 26 couples had one partner who spoke a different native language from their partner. Of these 21 couples, 15 incorporated some bilingual elements into their weddings. How, when, and why they chose to do this, however, differed. For Deborah and Tamara, the conscious selection of language and the premeditated "balance" of language and culture were important for symbolic and functional purposes. Bill, a 34-year-old Irish graduate student living in the United States for 8 years, selected a Gaelic–English-speaking priest to perform the Catholic ceremony to his American bride. Vows were printed in both languages and given to ritual audience members.

---

[1]The Hmong were farming people, originally from China, but due to persecution many migrated to Indochina, Vietnam, Laos, and Thailand. Today there is a substantial Hmong population in the midwestern United States.

Such conscious and unconscious balancing was expressed throughout selection and creation of artifacts and scripts from hybrid cakes and multiple flags to new kissing/bowing scripts and food variety. In some cases, a compromise was struck allowing for creative hybrids or dual ritual components (two wedding gowns, bilingual ceremonies, music from both cultures) resulting in accommodation for multiple values and traditions within one ritual. Emphasis was often placed on what was important for each partner or what was personally valued as a negotiation strategy (for examples, see Table 7.5). What was lost through doubling ritual elements may have been the "authenticity" of the ritual event according to one side or the other. However, the gain from accommodating diversity was mentioned overwhelmingly as a plus for this strategy.

Interestingly, for some couples, the balance continued into their married lives. For example, one couple spoke only Spanish on certain days of the week and English the others. Another couple chose to balance cultural identity in decorating their home: Each was assigned a different wall to include his/her own personal and cultural identity. Many couples also expressed promises to live in each other's country of origin at one point during their lives together.

Ritual elements related to other people forced couples to exert extra effort to consider the diverse audiences' special needs. Couples expressed concern over making audiences feel comfortable by including events and languages that they would understand. In this capacity, the couples acted as "hosts" for the ritual event,

TABLE 7.5
Worry About Different Ritual Audiences:
Coping by Organizing One Balanced Hybrid Ritual
(Excerpts from Data)

In terms of the wedding ritual, I think there are two layers of combination, one is what I liked and incorporated and one is what Robert liked and he incorporated and then of course both of what we liked reflected our cultural backgrounds, so I think it was those two layers. (Cheng, age 37, Chinese married to an American, interview)

I feel good about it 'cause it was very much our event, I think it was a statement of who we are, that we are an American Jew married to a Tanzanian and I think that's important. (Alician, age 33, American married to Tanzanian, interview)

Basically we tried to incorporate pieces of each other's culture … because the wedding was in New Zealand, it was very Western, but we had speeches in Japanese, dressed in Kimono, and drank Sake. (Janelle, age 31, New Zealander married to a Japanese, interview)

It is important for us to make as much of the wedding day as bilingual as possible…. The invitations, vows, readings, programs will have the entire ceremony in both languages, so that everyone can follow along. We'll have two MC's (one English, one Norwegian), speeches will be staggered English-Norwegian and will be kept short and sweet so no one gets bored or restless when they do not understand. (Deborah, age 30, Canadian married to a Norwegian, e-mail interview)

---

adding special services and informing audience members about the ritual because they understood the importance of the marriage ritual as a shared experience.

Typically, the "host" family would invite out-of-town guests to a function or "tourist" activities would be arranged. This is becoming more common even in same-culture weddings where families come from different parts of the country (Post, 2001). Christina explained activities planned for the Canadian and American audience members, "We are having a barbeque at my parents house before the wedding.... We are having both his family and relatives as well as mine all over so that they can get to know each other and have a day full of fun. We're also taking them all to one of the touristy places ... since they are all tourists to Victoria." Martha and Jeremy hosted a joint hen–stag party at a go-kart racing track during the week before the wedding and a rehearsal dinner that included ritual audience members as well as those who performed special roles. This couple often referred to their wedding as "the wedding week" rather than emphasizing one particular day. Hosting extra events added considerable planning time, money, and stress for the couple, but was seen as necessary for the smooth functioning of the wedding ritual and for managing extended family relations in the future.

Cross-cultural couples also worried that audience members may not understand foreign customs or rituals or be able to fully appreciate or participate in them. For example, Yamani (1998, p. 165) described what happened at the weddings for a Muslim couple from Saudi Arabia and Pakistan: "Although all belonged to the same religion, these differing customs and expectations made communication limited and full of misunderstandings ... and ... only partially understood by the visiting party." In our research, Gretchen, an American from a small town in Wisconsin, rejected many of her husband's Hmong rituals. She explained that she felt this way "for the reason that my parents wouldn't understand everything that was going on and they wouldn't know how to respond back to the typical things that you are supposed to do or say." Interestingly, Gretchen did not articulate concern over her partner's Hmong family and friends.

We also found examples where brides sometimes anticipated audience members' uncertainties and rectified the situation before it occurred. Martha and Jeremy informed American and English ritual audience members that hats (customary at middle- and upper-class English weddings) were optional so midwestern American guests would feel more comfortable at the English wedding. Florence described her apprehension about French guests' expectations regarding alcohol. She told us that wine is inexpensive and free at most French weddings but at her U.K. wedding the bar bill would be too great for her father to subsidize and guests would have to pay for their own drinks. Still, she described nightmares that her cousin would arrive at the wedding without any money and be thirsty and disappointed. She handled this fear by communicating cultural differences through word of mouth with her family. Elizabeth (U.S.) relayed her worry about getting her fiancé's Latin American ritual audience to the wedding on time. "We had to tell Javier's family that the wedding was 2 hours before it really was, so that they'd show up on time." Javier himself admitted that this was not an exaggeration and it was a necessity to "deceive them" in this way. "My sister's wedding was at 7, we told people 7 and it didn't start until 8:15 or later." This concept of time contrasted sharply with that of Elizabeth's midwestern U.S. family. To instruct guests at the wedding about unknown rituals, couples would sometimes go to elaborate lengths, including multilingual instruction booklets and a multilingual master of ceremonies.

Food and music were two ritual elements that allowed couples to offer variety as a way to satisfy diverse audience members. The danger with this strategy was that neither audience might be fully satisfied, but it avoids the greater danger that someone would be deeply dissatisfied. Music was also a way to entertain ritual audience members at the ceremony, reception, or celebration. For the dance, Javier explained how in Puerto Rico it was more typical to employ a band, but instead they hired a DJ who could play a combination of music. As it turned out, the DJ played "mostly Spanish music but a few polkas for the Wisconsin people—and the 'hokey pokey,' which was international." Florence found a DJ who would play both French and English/American music. In the beginning of the evening, the dance floor was segregated by song and nationality, but by the end of the evening, the bride's French father was dancing to the Rolling Stones with one of her Welsh friends. Songs from *Grease* acted as a cultural bridge as men and women, regardless of age or nationality, lined up to sing the words of the song.

Strategies for Coping with Worry About Different Ritual Audiences: Plan Separate Events.   Several of the couples in the study held one ceremony but also created two separate celebrations—one in each culture—to accommodate each partner's family and friends or to meet immigration requirements. Typically, the couple combined their honeymoon or next trip abroad to the other partner's culture where a special dinner or ritual event was organized in recognition of the wedding. In many cases, this was the first time one set of parents and extended families/friends would meet their new son or daughter-in-law.

Although this strategy avoided potential culture clash between the two ritual audiences, it also resulted in the fact that one partner's "side" was not equally present at the wedding ceremony, thus limiting an opportunity to feel and show (with pictures) family solidarity. Indeed, the absence of one family would be crystallized by their absence in the wedding album, possibly causing anxiety over loss of kin contact (Otnes & Pleck, 2003).

Only one couple in the study celebrated two complete wedding ceremonies with church weddings and receptions. When faced with the possibility of ritual audience members not traveling, Joan and Francisco decided to "go to them" instead. Joan discussed how they decided to hold two ceremonies:

> We decided this because his parents couldn't attend the ceremony in the U.S., so we had another ceremony and reception in Uruguay. Once

> we realized his family couldn't be there, his mom offered to host a re-
> ception. The reception grew to become another ceremony (but less for-
> mal). To have two ceremonies was a compromise so that his family
> could feel involved.

Other couples were forced to hold civil service weddings before any "wedding rituals" due to immigration issues. Vicki explained their first legal wedding was a
compromise and described her actions this way: "I will not wear white, I will not
wear my wedding band on my left hand or change my name until after the July
2002 wedding." By actively rejecting cultural customs for the "legal" wedding,
this bride also makes a strong statement about the lack of transformation, which
she is saving for her real wedding in the future.

Interestingly, the more formal the second celebration was (the more it re-
sembled another ritual ceremony), the more brides relished their first weddings
as "sacred." Joan described:

> I think of my "real" wedding as the wedding in the U.S. I wore a dress,
> had bridesmaids, prepared a whole bunch, decorated, had a reception. I
> was nervous. My father gave me away; Francisco cried. He wore a tux,
> etc. The ceremony in Uruguay was all planned out. All I had to do was
> show up dressed. Francisco wore a suit and I a pink dress. We walked
> down the aisle, the preacher said a few words, we greeted family and
> had a reception with lots of food.

In this case, Joan was not involved in the planning and was not emotionally invested.

Martha expressed ambivalence about their American reception held after her
English wedding: "A lot of people said I am coming to your wedding reception, but
(for us) ... it didn't feel like a wedding reception because we were married three or
four months before. I didn't wear a white dress, I wore a little black dress." For
Joan and Martha, their transformations had already taken place—and it did not feel
right to wear the "sacred" wedding dress a second time.

*Strategies for Coping with Worry About Different Ritual Audiences: Select a
Neutral Place.*   Almost all of the couples in the study noted the importance of
place, and they offered a conscious balancing of cultural elements as a way to
show egalitarian power or identity for the couple and ritual audiences. However, five couples chose to hold their weddings in a third culture, or a "neutral"
place, rather than host multiple events or create one hybrid ritual. Breger and
Hill (1998, pp. 166–167) discussed this strategy (typically for living arrangements) as a way for cross-cultural couples to "deflate the pressures of cultural
and economic differences by removing themselves from the particular cultural
context to a more neutral one." For Kumar, an Indian engaged to an American
from South Dakota, getting married in Africa while his fiancé was living there

temporarily seemed a fair option. He described their decision in considering where to get married in relation to their different ritual audiences, "So one way or another, I think we would have benefitted one side of the family more than the other. And I think this was a good alternative for us." Elizabeth, who was from Wisconsin, and Javier, who was from Puerto Rico, decided to have their wedding in Florida as a compromise because it was on "neutral grounds." Elizabeth said she could not imagine Javier's family coming to her small town and could not imagine her family in Puerto Rico. John, an American who married Japanese Kiyomi in the late 1980s when Japanese weddings were at their largest and most extravagant, explained how they consciously selected Switzerland, which was a "neutral" and less expensive choice: "It seemed natural that we would just go there and do this by ourselves."

Robert (Boston) and Cheng (China) decided to get married in Madison, Wisconsin, because of the neutrality. They also wanted to celebrate their new hometown, symbolic of their new life together, rather than focusing on their old lives. It is interesting to note that although same-culture destination weddings are commonplace, the decision process or rationale for holding ceremonies at these places probably differs from the political intent of cross-cultural couples. These five couples, for example, were actively avoiding selecting one culture over another to hold the first or only wedding ritual.

CONCLUSIONS

This chapter examines the antecedents to cross-cultural ambivalence and the strategies employed by cross-cultural couples when planning their wedding ritual. As such, it adds to the growing body of consumption literature on weddings by highlighting the special considerations made by cross-cultural couples. In addition, by illuminating conflicts with regard to personal values and cultural customs, and then by identifying strategies employed to cope with such conflicts, the work expands on theories related to cultural ambivalence.

In previous research, Otnes et al. (1997) showed some evidence for the existence of custom and value conflict in same-culture or cross-cultural weddings. These conflicts showed characteristics of cultural ambivalence, which were then resolved through coping strategies related to resignation, modification, and defiant nonpurchase. These strategies were also used by cross-cultural couples interviewed and observed in this study, but the discussion expands on how and when modification and nonpurchase (rejection) are utilized and offers new considerations and strategies related to ritual audiences.

It appears that a conscious realization of "cross-cultural ambivalence" or "being different" from same-culture couples allowed individuals and couples to deviate from cultural customs or dominant white wedding norms. Most couples observed in our research contained partners who had lived in multiple cultures and had probably "become oriented to differing sets of cultural values" (Merton & Barber, 1976, pp. 10–11; cf. Otnes et al., 1997). In addition, these couples had to choose whether to accommodate diverse role-players and audience members and so found themselves struggling over conflicting cultural values and norms. Conflicts between the couple and families/audience members could be explained according to cultural differences in values as well as demographic factors such as age of the couple, the level of economic dependence, and the geographic distance of bride and groom from their families. Typically, the older the couple, the higher the economic independence and larger the geographic distance from family members, the more the responsibility on the bride and the groom to negotiate and co-create the rituals among themselves. This is similar to what Breger and Hill (1998) noted in studies of cross-cultural couples: "How freely and how consciously customs are adopted and adapted also depend on whether the 'mixed family' is living under the influence of extended kin, or within an ethnic community where following perceived 'traditions' is considered important" (p. 19). Geographical distance from one's national culture often reduces kin influence because it allows cross-cultural families to actively choose cultural traditions and discount pressures to conform.

The couples in our study discussed how they consciously chose to modify ritual elements by showing their own (largely not materialistic) values in place of the selection of white wedding elements (e.g., expensive dresses, diamond rings, numerous attendants, and wedding registries). These findings conform to expectations laid out by Otnes and Pleck (2003), who predicted, "For ethnic weddings, excluding or toning down aspects of the white wedding and reception is often a statement of identity, and is found especially among middle-class couples who do not lead socially isolated lives" (p. 304). Perhaps the rejection of the white wedding (and materialism) enabled cross-cultural couples to deviate from dictated scripts and actively create their own scripts. White wedding elements were replaced according to strategies of creativity, simplicity, and modification. In addition, the older age of couples in the study may have contributed to rejection of white weddings and all the trimmings.

Most strategies employed by informants involved an active modification on the part of an individual or the couple in creating their wedding ritual(s). In some cases, however, the desire to modify the ritual was not fulfilled due to inability to attain customary items (Otnes et al., 1997). In these cases, the ambivalence led to disappointment and regret. Like the couples noted in Nelson and Otnes (forthcoming), several couples in our study were simply unable to provide cultural elements due to lack of services in the area. Such services related to bilingual role performers like priests or disc jockeys or artifacts such as invitations or music. For example, Ellen explained, "We couldn't find a bagpiper to hire for the reception in Hawaii!" Although a handful of wedding planners in the United States now advertise their cross-cultural experience, very few vendors currently offer cross-cultural services. In contrast to defiant nonpurchase noted in Otnes et al. (1997), the couples in this study suffered from a disappointing nonpurchase due to lack of availability.

Interestingly, the text also revealed additional conflicts and strategies not noted in Otnes et al. (1997) specifically related to considerations of others (ritual audience members). The selection of place for the wedding and the noted ramifications for power and identity were the primary considerations for cross-cultural couples in our study. Concern for two different ritual audiences at one event led many couples to create a ritual that contained a multiplicity of cultural elements so that each audience could understand and fully participate in the event. These hybridized weddings included bilingual ceremonies and doubled artifacts such as music and cake. The importance of equal recognition for each culture was often relayed so that couples consciously attempted to plan a balanced bricolage wedding ritual. In other cases, couples planned two separate celebration rituals when the two audiences were not both in attendance. This strategy was often considered a compromise in part because one partner's ritual audience was not represented at the "authentic" wedding ritual ceremony, but it also avoided the worry about culture clash and the difficulty of creating a hybrid wedding ritual. The third strategy employed by five cross-cultural couples was to simply select a neutral place without the influence of audience members. Rationale for this choice was often described in terms of a personal decision to adhere to the couple's choice rather than the accommodation of ritual audience members. Each of these strategies, however, resulted in discussion, negotiation, and compromise on the part of couples.

This study also outlines some of the disappointment or regret expressed by informants with regard to failed modifications or even successful modifications that resulted in an imbalanced wedding. Disappointment related to gaps in expectations and reality when hybrid solutions did not work out (e.g., Gretchen's disappointments in Table 7.6). Disappointment also was expressed with regard to decisions of place—especially when important ritual role players or audience members were unable to share the weddings.

Limitations and Directions for Future Research

Although there were brides (or couples) from more than 23 different national cultures in this study, most had one partner from North America. In addition, most informants were older than average (in their thirties) and were economically independent. Many were academics or had access to a computer/Internet and were therefore not representative of brides/couples worldwide. Still, the demographics seemed to mirror those of most cross-cultural couples (e.g., well-educated, middle class; Blau, 1977; Whyte, 1990). In addition, data were collected and interpreted from across qualitative methods, which helps in triangulation efforts.

Future research might examine the inclusion of symbolic ethnicity in weddings among second and third generation immigrants, as this appears to be a growing area, especially in the United States (Nelson & Otnes, forthcoming). Will the inclusion of symbolic ethnicity alter white wedding practices? Will conflicts arise between generations? Other differences could also be explored across or within cultures, such as religious or class: To what extent do institutional laws

TABLE 7.6
Disappointment as a Result of Compromise and Modification
(Excerpts from Data)

A) Food

My father really wanted to do the traditional Hmong thing and cook all the food, but it was too complicated. I think he was upset. (Wenxiang, age 23, Hmong married to Gretchen, American, interview).

We were going to try and have traditional Hmong food at the reception but that would have involved all of our family and relatives cooking and working all weekend and we didn't want them to work so we just had an Oriental Buffet, I don't know, it was OK. (Gretchen, age 21, interview)

B) Music

Once again, we tried to accommodate both cultures and it didn't work. He [the Hmong cousin who was DJ] didn't play a damn thing [any of her American songs] ... and then the band [Laotian-Hmong band selected by her husband/father-in-law] took over and played a lot of their music and then an uncle kind of took over as MC and he was speaking mostly all Hmong, really loudly so you know my relatives couldn't understand anything so they ended up leaving early.

We're just happy that it's over you know despite the somewhat crappy wedding. (Gretchen, age 21, American married to Hmong, interview).

C) Dress

I didn't know it was to be my wedding day.... I wear just new dress, not white, I was in blue. It's like my wedding dress now, and I was even without any makeup [regarding their civil service ceremony in Turkey]. But we will have a wedding in two years, when we go back to Turkey, we will have Turkish wedding, a wedding dress, and celebration. (Ellen, age 21, Russian married to Turk, interview)

D) Place

I don't know what I was thinking, I just thought it would be okay without them. And so, actually, none of my family came. And then, it's not their fault. It was like, if I told them to come, then they would have come, anyway. It's too far away and I guess I thought it would be kind of a burden to people then to come over, to fly over, ... but they would be fine financially, if they wanted to. I think, looking back, I kind of regret I didn't invite them actually. And when we went to Japan, my mother said, "Oh I really wish we had come to the wedding." (Kiyomi, age 30, Japanese married to an American, interview)

---

and practices or social norms influence weddings? Do couples differing in class or religion also deviate from traditional white wedding scripts? Other consumer rituals (e.g., holidays and funerals) could be investigated among multicultural families to discern if they rely on negotiation, compromise, and ritual creation and invention.

Our research also revealed issues related to power and compromise with respect to consumption issues, particularly when couples selected the place for the wedding. Cross-cultural couples were conscious of trying to achieve equal cultural representation, and often acted creatively to achieve this bricolage or actively "fought for" some issues each considered personally most important. Future research might investigate issues related to power and compromise more closely in other consumption contexts (e.g., purchasing a home, selecting a geographic location to live).

Research might also consider the ramifications of ritual modification for culture. Although critics warn that ritual entrepreneurship might cause a lack of authenticity and loss of traditional community, such improvisation within rituals is gaining social legitimacy in the postmodern world (Bell, 1997), and for global white weddings they are becoming "an amalgam of ever-changing elements of various origins" (Otnes & Pleck, 2003, p. 278).

REFERENCES

Barker, D. (1978). A proper wedding. In M. Corbin (Ed.), *The couple* (pp. 56–77). New York: Penguin.

Belk, R. (1989). Materialism and the modern U.S. Christmas. In E. Hirschman (Ed.), *Interpretive consumer research* (pp. 115–135). Provo, UT: Association for Consumer Research.

Belk, R., Wallendorf, M., & Sherry, J. (1989). The sacred and the profane in consumer behavior: Theodicy on the Odyssey. *Journal of Consumer Research, 16*, 1–38.

Bell, C. (1997). *Ritual perspective and dimensions.* New York: Oxford University Press.

Berry, J. (1980). Acculturation as varieties of adaptation. In L. Berkowitz (Ed.), *Acculturation: Theory, models and some new findings* (pp. 9–25). Boulder, CO: Westview Press.

Blau, P. (1977). *Inequality and heterogeneity.* New York: The Free Press.

Breger, R., & Hill, R. (1998). Introducing mixed marriages. In R. Breger & R. Hill (Eds.), *Cross-cultural marriage* (pp. 1–32). Oxford: Berg.

Bulcroft, K., Bulcroft, R., Smeins, L., & Cranage, H. (1997). The social construction of the North American honeymoon, 1880–1995. *Journal of Family History, 22*(4), 462–490.

Dobscha, S., & Foxman, E. (1998). Women and wedding gowns: Exploring a discount shopping experience. In E. Fischer & D. Wardlow (Eds.), *Gender, marketing and consumer behavior: Fourth conference proceedings* (pp. 131–142). Provo, UT: Association for Consumer Research.

Ellis, C., & Flaherty, M. (1992). *Investigating subjectivity: Research on lived experience.* Newbury Park, CA: Sage.

Glaser, B., & Strauss, A. (1967). *The discovery of grounded theory: Strategies for qualitative research.* Chicago: Aldine.

Gordon, M. (1964). *Assimilation in American life. The role of race, religion, and national origins.* New York: Oxford University Press.

Kates, S. (1998). With friends like her, who needs enemies? Weddings on film and the construction of womanhood. In E. Fischer & D. Wardlow (Eds.), *Gender, marketing and consumer behavior: Fourth conference proceedings* (pp. 41–54). Provo, UT: Association for Consumer Research.

Kendall, L. (1989). A noisy and bothersome new custom: Delivering a gift box to a Korean bride. *Journal of Ritual Studies, 3*, 185–202.

Kohn, T. (1998). The seduction of the exotic: Notes on mixed marriages in East Nepal. In R. Breger & R. Hill (Eds.), *Cross-cultural marriage* (pp. 67–82). Oxford: Berg.

Lincoln, Y., & Guba, E. (1985). *Naturalistic inquiry.* Beverly Hills, CA: Sage.

Lowrey, T. M., & Otnes, C. (1994). Construction of a meaningful wedding: Differences in the priorities of brides and grooms. In J. Costa (Ed.), *Gender issues and consumer behavior* (pp. 164–183). Thousand Oaks, CA: Sage.

Merton, R., & Barber, E. (1976). Sociological ambivalence. In R. Merton (Ed.) *Sociological ambivalence* (pp. 3–31). New York: The Free Press.

Nelson, M., & Otnes, C. (forthcoming). Exploring cross-cultural ambivalence: A netnography of intercultural wedding message boards. *Journal of Business Research.*

Nguyen, L. (August 4, 1996). Tied up in knots over cross-cultural wedding plans. *The Washington Post,* p. B01.

Otnes, C. (1998). Friend of the bride, and then some: The role of the bridal salon in wedding planning. In J. Sherry, Jr. (Ed.), *ServiceScapes* (pp. 229–258). Lincolnwood, IL: NTC Press.

Otnes, C., & Lowrey, T. M. (1993). Til debt do us part: The selection and meaning of artifacts in the American wedding. In L. McAlister & M. Rothschild (Eds.), *Advances in consumer research* (pp. 325–329). Provo, UT: Association for Consumer Research.

Otnes, C., Lowrey, T. M., & Kim, Y. (1993, September). Gift selection of "easy" and "difficult" recipients: A social roles interpretation. *Journal of Consumer Research, 20,* 229–244.

Otnes, C., Lowrey, T., & Shrum, L. (1997, June). Toward an understanding of consumer ambivalence. *Journal of Consumer Research, 24,* 80–93.

Otnes, C., & Pleck, E. (2003). *Cinderella dream: The white wedding in contemporary consumer culture.* Berkeley, CA: University of California Press.

Otnes, C., & Scott, L. (1996). Something old, something new: Exploring the interaction between ritual and advertising. *Journal of Advertising, 25*(1), 33–50.

Park, R. (1950). *The collected papers of Robert Ezra Park.* New York: The Free Press.

Pleck, E. (2000). *Celebrating the family: Ethnicity, consumer culture, and family rituals.* Cambridge, MA: Harvard University Press.

Post, P. (2001). *Emily Post's wedding etiquette* (4th ed.). New York: Harper Resource.

Roney, C. (1998). *The Knot's complete guide to weddings in the real world.* New York: Broadway Books.

Rook, D. (1985, December). The ritual dimension of consumer research. *Journal of Consumer Research, 12,* 251–264.

Rosenblatt, P., & Anderson, R. (1981). Human sexuality in cross-cultural perspective. In M. Cook (Ed.), *The bases of human sexual attraction* (pp. 215–250). London: Academic Press.

Spickard, P. (1989). *Mixed blood. Intermarriage and ethnic identity in twentieth-century America.* Madison: University of Wisconsin Press.

Spradley, J. P. (1979). *The ethnographic interview.* Harcourt Brace Jovanich.

Stanton, M. (1995). Patterns of kinship and residence. In B. Ingoldsby & S. Smith (Eds.), *Families in multicultural perspective* (pp. 97–116). New York: Guilford.

Triandis, H. (1994). *Culture and social behavior.* New York: McGraw-Hill.

Triandis, H. (1995). *Individualism & collectivism.* Boulder, CO: Westview Press.

Whyte, M. (1990). *Dating, mating and marriage.* New York: de Gruyter.

Yamani, M. (1998). Cross-cultural marriage within Islam: Ideals and reality. In R. Breger & R. Hill (Eds.), *Cross-cultural marriage* (pp. 153–170). Oxford: Berg.

8

Dowry: A Cherished Possession or an Old-Fashioned Tradition in a Modernizing Society?

Özlem Sandıkcı and B. Ece İlhan
Bilkent University

Tradition and modernity are generally viewed as polar opposites in classical sociological thinking. According to the linear model of development (e.g., Lerner 1958; Rostow, 1960), as societies modernize, tradition gradually loses its significance and its role as a support mechanism. An important assumption in this model of change is that traditions are impediments to the development of a modern society and are things of the past. It is now clear, however, that neither traditional societies are homogeneous and static structures, nor are tradition and modernity mutually exclusive systems. There is an increasing awareness that the old is not necessarily replaced by the new, and the outcome of the fusion of modern and traditional forces is often a hybrid formation, rather than clash of opposites.

The notion of "detraditionalization" appears, at first glance, as a reiteration of the tradition/modernity polarity but offers some important differences. Beck and Giddens, among other advocates, argued that at the early stages of modernization, many institutions depend heavily on traditions characteristic of premodern societies. But moving toward advanced phases of modernity—"reflexive modernization" in Beck's (1992) terms and "high" or "late" modernity in Giddens's (1991) terms—the role of existing traditions as support mechanisms for social activity become increasingly undermined. This does not mean that traditions altogether disappear in the modern world, but that their statuses change. No longer unquestionably true and taken for granted, they become subject to public debate, reinterpretation, and renewal. Thompson (1996) argued that in the modern world traditions lose their normative authority but retain their role as a means of making sense of the world and as a way of creating a sense of belonging. However, whereas traditions retain their significance, they become "uprooted from the shared locales of everyday life" and "are continuously re-embedded in new contexts and re-moored to new kinds of territorial units" (Thompson, 1996, p. 94). Mediated increasingly by the media and advertising industries and consumption goods, traditions become delocalized and less dependent on ritualized reenactment.

This study explores the relation between tradition and modernity by focusing on dowry practice—a form of marriage payment—in Turkey. It investigates the differences and similarities in meanings and experiences of dowry among different social groups, and discusses how dowry practices transform as a result of modernization and a rapidly developing consumer culture. Two reasons underlie this interest in the dowry practice. In some Asian cultures, including Turkey, dowry constitutes an important component of the wedding. The wedding is a major rite of passage and, as Cheal (1988) observed, it still retains its original significance even in postindustrial cultures. Several studies, including the research on the wedding cake (Charsley, 1987), the wedding gown (Freise, 1996), various wedding artifacts (Otnes & Lowrey, 1993), the wedding gifts (McGrath & Otnes, 1993; McGrath & Englis, 1995), the bridal magazines (Currie, 1993), and the bridal salons (Otnes, 1998), demonstrate the sociological and economic significance of the wedding. This study extends the literature by examining a component of the wedding that is not observed in Western contexts and contributes to the understanding of the ritual dimensions of consumption (e.g., Belk & Coon 1993; Lowrey & Otnes, 1994; Rook, 1985; Sherry & McGrath, 1989; Wallendorf & Arnould, 1991). Second, exploring contemporary practices of dowry in Turkey helps explicate the relation between dowry and patriarchy. Many regard the tradition of giving and taking dowries as an indication of the patriarchal power (Banarjee, 1999; Bhopal, 1997; Sharma, 1984; Tambiah, 1973). The fact that dowry is given only to women and not men may suggest that women are sold to men for marriage as property and, thus, dowry reproduces gender inequalities. This discussion explores how the changing social status of women transforms wedding practices, and to what extent dowry operates as a tool for reproducing patriarchy in Turkish society.

DOWRY PRACTICES

Along with bride price, dowry is a form of marriage payment that is mostly observed in South Asian cultures. Bride price refers to goods or money given by the groom's family to the family of the prospective bride in return for the realization of the intended marriage. Dowry, on the other hand, involves the gifts given to the bride, the groom, and the groom's family by the bride's parents. Gifts include embroidery, jewelry, kitchen items, bed linens, clothing, durables, and property. The total cost of the gifts given may be quite high, suggesting that the female's family begin accumulating these articles while their daughter is merely a baby. The motivation and the experience of dowry show great variety across the cultures in which it is practiced.

Most of the studies published to date focus on India, where the marriage institution is historically characterized by many forms of financial settlements (e.g.,

Caplan, 1984; Ifeka, 1989; Roulet, 1996; Tambiah, 1989). Traditionally, dowry practice was mainly restricted to propertied upper castes in Indian society and was mandated when a woman of inferior rank was to be married to a man of superior social rank. Traditional dowry included two components: a woman's inheritance and the direct gifts to the groom. In recent decades, as Banarjee (1999) observed, several changes have occurred in India with respect to marriage payments. Dowry has progressively displaced other forms of settlements and spread from upper castes to virtually all social groups (J. Caldwell, Reddy, P. Caldwell, 1983; Rao, 1993). Second, modern dowry has acquired the character of a transfer of assets from a woman's family to a man's family, involving periodic payments of cash or goods to groom's family even after many years of marriage (Banarjee, 1999; Billig, 1992). The shift from bride price to dowry is linked to demographic factors, namely, to the scarcity of grooms (Caldwell et al., 1983), as well as to the effects of industrialization, urbanization, and consumerism (Banarjee, 1999).

Bride price and dowry are also common in China despite the 1950 ban on all forms of marriage payments. Although the Communist regime perceived bride price and dowry as indicators of feudal extravagance, the practice of marriage payments never ceased (Croll, 1984; Siu, 1993; Yan, 1996). As Yan (1996) reported, since the economic reforms of the late 1970s, high bride price and lavish dowries have reappeared all over China. In contrast to India, bride price and dowry coexist in China, and are practiced among all social classes. Traditionally, dowries were subsidized through the bride price paid by the groom's family to the bride's family, a practice characterized by Goody (1990) as "indirect dowry." Recent studies report that there has been a change from indirect to direct dowry, and the nature of marriage payments has transformed from "a form of gift giving between families to a means of wealth allocation within the family" (Yan, 1996, p. 177). Furthermore, it is reported that brides and grooms play more active roles in contemporary marriage transactions and assume full control over the disposition of the bride price and dowry (Yan, 1996).

The meaning and experience of dowry in Turkey differ from the Indian and Chinese cases. Although both dowry and bride price exist, the practice of paying bride price is very limited and increasingly unwelcome. Dowry, however, remains to be a prevailing custom. Traditionally, dowry in Turkey was largely confined to textile products such as embroidery, clothing, bed linen, and carpets that are manually manufactured by the bride before her wedding (e.g., Çelik, 1987; Öztürk, 1983; Tezcan, 1997). This version of dowry had a clear pedagogical motivation. Dowry preparation was a major skill for young females living in the rural areas, who had little opportunities for education and employment. Typically, a daughter was instructed to start preparing her dowry between age 10 and 12 and was taught to knit, weave, and do needlework. In many instances, she was also given a wooden chest in which she could store her dowry. The daughter's interest in preparing her dowry was further encouraged by informal competitions organized among a neighborhood in which young females demonstrated their abilities and various items of dowry (Öztürk, 1983). Thus, traditionally, dowry functioned mainly as a symbolic tool to reflect the abilities and competencies of a bride-to-be in weaving, knitting, and embroidery. Her craft and labor of many years were finally appreciated and publicized through a ceremonial display of dowry just prior to the wedding day. The display of dowry not only honored the bride-to-be, but also publicly verified the content and scope of the dowry she was taking with her. In some areas, the dowry displayed was put into a written record and signed by the bride's and the groom's parents, as a reference in the case of a dispute or divorce in the future. If the marriage resulted in divorce, then it was customary for the husband to return the dowry back to the wife.

Studies conducted in different cultures suggest that dowry practice remains to be a strong tradition, but transforms as a result of various cultural, economic, social and political developments. Despite its significance and prevalence, however, there exists no ethnographically oriented research that investigates dowry practice and its transformation in contemporary Turkey. Motivated by this lack of research, this discussion explores dowry practices of different groups of consumers and seeks to understand how its meanings and experiences are negotiated, resisted, or accepted. Similar in many ways to India and China, the economic and cultural modernization of Turkey affects the role and composition of rituals and traditions, including dowry practices.

MODERNIZATION AND THE TRANSFORMATION OF MARRIAGE RITUALS IN TURKEY

The demise of the Ottoman Empire and the establishment of the Turkish Republic in 1923 mark a dramatic shift in the social, cultural, legal, political, and economic orientation of Turkey. At the core of the republican ideology was the desire to construct a "Western" society—modern, urban, secular, democratic, liberal, and rational—out of the Ottoman heritage of "the Oriental" that was equated with religiosity, traditionalism, backwardness, and peasantry. The first two decades of the republic witnessed a massive social reengineering project that aimed to restructure all domains of the public and private lives. As Robins (1996) noted for the republican elite, "It seemed as if the principles of modernity could be accommodated only on the basis of a massive prohibition and interdiction of the historical and traditional culture" (p. 68).

The republican ideology perceived the liberation of women as a necessary condition for the modernization of the society. Previous restrictions on education and employment were diminished and women were admitted to the public schools, the civil service, and the private professions. The 1934 Amendment to the Electoral Law granted suffrage to women and allowed them to be elected to public office. Several changes focused on redesigning marriage and family institutions. Civil law mandated secular marriage, abolished polygamy, prevented child marriages by setting minimum ages for marriage, recognized women as legal equals of men in inheriting and maintaining property, and gave women the right to file for divorce. However, the impact of the reforms was uneven across different social groups. Initially, the changes imposed by the state remained mostly ineffective in the rural areas. In villages far away from the reach of the administration, arranged marriages, polygamy, and religious weddings continued. Those who benefitted most from the new rights were urban middle- and upper-class women who had easier access to education and employment opportunities than rural women who more strongly felt the power of traditions and Islamic conservatism (Arat, 1994; Kadıoğlu, 1994).

Whereas the state attempted to reorganize the marriage institution and restate individuals' rights and obligations, it never explicitly interfered with the wedding traditions. Indirectly, however, it sought to promote Western styles of weddings (Lindisfarne, 2002). In place of old ceremonies, which were perceived as too exaggerated, rural, and religious, the republican elites favored simpler, secular, and "modern" ceremonies. The propaganda had stronger effects among the secular, urban groups of the population who associated themselves more with the republican ideology of modernization. Modern wedding ceremonies differed from traditional ones in many respects; some ritual components were abandoned altogether, others transformed substantially. Whereas traditional weddings lasted 3 to 7 days, modern weddings took place within a single day. In traditional ceremonies, it was customary for the groom's family to organize gender-segregated dinners. Typically, male and female guests were invited to separate houses and were served traditional Turkish food. Modern weddings, on the other hand, eliminated gender-based segregation and transported the ceremony from the confines of the homes to clubs and wedding salons. Female and male guests intermingled freely, danced, and listened to live music while enjoying beverages and snacks. The clothing styles of the modern weddings were also different. The mandatory replacement of traditional dressing with Western dressing code in 1925 has already transformed the clothing styles of the urbanites. Western-style wedding dresses were soon adopted by the secular elites, and it became customary for the bride to wear the white wedding gown and the groom to wear the black suit or tuxedo. Henna night ceremony was a prominent feature of traditional weddings (Üstüner, Ger, & Holt, 2000). Because henna night was strongly associated with Ottoman society, it was equated with backwardness and peasantry in the modern imagination and was abandoned in modern weddings.

The gap between the lifestyles, values, and gender role definitions of urban and rural populations widened over the years. Rapid industrialization during the 1960s and 1970s led to large-scale immigration from rural towns to big cities. Those who migrated settled in the periphery of the cities, creating not only shantytowns, but also a culture of their own that mingled their rural traditions with the values of modern city life (Bolak, 1997; Erman, 1998; Robins, 1996). Contemporary Turkish society is characterized by significant cultural, social, and economic differences and resultant varieties in lifestyles and consumption behaviors (Sandıkcı & Ger, 2002). Certain segments hold tightly on to traditions and face severe social and physical consequences in the case of deviation. Others disdain traditions as they perceive them to be a threat to their modern, secular, and urban identity. Yet, in other segments that have adopted a Westernized lifestyle but are not fully satisfied with the symbolism of the republican ideology, there is a return to traditions, an attempt to reinterpret traditions from the lens of the present. Üstüner et al. (2000), for instance, reported that a new, secular, and urban interpretation of the henna night ritual has emerged in recent years. According to the authors, the emergence of new forms of henna night ceremonies "can be seen as an example of the recent urban interest in the forgotten old and the authentic Turkey," and are indicative of the tensions between modern and traditional identities (Üstüner et al., 2000, p. 212). Wedding ceremonies and the various rituals they incorporate are rich symbolic phenomena through which culture and identities are not only enacted and reproduced but also contested and negotiated. In this respect, similar to the henna night ceremony, dowry practice is a symbolic domain in which various tensions between urban-rural and modern-traditional are played out.

METHODOLOGY

This study is explanatory in its nature and aims to offer a preliminary understanding of the dowry practices in Turkey. The explanatory and discovery-oriented character of the study required employing methods that provide in-depth understanding of the phenomena under investigation. Qualitative research with its "interpretive and naturalistic approach to subject matter" (Denzin & Lincoln, 1994, p. 2) better suited the objectives of this study than more structured approaches. The case study method (Hamel, 1993) was adopted and data was collected through "long-interviews" with a small set of informants (McCracken, 1988). Focusing on a select number of cases enabled interviewing and observing informants in-depth, and permitted a detailed understanding of the subjective meanings and experiences that characterize the dowry practices of the informants.

Informants were purposively selected to maximize chances of uncovering differences and similarities between urban and rural dowry practices (see Table 8.1 for the description of the informants). Previous studies on Turkey report significant differences among urban and rural populations regarding their attitudes toward traditions (Yazıcı, 2001; DIE, 2002). To understand rural dowry practices, informants living a small village located in southern Turkey were interviewed. In line with the demographic structure of Turkey (DIE, 2002), these informants were either illiterate or had only primary school education. They had been living in this small town for many generations, and were mainly responsible for household work. All of the urban informants live in capital city of Ankara. They are educated, with at least high school degrees, and are either employed outside or used to work as a professional. With their education, income levels, and lifestyles they are representative of urban middle- and upper-middle-class families in Turkey (Güvenç, 2001). The third group of informants is selected from shantytown dwellers, or those who have emigrated from small towns to big cities and occupy an in-between place in the socioeconomic map. Typical of the first generation immigrants (Erman, 1998), the older informant in this group has neither formal education nor paid employment. The younger informant, on the other hand, is a high school graduate and has a blue-collar job.

Given that dowry practice is primarily associated with brides, data was collected only from female respondents. In all three groups of informants, interviews were conducted with both the mothers and the daughters. Variations in age and life cycle allowed for explication of generational differences. All of the daughters were engaged and some got married during the course of the research. They all lived together with their parents, a behavior typical in Turkish society (Yazıcı, 2001). As a comparison, the study also interviewed one single and one divorced woman, both professionals that had been living independently for many years. Very few women in Turkey live alone, and such behavior connotes, sometimes pejoratively, an independent, modern identity and more liberal values (Yazıcı, 2001). There is some evidence in the literature that women who chose to live on their own or cohabit with their boyfriends have a more liberal attitude and tend to resist accepted norms and traditions associated with marriage, including the dowry practice (Banarjee, 1999; Bhopal, 1997). This comparison allowed for exploration of how economic and cultural independence transform women's relationships with marriage institution and traditions.

Data were collected through a series of semistructured "long interviews" (McCracken, 1988) conducted during the spring/summer 2001. The second author, who is a second year PhD student, interviewed the informants under the guidance of the first author. Both authors are single Turkish females, who have never been married and, thus, do not have personal experiences of dowry or other wedding-related rituals. The interviews were conducted in Turkish and sought to yield information on the artifacts, behaviors, actors, and audiences involved in dowry practice. The interviews were tape-recorded and transcribed by the second author. The transcriptions produced about 80 pages of single-spaced text, and were translated into English by the first author. To ensure correct translation, the texts were translated back and forth to Turkish and English until both authors reached to a consensus on their accuracy. In addition to interviews, visual data were collected. The interviewer visited the informants at their homes many times and took several pictures of their dowries. The photographs assisted as visual records of symbolism encountered in different dowry items and performances. Sample photographs are included in the text to clarify and illustrate various artifacts and themes.

TABLE 8.1

Description of the Informants

Arife: is 19 years old and engaged. She lives in a small village of Kas, a tourist town located in southern Turkey. Arife has a primary school education and, except for the summer months when she works at nearby farms as a harvester, she is not employed. She regards herself as a "housegirl"; she helps her mother in household chores and, in her spare time, prepares her dowry.

Arife's mother: whose family has been living in the same village for generations, is in her early forties. She is illiterate. She primarily takes care of the household. In the summer she also works as a harvester.

Dilek: is a 20-year-old high school graduate. She was born in a shantytown of Ankara and still lives in the same neighborhood with her parents. She works as an assistant hairdresser at a hair salon located at a middle-class neighborhood in Ankara. During the course of the interviews, she got married to a man whom her parents arranged for her.

Dilek's Mother: is a housewife in her mid-forties. She was born in a village in central Anatolia, participated in an arranged marriage, and then moved to Ankara with her husband. She is literate but does not have formal education. They live in the same shantytown area to which they first moved.

Şeyda: is a 25-year-old electrical engineer now completing her master's degree in the United States. She was born in Ankara and lived with her parents until she went to the States. She met her fiancé while she was studying there. The couple got married during the course of the research.

Şeyda's Mother: is a retired high school teacher in her early fifties. She and her husband, whom she married out of love, live in a townhouse located in a middle/upper-middle-class neighborhood of Ankara. She likes decorating her house and in her spare time attends to handcraft courses.

Almila: is a 25-year-old engineer currently looking for a job. She lives with her parents at a modern apartment complex. Her parents are both university graduates who have lived in big cities (Ankara and Istanbul) since they were born. Almilla is engaged to her boyfriend.

Almila's mother: is in her mid-fifties. She was born in Istanbul and lived there until she got married. She married her husband out of love. She is a lawyer and speaks English.

Elif: is a 32-year-old dentist. She is single and lives alone in Kas. She used to live with her boyfriend, but moved to her own place after they broke up. She moved out of her parent's house when she was 19 years old and has not lived with them since that time. Her mother is widow in her mid-fifties. She is a retired governmental employee.

Zeynep: is in her early thirties. She is from a wealthy and popular family in Kas. She is divorced and lives alone. She is a university graduate and works as a dealer at a casino. Her father is a yacht captain and her brother is a tour guide. Her mother is in her late fifties and a housewife.

Data analysis was guided by grounded theory, which is particularly appropriate when the goal of the analysis is the discovery of a theory from data (Glaser & Strauss, 1967; Straus & Corbin, 1990). Generating a theory from data means that the concepts and constructs "not only come from the data, but are systematically worked out in relation to the data" (Glaser & Strauss, 1967, p. 6). With such an orientation, the authors worked independently to identify key patterns and relationships in data, and then to relate emerging patterns to relevant theoretical concepts. Each stage involved several iterations and negotiations among the researchers. The analysis continued until the authors arrived at agreed on meanings. The discussions of the identified themes are illustrated through relevant quotes from the interviews. In order to preserve anonymity, the names of the informants have been changed.

FINDINGS

The analysis of the data suggests that dowry practice entails a multistaged process and each stage involves different artifacts, scripts, performances, and actors (Rook, 1985). The findings are discussed along three main stages that been have identified: negotiating, preparing, and selecting dowry. In each stage, the discussion highlights differences and similarities among different informant groups and various tensions that underlie their dowry practices. By examining variations across different socioeconomic groups and generations, this chapter aims to map out transformations in the meanings and experiences of dowry.

Negotiating Dowry

One of the key findings that emerged from the data is that there are multiple and sometimes contradictory definitions of what dowry is (or what it should be) and the discursive construction of dowry is contingent on the convergent and divergent practices of individuals. The varieties observed in the informants' experiences of dowry suggest that the process is negotiated differently among different social groups, and the way it actualizes largely depends on the individuals' proximity to or distance from traditional lifestyles. In villages and shantytowns, a dowry is still, as has been historically, exclusively for the bride-to-be and is prepared jointly by the daughter and her mother. The girl and the mother are enthusiastic about preparing and having a dowry and take pride in it. These informants' discourses and practices indicate that adherence to traditions enable them to assert their belonging to the community they live in and register their compliance to the expectations of the others. For these social groups, dowry not only valorizes marriage but more importantly operates as an indicator of the worth of the bride. If a girl has to marry without a dowry, then this shows the absence of her parents' support and puts her in a vulnerable position against her mother- and father-in-law:

Interviewer (I): What do you think of people who get married without dowry?

Mother of Dilek (M): When there is no dowry, of course it is not good. A girl without dowry feels very strange, as if she has nobody, as if she is an orphan.

I: As if she is an orphan?

M: Of course, as if she is an orphan. When a girl has her mother, I mean Dilek doesn't know anything, she doesn't purchase anything. But I know what a girl needs, whatever I use I get one for her.

In patriarchal societies, because women are regarded as socially inferior, dowry constitutes an important strategy to advance status and prestige of the bride's family (Comaroff, 1980; Tambiah, 1973). In Turkey, arranged marriages are still very common in rural areas, and marriage represents more of the union of two families than the union of two individuals (Erkut, 1982; Kağitçibaşi, 1986). Given the higher status of men as the "breadwinners," the groom and his family assume more authority and power in the marriage transaction. The bride's family uses dowry as a symbolic tool to boost their self-esteem and prestige. When dowry is adequately provided, this indicates that the bride's family has the competency, commitment, and resources to build a more egalitarian relationship with the groom's parents. If, on the other hand, the parents do not provide enough dowries for their daughter, they face the risk of being blamed and put down by the groom's family. Dowry-related criticism received from the groom's family not only weakens the status of the bride and her family but also signals deviation from norms. In order to avoid potential conflicts, the bride's mother takes control of the dowry process. It is mainly her responsibility to decide what the dowry will include and when it will be ready. As in one informant's case, this may even lead to the postponement of the wedding if the mother believes that dowry preparation requires longer time:

> My mother wanted my wedding to be on a later date. She said that my dowry was not complete yet and wanted to postpone the wedding to next year. That's why I also didn't want to get married immediately. My sisters-in-law said they would help us and provide whatever was missing. But they could blame me later. Because I didn't have full dowry they could put me down later. Even if they say they wouldn't I think they would do so. (Dilek)

> First they don't say anything of course. But then they blame you. I know this happens quite frequently, I keep hearing that happening. (Mother of Dilek)

The middle- and upper-middle-class urban informants' perceptions of dowry differ significantly from those of the rural and shantytown respondents. The difference stems partly from a different understanding of the marriage institution and partly from different meanings given to material goods. Middle- and upper-middle-class urban females typically choose the person they wish to marry rather than taking part in an arranged marriage (Yazıcı, 2001). Because the motivation behind the marriage is the romantic love between two individuals rather than an agreement between parents, these families do not perceive the marriage as a transaction. The parents of both sides place more emphasis on the happiness and well-being of the couple, and feel responsible for helping their children to successfully embark on a new life together. As they jointly share responsibility, it is a common practice that the parents of the groom-to-be also provide dowry to their son. This more egalitarian division of responsibility indicates a different understanding of dowry. For the informants from the village and the shantytown, dowry items reflect the prestige and social status of the bride and her parents, and its absence causes embarrassment and blame. For urban informants, however, dowry signifies the parents' goodwill and wish for a happy, loving, and lasting marriage. Dowry, in this case, resembles more the gift-giving practices that seek to strengthen the emotional bond between the children and the parents (Belk & Coon, 1993; Cheal, 1996; Fischer & Arnould, 1990):

> For me, material goods are not that important, it is important that they love each other. Other things happen over time, because it is impossible that some one can say "I have everything and I don't need anything else." You come across to something nice, and suddenly you change your mind. I mean goods can be acquired later, it is important that one finds a person to love.... I don't care what other people say. They might even say that Şeyda's dowry is not good enough. What we have done may not be important for them at all. But I have things that I'd like to give to my daughter, and those are important for me. If I am happy giving them and she is happy receiving them, that's what's important for me. (Mother of Şeyda)

When the our informants talk about dowry, they all refer to three different groups of items. However, the weight and significance given to each type of dowry differ among different social groups. First, there is *sandik çeyizi,* or chest dowry, which includes decorative textile products such as embroidery, needlecraft, and lacework (see Figs. 8.1, 8.2, and 8.3). According to the informants from the village, preparing a chest dowry is exclusively the responsibility of the daughter. No help is accepted from the mother, the sisters, or the friends. The girl consults her friends only to get ideas for patterns and designs. Overall, conformity rather than originality shapes the content of the chest dowry. The girls emulate each other and seek to produce similar types of dowry pieces. The more a girl's dowry is similar to

Fig. 8.1. Chest dowry: Example of manual needlework.

Fig. 8.2. Chest dowry: Tablecloth.

Fig. 8.3.   Chest dowry: Examples of embroidered bed linen.

those of other girls in the village, the more obvious it is that she is as competent as her friends in needlework. Because a hand produced dowry is a measure of a bride-to-be's skills, no pieces from the mother's dowry is included in her dowry. The dowry of a bride-to-be has to be as new and fresh as she is herself.

In rural areas, parents generally do not wish their daughters to gain an education beyond the primary school level. This is due to both difficulties in accessing to higher education in villages and the prevailing perception that the primary role of woman is to take care of the household and the children, which are chores that do not require formal education (Duben, 1982). In the shantytowns, however, girls attend school at least until they are 15 or 16 years old, and once they complete their education, they usually start working (Erman, 1998). In cities, the state enforces schooling more strictly than in rural areas, and most shantytown families need many members of the family to have paid employment outside the house in order to finance the higher cost of living in cities. Because these girls do not have too much free time at home, they do not learn how to do needlework. The modern lifestyle of the city enables them to acquire an education, and, to a certain extent, deviate from traditional female roles and responsibilities. However, their rural roots still dictate a traditional dowry. The tension between the old and the new gets resolved through a reallocation of roles and duties. The mother, in this case, assumes responsibility and becomes actively involved in preparing her daughter's dowry. She either hand produces dowry items herself or, to the extent she can afford, purchases mass produced pieces. Dilek's mother knows how to do needlework and prefers to hand produce dowry pieces herself, which she believes are much better than those that can be purchased:

> *I:* Did you all hand produce your daughter's dowry?
>
> *Dilek's Mother (M):* Of course, there is nothing that I purchased.
>
> *I:* Don't you like machine-produced items?
>
> *M:* Hand producing was common in the past. I like hand-produced pieces more. Because I only have one daughter I prepared everything myself.... Hand-produced dowry is far better than machined-produced dowry.
>
> *I:* Why is that?
>
> *M:* Because it reflects the labour, it is more beautiful. But now everybody prefers machine-produced pieces.
>
> *I:* Why do you think people prefer machine-produced pieces now?
>
> *M:* Not to be overburdened. They don't want to go through the trouble of producing them. It is very difficult to hand-produce things.

In contrast to the insistence on the uniformity of designs and pieces observed in the case of the village informants, there is more variety in the chest dowry of the shantytown informants. Trends rather than established norms influence the selection of the pieces to be included in the dowry. Dilek's mother revealed that she not only consulted her neighbors, relatives, and friends to find out which patterns were trendy, but also copied the designs and the pieces that she came across at the shops. Consequently, the dowry that the mother produces for her daughter differs significantly from the dowry that she had when she was a young woman.

The chest dowry of the village and shantytown informants is composed exclusively of white embroidery and lace. The color white symbolizes the innocence of the bride-to-be and the insistence on white pieces indicates the significance placed on her "purity." People living in villages and shantytowns tend to be highly conservative in moral values and especially when they take part in an arranged marriage, premarital sexual interaction between the parties is not permitted. The white embroidery that the bride-to-be takes with her, thus, symbolizes her virginity.

Chest dowry constitutes an important portion of the dowry of the urban informants as well. They value hand produced items; however, typically, neither the daughter nor the mother is interested in or able to do needlework. They do not wish to purchase machine produced pieces that they consider reflect a crass mass taste. Instead, they consult professionals who work as freelance laborers and hand produce dowry pieces in return of a fee. Depending on the complexity of the design and amount of labor, the fees can be quite substantial. Ordering pieces enables these families to choose the patterns, designs, and colors that best reflect their taste. The originality and authenticity of the pieces operate as a symbolic indicator of their aesthetic disposition and appreciation (Bourdieu, 1984; Holt, 1998). White, for instance, connotes a rural taste that they disdain, whereas the color beige symbolizes a more refined, elegant, and modern style. Irrespective of its color, however, chest dowry symbolizes, at least, the assumed purity and innocence of the bride-to-be for the urban informants as well.

A second type of dowry is the appliance dowry, which involves various kitchen items and household durables. In the villages, as the conventional female role in a marriage is structured around household chores, brides-to-be are expected to bring in articles that will be used in cooking and cleaning. Accordingly, the bride's family provides cutlery, plates, glasses, cooking pans, and even sponges, towels, and cleaning sets. The composition of the appliance dowry of the middle- and upper-middle-class urbanites, on the other hand, reflects their relative affluence and modern and professional lifestyles. Here, dowry items include timesaving household appliances (e.g., dishwashers, washing machines, and dryers) and leisure-oriented durables (e.g., big screen TVs, stereos, and DVD players). Given the egalitarian division of responsibility in helping out the new couple, the groom's and bride's families typically negotiate who is going to provide which appliance. For the informants from the shantytown, the appliance dowry, more than any other form, reflects the tension of living at the periphery of the city but not quite affording its material possibilities. Dilek, who was born in a shantytown, has been exposed to the lifestyle of the well-off urbanites, as have her friends. She desires to have a household full with appliances and goods that she sees in the shopping malls. Her notion of "ideal" dowry blends with the notions of "ideal" home (Öncü, 1997) filled with objects that she sees but cannot afford: "I mean, [if I had more money] I wish I had a beautiful home. I wish I could furnish it any way I like. I wish I could get everything I want. It [my house] is not going to be too bad but it could have been nicer."

Gift dowry is the third type of dowry and fulfills a different role than the other two types. Whereas chest and appliance dowries are for the use of the bride and the groom, gift dowry is given to relatives. Agonistic motives (Belk, 1988; Sherry, 1983) seem to underlie gift-giving practices of the informants from the village and the shantytown. These informants believe that it is required for the bride's family to give gift dowry to the groom's family, and use gifts to achieve some type of strategic personal gain. The gifts include hand-produced items such as headscarves, table clothes, and bed linen, and are given to the groom's parents, siblings, and relatives. Typically, the parents and the siblings receive more valuable items, whereas the relatives are given smaller gifts. By offering valuable gifts to the closest relatives, the bride's family symbolically reaffirms the relatively higher status of the groom's family, and hopes that the acknowledgment of power at the beginning will prevent any misbehavior in the future. In contrast to the unidirectional nature of gift giving in rural and shantytown informants, there is a reciprocal gift-giving behavior motivated by altruistic motives (Belk, 1988; Sherry, 1983) in urban middle- and upper-middle-class families. The gifts exchanged among these families typically include mass produced but high quality nightgowns, slippers, fabric, ties, and watches. Altruistic gift giving is inspired purely by the desire to give pleasure to the loved ones, and signifies a mutual expression of the goodwill of the families: "I think giving and receiving gift are very nice things. I mean it is an expression of love. Sometimes there can be some minor misunderstandings, conflicts during the weddings. Giving and receiving gifts remedy such misunderstanding. Besides, it is always a good thing to give a gift when you visit people" (Mother of Şeyda).

For those families who engage in the dowry practice, irrespective of the differences in their perceptions and underlying motivations, dowry is the symbolic expression of a new beginning. Its preparation and eventual transfer represent the transition from childhood to adulthood and from being a daughter/son to a wife/husband. Many of the informants liken dowry—and, in extension, marriage—to the rebirth of nature during spring. Like spring, dowry embodies all the excitement, joy, and sweetness of a new life.

But not all perceive dowry in such positive terms. Elif is a 33-year-old single woman who has never been married and has been living on her own for the past 17 years. As an independent woman living in a flat that she herself furnished, dowry is a thing of the past and reminds her "all the unused, unnecessary items" given to a daughter. She reveals that her mother had dowry but she has never seen her using any of those items. Elif acknowledges that many women in Turkey live with their parents until they get married. These women do not live in their own place, so for them dowry serves the very practical purpose of setting up a new household. She explains that she and her like-minded friends have a different attitude toward marriage and the customs associated with it:

> Now how we perceive marriage is different. I mean, for example, many
> couples do not even have wedding ceremony; they just have the legal

service. In the past, for example, there were engagements, weddings, and many preparations for all these ceremonies; they used to prepare lots of things in addition to dowry.... Now because the lifestyles are different, people really do not spend that much time at home. They set up more practical homes. I mean in the past people used to purchase big dining tables, chairs, furniture for the guest room and cupboards to put china. Now people want to live with less furniture, they have different lifestyles and they want to live more practically. For example, now, when we are together with friends we can dine over this coffee table. Those things used to be much more important in the past. People used to invite guests to dinner and they would have china sets for ten, twenty people and matching tablecloths, napkins, and things like that. And they would have these kinds of things in their dowry. Now we don't live like that any more.

Elif does not demand dowry from her mother, nor is her mother interested in preparing her dowry. However, she indicated us that she may consider having some of her mother's dowry one day, not to use but to keep as a memory: "The things that my mother or her mother did for her dowry, those belong to her. But they are important for her because she lost her mother. And I would like to keep a couple of things from her dowry as a memory of my mother." Select dowry items, such as hand produced embroidery and needlework, take the form of cherished objects to be transferred from the mother to the daughter, and, thus, represent metaphorical extensions of the mother into her daughter's future life (Price, Arnould, & Curasi, 2000).

Price et al. (2000) stated that ritual occasions and rites of passage can stimulate older people to dispose of their cherished objects. Zeynep's relationship with her mother suggests a similar pattern. Similar to Elif, Zeynep believes that dowry is already a thing of the past, and practiced only among more traditional segments of the Turkish society:

> Z: I think, today, there is no more dowry practice in some groups of the society. It has disappeared in the five percent of the population.

> I: Which five percent is that?

> Z: Five percent that has a very modern life. I never hear my friends talking about dowry when they are getting married. I don't even hear the term dowry any more.

However, although Zeynep did not need or want any dowry, she admits that her mother decided to transfer some of her own dowry items to her when she got married. She keeps these transferred items of embroidery and lacework "in a bag at the corner of the cupboard" but, nonetheless, appreciates them for their aesthetic and historical value and potential as family heirlooms: "They are mostly things that are not produced any more. They are all hand-produced. Things that require lots of labor and effort are not produced now. Or, they are machine-made. Old dowries are more valuable because of the labor put into them."

Preparing Dowry

Traditionally preparation of dowry starts at the birth of a daughter and the mother plays the key role in its preparation. In the villages, there exist clearly defined norms about how a girl's dowry should be. Following these norms, when the girl is old enough, the mother teaches her daughter how to hand produce dowry pieces. The informants related that each girl in the village has a very clear picture of dowry and wants her dowry to be similar to that of her friends. However, a different pattern was observed in the case of shantytown and urban informants. Although the mothers start preparing dowry early on, the daughters are not typically highly involved in its preparation until there is a prospective groom. They even despise their mother's interest in dowry as untimely and economically excessive. Yet, as soon as getting married becomes an immanent event, both their involvement level in its completion and appreciation of their mother's labor increases:

> My mother started to prepare dowry when I was just a kid. I used to say "mother, why are you preparing these, I'll never use them." Now, I am getting married and she says "see, how useful they are," and I agree. (Dilek)

> I started preparing Şeydas dowry when she was two and a half year old. Şeyda used to tell me "mom, don't prepare these, who is going to use them?" When we displayed her dowry, she liked it. She said "mom when did you prepare all these things?" She wasn't involved at the beginning now she likes them and says she will use them in the future. (Mother of Şeyda)

Two factors can explain this attitude. First, as most of the dowry pieces can be purchased, the preparation can be postponed to a later stage. Second, although the composition of dowry is relatively fixed in villages, fashion and social trends are powerful influences in the case of shantytown and urban informants. The girls living in the urban environment do not want to have outdated items in their "modern" homes and prefer to wait until the very end to acquire what is most trendy—of course subject to their financial means: "Now there is fashion. Everybody can follow fashion more or less. So there is no need to prepare lots of things beforehand. Because when there are new things on the market, you want to have them as well" (Mother of Almilla).

A shared understanding among almost all the informants is that every mother prepares a dowry for her daughter. The mother is influential in preparing as well as organizing the rituals associated with dowry. The active involvement of the mother in her daughter's dowry, first of all, is a sign of her ongoing and unconditional love for her daughter. Similar to gifts, dowry is a form of communication (Belk, 1979) that conveys messages of affection, support, and love, and is seen as part of the giver's—mother's—extended self (Belk, 1988). Mothers love their daughters and they show this through the efforts and sacrifices they put into the preparation of dowry. Because their love is endless, they want their daughters to have everything and live a life more comfortable than theirs:

> I used to save from our food money and buy things for her dowry. (Mother of Dilek)

> Even if dowry is not the most important thing in the life, you, as a mother, still want to give your best. I want her to have more than what I had…. The things that I didn't have, or the things that I see, let's say a simple tea drainer or a spoon holder, I mean these may not exactly constitute dowry but they look so original and when I purchase them for my self or even if I don't purchase them for myself, I always thinking of purchasing one for Şeyda. (Mother of Dilek)

> I want her to have everything, nothing should be missing. Only when she has everything you feel happy as a mother. (Mother of Almilla)

Dowry represents not only the embodiment of the mother's love, but is also an indication of the competency of the mother in preparing her daughter to the role of a wife. Because women mostly live with their parents until they get married, mothers feel that their daughters are neither experienced in taking care of a household, nor knowledgeable about the requirements of a running a good home. Thus, it is the mother's responsibility to foresee and provide whatever her daughter will need in effectively performing the roles of a wife and, later, a mother: "A mother knows better what her daughter will need. Because she has never run a household she doesn't know what she needs" (Mother of Almilla).

In contrast to the dominant role of the mother, the father remains generally inactive in the process. Because dowry is perceived as a female ritual, the father's role is typically limited to providing financial support. Like in many other rituals, females take more responsibility in maintaining and performing the ritual (Fischer & Gainer, 1993; McGrath & Englis, 1996; Wallendorf & Arnould, 1991). In all social groups, the father's duty only involves paying for the dowry items. Whereas the fathers desire their daughters to have dowry, they influence the extent of dowry by pressuring their wives not to overspend. The mothers typically negotiate between the daughter and the father, and come up with a solution that will satisfy both sides. Often, the mothers resort to their own savings to acquire the missing items. Even if there may be many arguments and conflicts over how much to spend between the mother and the father during the preparation process, the fathers, at the end, are generally proud of their wives and appreciate their efforts once they see the results:

> He [the father] told me that I was such a good mother. He asked "when did you prepare all these?" He said that he was not aware of all these beautiful things that I prepared. He, of course, saw individual items at the beginning. Then, when we displayed them, he saw all of it, and examined them at length. He even joked if she [daughter] is not going to use all of it, we could take some and use! He really really liked them. (Mother of Şeyda)

The role of the groom-to-be and his parents differ in the villages, the shantytowns, and the cities. In the villages, the groom-to-be does not interfere with the dowry preparation. If there is something additional required of which to the bride-to-be's family must be reminded, then it is his mother's responsibility to negotiate this issue with the mother of the bride-to-be. Because what is expected from each family is clearly defined and strictly followed in the villages, the two families conform to the expectations. There is little hesitation about what is to be done and the way it is to be done. The groom-to-be's family therefore assumes a rather passive role in the process. The family of the bride-to-be remains as the key actor in the case of the shantytown dwellers; however, negotiation between the two families is generally more complicated and potentially conflicting. Shantytowns involve people who have emigrated from different parts of Turkey. When two families are to be connected through marriage, this often means union of families from different rural backgrounds who have different local customs. If the expectations are not clearly laid out and agreed on, then arguments and conflicts may arise. The conflicts arising as a result of regional differences in values suggest cultural ambivalence (Otnes, Lowrey, & Shrum, 1997), which may force the parties involved to readjust, often unwillingly, their behavior: "In my village, the girl's family buys the chest and brings it to the new house. Here, groom's family takes the dowry to the house. Groom should bring the chest with him. But, I cannot tell, I cannot tell them to bring a chest to put dowry" (Mother of Dilek).

Traditionally, parents have strong authority and power over their children, and expect them to be submissive (Tekeli, 1991). In the villages, this family structure prevails and the parents strictly monitor and control marriage decisions and preparation. In the shantytowns, the authority of the parents remains strong, but the couple is given some freedom to negotiate various marriage related practices. In urban families, there is a more egalitarian relationship between the children and the parents that allows the children to better assert their individuality and take more responsibility in planning of the marriage. These families feel themselves responsible for supporting their children financially to reach at their dream without dictating how the dream should unfold.

Displaying Dowry

Once the dowry is prepared and the wedding date is finalized, there remains one last step in the ritual: displaying dowry. Dowry display is essentially the showing-off of the dowry prepared for/by the bride to the relatives and friends. Time and place of the display varies; it might take place in the home of the bride's parents, the groom's parents, or the new couples, and it might happen before or after the marriage. Dowry displays, like baby showers, are rites of passage signifying one of the major role transitions that most women undergo during their lives (Fischer & Gainer, 1993). Similar to traditional baby showers, dowry displays are attended exclusively by female guests. The absence of men suggest that the display, like other forms of female-only rituals, such as baby showers or home shopping parties, aims to foster female solidarity and facilitate the transition from girlhood to womanhood.

In the villages, dowry display typically happens a few days before the wedding. The groom's family, the relatives, and the neighbors visit the house and examine the individually displayed items. The display allows the guests, and especially the groom's family, to assess the amount of dowry the bride is bringing with her and the extent of her abilities in hand producing dowry pieces. In extreme cases, if the groom's family is not satisfied with the dowry, then they may decide to cancel the wedding. When everyone sees the dowry and if there are no disagreements between the two parties, then the single girls of the village take the dowry from the bride's parent's house, bring them into the couple's new house, and ceremonially place them. The ceremonial transfer and replacement of dowry functions as an encouragement for the unmarried girls who are expected to be inspired by the effort the bride has put into her dowry. The display reproduces the expectations, re-affirms the significant role dowry plays in reaching the happy ending (e.g., the wedding), and motivates the single girls to emulate the behavior of the bride.

The tradition of displaying dowry continues in the shantytowns but it has to be modified due to economic and physical limitations faced by these families. Dilek's mother wanted to display her daughter's dowry. However, she was hesitant to invite her neighbors and distant relatives. When a guest comes to see the dowry, it is customary that she brings along a gift for the bride-to-be. Well aware of the financial difficulties that the families living in shantytowns endure, Dilek does not want to be perceived as someone asking for gifts, and thus limits the number of people she invites:

> *Mother of Dilek (M):* I didn't invite many people; it would be like asking for gifts.

> *I:* Do they usually bring gifts?

> *M:* Yes. When you invite everybody it is like you have to bring gifts.

I: What kind of gifts do they typically bring along?

M: Things like glasses, plates, bowls.

I: Do they bring hand-produced items?

M: No, sometimes things like socks, things that are not very expensive.

I: What kind of gifts do you bring along when you go to a dowry display?

M: Sometimes small gifts, sometimes, when you visit someone that you don't want feel embarrassed you have to bring something more valuable.

Furthermore, reciprocity principle requires that when a guest brings a gift to the dowry display, she and her family are invited to the wedding ceremony in return (Yan, 1996). This, of course, means additional financial burden for the groom's family, who covers the cost of the wedding ceremony. In the cities, weddings are typically performed in rented parlors where cost is calculated on a per-person basis, so that the more people invited, the more the total cost. Because the families cannot afford to invite too many people to the wedding, they do not want to heavily publicize the wedding and, hence perform only a small-scale dowry display. In addition to the economic difficulties, the constraints of the physical space affect the scope of the display (see Figs. 8.4 and 8.5). Shantytown dwellers typically do not live in spacious houses where they can devote rooms or part of the garden to display dowry. They can display whatever they can place in a small room:

> *Dilek (D):* You display dowry a couple weeks before the wedding. In the past people would empty a room and hang the dowry pieces on the wall.

> *I:* Did you do that?

> *D:* No. We used one of the rooms, and there was bed and other furniture there. So it was really jammed. My mother didn't want to hang them on the wall. So we placed the pieces on top of each other on the bed.... Actually, they had to be displayed for week and you had to have a big room where you can display everything individually. But my dowry remained in boxes; because we didn't have enough space we could not display them. We couldn't have used the living room either; it is already small and we had relatives staying with us.

Fig. 8.4.   Dowry display: Examples of bed linen and Kitchen Utensils.

In urban middle- and upper-middle-class families, display of dowry continues, but in a substantially modified form. The informants indicate that, because
they regard such ceremonies as "rural" practices, they do not organize a special
day for the display. Instead, after the wedding, when the couple is established in
their new house, they invite their friends and relatives. Every guest visiting the
couple for the first time is given a tour of the house. The guests, both male and female, walk through the rooms (including the bed- and bathroom), examining the
furniture, the decoration, and various objects on display. Although the
mixed-gender nature of urban dowry displays suggests more egalitarian gender
role attitudes (Fischer & Gainer, 1993), the extension of the display from dowry
items to the house of the newly wed couple indicates a higher emphasis given to
the conjugal bond.

Fig. 8.5.   Dowry display: Examples of gifts to groom's relatives.

CONCLUSIONS

The social rules of marriage in Turkish society developed in the context of an Islamic peasant society characterized by high levels of social and economic dependency on the family. In the traditional peasant family, the family head has control over economic resources and this control augments the social basis of patriarchal authority. The household unit, through the distribution of domestic labor and domestic financial organization, operates as the key site in which patriarchy is reproduced. Turkish society remains highly patriarchal (Kandiyoti, 1991; Erman, 1998). In villages and shantytowns, parents exert control over spouse selection, and arranged marriage remains a widely accepted behavior. The mother and the father strictly control marriage-related practices, and comply with established norms and customs. This analysis indicates that dowry is still perceived as a requirement for a successful marriage in villages, and its absence causes personal and social embarrassment and disadvantages. The fact that dowry is prepared only for the bride and is required as a condition of marriage can be read as an expression of patriarchal authority. As Kandiyoti (1988) argued, in classic patriarchy, "dowries do not qualify as a form of premortem inheritance since they are transferred directly to the bridegroom's kin and do not take the form of productive property" (p. 279). The bride enters her husband's household as a dispossessed individual without any bargaining power.

However, the results also indicate that, in the villages and the shantytowns, the mother of the bride plays a key role in the preparation of dowry. She assumes full responsibility in guiding the behaviors of her daughter, and in selecting, organizing, and transferring dowry items. The authority of the mother suggests the existence of matriarchal power as well, at least within the context of dowry practices. Dowry practices of the urban informants present a more egalitarian perception of gender roles. Even though these families provide dowries, they reframe dowries as symbols of support rather than necessity. More importantly, the groom's family provides dowry for their son, a behavior observed in neither India nor China.

Although ritual behaviors are regarded as "extremely resistant to innovation or deviation" (Rook, 1985, p. 253), this study indicates that they do transform, albeit gradually. As individuals adopt more modern lifestyles, traditional dowry practices become recontextualized and are renegotiated. However, the transformations observed in the context of the Turkish society differ from the transformations reported for India and China. This suggests a culture-specific process through which the tensions between traditions and modernity are played out. Although effects of urbanization, commercialization, and female employment enable changes in dowry practices, the way responsibilities and gender role definitions are negotiated depends on the context of situational constraints and opportunities. The experiences of the informants from the shantytown suggest a transitional stage in which the tensions between the traditions of the rural past and the norms of urban life are most severely felt. The practices of the urban informants, on the other hand, represent more flexible experiences of dowry, which are guided by less binding and more spontaneous scripts.

The permanence of dowry, albeit in transformed forms, suggests that it continues to serve important functions in the Turkish society. Apart from the symbolic and ideological reasons underlying the continuity of dowry practice, socially accepted norms about parent–child relationship are influential in perseverance of dowry. Children of both genders typically live with their parents until they get married. Expressive enough, the term getting married in Turkish, *evlenmek*, literally means "acquiring a house," reflecting the expectation that individuals can move into their new house only when they get married. From this perspective, dowry serves a very practical purpose, helping children to set up a new household. The fact that only the single and divorced informants perceive dowry as an old-fashioned and redundant practice supports this view. These women, who are experienced in living alone and define their identities as "modern," distance themselves from dowry and its "traditional" connotations. However, this distancing does not necessarily lead to rejection. Rather, these informants strategically reconstruct dowry as an heirloom or an aesthetic object. Such recontextualizations resonate with the modern reinterpretations of the henna night ritual (Üstüner et al., 2000).

Several factors might trigger transformations in traditional dowry practices. Women's increasing participation into the labor force (DIE, 2002) weakens the material basis of patriarchal authority, enabling renegotiation of gender roles. Women's education and employment outside the home practically eliminates the expectation that she has to hand produce her dowry pieces, which necessitates a redefinition of dowry and reallocation of responsibilities. The emphasis on nuclear family and the discouragement of arranged marriages in urban modernist discourse accentuates the importance of romantic love and the conjugal bond, permitting the bride and the groom to play more active roles in marriage arrangements. Consumerism and proliferation of consumer goods transform the composition of dowry by enabling families to purchase pieces and legitimating new items—appliances—as dowry. As Goldstein-Gidoni's (2000) study of contemporary Japanese weddings indicates, traditions can be and are often commodified, and the reciprocal and complex relationship between the producers of tradition and the consumers of their products requires careful analysis. The analysis of the production side—the role of dowry shops, branded dowry products, and the marketing discourse behind them—to future studies.

Marriage traditions and rituals are expressive of the historical, social, and cultural norms and assumptions about gender identities and roles, family dynamics, and consumption practices. Given the lack of academic interest on the topic, it is impossible to state if there are similar transformations in other wedding-related rituals in Turkey (for an exception, see Üstüner et al., 2000). However, the case of dowry demonstrates that new meanings attached to old traditions indicate a dynamic negotiation process whereby traditions and rituals do not merely reproduce a culture but are used as cultural resources to define new social boundaries and identities. The confrontation between tradition and modernity can be a source of tension, but it is also a source of cultural creativity and dynamism.

REFERENCES

Arat, Z. (1994). Turkish women and Republican reconstruction of tradition. In F. Göcek & S. Balaghi (Eds.), *Reconstructing gender in Middle East: Tradition, identity and power* (pp. 57–78). New York: Columbia University Press.

Banarjee, K. (1999). Gender stratification and the contemporary marriage market in India. *Journal of Family Issues, 20*(5), 64–676.

Beck, U. (1992). *Risk society: Towards a new modernity* (M. Ritter, Trans.). London: Sage.

Belk, R. (1979). Gift-giving behavior. In J. N. Sheth (Ed.), *Research in marketing* (pp. 95–126). Greenwich, CT: JAI Press.

Belk, R. (1988). Possessions and the extended self. *Journal of Consumer Research, 15*, 139–168.

Belk, R., & Coon, G. (1993). Gift giving as agapic love: An alternative to the exchange paradigm based on dating. *Journal of Consumer Research, 20*, 393–417.

Bhopal, K. (1997). South Asian women with households: Dowries, degradation and despair. *Women's Studies International Forum, 20*(4), 483–492.

Billig, M. (1992). The marriage squeeze and the rise of groom price in India's kerala state. *Journal of Comparative Family Studies, 23*, 197–216.

Bolak, H. (1997). When wives are major providers: Culture, gender, and family work. *Gender Studies, 11*(4), 409–433.

Bourdieu, P. (1984). *Distinction: A social critique of the judgment of taste.* London: Routledge & Kegan Paul.

Caldwell, J., Reddy, P., & Caldwell, P. (1983). The causes of marriage change in South India. *Population Studies, 37*, 343–361.

Caplan, L. (1984). Bridegroom price in urban India: Class, caste and "dowry evil" among Christians in Madras. *Man, 19*, 216–233.

Çelik, A. (1987). Uşak, Sivaslı, Tatar kasabası düğün adetleri [Marriage customs of Tatar village of Sivaslı township of the city of Uşak]. *Türk folklorundan derlemeler* (pp. 31–46). Ankara: Kültür Bakanlığı Yayınları.

Charsley, S. (1987). Interpretation and custom: The case of the wedding cake. *Man, 22*, 93–110.

Cheal, D. (1988). Relationships in time: Ritual, social structure and the life course. In N. Denzin (Ed.), *Studies in symbolic interaction* (pp. 83–109). Greenwich, CT: JAI Press.

Cheal, D. (1996). Gifts in contemporary North America. In C. Otnes & R. Betramini (Eds.), *Gift giving: A research anthology* (pp. 85–97). Bowling Green, OH: Bowling Green State University Popular Press.

Comaroff, J. (1980). Introduction. In J. Comaroff (Ed.), *The meaning of marriage payments* (pp. 1–47). New York: Academic Press.

Croll, E. (1984). The exchange of women and property: Marriage in post-revolutionary China. In Renee Hirschon (Ed.), *Women and property—Women as property* (pp. 44–61). London: Croom Helm.

Currie, D. (1993). "Here comes the bride": The making of a "modern traditional" wedding in Western culture. *Journal of Comparative Family Studies, 24*, 403–421.

Denzin, N., & Lincoln, Y. (1994). *Handbook of qualitative research.* Thousand Oaks, CA: Sage.

DIE (Devlet Istatistik Enstitusu) [Republic of Turkey, Prime Ministry State Institute of Statistics]. (2002). Kadin istatistikleri ve göstergeleri [Women's indicators and statistics] *http://www.die.gov.tr/toyak/cover1/index.html*, Ankara, Turkey.

Duben, A. (1982). The significance of family and kinship in urban Turkey. In Ç. Kağıtçıbaşı (Ed.) *Sex roles, family and community in Turkey* (p. 3). Bloomington: Indiana University Press.

Erkut, S. (1982). Dualism in values toward education of Turkish women. In Ç. Kağıtçıbaşı (Ed.) *Sex roles, family and community in Turkey* (p. 3). Bloomington: Indiana University Press.

Erman, T. (1998). The impact of migration on Turkish rural women: Four emergent patterns. *Gender and Society, 12*(2), 146–167.

Fischer, E., & Arnould, E. (1990). More than a labor of love: Gender roles and Christmas gift shopping. *Journal of Consumer Research, 17,* 333–345.

Fischer, E., & Gainer, B. (1993). Baby showers: A rite of passage in transition. *Advances in Consumer Research, 20,* 320–324.

Freise, S. (1996). *The function of a consumer good in the ritual process: The case of a wedding dress.* Working Paper, University of Hohenheim, West Germany.

Giddens, A. (1991). *Modernity and self-identity: Self and society in the late modern age.* Stanford: Stanford University Press.

Glaser, B., & Strauss, A. (1967). *The discovery of grounded theory.* Chicago: Aldine.

Goldstein-Gidoni, O. (2000). The production of tradition and culture in the Japanese wedding enterprise. *Ethnos, 65*(1), 33–55.

Goody, J. (1990). *The oriental, the ancient and the primitive.* Cambridge, England: Cambridge University Press.

Güvenç, M. (2001). *Kentlerin yan anlamları: Toplumsal coğrafyalar, farklılıklar, benzerlikler* [Connotations of cities: social geographies, similarities, differences]. *Istanbul, 36,* 80–83.

Hamel, J. (1993). *Case study methods. Jacques Hamel, with Stephane Dufour and Dominic Fortin.* London: Sage.

Holt, D. (1998). Does cultural capital structure American consumption? *Journal of Consumer Research, 25,* 1–15.

Ifeka, C. (1989). Hierarchical woman: The "dowry" system and its implications among Christians in Goa, India. *Contributions to Indian Sociology, 23*(2), 261–285.

Kadıoğlu, A. (1994). Women's subordination in Turkey: Is Islam really the villain? *Middle East Journal, 48*(4), 645–660.

Kağıtçıbaşı, Ç. (1986). Status of women in Turkey. *International Journal of Middle Eastern Studies, 18,* 485–499.

Kandiyoti, D. (1988). Bargaining with patriarchy. *Gender and Society, 2*(3), 274–290.

Kandiyoti, D. (1991). Patterns of patriarchy: Notes for an analysis of male dominance in Turkish society. In Ş. Tekeli (Ed.) *Women in modern Turkish society* (pp. 306–318). London: Zet Books.

Lerner, D. (1958). *The passing of traditional society.* Glencoe, Ill. Free Press.

Lindisfarne, N. (2002). *Elhamdülillah Laikiz* [Thank God, we're secular]. İstanbul: İletişim Yayınları.

Lowrey T. M., & Otnes, C. (1994). Construction of a meaningful wedding: Differences between the priorities of brides and grooms. In J. Costa (Ed.), *Gender and consumer behavior* (pp. 164–183). Beverly Hills, CA: Sage.

McCracken, G. (1988). *The long interview.* Qualitative Research Method Series (Vol. 13). Newbury Park, CA: Sage.

McGrath, M., & Englis, B. (1996). Intergenerational gift giving in subcultural wedding celebrations: The ritual audience as a cash cow. In C. Otnes & R. F. Beltramini (Eds.), *Gift giving* (pp. 123–141). Bowling Green, OH: Popular Press.

McGrath, M., & Otnes, C. (1993, February). *Communal exchange in the context of intergenerational giving of wedding gifts.* Paper presented at the American Marketing Association winter educators' conference, Newport Beach; CA.

Öncü, A. (1997). The Myth of the "Ideal Home" Travels Across Cultural Borders to Istanbul. In A. Öncü & P. Weyland (Eds.), *Space, culture and power* (pp. 56–72). London: Zed Books.

Otnes, C. (1998). "Friend of the bride"—and then some: Roles of the bridal salon during wedding planning. In J. Sherry, Jr., (Ed.), *ServiceScapes* (pp. 229–258). Lincolnwood, IL: NTC Press.

Otnes, C., & Lowrey, T. M. (1993). The selection and the meaning of artifacts in the American wedding. *Advances in Consumer Research, 20,* 325–329.

Otnes, C., Lowrey, T. M., & Shrum, L. J. (1997, June). Toward an understanding of consumer ambivelance, *Journal of Consumer Research, 24,* 80–93.

Öztürk, İ. (1983). *Evlilikte çeyiz hazırlamanın ve çeyiz çevresinde oluşan toplumsal kuralların tekstil el sanatlarının yaşamasına etkisi* [The effects of dowry preparation and the establishment of social rules around the dowry on the survival of handmade textiles]. II. Milletlerarası Türk Folklor Kongresi Bildirileri. Ankara, Kültür Bakanlığı [Proceedings of the II International Congress on Turkish Folklore], 165–199.

Price, L., Arnould, E., & Curasi, C. (2000). Older consumers' disposition of special possessions. *Journal of Consumer Research, 27,* 179–201.

Rao, V. (1993). The rising price of husbands: A hedonic analysis of dowry increases in rural India. *Journal of Political Economy, 1101,* 666–677.

Robins, K. (1996). Interrupting identities: Turkey/Europe. In S. Hall & P. du Gay (Eds.), *Questions of cultural identity* (pp. 61–86). London: Sage.

Rook, D. (1985). The ritual dimension of consumer behavior. *Journal of Consumer Research, 12,* 252–264.

Rostow W. W. (1960). *The stages of economic growth.* Cambridge: Cambridge University Press.

Roulet, M. (1994). *The idea, practice, and politics of dowry in two North Indian villages.* Unpublished PhD dissertation, University of Michigan.

Sandıkcı, Ö., & Ger, G. (2002). In-between modernities and postmodernities: Investigating Turkish consumptionscape. In S. Broniarczyk & K. Nakamoto (Eds.), *Advances in Consumer Research, 29,* 465–470.

Sharma, U. (1984). *Women, work and property in north west India.* London: Tavistock Publications.

Sherry, J. (1983). Gift giving in anthropological perspective. *Journal of Consumer Research, 10,* 157–168.

Sherry, J., & McGrath, M. (1989). Unpacking the holiday presence: A comparative ethnography of two gift stores. In E. Hirschman (Ed.), *Interpretive consumer research* (pp. 148–167). Provo, UT: Association for Consumer Research.

Siu, H. (1993). Reconstituting dowry and brideprice in South China. In D. Davis & S. Harrell (Eds.), *Chinese families in the Post-Mao era* (pp. 165–188). Berkeley: University of California Press.

Strauss, A., & Corbin, J. (1990). *Basics of qualitative research: Grounded theory procedures and techniques.* Newbury Park, CA: Sage.

Tambiah, S. (1973). Dowry and bridewealth and the property rights of women in South Asia. In J. Goody & S. Tambiah (Eds.), *Bridewealth of dowry* (pp. 59–169). Cambridge; England: Cambridge University Press.

Tambiah, S. (1989). Bridewealth and dowry revisited: The position of women in Sub-Saharan Africa and North India. *Current Anthropology, 30,* 413–435.

Tekeli, Ş. (1991). Introduction: Women in Turkey in the 1980s. In Ş. Tekeli (Ed.), *Women in modern Turkish society* (pp. 1–22). London: Zet Books.

Tezcan, M. (1997). Türk evlenme ve düğün gelenekleri modeli. [A model for Turkish marriage and wedding traditions.] *Türk halk kültürü araştirmalari* (pp. 219–230). Ankara: Kültür Bakanlığı Yayınları.

Thompson, J. (1996). Tradition and self in a mediated world. In P. Heelas, S. Lash, & P. Morris (Eds.), *Detraditionalization: Critical reflections on authority and identity* (pp. 89–108). Oxford: Blackwell.

Üstüner, T., Ger, G., & Holt, D. (2000). Consuming ritual: Reframing the Turkish henna night ceremony. In S. Hoch & R. Meyer (Eds.), *Advances in Consumer Research, 27,* 209–214.

Wallendorf, M., & Arnould, E. (1991). "We gather together": The consumption rituals of Thanksgiving Day. *Journal of Consumer Research, 18,* 13–31.

Yan, Y. (1996). *The flow of gifts: reciprocity and social networks in the Chinese village.* Stanford; CA: Stanford University Press.

Yazıcı, E. (2001). *Üniversite gençliği 2001: Üniversite gençliğinin sosyo-kültürel profili üzerine bir alan çalişmasi* [The university youth 2001: A field study of sociocultural profile of the university field]. Ankara: Gazi Üniversitesi Yayınları.

Part IV

Gift Exchange

9

Gift Exchange Rituals in the Workplace: A Social Roles Interpretation

Julie A. Ruth
Rutgers University

Consumer research on gift giving has focused on the ritual as a means of creating and maintaining family and friendship relationships (Belk, 1976; Belk & Coon, 1993; Cheal, 1988; Ruth, Otnes, & Brunel, 1999). The scant research in workplace contexts has typically examined interorganizational gifts exchanged between a firm, or its representatives, and those outside of the firm such as suppliers or customers (Beltramini, 1992, 1996; Dorsch, Grove, Pickett, & Kelley, 1997).

Omitted from inquiry has been research on consumption rituals among intra-organizational representatives in the form of gift giving among a firm's employees or coworkers, such as those to mark coworker birthdays or retirements. The term *coworker* is used broadly here to denote any type of giver or recipient within the firm, including an employee, supervisor, subordinate, or peer. Gifts among coworkers can be distinguished from those among non-coworker friends and family because kinship ties typically do not exist to support the obligation to give. Moreover, participation in gifting activities in the workplace may require dual performance roles (e.g., the giver and recipient in an interpersonal relationship such as friend or acquaintance, as well as that same person in the role of employee with work roles and responsibilities). As such, gifting rituals among coworkers may blend rules-of-friendship and rules-of-work because intraorganizational gift givers and recipients are likely to hold beliefs about organizational culture and work role responsibilities (O'Reilly, Chatman, & Caldwell, 1991), as well as norms believed to underlie gift giving such as reciprocity (Gouldner, 1960; Mauss, 1954). Gifts within the firm can also be distinguished from gifts between firms because of the shared cultural meanings held by employees of the same firm (Schein, 1992; Trice & Beyer, 1984). Further, gifts between firms are often viewed as means of gaining future business (Dorsch & Kelley, 1994; Dorsch et al., 1997), an objective that does not necessarily apply to within-firm gift practices.

The current study addresses this gap in ritual research through interpretation of critical incident survey data and interviews with people regarding their experiences as givers and recipients of gifts in the workplace. More specifically, the interpretation focuses on the expression of social roles (Otnes, Lowrey, & Kim, 1993) among givers and recipients in workplace settings in light of prior research on gift exchange, rituals, interpersonal relationships, and organizational culture. The social roles perspective encompasses the giver's intended message with respect to the giver–recipient relationship, and aids in uncovering the dynamics of balancing beliefs, norms, and roles associated with gift giving and the workplace. This research will contribute to the understanding of gift giving as a consumption ritual that affects accomplishment of work-related symbolic communication and the maintenance of ongoing interpersonal relations in the workplace. This research will also provide insight into the generalizability of consumer gift exchange theories, as well as the dynamics of consumers who are attuned to consumption rituals, interpersonal relationships, and organizational roles and norms.

CONCEPTUAL FOUNDATIONS

It is widely believed that people engage in giving and receiving as a means of entering into and maintaining social relationships. In investigating how meaning is manifested in gift exchange, Otnes et al. (1993) introduced the notion of social roles, where gifts are imbued with meaning about the giver's intentions in their social relations with the recipient. The six social roles include givers who are *Pleasers* that seek to make the recipient happy, *Providers* of what the recipient needs, *Acknowledgers* of nonclose recipients, *Compensators* for something the recipient has lost or does not have, *Socializers* who seek to place certain values or knowledge with the recipient, and *Avoiders* who communicate symbolically through the absence of a gift.

Because gifts are "movements in the management of meaning" (Sherry, 1983, p. 157), it is important to understand how participants in gift relationships communicate such meaning. As Duck, West, and Acitelli (1997, p. 16) note, relationship interactions such as gift giving are embedded in the social context of "shared meaning system[s] … [including] cultural meanings, social meanings … and the meaning systems constructed between" the giver and recipient. In addition to the social and psychological meanings that shape family and friendship gift relationships, the workplace is, and has, its own culture that is associated with emotionalized, collectively held beliefs and norms impelling members to act in certain ways (O'Reilly et al., 1999; Schein 1992; Trice 1993). Beliefs are expressed through symbols of all sorts, including firm logos, mascots, buildings, and employee participation in ceremonies, rituals, and workplace duties (Trice, 1993). Work norms are rules for behavior that are understood by work group members (Cialdini, Bator, & Guadagno, 1999). Notwithstanding the variety and sources of beliefs and norms that ultimately reflect a firm's culture, organizational culture is pervasive and affects a wide array of individual- and firm-level activities, including decision-making styles, marketing strategies, human resources policies and procedures, and the day-to-day atmosphere of the workplace (Deal & Kennedy, 1999; Rousseau, 1997; Schein, 1992).

RESEARCH FOCUS

Participation in rituals is one way in which the workplace is likely to both reflect and (re)create workplace culture (Trice & Beyer, 1984). Indeed, "rituals bind [people] through community and culture-building, individual and communal celebration" (Manning, 2000, p. 1). Yet little is known about the ways in which gift rituals are undertaken in the workplace, the social roles expressed through workplace gifts, and how a firm's culture along with an individual's work roles and responsibilities relate to the meanings associated with gifts in this context. Thus, this research examines the specific issue of the social roles expressed through gifts in the workplace. In doing so, an enriched understanding of how the setting—in this case, the workplace—contextualizes gift-giving practices is obtained.

METHODS

To investigate these issues through interpretation, two complementary data collection methods were used: depth interviews and critical incident surveys. Interpretation is appropriate here because of the goal of uncovering the meanings associated with gift giving in this context. Depth interviews were used because of the ease with which informants could relate their gift experiences and because of the opportunity to probe for fuller understanding of situations and experiences. Because critical incident surveys can be distributed across a broad sample, their complementary use provided access to gift experiences in a variety of work settings.

Interviews

Eight semistructured interviews were conducted, audiotaped, and then transcribed for analysis. Following McCracken's (1988) recommendations, a guide for questions and prompts was developed for the interviews. The discussion guide provided a template for the interview, while also permitting informants to freely describe their own experiences as gift givers or recipients at work. The interview began with a question asking informants to describe their job and their workplace as if an acquaintance had expressed interest in seeking employment at their firm. This opening question was used to put the informant at ease and to elicit important background information about workplace culture, roles, and responsibilities. The interview turned next to the issue of gifts in the workplace by eliciting information about the types of occasions when gifts are given and received in their workplace. Informants volunteered these occasions, ranging from anniversary of employment to birthdays to unexpected illness. The interview was then structured around specific incidents for each of the occasions listed by the informant. Probes were used, as needed, to prompt recollection about ritual context, emotions experienced, workplace culture, and relationships with givers, recipients, and other coworkers. The depth interviews yielded a total of 56 gift experiences.

Appendix A provides a description of the informants, who were paid $10 for participating. Each interview lasted between 45 minutes and 1½ hours, and yielded a total of 125 single-spaced pages of data. All interviews were conducted with informants in the eastern United States. Informants were acquaintances or strangers introduced to the interviewer by acquaintances. Informants ranged from age 23 to 60, and also ranged in number of years of employment with their organization (e.g., 1 year to 29 years with the same employer). Three of the informants did not attend a 4-year college; three have advanced degrees.

Critical Incident Surveys

Critical incident surveys on gift giving and receiving experiences were collected on three occasions over the 1993–1998 time period (see Ruth et al., 1999; Ruth, Brunel, & Otnes, 2002). Although not a focus of those data collection efforts, 33 individuals described gift giving or gift receiving experiences in workplace situations. These data were incorporated into the current project. The average age of the 33 critical incident respondents was 38 years and 66% were women. Their employers and occupations were quite diverse (e.g., school teachers, restaurant waitresses, self-employed attorneys, etc.).

Overview of the Combined Data Set

In total, the data for interpretation involve 89 gift experiences encompassing 26 receipt and 63 giving contexts, equally divided between noncalendrical occasions such as leaving a job, and calendrical events such as birthdays, holidays, or employment anniversaries. Depth interview informants are identified by DI and their pseudonyms (see Appendix). Critical incident reports, identified by CI, include the informant's gender and age.

INTERPRETATION

The interpretation focuses on uncovering the social roles expressed between coworker givers and recipients and the relationship of corporate culture, norms, and job roles to gift ritual practices in the workplace. Such an interpretation provides a foundation for further examining the prominent tensions between rules-of-friendship and rules-of-work in gift-giving practices.

Social Roles Expressed in the Workplace

Table 9.1 summarizes the social roles that emerged in workplace contexts along with an example, occasions, giver emotions, and gift strategies for each. Among the social roles observed in family and friendship settings (Otnes et al., 1993), the Acknowledger role was prominent in workplace settings, as was Avoider. Pleaser, Provider, Socializer, and Compensator were evident but not prominent. Newly emergent were the social roles of Appreciator, Booster, Manipulator, Humanizer, and Changer.

Acknowledger and Avoider

In Acknowledger role situations, givers typically engage in obligatory (and often token) gift selection for recipients who are on the fringe of their network of relations at work. Gifts expressing the Acknowledger role can be described as low on sentiment and value (Sherry, McGrath, & Levy, 1993). A variety of occasions may precipitate Acknowledger expression, including birthdays, holidays, and retirements.

Much like the givers in family and friendship social networks, Acknowledgers at work often participate in group gifts and settle for what suffices, as opposed to what the recipient would truly like, in order to ease the burden of gift giving (Otnes et al., 1993). For example, as a matter of personal policy, Audrey typically contributes to all group gift requests, but she does not suggest gifts or track what is being given by the group to a coworker recipient. Instead, her senior vice president's administrative assistant typically handles the process of gift giving for occasions such as marriage or illness of a coworker. As Audrey says, "I'm too busy for that."

Moreover, some workgroup norms can be in place (Cialdini et al., 1999), where Acknowledger expressions are expected and it is customary for all workgroup members to give, even if the recipient is not close or well liked. Because the pressure to conform to such behavioral norms is high, some coworker givers participate reluctantly and with some negative emotions (Cialdini et al., 1999; Trice, 1993): "I don't like feeling obligated to give just for its own sake. Lack of interest in the coworker was harder to explain than giving a donation and avoiding an unpleasant situation" (CI, Male, age 40).

Although such behavioral norms are widely known but often unspoken, some workgroups arrive at a negotiated strategy for acknowledging others. Secret Santa or Pollyanna gift exchanges may reflect negotiated Acknowledger strategies, as each person in the workgroup draws a recipient name at random and is typically subject to a group-determined limit on the amount to be spent on gifts.

TABLE 9.1
The Expression of Social Roles in the Workplace

Social Role	Definition	Workplace Example	Workplace Occasions	Workplace Giver Emotions	Gift Strategies in Workplace Settings
Acknowledger*	The giver is engaged in obligatory gift selection for a recipient on the fringe of their social network, with the (often-times token) gift symbolizing that a relationship exists.	The vice president of a large unit announced that the workgroup would be giving a gift basket to a hospitalized coworker. Audrey did not know the coworker well at all ("Would I have any personal information? No."). Nevertheless, she contributed to a group gift.	Christmas/end-of-year parties and accompanying gift exchanges such as Secret Santa or Pollyanna; personal events such as marriage, birth of child, birthday of a non-close work associate	Mild positive emotions to negative emotions, such as resentment and frustration, if obligated to participate	"Settle," let someone else handle details of gift selection and presentation, group negotiation on how to acknowledge everyone
Avoider*	A deliberate symbolic message is sent by the absence of gift exchange.	"We didn't do anything for her [the boss] last year [even though the group had given the boss a gift in the past]. When you're in there running someone else's business who is not really appreciating it or getting the fact	Although not likely when highly visible and/or negatively sanctioned for doing so, the Avoider role can be communicated in conjunction with any gift-giving occasion.	Negative emotions	None, by definition

	that she's not really taking care of her business, you don't want to get her a present.... There developed an us-against-her [mentality] so she was not included in the group of *us* who were struggling together.... So, she just wasn't part of the group."		Positive emotions	"Buy what they like," give organizational (e.g., logo items) or occasion symbols (e.g., certificate of appreciation, watch to symbolize time for retirement)
Appreciator	The giver knows, and wishes to demonstrate the knowledge, that the recipient has completed his/her work duties in a noteworthy fashion.	"I give as an additional token of my appreciation, coming from me personally as opposed to maybe what the bank would give them or what they may get from their families. I work closely with these people and they do a tremendous job."	Any positive occasion such as retirement, anniversary of employment, holiday, birthday, etc.	
Booster	A gift and/or the occasion of recognizing a recipient provides an opportunity to promote the organization to an audience that can be internal or external to the workplace.	Upon the occasion of a high-ranking manager's 20th anniversary in a difficult leadership job, Michael presented the manager with a certificate of appreciation and clothing items	All occasions, including Christmas/end-of-year occasions, anniversary of employment, and retirement	Muted with respect to the giver's feelings toward the recipient; range of emotions depending on planning and executing the ritual event itself
				"Buy what I want you to have"

(continued)

TABLE 9.1
(*continued*)

Social Role	Definition	Workplace Example	Workplace Occasions	Workplace Giver Emotions	Gift Strategies in Workplace Settings
		embellished with the organization's official symbols and logos. He said, "We really have been playing up [the corporate name, logo, and image] a lot.... So I have to say that there was nothing in the gift decision [that was personalized to the recipient or the occasion of 20 years of service]."			
Manipulator	The giver seeks, directly or indirectly, to achieve workplace goals.	"Some of the folks referred to it as, 'Let's leverage Daniel one more time.' It wasn't if you worked at the bank or you reported to Daniel	All occasions, including Christmas/end-of-year occasions, anniversary of employment, and retirement	No pattern	"Buy what they like," "Buy what I want you to have," "Buy what will elicit the outcome I seek"

| Humanizer | Gifts serve to communicate that, more than merely being a worker, the giver or recipient is a human being with human qualities. | "It's just more from the standpoint that instead of just looking at me as a boss or supervisor, I think it brings the relationship to a more personal level." | [that determined if you were invited to the retirement reception]—you needed to have acquired one of his customers.... The fact is that the bank sort took a situation and did one thing ['leverage Daniel'] and had it appear they were doing something else [honor their employee with gifts and a party]." | Christmas/end-of-year holiday occasions, birthdays. Not anniversary of employment because that might emphasize work-related qualities rather than more personal ones. | Mostly positive emotions | "Buy what they like" "Buy what I like" |

(continued)

TABLE 9.1
(continued)

Social Role	Definition	Workplace Example	Workplace Occasions	Workplace Giver Emotions	Gift Strategies in Workplace Settings
Changer	The giver desires to begin a new type of relationship with the recipient, typically a personal, rather than workplace, one.	"He handed me a box and said he appreciated my willingness to work with him.... I was immediately embarrassed because there was no need for the gift, but put it aside with a strained, 'Thank you.' I opened the box later and was flustered and angry as well as embarrassed.... This type of gift [lingerie] was totally out of line."	"No occasion," emergent occasions (e.g., completing a special project), or personal occasions such as birthdays	Positive, except for uncertain emotions regarding the recipient's reaction	"Buy what I think they will like," "Buy what I want you to have"

[a]From Otnes et al. (1993)

Another version of this is a birthday club where the coworker whose birthday was last recognized is now the person to make arrangements for a cake/gift in honor of the coworker with the birthday, a form of generalized reciprocity (Sahlins, 1972). This behavior is similar gift-giving practices in contemporary Hong Kong, where third-tier friends engage in collective gift-giving efforts orchestrated by someone closest to the birthday person (Joy, 2001).

Expressing Acknowledgment is facilitated by formal and informal workplace communication tools, including published lists of birthdays and public dissemination of information regarding the recipient's likes and dislikes:

> At [one of the bank's retail locations] they have thirteen tellers and three people on the platform, so that's sixteen people, and they go so far as they have a list in their lunchroom and the people put down their preference of a cake. They even go one step further. I think in some cases they put down what they do *not* want. (DI, Jane)

These mechanisms are workplace examples of two characteristics important to successful gift giving: personalization of the gift to the wants/needs of the recipient (Belk, 1996) and equipollence among equivalent recipients by ensuring everyone in the group is acknowledged (Lowrey, Otnes, & Robbins, 1996; Lowrey, Otnes, & Ruth, forthcoming).

Because workgroups are not necessarily easily defined, one of the challenges faced by Acknowledgers is the size and membership of the work network to acknowledge. Relevant social networks may include cliques of coworkers who identify more closely with a subset of a workgroup, those individuals who are formal members of a work unit, or those at various levels that are involved in work flow (Trice, 1993). With the ambiguity about relevant work networks, some givers rely on personal heuristics to reduce the burden. For example, Jane stated, "Generally, everybody I work with I do like, and even with the people that I don't like, I contribute anyway." Others, such as Karen, evaluate each request separately according to a social exchange framework (Belk & Coon, 1993; Cheal, 1988). Karen admitted, "I'm such a *quid pro quo* person, it's sad." When Karen was asked to participate in a group gift for a coworker who was getting married, she refused because the bride-to-be had not contributed when Karen had sought out, over the course of 3 years, coworkers to sponsor her efforts in charity fund-raising events.

In such situations, the Avoider role is enacted, where a deliberate symbolic message is sent by the absence of a gift (Otnes et al., 1993). Other mechanisms may permit an unseen expression of the Avoider role. For example, in some work settings, gift contributions are solicited by sending an envelope sequentially to all potential contributors; individuals check off their name as the envelope is passed, permitting people to contribute as much or as little as they like or to make no contribution at all. This method minimizes public display and comparison of individual contributions to group gifts (Cheal, 1988), reducing the likelihood of sanctions for not engaging in the normative behavior to give (Cialdini et al., 1999).

Whereas the Acknowledger role emerged as a prominent form of social role expression identified by Otnes et al. (1993), five new social roles emerged in a close reading of the data regarding gifts in the workplace: Appreciator, Booster, Manipulator, Humanizer, and Changer.

Appreciator

Across workplace conditions and characteristics, gifts formally recognize the efforts of the recipient and the results of their work. Oftentimes, work contributions appear to go unnoticed or unacknowledged, and gifts are a means of symbolically communicating that the giver not only knows about, but also wants to take the additional step to communicate about the extent of the coworker's contributions. The Appreciator is clearly distinguished from the Acknowledger because the former is not acting in an obligatory fashion. Moreover, the Appreciator is communicating that the recipient plays an integral role in work functioning and effectiveness. As a result, the Appreciator willingly, rather than out of obligation, seeks out a way to validate the recipient and their work.

Appreciator gifts are generally geared toward recipient's tastes and interests ("buy what they like"; Otnes et al., 1993) or are symbols associated with the organization or that particular occasion (e.g., items emblazoned with organizational symbols and logos; a watch or clock upon retirement). During the process of giving, Appreciators generally experience positive emotions. Emotional reactions to Appreciator gifts range from surprise to frustration to enjoyment, depending on the recipient's view of whether they are merely doing their job or are deserving of the additional recognition.

The Appreciator role is communicated on holidays such as Christmas, the anniversary of employment, or on separation from the firm. In these settings, givers express their appreciation for a job well done:

> I give as an additional token of my appreciation, coming from me personally as opposed to maybe what the bank would give them or what they may get from their families. I work closely with these people and they do a tremendous job, and Christmas is traditionally a gift-giving season. (DI, Jane)

Recipients often interpret the gift in a similar manner, even if they believe that an Appreciator gift is not required:

> The gift came as a total surprise for work I did [to organize an association meeting] that was so natural to me, and normal, and my usual way of functioning, that I could not imagine being given a gift in ac-

knowledgment. I had only done my job. I felt deeply touched. (CI, Male, age 56)

Other recipients interpret such gifts as getting what they deserve for their work, as reflected in the comments of Martha, who is viewed as indispensable and always willing to go above and beyond the call of duty in her workplace:

> I think it's a sign of appreciation. Because I think when you're in a job, you get paid, and a lot of employers feel that paycheck is their show of appreciation. I don't agree with that, being on the employee's side of that chair.... Whether you're a play-it-by-the-game person who does the least they have to do or the person who comes in early, leaves late, and does all the extra things, you still get paid the same. So how does that person who goes above and beyond ever know they're appreciated? I think that [gift giving in the workplace] is how you do that. (DI, Martha)

Departure/retirement and anniversary of employment are also occasions associated with expression of appreciation to recipients:

> It was during an opening night party, where we toasted the cast and crew of the play. It was my last week of work, concluding three and a half years of work for the theater. This gift of two beautiful candlesticks was given by the president of the board, who also made a speech in my honor. I felt that they acknowledged everything I had done ... the difference I had made. I had an incredible warm feeling in my heart and stomach. I began to cry. (CI, Female, age 30)

Such Appreciator gifts and ritual occasions provide an opportunity to hold rites-of-passage ceremonies whose essential purpose is to enable the individual to pass from one defined position to another (van Gennep, 1960, p. 3). Rites of passage can occur with any change of physical being, place, or social status, including occasions such as retirement and separation from the firm (Trice, 1993). These changes can create disturbances in the group and disturbances for the recipient. For example, Sylvia indicated that she had no negative emotions about participation in the workplace rituals associated with her retirement but had reservations about postretirement life: "I was going into my next passage of life, which was a little frightening to me.... So my mixed bag was fright, anticipation, and excitement.... So I was very happy for all the years but sad that I was leaving it" (DI, Sylvia).

Rites of passage, including the rituals accompanying retirement such as parties and gifts, provide opportunities to facilitate the transition and may help to make that new status apparent (van Gennep, 1960). Workplace gifts can communicate the person's new status (e.g., retired) by personalizing the gift according the individual's plans for the time ahead (e.g., money for an extensive vacation).

Moreover, in the Appreciator role, extensiveness of gifts and other ritual artifacts signal level of appreciation, much like the size and largesse of gift giving can be viewed as symbols of love in family and friend relationships (Belk & Coon, 1993; Cheal, 1987):

> I think what [the employee's boss] did for [the person who resigned] was really something *above* what should have been expected.... We could have all taken him out to lunch and all paid ... or we could have had a potluck kind of thing here and given him a gift ... or we all could have gone to dinner somewhere, not on company time and said good-bye.... I think the fact that [the boss] did that [had a company-paid, sit-down dinner with the immediate workgroup as well as other invited guests] was his acknowledgment to [the departing employee] that he really appreciated all that he did. And that he wished him well [in graduate school]. (DI, Martha)

Furthermore, not all types of separation from the employer are deemed worthy of the Appreciator expression through gifts. A worker's voluntary decision to seek employment elsewhere would not necessarily be Appreciator-worthy, because seeking employment elsewhere may signal that the departing employee views the current workplace as less than satisfactory ("I think if he was leaving to go to another job, I don't think there would have been a party"; DI, Martha). However, departures to retire or seek higher education are contexts that may be worthy of Appreciator gift giving.

Booster

A gift and/or recipient can be the vehicle through which promotion of the organization occurs. The giver typically seeks to communicate favorable qualities of the firm such that important audiences see the organization in a (more) positive light. Two different audiences may be the targets of boosterism messages via gifts: (a) audiences *internal* to the organization, including the immediate workgroup or employees at large (Gilly & Wolfinbarger, 1998), and (b) audiences *external* to the organization (Duncan & Moriarty, 1998; Dutton & Dukerich, 1991; Lawler, Yoon, Baker, & Large, 1995).

Anniversaries of employment are occasions associated with boosterism. These occasions, if recognized, involve firm-related gifts such as those emblazoned with the firm's name and logo that serve as reinforcements of the organization name (Duncan & Moriarty, 1998). Unlike Appreciator gifts that focus on the recipient, here greater emphasis is placed on promoting the organization through gifting activities. Michael related that, given his gregarious personality and job responsibilities as one of two high-level chief operating officers of his firm, he has been earmarked as the organization's gift giver. Upon the occasion of a high-ranking manager's 20th anniversary in a difficult leadership job, Michael acted on behalf of the organization to present the manager with a certificate of appreciation and clothing items embellished with the organization's official symbols and logos:

> So, I guess the thing that we tried to do is, in the last couple of years ...
> we really have been playing up [the corporate name, logo, and image] a
> lot.... So I have to say that there was nothing in the gift decision [that
> was personalized to the recipient or the occasion of 20 years of service]
> other than ... I got him a golf shirt.... I mean I wouldn't see [the recipient] wearing a t-shirt. I would see him wearing a golf shirt. So, I mean,
> that kind of decision was made, but the concept wasn't, What would
> [the recipient] really want? (DI, Michael)

Indeed, in his personal life, Michael prides himself on highly personalized gifts. In this situation, however, the CEO "who is definitely a non-gifty kind of guy" sent a strong signal to Michael on gift giving:

> *Michael:* Actually I was thinking about doing something more spectacular, one of those glass things with something engraved on it. But I didn't
> get the sense that's what [the CEO] wanted to do.
>
> *I:* How did you get the sense that's not what he wanted to do?
>
> *Michael:* You could tell he lost interest in what I was saying. And so I
> quickly got that he didn't want to go to any great lengths.... [You can
> tell when the CEO] turns to his computer and he's checking his email.

What leaders pay attention to, or do not pay attention to, are mechanisms for influencing organizational culture (Schein, 1992), here moving the social role expression from Appreciator to Booster. Morever, the invited guests and audience for the anniversary celebration were largely the high-ranking manager's subordinates. Thus, the celebratory ritual associated with presentation of the gift itself served to reproduce shared enthusiasm for the firm and its symbols (Rook, 1985; Trice, 1993; Trice & Beyer, 1984).

Year-end gifts associated with Christmas are also occasions for the expression of boosterism through logo gifts to employees, as reflected in this exchange with Karen:

> *Karen:* Lands' End will come in [as a supplier] with different things
> that have [the firm's] name on it like a big duffel bag. You could get a

bathrobe. You can get a backpack.... All kinds of different things with the [firm's] logo that you could choose....

I: You said all the choices have the [firm's] name. What do you think about that?

Karen: I think that it's self-promotion but if they didn't do it, then I would be surprised. Why wouldn't they? My duffel bag goes with me all over.... It's actually pretty brilliant marketing.

I: Are there people who don't care for it?

Karen: Yeah, there are some people who would rather ... like if they are going to get a towel, they would rather just have a towel and not have the company name on it. Some people feel that way.... Besides the flat out marketing of it, I think their intention is to make everyone feel like they are getting a little Christmas bonus.

Customers, suppliers, and other external stakeholders can also be the target audience. Here, boosterism typically takes the form of generating goodwill in the community, a key component of corporate reputation (Dutton & Dukerich, 1991; Fombrun, 1996). Audrey and her coworkers at all levels—including the factory workers who often are newcomers to the United States—receive a turkey as a gift from the firm each Thanksgiving. Audrey believes that the gift is given primarily to say thank you to the factory workers, through the turkey's monetary value as well its symbolism of American culture. For those who do not wish to take possession of a turkey, Audrey among them, the company makes it possible to donate the turkey to a local branch of a well-known, nationwide charity. The firm's CEO is on that charity's board of directors, and he is recognized for the company's various donations to the charity throughout the year. Thus, gifts to employees can also be seen as a vehicle to either directly or indirectly achieve greater goodwill among important stakeholders outside of the firm (Duncan & Moriarty, 1998; Fombrun, 1996).

Manipulator

The Manipulator social role acknowledges that some gifts are given not to express appreciation for a job well done or boost overall goodwill toward the organization, but to achieve specific work goals such as improved customer satisfaction or reinforced employee loyalty. Audrey sees some requests from her boss to contribute to group gifts as directives rather than a choice and an attempt on his part to be perceived by subordinates as a caring boss via impression management (Goffman, 1959). Karen believes she and her coworkers receive gifts from the firm at holiday time because customers are in the holiday spirit and feeling happy; without gifts from the firm to its employees, customer service representatives would not be matching the emotions of their clients, and customer service would suffer.

Other business objectives include solidifying retention of key customers during employee transitions such as retirement:

> Daniel was the regional supervisor, and when he retired, they had sort of an interesting get-together. Some of the folks referred to it as, "Let's leverage Daniel one more time." What they did is they invited so many of Daniel's customers, so many of his coworkers ... and they had a reception.... It wasn't if you worked at the bank or you reported to Daniel [that determined if you were invited to the reception]—you needed to have acquired one of his customers.... The bank believes that social work is important to our business. The fact is that the bank sort of "took a situation and did one thing ["leverage Daniel one more time"] and had it appear they were doing something else [honor their employee with gifts and a party]. It appeared this was a retirement party for Daniel, and a lot of people who worked at the bank who were not invited assumed that that was what it was. The people who were invited from the bank understood why they were invited, but the interesting part was the people who were not invited from the bank. A lot of those folks did not understand why they weren't invited and in fact, that created some ill will. (DI, Jane)

Along with the intention to smooth the transition for Daniel's clients and the new sales staff, the attention to ritual audience moved this event from an Appreciator context of a job well done to a Manipulator role expression. If Appreciator had been the predominant value to be communicated, those orchestrating this rite of passage would have likely invited people who wished to express appreciation of a job well done, including those the retiree supervised and worked with internally.

Employees' attitudes toward the firm are influenced by their perceptions of the motives that underlie reward systems and other practices such as the conduct of organizational ceremonials and rites (Rousseau, 1997; Trice & Beyer, 1984). Compared to Acknowledger, Appreciator, and Booster social roles, expressing the Manipulator role seems to have strong potential to be viewed negatively because of the contradictions between ideals of the perfect gift (Belk, 1996) and the underlying characteristic of expressing this role. In the latter, the giver seeks to achieve work-related objectives, whereas in the former the gift should be given solely to please the recipient, and should not be given to benefit a third party such as the firm or its customers. Thus, gifts that are received and understood as Manipulators may be suspected of not being pure gifts (Carrier, 1991; Malinowski, 1922) because they carry with them the suspicion of ulterior motives beyond pleasing the recipient. Such gifts and gift situations may elicit mixed or negative emotions (Otnes, Lowrey, & Shrum, 1997; Ruth et al., 2002).

Humanizer

As the United States has shifted toward an information or knowledge economy, employees and their talents have become increasingly important raw materials in the accomplishment of the work of business (Rousseau, 1997). Both givers and recipients express the view that workplace gifts can communicate that the giver sees the recipient not merely as a producer, but as a human being with human qualities and experiences. Even in the face of a tumultuous merger and the dehumanizing aspects of longtime business relationships negated by new management, Jane seeks to communicate with her subordinates in a human, one-to-one way: "It's just more from the standpoint that instead of just looking at me as a boss or supervisor, I think it brings the relationship to a more personal level" (DI, Jane). Recipients also receive the Humanizer meaning, as expressed by Andy, who works in the fast-paced, high employee turnover advertising business:

> They would say, "Be quiet. It's a surprise."... When people weren't looking, they would bring birthday cards around so you could sign them. It was a nice thing. You get away from the hustle and bustle of work everyday to take time out to do things like that. It makes you feel like a person, not a machine.... It seemed they were interested in people as people rather than as employees. (DI, Andy)

The social role of Humanizer may not be expressed in family and friendship settings, because human qualities are taken as a given in those contexts. The Humanizer role emerges in this context because the more instrumental qualities of worker and producer may generally dominate the workplace.

Such expressions of the human qualities of givers and recipients may open up channels of communication and create shared meaning across divisions of hierarchy, work units, and other workplace differences such as gender and age (Deal & Kennedy, 1999). Acknowledging that the giver or recipient coworker is human may also confirm that personal sacrifices are being made to accomplish work goals. Such messages, if successfully transmitted and received, may open up new lines of communication and serve as an investments or a banked resource that can offset past or future demonstrations of negative human qualities, such as errors in judgment or action (Wiseman & Duck 1995).

Changer

In the Changer role, givers seek to express a desire to begin a new type of relationship with the recipient (Sherry, 1983), typically a personal rather than workplace one. Some gifts, particularly those that are the first ones between coworkers, may signal a sense of friendship or romantic interest on the part of the giver (Ruth et al., 1999), as exemplified by this coworker gift-giving situation:

> He [a coworker] saw me admiring four kittens in a hand-woven basket when were at a store together. The kittens were homemade cotton, stuffed in fabric. I liked the item because it reminded me of my boyfriend, who likes kittens a lot. When I visited him [her boyfriend], we even played with the kittens his cat recently had. This other guy, my coworker, had already told me he liked me…. He bought the kittens in a basket for me, and I felt guilty. He didn't know I had a boyfriend…. I got nervous and felt terrible that I hadn't told him sooner. Soon after the gift was given to me, I thanked him and let him know I had a boyfriend. He [then] told me to think of the gift as one from a friend to a friend.

Attempts of one person to change a relationship are inherently risky, because the target of the change attempt may not share the same views about the relationship's trajectory (Duck, 1994). When the recipient does not share the sentiments expressed by the gift, mixed and negative emotions are likely to be elicited in conjunction with a shift toward a weakened or severed relationship (Ruth et al., 1999):

> The coworker and I were to teach a class after work, but across town. We agreed to stop for a burger on the way. While we were eating, he handed me a box and said he appreciated my willingness to work with him on the course. I was immediately embarrassed because there was no need for the gift, and the fact that one was being offered seemed inappropriate. I did not open the gift, but put it aside with a strained, "Thank you." I opened the box later and was flustered and angry as well as embarrassed…. This type of gift [lingerie] was totally out of line. I returned it—to his knowledge, unopened. (CI, Female, age 40)

Consistent with Belk (1979; Belk & Coon, 1993), the more intimate the gift, the more intimate the desired relationship. The workplace adds additional risk in attempting to change the relationship trajectory toward greater intimacy, because business norms typically seek to dampen such relationships and since such giver actions may be construed as workplace harassment (Rotundo, Nguyen, & Sackett, 2001).

Some workplace recipients who are targets of unwanted Changer expressions might elect to merely change the culture of the relationship by such actions as avoiding contact with the giver or relating to the giver in the company of other co-workers. Other situations call for a more direct intervention, even if considered to be a relationship taboo (Baxter & Wilmot, 1984). In the following Changer experience, an intimate gift was given at the workplace, in front of the boss. The recipient reported:

> My boss was not at all pleased with the gift [lingerie]. He thought it extremely inappropriate and was unsure as to how he should deal with the situation. It took a couple of meetings with our supervisor to resolve the situation. I was afraid that something similar might happen again when he [the giver] was alone with me. If he was going to give me that type of gift, he should have done so away from our place of employment. (CI, Female, age 25)

The supervisor's intervention provided "unmistakable clues" that "all was not well" in this coworker relationship and their network of relations with others in the workplace (Wiseman & Duck 1995, p. 63). Indeed, as the recipient noted, the workplace is not considered to be an appropriate context for highly personal and intimate, nonwork-related gifts and their meanings.

TENSIONS IN GIFT EXCHANGE
IN THE WORKPLACE

The interpretation of five new social roles has provided a foundation for examining two hallmark characteristics widely observed in North American friendship and family gift-giving contexts: reciprocity and equipollence. These characteristics are sometimes at odds with rules-of-work, or norms associated with the workplace.

The Tension of Reciprocity Versus Hierarchy Norms
in the Workplace

The gift-giving norm of reciprocity is felt in the workplace to some degree, as has been demonstrated with the generalized reciprocity associated with round-robin Acknowledger gifts, particularly among peers. Reciprocity is clouded, however, with respect to how gift exchange should be handled among nonpeers. For example, some organizations have explicit policies forbidding gifts among bosses and those they supervise because of the appearance of favoritism. One recipient indicated she felt guilty in receiving a gift from her subordinates because there was a policy against such acts and also, in accepting the gift, which she felt was genuinely given without expectation of favors, she "was receiving more than I was giving. I felt I should be giving them each a gift, in return" (Female, age 63).

It appears that downward gifts, from bosses to those they supervise, are more common than upward ones for a variety of reasons. First, Appreciation gifts are common in work settings, and bosses may appreciate the work done by those they supervise. Second, individuals perceived as status subordinates generally carry no expectation of an equivalent return in gift giving (Sherry, 1983). Third, gifts as resources are generally directed toward those with fewer resources (Cheal, 1987, 1988), paralleling the typical wage and resource disparity between bosses and those they supervise.

Upward workplace gifts emerged in two situations: (a) a group gift is given to the superior; and (b) knowingly going against norms, an individual decides to give an upward gift. Regarding the former, Martha indicated the intention of a group expression of appreciation and stated:

> I know it wasn't normal for the girls to give [the boss] a gift, but it's just ridiculous, because he's one of the best-ever bosses. And it's ridiculous for him to buy us something and then we don't buy him anything.... We do buy [the boss] something because he's so great. Get somebody else in here—we won't buy them something! (DI, Martha)

Regarding the latter, impression management attempts directed from subordinates to superiors have been found to affect performance ratings and rewards beyond an individual's actual level of performance (Rousseau, 1997). Because an upward gift may be considered to be such an influence attempt, coworkers may make negative attributions about an individual giver's intentions with an upward gift. Those individuals who do not witness directly but learn of upward gifts can act as a sanctioning audience that shapes meaning in the workplace because of the negative connotations associated with upward gifts (Wayne, Liden, Graf, & Ferris, 1997; Yukl & Falbe, 1990). As one employee put it, "I just don't think it's really appropriate if you do that [give an individual gift to your superior], and your coworkers find out about it, then they will think that you are 'brown-nosing.' That's how it's looked at. 'Oh, she's kissing [the boss's] ass'" (DI, Karen). Because gift giving can be seen in such a light, and to avoid sanctions that come with such attributions (Cialdini et al., 1999), some individual givers attempt to keep such gifts from public view and discussion.

The Tension of Equipollence Versus Personalization in the Workplace

Equipollence norms are also evident in the workplace, where there is an expectation of equivalent gifts for equivalent recipients (Lowrey et al., 1996), as reflected by Karen, who stated, "You can't just give one person a party and then ignore the next person because the person who is ignored feels like crap." In the same way that similar family members should be treated equivalently (see Lowrey et al., forthcoming), there exists a norm that equivalent coworkers should be recognized equivalently. Thus, many givers offer nearly the same gifts to equivalent recipients, as exemplified by this exchange with Jane:

> *Interviewer (I):* Did you like doing that or did you feel like it was a burden?
>
> *Jane (J):* It is a burden ... to find ... different gifts that people will appreciate, that they will use and is fitting to a diverse group of people ... maybe in age, or male or female, whatever the diversity. I always tried to keep the gifts the same.
>
> *I:* You thought it had to be the same?
>
> *J:* Yes, I felt it did. Because if you have five tellers who are doing essentially the same job ... I don't think it would be fair to get one one thing and one another thing unless the difference would be just in the color.
>
> *I:* ... I guess it's hypothetical for someone to say I'm going to spend $5 on everybody but I'm going to get something different for everyone.
>
> *J:* Yeah, but again that leaves the door open to speculation and people thinking in the back of their mind, Well you spent $5 and you got this. But they don't know, "Really, did she spend $5 or did she really spend $10? My co-workers got the $10 gift and mine was only a $5 gift. It looks like there's a difference." It usually makes it easier if you get everyone the same thing and maybe just differentiate by color.

On the other hand, in family and friendship contexts, the desire for personalization means that gifts should be geared to a specific recipient and their tastes (Belk, 1996; Cheal, 1984). However, work relationships are not necessarily close for a variety of reasons, such as differences in gender, age, and cultural background (Deal & Kennedy, 1999), and potentially limited opportunities for sharing personal information (Schein, 1992). This tension between the same—but personalized—gift is difficult for givers to resolve and frequently leads to the expression of the Acknowledger role, rather than something more meaningful.

Several gift selection strategies help to manage equipollence versus personalization demands in the face of adverse conditions. For example, many Acknowledger gift situations satisfy equipollence norms by recognizing each person at one time (e.g., random drawing of names at Christmas) or serially over time (e.g., birthday club). Personalization can be accomplished through creative means. For example, Sarah indicated her pleasure when her coworkers remembered that she does not like cake. The coworkers gave her a birthday "cookie cake" instead, to most closely suit her tastes. Similarly, a retirement cake was a source of great pleasure for a giver, who expended a great deal of effort to decorate the customary retirement cake with the likeness of the retiree. As the giver noted:

> I opened the box to display the cake. There were several favorable comments about the cake's appearance, especially from the recipient.... I enjoyed seeing the delight in the face of the recipient. The recipient was so delighted with the decoration on the cake he didn't cut it. He took pieces off the side, but saved the design. (DI, Male, age 41)

Newly recognized in the workplace setting—but likely to hold in family and friendship settings as well—is the notion of equipollence among givers, where candidate givers who are at the same level may feel pressure to give/not give if their equivalents are giving/not giving. Karen believes equipollence pressures were in place when she declared: "I think she did it because she felt an obligation to do it, because she probably found out that a lot of other managers do [give gifts to subordinates] and she didn't want us to feel left out. I don't think she put any thought into it.... Not to make anybody feel good or feel holiday-ish. She just did it just to do it." Clearly, impression management attempts can fail, reflected in the notion that the manager gave little thought, effort, or attention to personalization in this situation.

CONCLUSION AND FUTURE RESEARCH

As the previous interpretation reflects, gifts are given between coworkers of all sorts, including the firm to employees, bosses and those they supervise, and employee peers. Gifts in the workplace are largely contextualized by a social exchange framework (Belk & Coon, 1993; Cheal, 1988; Rousseau, 1997), where reciprocity may be expressed in the form of direct work performance, an immediate or delayed nonwork gift in return, or a more generalized form of reciprocity through participation in similar gift-giving occasions in the future (Sahlins, 1972). Further, workplace givers and recipients indicate a desire for three characteristics that shape gift giving in general: personalization, voluntary participation, and surprise. In opposition to these perfect gift characteristics (Belk, 1996), however, are the characteristics of many workplaces: networks of people who share work but perhaps little else that may be useful in personalizing gifts, and the presence of normative pressures guiding all sorts of work-related behaviors, including whether or not to participate in gift giving (Cialdini, et al. 1999). Viewed from this perspective, work gifts are seen as having the potential to make the environment more pleasant but can also be associated with mixed emotions, including negative feelings associated with obligation, burden, and uncertainty (Ruth, 1996; Ruth et al., 2002; Sherry, McGrath, & Levy, 1993; Wooten, 2000). Thus, although gift giving in the workplace may facilitate the accomplishment of many positive interpersonal and organizational outcomes, (e.g., building teamwork and making the workplace more pleasant through breaks from work routines), workplace gift giving also has the potential to create ambivalence and tensions as norms of equipollence, reciprocity, hierarchical and peer relationships, and the workplace in general come into play.

Seven social roles emerged in conjunction with gifts in the workplace: Acknowledger, Avoider, Appreciator, Booster, Manipulator, Humanizer, and Changer roles. It appears that Avoider and Changer roles place greater emphasis on personal considerations rather than workplace ones. That is, Avoiders place higher priority on their own desires to not give, than on any pressures exerted in the workplace to participate in, or conform to, giving efforts. Similarly, Changers give greater weight to personal considerations, as they attempt to use gifts to establish more intimate rather than workplace relationships with coworkers, even in the face of norms against such moves. In contrast to the Avoider and Changer roles, Boosters and Manipulators place greater weight on work compared to personal goals when gifts are used to promote organizational goodwill or achieve business goals such as retention of key customers. Whereas the Appreciator role emerged in the workplace setting and may indeed underlie much of interpersonal gift giving in the sense that the giver "appreciates" the interpersonal relationship with the recipient, the Humanizer role appears to have meaning only in a work-related setting because family and friends acknowledge the human, subjective, and interpersonal qualities of one another by the very nature of their relationships. That is, interpersonal gifts that signal "I am a human being" and "I see you as a human being" may be entirely redundant with everyday, interpersonal relationships, and may be unnecessary. In contrast, the overall culture of work, where employees are seen as resources to be deployed, may constitute a dehumanized environment, to one degree or another. As a result, human and humane symbolic communications may be welcomed in the workplace, particularly at times when gift giving is pervasive in the culture (e.g., Christmas).

Although the overall culture of work fosters the expression of some social roles, a particular organization's culture may also affect a whole host of activities (Schein, 1992), including coworker gift practices. Audrey, who works for a large, well-known, successful Japanese firm with many facilities in the United States, explained, the firm is hierarchical and formal to the point that "we have cube etiquette policies here [explicit, formal policies about how work cubicles can be decorated].... Our corporate services unit monitors cube decorating. Gifts in her workplace are rarely accompanied by food, parties, and casual behavior. In contrast, Sarah works for a very small, privately and informally run firm. All of her coworkers are women who are "close knit" and "know everybody's business all the time." For example, Sarah and her coworkers had a "farewell-to-her-uterus" party on the occasion of a coworker's hysterectomy. Gift exchange in Sarah's work environment is frequent, informal, and oftentimes has a joking quality that is not likely to be replicated in more formal, hierarchical organizations with greater coworker diversity.

Moreover, although each firm may have an overall culture affecting workplace behavior, it is also well known that organizations also have subcultures comprised of smaller informal or formal groups that share certain beliefs (Schein, 1992; Trice, 1993). Gift practices that occur in one subcultural group (e.g., upper management) may not be present in another group (e.g., those on the factory floor). It may be possible that the sphere of gift giving or its ritual audience maps to whether the norms of the organizational culture or subculture predominate.

Evidence has been provided on the influence of the culture of work overall, a particular organization, and or a particular subculture with an organization, and it is also very likely that workplace gift giving can profoundly affect the organization itself. Because gift-giving rituals are formed and reformed with each performance, they can restate what is "true" about people and the organization. Because gifts in the workplace are often offered in conjunction with elaborate rites and ceremonies (Trice & Beyer, 1984), much about an organization's culture is revealed through the snapshot of such occasions and activities. The availability of benefits and employee perceptions of an organization's standing contribute to employee commitment (Rousseau, 1997). Indeed, in the decline or absence of gift-giving rituals, employees may feel a commensurate dilution of regard for, and adherence to, the firm and its prospects:

> Slowly, as our financial results came out and became worse and worse, all those things [gifts and parties given by the firm] started to be taken away. They just cut every corner they possibly could…. The holiday party … usually they have a big fancy dinner, everyone gets dressed up, people look forward to it. In the last year, they had it in the conference room and I think they ordered pizza or something like that. They took away all these little things but it added up to a lot of disappointment and people feeling uncomfortable about working there…. It's human nature, I think, that when you work really hard, that you will be treated well. People worked really hard and they were still getting treated like crap…. But in my new job, we just had a birthday party for three people who were having their birthday this week, and everyone came into the conference room and it was a big surprise…. It makes for a much happier environment. (DI, Andy)

Employees infer qualities about the firm through changed social roles of gift giving (i.e., for this worker's first employer, moving from Pleaser/Acknowledger to Avoider). Lack of rituals and accompanying artifacts can serve as cultural symbols of corporate decline and may be associated with other negative workplace outcomes such as lowered morale and reduced loyalty (Trice, 1993).

Future Research

Many areas of future research on gift giving are suggested by this investigation. For example, consistent with gender differences observed in family and friendship settings (Fischer & Arnold, 1990; Otnes, Ruth, & Milbourne, 1994), future research should examine the roles of men and women in ceremonies and rituals in the workplace. Jane indicated that the men in her workplace would not be likely to initiate or organize workplace parties and gift occasions, but if contributions were requested, the men are included and they give. She further volunteered that because food typically accompanies such workplace ceremonials, instead of bringing in a food dish the men will contribute money to a meat platter. These comments, and others, reflect the possibility that women may orchestrate—by desire, ability, assignment, or default—a disproportionate amount of gift activities in the workplace, much like their labor of love in orchestrating gifts among family and friends (Fischer & Arnold, 1990). Alternatively, it may be possible that men seek to be more active givers in the workplace rather than the homeplace because of their attention to achievement orientation in work settings. Because gender was not the focus of this research, it was not possible to determine if differences exist between men and women in their participation in workplace gifting. If differences were observed, it would be important to understand whether they are due gift-giving expertise, workplace roles and responsibilities, or socialization regarding relationships in general.

Moreover, cross-cultural investigations of gifts in family and friendship contexts have yielded important insights into boundary conditions and generalizability of underlying concepts (see Joy, 2001). Some research has shown that Koreans participate more than Americans in workplace gift activities (Park, 1998), suggesting the potential insights to be gained from cross-cultural research in this area. Comparable investigations of workplace givers and recipients in a variety of cultures would also be expected to uncover important insights, because corporate culture and norms are known to vary widely across country cultures (e.g., Japan; Ouchi, 1981).

Future research should examine thoroughly the distinction between individual versus collective gifts in the workplace. Gifts given by a group of coworkers appear to be prevalent, but it is unclear how a sense of the group emerges and how such group gifting efforts are accomplished. Perhaps in addition to social roles, coworkers may adapt organizational buying tasks (e.g., gatekeeper, influencer, and purchaser) to gift-giving tasks in the organizational context (e.g., contributors, purchasers, organizers, etc.). Further research into the formation of group identity and performance roles within the gift-giving group will yield fresh insights into the multifaceted nature of gift giving in the workplace (see Wooten & Wood, this volume).

More broadly, neither consumer researchers nor organizational behavior scholars have paid sufficient attention to the ways people utilize products and services to accomplish work objectives rather than personal or family ones. Given the time and attention people in this culture allocate to work, consumer researchers may be overlooking one of the most influential contextual factors shaping micro- and macrolevel consumption decisions and activities. Whereas this research seeks to examine a specific intersection of consumption and work life—namely, gift giving in the workplace—the broader question of how individuals use products and services to facilitate participation and achievement in work life remains a fruitful area of research to be plumbed.

ACKNOWLEDGMENTS

The author thanks Cele Otnes, John F. Sherry, Jr. and David Wooten for comments on an earlier version of this chapter.

APPENDIX A:
DESCRIPTION OF DEPTH INTERVIEW
INFORMANTS

Sylvia   is a married woman in her early sixties who did not attend college. She recently retired from a large organization (more than 10,000 employees) after working there for 25 years, most recently as an executive assistant to a high-level manager. Sylvia was highly respected by her boss and work colleagues. At the time of the interview, she had recently retired, and she and her husband had moved from the suburban community where they raised their children to a retirement community.

Martha   is a married woman in her mid-fifties who did not attend college. She lives in a small town near a large metropolitan area, and her children and grandchildren live nearby. Because of her personal work ethic, experience in the organization (20 years), engaging personality, and role as administrative assistant, she is widely viewed by bosses and coworkers as indispensable to all workplace activities. She is the social "glue" in her work unit.

Michael   is a 50-year-old married father of one teenage daughter. He has spent his entire work life with his firm (25 years), steadily working his way up the organizational hierarchy. He now oversees the day-to-day management of numerous, diverse work units and employees (about 100). He is gregarious and important to the organization because of his relationship-building efforts, both internally and externally. He earned a graduate degree and lives in the suburbs of a major metropolitan area.

Jane   is a 45-year-old married woman with an elementary school-age daughter. Jane obtained an associate's degree and lives and works in a city of

50,000 residents. She began her career as a bank teller and steadily worked her way up to assistant vice president of a small, regional bank, where she has worked for 27 years.

Audrey   is a 30-year-old single woman who works for a large, well-known Japanese firm. She has worked for the firm for 4 years, and was recently promoted to her current position as promotions manager. She recently completed an advanced degree in business management. She lives and works in the suburbs of a large metropolitan city.

Karen   is a 28-year-old single woman. She does systems and marketing customer service work at a large corporation, where she has worked for 6 years. She recently completed a part-time advanced degree program, and seeks to increase her salary as a result. She lives with her brother, whom she considers to be her best friend, and works in the suburbs of a large metropolitan city.

Andy   is a 24-year-old man. He recently moved from the West Coast to the East Coast to gain entry into the advertising business and also to be nearer to his girlfriend. He began his advertising career with a large, well-known advertising agency, and then was laid off after the agency lost a key business account. He rebounded with a higher level job in a new agency that serviced dot.com businesses, and was again laid off as the dot.com business environment declined in spring 2001. At the time of the interview, he was as assistant account executive for a medium-sized advertising agency in a large metropolitan city and was engaged to be married.

Sarah   is a 23-year-old single woman. She is office manager of a privately owned hair salon. She has been working full time at the salon for 4 years while completing her undergraduate degree. She lives at home with her mother in a suburban community and is very family oriented.

REFERENCES

Baxter, L., & Wilmot, W. (1984). Secret tests: Social strategies for acquiring information about the state of the relationship. *Human Communication Research, 18*(March), 336–363.

Belk, R. (1976). It's the thought that counts: A signed diagraph analysis of gift giving. *Journal of Consumer Research, 3*(December), 155–162.

Belk, R. (1979). Gift giving behavior. In J. Sheth (Ed.), *Research in marketing* (Vol. 2, 95–126). Greenwich, CT: JAI Press.

Belk, R. (1996). The perfect gift. In C. Otnes & R. Beltramini (Eds.), *Gift giving: A research anthology* (pp. 59–84). Bowling Green, OH: Bowling Green University Press.

Belk, R., & Coon, G. (1993). Gift giving as agapic love: An alternative to the exchange paradigm based on dating experiences. *Journal of Consumer Research, 20*(December), 393–417.

Beltramini, R. (1992). Exploring the effectiveness of business gifts: A controlled field experiment. *Journal of the Academy of Marketing Sciences, 20*(1), 87–91.

Beltramini, R. (1996). Business believes in gift giving. In C. Otnes & R. Beltramini (Eds.), *Gift giving: A research anthology* (pp. 163–173). Bowling Green, OH: Bowling Green University Press.

Carrier, J. (1991). Gifts in a world of commodities in America: The ideology of the perfect gift in American society. *Social Analysis, 29*, 19–37.

Cheal, D. (1984). Rule enforcement without visible means: Christmas gift giving in Middletown. *American Journal of Sociology, 94*(Suppl.), S180–S214.

Cheal, D. (1987). Showing them you love them: Gift giving and the dialectic of intimacy. *Sociological Review, 35*(February), 150–169.

Cheal, D. (1988). *The gift economy.* New York: Routledge & Kegan Paul.

Cialdini, R., Bator, R., & Guadagno, R. (1999). Normative influences in organizations. In L. Thompson & J. Levine (Eds.), *Shared cognition in organizations: The management of knowledge* (pp. 195–211). Hillsdale, NJ: Lawrence Erlbaum Associates.

Deal, T., & Kennedy, A. (1999). *The new corporate cultures.* Reading, MA: Perseus.

Dorsch, M., & Kelley, S. (1994). An investigation into the intentions of purchasing executives to reciprocate vendor gifts. *Journal of the Academy of Marketing Science, 22*, 315–327.

Dorsch, M., Grove, S., Pickett, G., & Kelley, S. (1997). Responses to gift-giving in a business context: An empirical examination. *Psychological Reports, 81*(3, P1), 947–955.

Duck, S. (1994). Steady as (s)he goes: Relational maintenance as a shared meaning system. In D. Stafford & L. Stafford (Eds.), *Communication and relational maintenance* (pp. 45–60). New York: Academic Press.

Duck, S., West, L., & Acitelli, L. (1997). Sewing the field: The tapestry of relationships in life and research. In S. Duck (Ed.), *Handbook of Personal Relationships* (pp. 10–23). New York: Wiley.

Duncan, T., & Moriarty, S. (1998). A communication-based marketing model for managing relationships. *Journal of Marketing, 62*(April), 1–13.

Dutton, J., & Dukerich, J. (1991). Keeping an eye on the mirror: Image and identity in organizational adaption. *Academy of Management Journal, 34*(3), 517–554.

Fischer, E., & Arnold, S. (1990). More than a labor of love: Gender roles and Christmas gift shopping. *Journal of Consumer Research, 17*(December), 333–345.

Fombrun, C. (1996). *Reputation: Realizing value for the corporate image.* Cambridge, MA: Harvard Business School Press.

Gilly, M., & Wolfinbarger, M. (1998). Advertising's internal audience. *Journal of Marketing, 62*, 69–88.

Goffman, E. (1959). *The presentation of self in everyday life.* New York: Anchor.

Gouldner, A. (1960). The norm of reciprocity: A preliminary statement. *American Sociological Review, 25*, 161–178.

Joy, A. (2001). Gift giving in Hong Kong and the continuum of social ties. *Journal of Consumer Research, 28*(2), 239–256.

Lawler, E., Yoon, J., Baker, M., & Large, M. (1995). Mutual dependence and gift giving in exchange relations. *Advances in Group Processes, 12*, 271–298.

Lowrey, T. M., Otnes, C., & Robbins, K. (1996). Values influencing Christmas gift giving: An interpretive study. In C. Otnes & R. Beltramini (Eds.), *Gift giving: A research anthology* (pp. 37–56). Bowling Green, OH: Bowling Green University Press.

Lowrey, T. M., Otnes, C., & Ruth, J. (forthcoming). Extradyadic effects in gift giving: A social networks perspective. *Journal of Consumer Research.*

Malinowski, B. (1922). *Argonants of the western Pacific.* London: Routledge & Kegan Paul.

Manning, K. (2000). *Rituals, ceremonies, and cultural meaning in higher education.* Westport, CT: Bergin & Gervin.

Mauss, M. (1954). *The gift.* London: Cohen & West.

McCracken, G. (1988). *The long interview.* Newbury Park, CA: Sage.

O'Reilly, C., III, Chatman, J., & Caldwell, D. (1991). People and organizational culture: A profile comparison approach to assessing person-organization fit. *Academy of Management Journal, 34*(3), 487–516.

Otnes, C., Lowrey, T. M., & Kim, Y. (1993). Gift selection for easy and difficult recipients: A social roles interpretation. *Journal of Consumer Research, 20*(December), 229–244.

Otnes, C., Lowrey, T. M., & Shrum, L. J. (1997). Toward an understanding of consumer ambivalence. *Journal of Consumer Research, 24*(June), 80–93.

Otnes, C., Ruth, J., & Milbourne, C. (1994). The pleasure and pain of being close: Men's mixed feelings about participation in Valentine's day gift exchange. In C. Allen & D. Roedder John (Eds.), *Advances in consumer research* (pp. 159–164). Provo, UT: Association for Consumer Research.

Ouchi, W. (1981). *Theory Z: How American business can meet the Japanese challenge.* New York: Avon.

Park, S. (1998). A comparison of Korean and American gift-giving behaviors. *Psychology & Marketing, 15*(6), 577–593.

Rook, D. (1985). The ritual dimension of consumer behavior. *Journal of Consumer Research, 12*(December), 251–264.

Rotundo, M., Nguyen, D., & Sackett, P. (2001). A meta-analytic review of gender differences in perceptions of sexual harassment. *Journal of Applied Psychology, 86*(5), 914–922.

Rousseau, D. M. (1997). Organizational behavior in the new organizational era. *Annual Review of Psychology, 48,* 515–546.

Ruth, J. (1996). It's the feeling this counts: Toward a framework for understanding emotion and its influence on gift-exchange processes. In C. Otnes & R. Beltramini (Eds.), *Gift giving: A research anthology* (pp. 195–214). Bowling Green, OH: Bowling Green University Press.

Ruth, J., Brunel, F., & Otnes, C. (2002). Linking thoughts to feelings: Investigating cognitive appraisals and consumption emotions in a mixed emotions context. *Journal of the Academy of Marketing Science, 30*(2) 44–58.

Ruth, J., Otnes, C., & Brunel, F. (1999). Gift receipt and the reformulation of interpersonal relationships. *Journal of Consumer Research, 25*(March), 385–402.

Sahlins, M. (1972). *Stone age economics.* New York: Aldine.

Schein, E. (1992). *Organization culture and leadership.* San Francisco: Jossey-Bass.

Sherry, J., Jr. (1983). Gift-giving in anthropological perspective. *Journal of Consumer Research, 10*(September), 157–168.

Sherry, J., Jr., McGrath, M., & Levy, S. (1993). The dark side of the gift. *Journal of Business Research, 28,* 225–244.

Trice, H. (1993). *Occupational subcultures in the workplace.* Ithaca, NY: Industrial and Labor Relations Press of Cornell University.

Trice, H., & Beyer, J. (1984). Studying organizational cultures through rites and ceremonials. *Academy of Management Review, 9*(4), 653–669.

van Gennep, A. (1960). *The rites of passage.* M. B. Vizedom & G. L. Caffee (Trans.). London: Routledge & Kegan Paul.

Wayne, S., Liden, R., Graf, I., & Ferris, G. (1997). The role of upward influence tactics in human resource decisions. *Personnel Psychology, 50,* 979–1006.

Wiseman, J., & Duck, S. (1995). Having and managing enemies: A very challenging relationship. In S. Duck & J. Wood (Eds.), *Confronting relationship challenges* (pp. 43–72). Thousand Oaks, CA: Sage.

Wooten, D. (2000). Qualitative steps toward an expanded model of anxiety in gift giving. *Journal of Consumer Research, 27*(1), 84–95.

Yukl, G., & Falbe, C. (1990). Influence tactics and objectives in upward, downward, and lateral influence attempts. *Journal of Applied Psychology, 75*(2), 132–141.

10

In the Spotlight:
The Drama of Gift Reception

David B. Wooten
University of Michigan

Stacy L. Wood
University of South Carolina

Gift exchange is a consumption ritual of great economic (e.g., Camerer, 1988), social (e.g., Cheal, 1987), and psychological significance (e.g., Neisser, 1973). Although the form and functions of these rituals vary across the occasions and cultures they span, some aspects are common across gift exchange rituals (Green & Alden, 1988). For instance, with few exceptions (e.g., Mick & DeMoss, 1990; Sherry, McGrath, & Levy, 1995), gift rituals involve giver and recipient as primary performance roles. The two principal cast members have freedom to choose how they enact their roles, but ritual scripts cue them to incorporate certain acts and props into their performances.

Although givers and recipients are coperformers in gift exchange rituals, they rarely receive equal billing in the literature. For instance, recent studies have explored motives that influence how givers enact their roles (e.g., Otnes, Lowrey, & Kim, 1993) and factors that make them agonize over their performances (Wooten, 2000). In contrast, researchers have paid little attention to the performance of gift reception (Sherry, 1996). This inattention is surprising given the excessive attention paid by givers, especially as recipients unwrap and respond to their gifts (Schwartz, 1967). Recipients' performances are part of the interaction ritual that occurs after gifts are presented (Sherry, 1983). Moreover, gift receipt experiences shape and reflect relationships between givers and recipients (Ruth, Otnes, & Brunel, 1999). These insights suggest that greater knowledge of gift reception can provide a deeper understanding of gift exchange rituals.

This chapter addresses a gap in the gift-giving literature by exploring the ritual behaviors of gift recipients. Gift recipients were interviewed, their public reactions to gifts were observed, and their written expressions of gratitude were analyzed in order to understand their internal scripts and expressive behaviors. Because recipients' behaviors influence the affective outcomes experienced by givers (Sherry, 1983), a dramaturgical analysis of their ritual role performances is warranted. The goal of this chapter is to complement insights from recent examinations of gift reception (e.g., Pieters & Robben, 1998; Ruth et al., 1999) by shedding light on how gift reception rituals are performed.

ON THE RECEIVING END

Although few studies have focused specifically on gift recipients, examinations of gift exchange, in general, may help to illuminate important aspects of gift reception. For instance, descriptive models of gift exchange processes (e.g., Banks, 1979) have offered insights about recipients' behaviors, motives, and emotions. Recipient involvement is evident in each of Sherry's (1983) three stages of the gift exchange process.

The *gestation stage* includes activities antecedent to the actual exchange (Sherry, 1983) and can be filled with suspense and anticipation (Banks, 1979). Opportunistic recipients elicit gifts from prospective givers (Sherry, 1983). They drop hints (Banks, 1979) and use registries (Chen, 1997) to influence gift choices. Savvy retailers encourage recipients to elicit gifts in order to minimize disappointment among recipients and anxiety among givers. Sears distributes its "Wish Book" toy catalog in time for kids to construct wish lists for Santa. Would-be recipients can even register online at Wishbook.com. Benefits to retailers include fewer items returned and increased store traffic. Critics argue that elicitation threatens sacred elements of gift rituals (Schor, 1998), like the pretense of gift giving as an act of altruism (Belk, 1993) and the suspense that sustains the joys of receiving (Hagerty, 1998; Harris, 1972).

The *prestation stage* involves the actual exchange (Sherry, 1983). During prestation, recipients unwrap and interpret gifts. Cultural norms dictate where (e.g., Green & Alden, 1988) and how (e.g., Searle-Chatterjee, 1993) gifts should be unwrapped. Recipients' appraisals of gifts depend on the gifts, occasions, and relationship between exchange partners (Pieters & Robben, 1998). However, recipients' public reactions do not always reflect their private appraisals (Sherry, 1983). Mauss (1954) argued that recipients must accept gifts, praise them, and eventually repay givers. Intervals between reciprocal exchanges constitute periods of indebtedness that shift back and forth between exchange partners. The balance of debt sustains relationships by creating mutual feelings of gratitude (Schwartz, 1967). Although repayment is expected, it is usually deferred in order to sustain the illusion that reciprocal acts of giving are voluntary (Bourdieu, 1994). Meanwhile, recipients are expected to show indebtedness to givers. These expressions of gratitude are central to the interaction ritual that occurs during prestation.

Reformulation is the final stage of gift exchange, during which a newly presented gift can both affect and reflect the relationship between giver and recipient (Ruth et al., 1999; Sherry, 1983). Communication and consumption are focal activities at this stage (Banks, 1979). Thank you cards are common communication channels. They confirm receipt when time or distance separates offer and acceptance, they convey initial reactions when givers are not present to witness unwrapping, and they reinforce initial appraisals. Givers discount these obligatory verbal expressions of gratitude and monitor actual behaviors for hidden truths about recipients' feelings, and recipients respond by displaying gifts strategically (Banks, 1979).

Consumption offers evidence of appreciation. Regular use or display implies liking while premature storage or disposal implies disregard. Recipients forfeit property rights when they accept gifts (Sherry, McGrath, & Levy, 1992). Acceptance implies consumption and retention, especially of nonperishable items, so gifts cannot be discarded as easily as nongift possessions. Returning items to stores or redistributing them as gifts for others creates discomforts for both exchange participants (Sherry et al., 1992). Exceptions are granted for poorly fitting articles of clothing (Rucker et al., 1991).

This review has summarized descriptive insights and empirical findings about recipient behavior. Empirical efforts have focused on issues relevant to the reformulation stage, but few have explored recipient behavior earlier in the process. Recipients' efforts to guide gift selections during gestation and sustain gaiety during prestation are important acts in their ritual performances. These behaviors influence givers' impressions of gifts, recipients, and relationships and, therefore, lend themselves to dramaturgical analysis with its focus on creating and sustaining desired impressions.

DRAMATURGY AND RITUAL BEHAVIOR

The dramaturgical perspective argues that social scripts and impression management influence social behavior (Goffman, 1959). Dramaturgical analysts view social life as theater with social interactions as performances featuring actors, roles, scripts, settings, costumes, and props. Some (e.g., Messinger, Sampson, & Towne, 1962) argue that the perspective is only a metaphor for social life (i.e., life is *like* theater), and others (e.g., MacCannell, 1973) favor a literal interpretation (i.e., life *is* theater). Critics argue that life is not theater, nor is it like theater. Equating the two obscures crucial differences between reality and fiction (Wilshire, 1982). This discussion shares the perspective of Goffman (1959) and others (e.g., Brissett & Edgley, 1990; Overington & Mangham, 1982), who view the dramaturgical model as a useful analytic device to shed light on social behaviors that are contextually bounded, expressive, and ritualistic.

Rook (1985) utilized the dramaturgical metaphor to illuminate the ritual dimensions of consumption. In particular, he identified ritual artifacts (e.g., greeting cards and gifts), scripts, performance roles, and audiences as important elements of ritual experience. His framework addressed consumption rituals, in general. This chapter examines an understudied aspect of a specific ritual—gift giving. It uses the dramaturgical metaphor to enhance understanding of the expressive and ritualistic behaviors of a key performer in this ritual—the gift recipient.

METHODS

The analysis here is based on data obtained from multiple sources. The study conducted 19 semi-structured interviews focusing on givers' expectations of recipients and recipients' thoughts, feelings, and behaviors when they expect and receive gifts (prerecipient data). These interviews served three purposes. First, aided discovery of the mental scripts that guide recipients' behaviors throughout the gift exchange process. Second, they facilitated an understanding of how givers' expectations shape recipients' performances. Third, they enabled the indentificaiton of additional data needs.

Gift presentations were videotaped at seven baby showers (Shower data). These data enabled observation of recipients' actual behaviors during the prestation stage. Based on preliminary interviews, researchers collected thank you cards from family members, friends, and colleagues (Card data). Respondents in the preliminary interviews identified thank you cards as important ritual artifacts that enhance recipients' performances during the reformulation stage. The study also recorded stories told by acquaintances after they discovered the focus of the research (Story data). Based on insights from these stories and gaps in existing data, supplementary interviews were conducted to obtain additional stories highlighting recipients' behaviors during the gestation and reformulation stages of the process (Postrecipient data). Table 10.1 contains detailed information about the data.

An emergent design and multimethod approach are evident in Table 10.1. For instance, thank you cards were collected after preliminary interviews revealed a need for them and supplementary interviews were conducted to fill gaps not addressed by our other data sets. The multiple method approach yielded complementary data sets that enabled researchers to offset limitations associated with each individual data set. Overall, the data include actual and self-reported behavior, public and private reactions to gifts, adlibbed and scripted responses from recipients, and stories relevant to multiple stages of the process.

TABLE 10.1
Data Sources and Uses

Dates	Data Sources	Uses	Description
12/96–11/97	Videotaped baby showers (Shower)	To observe recipients' behaviors in natural settings, especially the impromptu expressive behaviors they perform as they open gifts and offer initial expressions of gratitude.	We videotaped the gift presentation segments of 7 baby showers. There were 119 reactions by 13 recipients (4 showers were co-ed and 2 grandmothers received gifts). We recorded actions and words of actors and salient audience members. We described audience composition and physical settings in field notes. We interviewed the videographer immediately after the two showers not attended by either author.
1/97–2/97	Preliminary interviews (Pre)	To explore givers' expectations of recipients, examine recipients' self-reported concerns and behaviors throughout the process, and determine additional data needs.	We conducted 19 interviews with 20 university employees (13 women, 5 men, and 1 married couple). Each semistructured interview was conducted and recorded on campus. We employed member checking by returning interview transcripts to interviewees and discussing our interpretations with them.

(continued)

TABLE 10.1
(continued)

Dates	Data Sources	Uses	Description
2/97–7/99	Thank you cards (Card)	To observe actual reactions, especially the carefully scripted ones conveyed through private communications.	We collected thank you cards from family members, friends, and coworkers. In addition, we photocopied thank you cards that were posted on departmental bulletin boards throughout the business school. Overall, we collected and analyzed 107 cards from males, females, children, and adults.
6/99	Stories obtained via conversations (Story)	To highlight concerns and behaviors that were not addressed by other data sets.	Three female associates or acquaintances expressed interest in the research and offered stories about their experiences. We later contacted them by phone and asked permission to audiorecord their stories.
2/01	Supplementary interviews (Post)	To obtain stories about recipients' gift receipt experiences, especially during gestation and reformulation.	We interviewed 16 university employees (13 women and 3 men) on campus and audiorecorded each semistructured interview. We accomplished member checking through follow-up interviews with a subset of informants.

ANALYSIS

Acts of Gift Reception

Literature and data were synthesized to identify four important acts of gift reception. Acts are segments of performances separated by lapses of time and differentiated by changes of actors, scenes, or actable ideas (Hare & Blumberg, 1988). Recipients convey gift expectations to prospective givers (elicitation), open gift packages (revelation), provide evaluative information (reaction), and use, store, or discard gifts (consumption). The pretexts, region dynamics, audience roles, and performance pressures are identified as important aspects of these acts.

In theatrical contexts, dramatists refer to written scripts as pretexts and actual performances as texts of dramas (Hare & Blumberg, 1988). In social contexts, Lyman and Scott (1975) considered actors' expectations about appropriate role performances as pretexts for social interaction. Pretexts shape performances, but do not necessarily determine them. Social actors make and evaluate performances based on samplings of past performances, reciprocal actors' performances, and expected behavior in the chosen setting (Allen & Scheibe, 1982). In gift reception contexts, many recipients are aware of behavioral guidelines, but difficult recipients often deviate from them (Otnes et al., 1993).

Region dynamics refers to actors' tendencies to alter their behaviors across regions (Tewksbury, 1994). Goffman (1959) differentiated among front-, back-, and offstage regions. Frontstage regions are places where performances are presented for audience consumption (Tewksbury, 1994). Backstage regions are devoted to preparing frontstage performances. These regions are places where the impressions fostered by performances are knowingly contradicted (Goffman, 1959). For instance, a gift recipient who receives a new outfit may leave the room to try it on for the giver. She is backstage while she changes her clothing, poses, or assesses its style and fit privately, but she is in a frontstage region as soon as she and the garment are on display before the giver. Offstage regions are removed physically, temporally, or behaviorally from frontstage performances (Tewksbury, 1994). The hypothetical recipient is offstage (as a recipient of the outfit) when she, the giver, and others are not attending to the evaluative implications of her talk and use of the garment. Recipients may not be aware of being onstage and may not be able to prepare backstage.

Audiences validate role enactments, cue appropriate behaviors, provide social reinforcement, and contribute to role maintenance over time (Sarbin & Allen, 1968). In the context of gift reception, givers fulfill these functions as coperformers and audience members. Their audience role becomes more salient after the tasks of selecting gifts and preparing them for presentation are accomplished. Goffman (1974) distinguished between theatergoers and onlookers as roles of audience members. These roles reflect different levels of preoccupation with on- and offstage activities. Theatergoers attend to offstage activities (e.g., buying tickets and breaking for intermissions). These audience members are critical viewers who look for flaws in performances or other cues that behaviors are contrived. Onlookers are engaged in the performance. These audience members ignore offstage factors that prevent them from being taken in by a performance. In the context of gift giving, theatergoers might think about the time and money invested in the gift as they await the recipients' reaction. Consequently, the giver may expect the reaction to be commensurate with the investment in the gift. An onlooker, on the other hand, focuses primarily on the recipient's reaction and accepts it at face value. The role that audience members favor varies during and across acts and performances.

Performance pressures are often influenced by audience factors (Latane, 1981). The presence of others prompts dramaturgical awareness (Brissett & Edgley, 1990) and self-presentational concerns (Goffman, 1959), especially when interpersonal evaluation is salient and social consequences are high (Schlenker & Leary, 1982). Feelings of being watched and evaluated, and attention to one's expressive behaviors and their relational consequences are characteristic of gift reception. Table 10.2 summarizes the four acts of reception in terms of the dramaturgical concepts discussed earlier.

Table 10.2 summarizes each act in its prototypical form. However, recipients omit or alter the performance of certain acts. Characteristics of gifts, recipients, occasions, and relationships between partners often shape these performances. For instance, recipients may not perform expressive behaviors that are viewed as "out of character" for them (i.e., inconsistent with their personalities). In addition, recipients who have not been socialized (e.g., children) or have been socialized in a different cultural context may deviate from the script suggested in Table 10.2.

Recipients' performances are also shaped by the gifts they receive. For instance, rules of etiquette call for rejecting inappropriate gifts (Post, 1992). If not, recipients accept the obligations and identities implied by the gifts (Belk & Coon, 1993; Schwartz, 1967). In addition, the perceived sacrifice reflected in gifts influences the way recipients perceive and react to gifts. Sacrifice is a function of the time, effort, and money that one gives up for the sake of another (Katz, 1976). Substantial sacrifice is viewed as a sign of love and a characteristic of the perfect gift (Belk, 1996), whereas minimal sacrifice is taken as a sign of indifference (Belk & Coon, 1993). The data also suggest that elaborate packaging affects recipients' performances during acts of revelation and reaction.

The literature and data suggest that relationships between exchange partners also shape performances by recipients. Characteristics of relationships both reflect and affect the experience of gift reception (Ruth et al., 1999). It was found that the duration, distance, and nature of relationships do influence whether and how certain acts are performed. For instance, recipients are less tentative about eliciting gifts from family members than from distant relatives or new romantic partners. Expectations about thank you cards also depend on the relationship between exchange partners. Moreover, opportunities for the

TABLE 10.2
Acts of Gift Reception

Acts	Stage	Pre-text	Region Dynamics	Audience Roles	Performance Pressures
Elicitation	Gestation	Recipients attempt to convey gift expectations while trying to avoid negative attributions.	Front stage with varying back stage preparation. The line between on and off stage can be unclear.	Theatergoer. Givers watch recipients for gift ideas and they do the "business" of gift shopping.	Low to moderate depending on elicitation mode, gift occasion, and familiarity with givers. Plus there are opportunities to rehearse.
Revelation	Prestation	Recipients show gratitude for gifts and eagerness to open them.	Mostly a front stage activity in western cultures.	Onlooker. Givers look for signs of anticipation and appreciation.	Low to moderate depending on whether givers are present to witness unwrapping.
Reaction	Prestation to reformulation	Recipients express appreciation for gift and giver.	Initial reactions are adlibbed, but thank you cards allow back stage practice.	Theatergoer. Watches recipient to (in)validate role enactments.	High. Recipients' reactions are crucial and their relationships with givers can be affected.
Consumption	Reformulation	Recipients show that gifts are valued objects by using them as givers intended.	Recipients are onstage initially, but it is unclear when they are finally off stage.	Onlooker. Givers tend to view consumption as reality, not as a performance	Moderate to high. Givers infer liking from usage. So it may be necessary for recipients to use or display gifts strategically.

221

strategic display of gifts increases with the psychological and physical distance between exchange partners.

Finally, the gift occasion influences the performance of gift reception. For instance, elicitation tends to be more formalized for highly ritualized gift occasions (e.g., weddings, showers, and Christmas). However, formal modes of elicitation (e.g., gift registries) have been used for other gift occasions (Chen, 1997). Occasions involving mutual giving or large audiences also affect recipients' performances. Exchange partners may be motivated to establish guidelines when they exchange gifts simultaneously in order to reduce performance pressures (Wooten, 2000). Moreover, occasions with large audiences often require considerable amounts of face time, resulting in increased performance pressures for gift recipients. Figure 10.1 presents a framework outlining the factors that affect the performance of reception. The remainder of this section provides details about each act and includes examples from the data that informed the analysis.

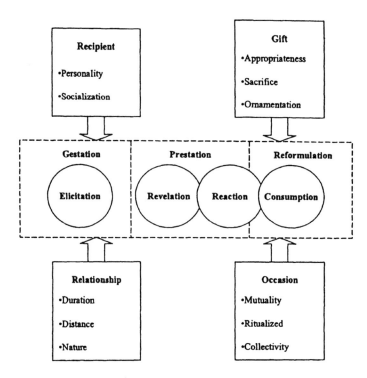

Fig. 10.1.   Factors shaping acts of reception.

Act I: Elicitation

Elicitation involves any means, intentional or not, by which recipients convey gift expectations to prospective givers (Sherry, 1983). Elicitation tactics vary in subtlety and specificity. Key props include gift registries, store catalogs, and coveted items. The following excerpt illustrates elicitation by a recipient who previously expressed her desire to have a cookbook like the one her mother owns:

> My daughter made a big to-do over a cookbook. So I bought her one and gave it to her. She looked at it and she said, "Oh, I finally have my own." And you knew that's what, well, she already told me when she looked at my book, how much she would like to have a book just like it. So when I bought it and gave it to her as a gift, well she hugged me and said, "Thanks, Mom. You knew I wanted this, didn't you?" (Susan, Pre #2)

Susan's comments show how exchange relationships benefit when givers pay attention to the wants, needs, tastes, or preferences of recipients. A benefit to givers is highlighted in Jan's assertion that she rarely second-guesses her gift choices because she tunes in to her recipients as gift occasions approach. When asked if she ever doubts her gift choices, Jan replied:

> Maybe, rarely. Usually I'm the type of person, I tend to listen to what people like or say what they'd like to have and cue in on those kinds of things. Sometimes, you know a lot of times when you're carrying on a conversation with someone, they'll go, well, gee, "I'd sure like to get this" or "I'd like to have this." You remember that. If it is close to their birthday or Christmas and you're buying for them, you'll think back and somewhere in a conversation you'll go, "Did you ever get" whatever you remember them saying, and if they say, "No" then you go okay, that's something I can buy. (Jan, Pre #6)

The comments by Susan and Jan illustrate the difficulty of separating on- and offstage behavior for some acts of elicitation. Recipients may give subtle hints when givers are not tuned in. Inversely, recipients have audiences even when they are not aware of being onstage. Although givers are the primary audience members for acts of elicitation, audience member is not the primary role of givers during gestation. Their major concerns involve selecting gifts and preparing them for presentation.

Acts of elicitation like registering for gifts or writing letters to Santa strengthen associations between gift rituals and the ritual occasions (e.g., weddings or Christmas) in which they are embedded. On the other hand, critics (e.g., Hagerty, 1998; Harris, 1972; Schor, 1998) argue that elicitation violates the spirit of gift exchange rituals. Moreover, recipients who elicit gifts risk imputations of greed, even when elicitation is understood to be part of the ritual occasion (e.g., bridal gift registries). For instance, Kimberly was concerned about the prices of items on her bridal registry, so she registered for an inexpensive china pattern that she liked instead of the expensive one that she loved. She laughed and explained that she ultimately settled for the less expensive pattern because "I didn't want to do a Natalie." She explained that Natalie registered for expensive items that she would never consider purchasing with her own money. Kimberly wanted to avoid appearing greedy and to consider her guests, most of whom had lower incomes than she and her groom. She even considered exchanging pieces of the inexpensive china for the expensive china and paying the substantial price difference, but she was afraid someone would notice (Kimberly, Story #3).

Act II: Revelation

Givers decorate gifts in elaborate packaging to decommoditize concealed objects (Belk, 1993). Recipients unwrap them to discover their contents, which is the act of revelation. Key props include giftwrap, bows, ribbons, cards, and gift bags. Suspense builds as revelation approaches (Banks, 1979), especially with Christmas gifts that are wrapped and displayed long before recipients unwrap them (Caplow, 1984). Impatient recipients sometimes shake packages and ask for hints about package contents. The following quote is illustrative:

> First, I try to guess what it is, and when I guess what it is, I'm tickled. I'm the type that wants to be surprised, but I bug [givers] to death to try to get them to tell me what it is. And then I admit I'm a little disappointed because I should have never tried to guess. In my mind I try not to guess because I like being surprised. But, I'm my worst enemy because I've bugged them to death until they give me a hint, and then I figure it out. (Rachel, Pre #13)

On cue, eager recipients tear open giftwrap. Greg referred to overzealous efforts to rip open gift packages as the "slash and burn" approach (Greg, Pre #8). Some cultures discourage this practice as a sign of greed and materialism (Searle-Chatterjee, 1993). It can also offend givers who invest time, effort, and self in decorating packages. Whitley appeared to be aware of the negative implications of the "slash and burn" approach when she offered a disclaimer as she tore giftwrap from a shower gift. She said, "Alright I rip paper off, I'm not one of those neat people. I'm not one of those people who tears the paper neatly. No, go for it!" (Whitley, Shower #7). Disclaimers are statements people make before their performances in order to deflect negative implications of forthcoming acts (Hewitt & Stokes, 1975). Whitley wanted everyone to know that her style of unwrapping gifts is not intended as a reflection of the gifts or their packaging, but of her brash personality.

Some recipients adjust their unwrapping style to the quality of the packaging. For instance, Rachel advocates a slow, methodical approach to unwrapping gifts that are nicely wrapped. She notes that "some people put tons of tape on, some people put all those little fancy things and it's like you don't want to hurt their feelings by messing up all of that" (Rachel, Pre #13). Packaging alternatives like gift bags have emerged to threaten traditional unwrapping rituals and artifacts. In public settings like the showers it was observed that recipients often acknowledge givers and read greeting cards before they unwrap presents. Recipients may perform differently in private settings. Cultural norms, individual differences, and packaging characteristics shape their public performances.

Although recipients show concern about how they perform acts of revelation, these concerns are overshadowed by their concerns about reacting appropriately to gifts after they open them. Their dramaturgical awareness and subsequent concerns about their forthcoming reactions are evident in the following comments from Cindy:

> When I'm at home and I'm opening [a gift] and it's from my kids, I think I have to show that I'm really excited about this. I have to show that I'm really grateful for what they've done and, no matter what, I have to let them know I appreciate it. To me it doesn't even matter what's in there. It's not just with them, it's with everybody. I don't care what anyone gives me. I mean, well I shouldn't say I don't care. I appreciate everything and so, whatever someone gives me, I'm thinking I've got to show this, that I appreciate it. (Cindy, Pre #12)

Cindy's remarks reflect her awareness of the spotlight shone on recipients during prestation. The glare of the spotlight is evident in her attention to detail and concerns about performing well. She "has to show that she is really excited" and "really grateful" for her gifts, "no matter what" is in the package. Recipients feel various emotions throughout the gift experience (Ruth, 1996), but Cindy's comments reflect greater concerns about what she shows than what she feels. She indicated that she is not overly concerned about what she gets. That is, she cares less about material objects, than she does about the interpersonal dimension of gift relationships. Her most pressing concerns during revelation are related to the meatier part of her role as recipient, that is, her forthcoming lines that convey her reaction to the gift.

Act III: Reaction

Recipients' reactions are crucial to givers (Schwartz, 1967), so this act is often the featured act of gift reception. Reactions are shaped by norms of considerateness and self-respect. Considerateness involves going to appropriate lengths to protect others' faces because of emotional identification with them. Self-respect involves avoiding some behaviors and performing others in service of impression management (Goffman, 1967). Recipients should accept gifts and show gratitude (Mauss, 1954). They should not reject gifts unless the gifts are inappropriate (Post, 1992). Those who reject suitable gifts risk imputations of difficulty (Otnes et al., 1993) and their relationships with givers (Ruth et al., 1999). Those who accept inappropriate gifts accept the identities implied by their gifts (Schwartz, 1967).

When gifts are opened in frontstage regions, recipients convey their reactions in two stages. First, they express initial reactions in impromptu performances immediately after they open their gifts. Second, they supplement these adlibbed performances with carefully scripted thank you cards prepared in backstage regions. When recipients do not open gifts in a frontstage region, the carefully scripted thank you cards become even more important.

The gift and thank you cards are key props for this act. Recipients are expected to mention the gift when they respond to givers, especially in written form. Thank you cards from a variety of occasions and verbal responses from baby showers were content analyzed and it was found that recipients commonly praise givers and their gifts. However, unlike Pieters and Robben's (1998) findings regarding private appraisals, it was found that public expressions rarely address gift occasions. In their communications with givers, recipients acknowledge occasions, but they praise gifts and givers. Perhaps their spoken responses reflect their efforts to praise givers only for things for which they can take credit. Unless gifts are given "just because," givers do not control gift occasions. When recipients mentioned occasions in thank you cards, they were usually crediting the giver and gift with making an occasion special. The following response from a 10-year-old boy is illustrative: "Thank you so much for the Allie Baby especially with Prince, I never thought I'd get another one. And also for the Lego set, it can lift a full box of crayons and a calculator. Again thank you for making this my best Christmas ever!" (Donald, Card #1).

Donald expressed gratitude for receiving a duplicate of a stuffed doll that he slept with since early childhood. The original was damaged from years of wear and tear. The replacement even included the stuffed dog that he lost years ago. Consistent with givers' expectations of recipients, Donald demonstrated his use of the gift by commenting on the lifting capacity of his Lego set. He concluded by crediting the givers for making the occasion special.

Many givers identified a positivity bias that affects recipients' performances and favors deception. Recipients are responsible for creating and sustaining impressions that gifts are valued. Others may attest to the goodness of gifts, but recipients are the final arbiters of value because givers are expected to consider recipients' wants or needs when they make gift choices (Belk, 1979). The goodness of gifts lies not as much in their monetary value or popular appeal as in their suitability to be given by specific givers to designated recipients (Belk, 1996). Because recipients are best suited to make this determination, only they can designate objects as treasured gifts. This designation is one of the rewards that givers seek

(Schwartz, 1967), but cannot attain without credible shows of gratitude by recipients. The credibility of recipients' reactions is threatened if they are at odds with a consensus, out of character for individual actors, or inconsistent with actual consumption. Sometimes these shows of appreciation are literally acts. Recipients feign emotions (Sherry, 1983) and other conditions of the perfect gift (Belk, 1996). This deception results from a preference system that promotes acceptance and hides rejection (Rodriquez & Ryave, 1990). Consequently, givers adopt the mindset of theatergoers and watch closely for inconsistencies in performances (Banks, 1979). Greg indicated that he listens carefully for expressive language and voice inflection. As an example, he imitates the dramatic responses of his daughter who, like other children, gives genuine responses.

> "Ohhhh!" or "Thaaannk youuuu!" or "You shouldn't haaavve!" or "It's wonnnderful!" My daughter says, "Ooooh, wowww!" They're still at a very young age where everything is just right on the surface. There's no deception or guile. I think that at their age if they were to open something that they didn't like, their faces would let you know. (Greg, Pre #8)

The expressive language that Greg described is similar to the responses that were observed from recipients of baby shower gifts. According to Schlenker (1980), paralanguage like voice inflection, pace, and repetition conveys meaning and emotion. Givers monitor paralanguage to judge consistency in recipients' performances. Body language and facial expressions also convey meaning (Schlenker, 1980). Nonverbal cues that support verbal expressions enhance perceptions of sincerity (Leary, 1995). Inconsistencies occur not only when expressive cues and spoken words offer conflicting appraisals, but also when levels of expressiveness fail to match expected levels of enthusiasm (Graham, Gentry, & Green, 1982). Recipients who lack expressiveness are seen as unappreciative. Those who are overly expressive are also viewed with suspicion (DePaulo, 1992). Some givers, like Laverne, consider individual differences when they assess recipients' reactions.

> A five-year old is screaming and yelling. To my mom when she was 60, it was crying and tears. You know, it kind of depends on the person. If they're, I have some friends who are real emotional, who tend to get real emotional. My boys tend to be rather loud when they, you know, either that's cool or that's great or, you know, "Hey Mom that was wonderful." It's just kind of their reaction, and it's different for different people. (Laverne, Pre #5)

Givers also pay close attention to expressive cues that are not easily controllable. For instance, Greg emphasizes the diagnosticity of nonverbal cues like body language and facial expressions. According to Greg:

> I think that's an awful lot better indicator than the words because I've never seen anybody open a gift and say, "Why in heaven's name did you buy this?" I've never seen somebody offer a direct verbal response that is negative, like "This sucks!" But I know I've seen cases where someone opens something up and there's just this look of crestfallen, or confused, or whatever, but there's a look. (Greg, Pre #8)

Greg recognizes that recipients are socialized to say the right things, but their bodily instincts do not always cooperate. Actors attempt to use nonverbal cues strategically (Goffman, 1959), but they can be difficult to control (DePaulo, 1992). Mike (Pre #18) and Sam (Pre #19) agree that nonverbal cues often betray one's true feelings and they are not easily controllable, but that does not stop recipients from trying. Mike and Sam try to catch the facial expressions that recipients have immediately after they open their gifts. According to them, once recipients compose themselves for the performance, even their nonverbal behaviors can be contrived:

> Well, I think it's the moment when they're trying to figure out what it is. Sort of try to catch the moment before they try to compose themselves. Sort of a genuine reaction. I mean, I guess that you know, their face … it's probably their face … probably it's the facial expression that is primary. You sort of catch, you know, that specific moment for the uh, the … when the reaction is … before the mind has caught up with reaction. Of course then you're never sure. You look for that, but I don't think you're particularly confident in it. The thing with my wife about jewelry, it's always like that. "Are you sure you like it? Do you really like it?" Sort of asking questions a lot to try to get sort of, you know, see if you can read into the response anything that's less than genuine or it's uh … Well that doesn't really work with my wife, not with my wife. If she doesn't like it she'll just say so (laugh), eventually. (Mike, Pre #18)

> It's probably based upon non-verbal kinds of cues that they send off, like their facial expressions and body language. And, then of course, they say "thanks" and "it's a great gift" and all that, but you try to make an assessment based on their non-verbal cues.… I mean, it's probably facial expressions more than anything. You know, you want to see what that initial reaction is when the present is unwrapped or when, you know, it is presented to the individual. I mean, that's what you're looking for initially. I mean, you know, if you get clothes for your child for their birthday and they open, you know, unwrap the present and they see that it's clothes (laughs).… its easier to read the emotions of a three year old than it is for a 33 year old. But it's the same process although somewhat easier to do than for older adults. (Sam, Pre #19)

Both interviewees suggest that face-to-face reactions are often feigned, but doing so requires a little time and a lot of effort. Sam's comparison between children and adult recipients and Greg's remarks about the candor of his daughter suggest that recipients must learn how to act. According to Laverne, recipients are taught not only to give praise in person, but also to follow it up with written expressions of gratitude.

> I wasn't raised giving thank-you cards with gifts and stuff. And I have friends who are adults, who were raised giving thank-you cards. And it's something I wish I had a better habit of doing because when I get thank-you cards back it's like it's a further confirmation that the thought and effort that goes into purchasing a gift was really appreciated. And I don't personally do it as much as I would like. I do it more now because I've known people who do it. So I think it's something that people did more prevalently 30 or 40 years ago that's a little bit lost some today. Something we could give back. (Laverne, Pre #5)

Some people were taught to give thank you cards when they receive gifts, so they are offended when they do not receive them when they give gifts. Moreover, those who believe that thank you cards are obligatory tend to discount them as evidence of a good gift and scrutinize them for signs of insincerity. Interviewees stressed the importance of receiving personalized messages. For instance, Blanche indicated that personal touches enhance appearances of sincerity. According to Blanche:

> When you give wedding gifts you know they have gotten many, many gifts. If they've taken the time to write the thank-you note, and thank you specifically for what you got, where you don't think they're just sitting there doing form thank-yous, but a little bit of a personal touch or telling you "This will go great in my bathroom with my so and so and so and so." You know, really relating to you what they're going to do with it or how they're going to use it. And I think that it's really sincere, it means more. But so many times you get a thank-you, "Well, thank you for your wedding gift" or "Thank you for the towels." Well, do they know that I gave them blue towels or did I give them green towels that won't match, you know. (Blanche, Pre #3)

Some interviewees indicated a desire for handwritten notes on personal stationery instead of store bought cards with pre-printed messages. Some were extremely critical of anything that resembles a form letter. For instance, references to "the gift" in generic terms violated their expectations of receiving a thank you card that contains a different message than what others receive. Paradoxically, people advocated standard formats to ensure unique content. A greeting card manufacturer even mass-produces a "fill-in-the-blank" thank you card to train young recipients to personalize their messages (Card #48). Because recipients learn how to craft their performances when they react to gifts, givers rely on the act of consumption to convey information about recipients' true reactions to gifts.

Act IV: Consumption

Consumption involves the various ways recipients use gifts after they receive them. In this context, use of the term "consumption" is similar to Sherry's (1983) use of "disposition." Givers expect recipients to use gifts for their intended purposes (Sherry et al., 1992). They interpret immediate or regular use as a sign of appreciation and liking. Otherwise, givers assume that recipients do not appreciate their gifts or the relationship. For instance, Alice, a mother of two adult sons, often gives home furnishings and infers appreciation from how prominently they are displayed in the recipients' homes. She described being elated to find that a framed and matted photograph from her was displayed above the mantle in her son's new home. However, she was disappointed when she house sat for him and found that a statue from her was left molding in his back yard (Alice, Pre #10).

The interviewees complained about recipients neglecting gifts, storing them prematurely or in the original packages, exchanging them for other items, returning them to givers, or redistributing them as gifts to others. These forms of rejection are hurtful to givers (Rucker et al., 1991) and embarrassing for recipients who are discovered doing them (Sherry et al., 1992). Maxine conveyed her embarrassment and frustration over her struggles to conceal her decision to return a sweater she received as a gift from her grandmother:

> My other grandmother tries to get us clothes and it's just impossible because we're totally different. She thinks I'm an extra small or smaller, and it's like, "No, Grandma." You know, and a sweater she bought me at Christmas, it's like, "Oh Grandma." It's like you've got to say, "Thanks, Grandma!" and smile, but when you see her, she's like, "Oh, you should have worn the sweater I got you," and really you already returned it. 'Cause my mom was saying, "Well, your Grandmother's asking me again about that sweater," and she was just so proud of picking that out. It was a cream sweater with silver threads. It was not anything I would wear at all. And she was asking, but what would I tell her, and I'm, well I'm just going to have to probably, not to say that I would lie, but I would just say that "It got a hole in it" or something. I don't want to hurt her feelings by saying, "Well, Grandma, I took it back." I don't know what I'm going to do. It will be summer and I hope she'll forget about it. (Maxine, Post #2)

Maxine admitted to forcing a smile and feigning satisfaction when she received an unattractive sweater as a gift from her grandmother. Now she is worried because she returned the sweater before her grandmother could see her wear it. She has not seen her grandmother since she received the gift and is not looking forward to their next encounter because her grandmother has been asking about the sweater. She was hoping for an easy way out (e.g., summer would come or her grandmother would forget), but reluctantly admitted that she would lie to avoid hurting her grandmother's feelings. This episode is consistent with previous findings (e.g., Sherry et al., 1992) that gift recipients have fewer degrees of freedom than do consumers who purchase objects for personal use.

Pressures to use gifts as intended prompt strategic consumption from recipients (Banks, 1979). For instance, Halle recalled receiving a calendar from her boyfriend and displaying it in her bedroom even though she really did not like it.

> This year with my boyfriend, he gave me … last year he gave me an Ally McBeal calendar. At first I went, "Oh," it was kind of weird, but anyway, I hung it up in my room, I wasn't going to bring it to work. And then the next year he got me another one, which bless his heart.… So I think I'll be getting them for the next 20 years! (Halle, Post #5)

Halle was too embarrassed to display the calendar at work where others could see it, so she hung it in her room where her boyfriend would notice. Her boyfriend was so convinced that she liked the calendar that he latched on to the gift idea and bought the next edition the following year. Halle joked that she will probably continue to get Ally McBeal calendars for the next 20 years. Although deception was involved in this example, it is not always involved when recipients display gifts strategically. For instance, Maxine described how she displayed a hand-made Christmas gift from her 6-year-old daughter in order to reassure her daughter that the gift is valued. Her daughter, Amber, made the gift as an art project. The gift was intended as a surprise, but Amber was so excited that she almost revealed the secret on numerous occasions. She came home every day with reports about her progress, but Maxine was determined not to let her daughter spoil the surprise. According to Maxine:

> So when Christmas came, it was like the first present she wanted me to open. She comes bringing it over to me and it was the cutest thing, it was on white paper and it had little stamps. She just peppered it with them. This big bow was all taped galore, you know. And I opened it up and it was a calendar and every month has a scene with her hand. Like for June it was sunshine and the rays were her hands, and then of course, Thanksgiving was a turkey with her hand. Every month had something made out of her hand. And she was just, "See, Mom, look at it," and it just made me cry. I was looking at it and like, "Amber, this is so precious, I'll remember this forever, you know, it's got your hands," and I was just crying and crying. And she said, "Don't you like it?" (Maxine, Post #2)

This episode reveals the ambiguity associated with tears. Amber interpreted Maxine's tears of joy as evidence of disappointment. The excerpt highlights Maxine's reaction, but her solution to the problem that her reaction created illustrates strategic display without deception. She hung the calendar on the refrigerator so she could see it every day and Amber could see how much she adores it. She told her daughter that people sometimes cry when they are happy. Amber now understands that, "the happiest gifts make people cry—because they make you feel warm and moushy."

Although it is not obvious from the episode described by Maxine, some strategic displays can be difficult when givers and recipients reside in the same household because there are few structural barriers to separate front- and backstage regions. Sophia illustrates this problem when she describes how her husband's assurances that he likes certain gifts from her are betrayed by his tendency to store them in his closet. According to Sophia, he would say, "I love it Sophie!" but the gift would be in the back of his closet (Sophia, Pre #15). The moment when recipients are offstage is rarely clear, so recipients sometimes feel like they are constantly on display.

CONCLUSIONS

This chapter presented a dramaturgical analysis of gift reception to illuminate the role of gift recipient and shed light on the ritual script that guides recipients' performances. This analysis enlarges the understanding of gift exchange by devoting attention to the role of recipient, which is an important role that has been under-researched (Sherry, 1996). Recipients are often concerned about managing interpersonal impressions and protecting the situated identities of their exchange partners. The salience of interpersonal evaluation and the interpersonal stakes involved, especially after gifts are presented, prompt them to monitor and control their expressive behaviors for the sake of self and others.

Based on a synthesis of literature and data, four important acts of gift reception—elicitation, revelation, reaction, and consumption—are identified. Although revelation constitutes the climactic moment for recipients, the reaction is the featured act for givers who eagerly await feedback from recipients (Schwartz, 1967). The four acts differ in terms of the region dynamics, audience roles, and performance pressures associated with them. However, some common factors influence if and how they are performed.

Throughout the analysis a tension between appropriateness and sincerity was evident. For instance, sincere efforts to elicit desired gifts are often deemed inappropriate (Hagerty, 1998; Harris, 1972; Schor, 1998). Earnest efforts to discover the contents of gift packages can be viewed as displaying inappropriate levels of greed or materialism (Searle-Chatterjee, 1993). Recipients sometimes try to suppress instinctive reactions to gifts in favor of more acceptable contrived responses (Belk, 1996; Sherry, 1983). They are also encouraged to use templates to help them convey personalized messages that sound sincere (e.g., Post, 1992). Finally, they feel pressured to use or display unwanted gifts for fear of hurting others' feelings and violating standards of propriety. Despite a number of notable exceptions, especially children and difficult recipients (e.g., Otnes et al., 1993), recipients' concerns about propriety appear to overshadow their concerns about sincerity. However, appropriate behavior includes appearing sincere, so recipients try to give credible performances. Although sincerity undoubtedly enhances credibility, credible performances are not always sincere. Moreover, because audiences are sometimes skeptical and emotional reactions (e.g., crying) are sometimes ambiguous, sincere performances are not always credible.

Limitations

This chapter presented a dramaturgical analysis of gift reception. The decision to focus primarily on the expected and actual behaviors of recipients downplays the fact that givers and recipients are coperformers in gift exchange rituals. This analysis treated givers as though audience member was their primary role. Future research is needed to explore giver–recipient interactions as performance teams (e.g., Goffman, 1959). For instance, a man who receives a gift from his spouse may feign delight while others (e.g., children and friends) are present in order to protect the situated identities of himself and his wife. However, he may express his true disappointment in a private conversation with his wife. The authors actually observed teamwork by exchange partners during a few baby showers when someone in the audience heckled another about the suitability of a gift. In a few cases, givers attempted to defend their choices and recipients gave supportive responses that protected givers' faces and preserved the festive atmosphere surrounding the occasion.

ACKNOWLEDGMENTS

We thank Russ Belk, Cele Otnes, Julie Ruth, and John Sherry for comments on earlier versions of this chapter. We also thank Jo Anne Cullip, Mary Ellen Dickerson, Deloris Perry, Julie Ritter, Mary Stallings, Marcia Wood, and Lynn Wooten for assistance with data collection.

REFERENCES

Allen, V., & Scheibe, K. (1982). *The social context of conduct: Psychological writings of Theodore Sarbin*. New York: Praeger.

Banks, S. (1979). Gift-giving: A review and an interactive paradigm. In W. Wilkie (Ed.), *Advances in consumer research* (Vol. 6, pp. 319–324). Ann Arbor, MI: Association for Consumer Research.

Belk, R. (1979). Gift-giving behavior. In J. Sheth (Ed.), *Research in marketing* (Vol. 2, pp. 95–126). Greenwich, CT: JAI Press.

Belk, R. (1993). Materialism and the making of the modern American Christmas. In D. Miller (Ed.), *Unwrapping Christmas* (pp. 75–104). Oxford: Clarendon.

Belk, R. (1996). The perfect gift. In C. Otnes & R. Beltramini (Eds.), *Gift giving: A research anthology* (pp. 59–84). Bowling Green, OH: Popular Press.

Belk, R., & Coon, G. (1993). Gift-giving as agapic love: An alternative to the exchange paradigm based on dating experiences. *Journal of Consumer Research, 20*(December), 393–417.

Bourdieu, P. (1994). *Practical reason.* Stanford, CA: Stanford University Press.

Brissett D., & Edgley, C. (Eds.). (1990). *Life as theater: A dramaturgical source book.* New York: de Gruyter.

Camerer, C. (1988). Gifts as economic signals and social symbols. *American Journal of Sociology, 94*, S180–S214.

Caplow, T. (1984). Rule enforcement without visible means: Christmas gift giving in Middletown. *American Journal of Sociology, 89*, 1306–1323.

Cheal, D. (1987). "Showing them you love them": Gift giving and the dialectic of intimacy. *Sociological Review, 35*, 150–169.

Chen, D. (1997). Wishful thinkers are using gift registries for all occasions. *New York Times*, July 27, p. 10.

DePaulo, B. (1992). Nonverbal behavior and self-presentation. *Psychological Bulletin, 111*, 203–243.

Goffman, E. (1959). *The presentation of self in everyday life.* New York: Anchor Books.

Goffman, E. (1967). *Interaction ritual: Essays on face-to-face behavior.* New York: Anchor Books.

Goffman, E. (1974). *Frame analysis: An essay on the organization of experience.* Boston: Northeastern University Press.

Graham, J., Gentry, K., & Green, J. (1982). The self-presentational nature of emotional expression: Some evidence. *Personality and Social Psychology Bulletin, 7*, 467–474.

Green, R., & Alden, D. (1988). Functional equivalence in cross-cultural consumer behavior: Gift giving in Japan and the United States. *Psychology & Marketing, 5*, 155–168.

Hagerty, J. R. (1998, December). Ever receive slippers when you wanted black cha-cha heels?—Sick of bad Christmas surprises, people demand to know what's under the tree. *The Wall Street Journal*, 24, p. A1.

Hare, A., & Blumberg, H. (1988). *Dramaturgical analysis of social interaction.* New York: Praeger.

Harris, M. (1972). Bah humbug. *Natural History, 81*, 21–25.

Katz, J. (1976). How do you love me? Let me count the ways (The phenomenology of being loved.) *Sociological Inquiry, 46*(1), 17–22.

Latane, B. (1981). The psychology of social impact. *American Psychologist, 36*, 343–356.

Leary, M. (1995). *Self-presentation: Impression management and interpersonal behavior.* Madison, WI: Brown & Benchmark.

Lyman, S., & Scott, M. (1975). *The drama of social reality.* New York: Oxford University Press.

MacCannell, D. (1973). Nonviolent action as theater: A dramaturgical analysis of 146 demonstrations (Monograph 10). Haverford, PA: Haverford College, Nonviolent Action Research Project.

Mauss, M. (1954). *The gift: The form and reason for exchange in archaic societies.* New York: Norton.

Messinger, S., Sampson, H., & Towne, R. (1962). Life as theater: Some notes on the dramaturgic approach to social reality. *Sociometry, 25,* 98–110.

Mick, D., & DeMoss, M. (1990). Self-gifts: Phenomenological insights from four contexts. *Journal of Consumer Research, 17,* 322–332.

Neisser, M. (1973). The sense of self expressed through giving and receiving. *Social Casework, 54,* 294–301.

Otnes, C., Lowrey, T. M., & Kim, Y. (1993, September). Gift selection for easy and difficult recipients: A social roles interpretation. *Journal of Consumer Research, 20,* 229–244.

Overington, M., & Mangham, I. (1982). The theatrical perspective in organizational analysis. *Symbolic Interaction, 5,* 173–185.

Pieters, R., & Robben, H. (1998). Beyond the horse's mouth: Exploring acquisition and exchange utility in gift evaluation. In J. Alba & J. Hutchinson (Eds.), *Advances in consumer research* (Vol. 25, pp. 163–169). Provo, UT: Association for Consumer Research.

Post, E. (1992). *Emily Post's etiquette* (15th ed.). New York: HarperCollins.

Rodriquez, N., & Ryave, A. (1990). Telling lies in everyday life: Motivational and organizational consequences of sequential preferences. *Qualitative Sociology, 13,* 195–210.

Rook, D. (1985). The ritual dimension of consumer behavior. *Journal of Consumer Research, 12,* 251–264.

Rucker, M., Leckliter, L., Kivel, S., Dinkel, M., Freitas, T., Wynes, M., & Prato, H. (1991). When the thought counts: Friendship, love, gift exchanges and gift returns. In R. Holman & M. Solomon (Eds.), *Advances in consumer research,* (Vol. 18, pp. 528–531). Provo, UT: Association for Consumer Research.

Ruth, J. (1996). It's the feeling that counts: Toward an understanding of emotion and its influence on gift-exchange processes. In C. Otnes & R. Beltramini (Eds.), *Gift giving: A research anthology* (pp. 195–214). Bowling Green, OH: Popular Press.

Ruth, J., Otnes, C., & Brunel, F. (1999). Gift receipt and the reformulation of interpersonal relationships. *Journal of Consumer Research, 25,* 385–402.

Sarbin, T., & Allen, V. (1968). Role theory. In G. Lindzey & E. Aronson (Eds.), *Handbook of social psychology* (2nd ed., pp. 488–567). Cambridge, MA: Addison-Wesley.

Schlenker, B. (1980). *Impression management: The self-concept, social identity, and interpersonal relations.* Monterey, CA: Books/Cole.

Schlenker, B., & Leary, M. (1982). Social anxiety and self-presentation: A conceptualization and model. *Psychological Bulletin, 92,* 641–669.

Schor, J. (1998). *The overspent American: Upscaling, downshifting, and the new consumer.* New York: Basic Books.

Schwartz, B. (1967). The social psychology of the gift. *American Journal of Sociology, 73,* 1–11.

Searle-Chatterjee, M. (1993). Christmas cards and the construction of social relations in Britain today. In D. Miller (Ed.), *Unwrapping Christmas* (pp. 176–192). Oxford: Clarendon.

Sherry, J., Jr. (1983). Gift giving in anthropological perspective. *Journal of Consumer Research, 10,* 157–168.

Sherry, J., Jr. (1996). Reflections on giftware and giftcare: Whither consumer research. In C. Otnes & R. Beltramini (Eds.), *Gift giving: A research anthology* (pp. 217–227). Bowling Green, OH: Popular Press.

Sherry, J., Jr., McGrath, M., & Levy, S. (1992). The disposition of the gift and many unhappy returns. *Journal of Retailing, 68,* 40–65.

Sherry, J., Jr., McGrath, M., & Levy, S. (1995). Monadic giving: Anatomy of gifts given to the self. In J. Sherry, Jr. (Ed.), *Contemporary marketing and consumer behavior: An anthropological sourcebook* (pp. 399–432). Thousand Oaks, CA: Sage.

Tewksbury, R. (1994). A dramaturgical analysis of male strippers. *Journal of Men's Studies, 2,* 325–342.

Wilshire, B. (1982). The dramaturgical model of behavior: It's strengths and weaknesses. *Symbolic Interaction, 5,* 287–297.

Wooten, D. (2000). Qualitative steps toward an expanded model of anxiety in gift-giving. *Journal of Consumer Research, 27,* 84–95.

11

Ritual Desire and Ritual Development: An Examination of Family Heirlooms in Contemporary North American Households

Carolyn Folkman Curasi
Georgia State University

Eric J. Arnould and Linda L. Price
University of Nebraska–Lincoln

> I hope this will become a family tradition. The ring is the only object I will pass down. I never bought anything or received any other thing that is important enough to me to pass down to my family.... I want the ring to start becoming a family heirloom, and to be passed on to generations. When it's passed down, I want my daughter to tell her daughter, Amanda, the story behind it. (Mrs. Thompson, Female, age 72)

This investigation examines rituals associated with heirlooms in contemporary North American society. In particular, we draw attention to consumers' longing for ritual. Woven through our interview data, we are struck by the presence of an affective state that might be described as a desire or longing for ritual, as illustrated in the opening quote and as echoed by other informants. This desire for ritual seems to reflect a tacit understanding of ritual's role in broadcasting, enacting, and commemorating important family values. This affective state translates into a desire for ritual action often played out in individual middle-class families in North America through the development and ritualized use of family heirlooms.

We also draw attention to consumers' desire to both create and to sustain family heirloom rituals. Families compose ritualized activity as *bricolage*, a French term, that literally translates as "puttering," or "do-it yourself," and was introduced by Levi-Strauss to describe the compositional tactics found in traditional mythology. The behavioral latitude that ritual development can absorb struck us as we studied family heirlooms and informal disposition rituals in contemporary American families. Family storytelling plays a significant role in heirloom use and the associated disposition rituals.

Our contribution falls into several domains. First, both classic and contemporary accounts of American kinship and the American household are virtually silent on the subject of ritual actions related to inheritance (e.g., Hollingshead, 1949; Komarovsky & Waller, 1945; Mead, 1948; Parsons, 1943; Schneider, 1980). Further, discussions of family heirlooms have focused on what is transferred (Hurd, 1985), the extent to which rich families distribute or preserve their wealth (Wilhelm, 1997), the extent to which wealth is inherited equally between offspring (Lavely, 1992), and on simple classifications of the gendered transfer of particular goods (Sussman, Cates, & Smith 1970).

By contrast, our research identifies how families make use of heirlooms to develop a sense of tradition. Through rituals involving heirlooms, our informants speak and act in a subjunctive mode, that is, in ways that privilege a future molded in tradition. Often informants will reach back to a virtual, mythic, "subjunctive" past to which Schechner (1996) and Turner (1967) referred to as a source of ritual meanings generally. This is a past of the world "as if," steeped in ambiguity and nostalgia (Gillis, 1996; Holak & Havlena, 1992), that can be recreated to serve the needs of the future. Informants' behavior suggests they believe traditions, even those constructed today, can endure indefinitely. In addition, our data is rich in informants' presumptions that mythical future heirs will provide symbolic immortality to the living through his or her subsequent actions. This temporal framing of tradition calls into question postmodern theories of tradition's end and the decentered subjectivity of historical actors. Our data show how rituals that collect around particular cherished possessions constitute meaningful, elective descent groups for particular families. Thus, this research identifies emergent social structures for ritual action in a North American context. These shallow bilateral descent groups are disparate from the corporate local groups examined in much of the anthropological literature on ritual (e.g., Turner 1967, 1969).

Second, virtually all of the research on favorite objects (Belk, 1988, 1991a, 1991b; Belk, Wallendorf, & Sherry, 1989; Csikszentmihalyi & Rochberg-Halton, 1981; Wallendorf & Arnould, 1988) focuses on their meanings to individuals. Research on object meaning (see Mick, Burroughs, Hetzel, & Brannen, 1999, for a review) focuses on more general social meanings or the subcultural meanings of objects. Thus, there is little research on the creation and transfer of shared communal meanings of objects at the family or household level (but see Olsen, 1995). Our research contributes to closing this gap in knowledge.

Third, in Western consumer societies people naturally have recourse to consumer goods, the ubiquitous material of consumer culture in the constitution of cultural meaning. Rituals seem to play an active role in animating consumer goods with the roles ascribed to them by Douglas and Isherwood (1979) as stabilizing cultural categories. But goods, especially mass-marketed consumer goods, do not provide a transparent catalogue of cultural categories. We maintain that performances, especially ritual performances, are required to activate object meanings pertinent to social life. Marketers use advertising to activate object meaning. Consumers develop their own rituals to activate object meaning. Without ritual, the categories are at best merely potential, and the objects inert. Phrased another way, our data shows that consumers' ritual performances, often addressed to the "little community" of the household or extended family, are capable of creating and fixing cultural categories (see also Holt, 1998).

In the first section of the paper we begin with some background on the role heirloom objects play in consumer societies and then discuss the nature of ritual in Western consumer societies. Next, we detail the desire for ritual that accompanies the actual transfer and imagined transfer of cherished possessions. We illustrate this desire for ritual and we demonstrate how it is manifested in ritual *bricolage*, or elective forms that integrate lived experience, imagined tradition, successful examples, and ancestral customs. We do not wish to recapitulate the excellent syntheses of ritual theory provided by others (e.g., Bell, 1997, Rivière, 1995; Segalen, 1998). Instead we prefer to highlight the literature on cherished possessions and family heirlooms that is germane to our investigation.

CHERISHED POSSESSIONS
AND HEIRLOOMS

The possessions for which we have the deepest feelings are those that provide the greatest symbolic meanings. Often these items evoke fond memories of loved ones, special places, and cherished experiences (Belk, 1991a; Tobin, 1996): "Memory laden possessions act as nostalgic mnemonic devices that evoke affective experiential knowledge" (Belk, 1991a, p. 29). Individuals value them for the nostalgic feelings they can evoke, not for an ability to remind us of factual historic data. Cherished items permit us to archive our past. Photographs, medals and mementos can attest to our achievements and to our participation in the significant events of our lives (Belk, 1991a; Kaufman, 1980). Mementos have the power to document success, as well as when received as gifts, to document that we are loved.

Select cherished objects have the unique capacity to allow us to author our past. We judiciously cull as our most cherished possessions those objects to which our fondest and preferred memories are attached (Belk, 1991a; Katriel & Farrell, 1991; Stone, 1988). Cherished objects allow us to author a past, as we prefer to remember it (Kamptner, 1989). Unruh (1983) and Price, Arnould, and Curasi (2000) show that older individuals often craft the way they hope to be remembered through the possessions they choose to transfer, and the people they select to transfer them to.

Material culture is widely used to memorialize the deceased. Gravestones, memorials, mementos, and their care are indicative of a widespread desire to ritualize and reify deceased loved ones (Belk, 1991a; Stones from Bones, 2002; George & Nelson, 1982; Warner, 1959; Zelinsky, 1976). Selective retention of some of deceased loved ones' possessions comforts the living with symbolic assurances of remembrance. Retaining a loved one's possessions may also ease the separation anxiety that can accompany his or her death (Belk, 1991a). These items can provide survivors with a sense of continuity in the face of loss and change (Tobin, 1996). Belongings of the deceased are sometimes thought of as totemic remains, especially when viewed as part of the deceased's extended self (Belk, 1988; Price et al., 2000). Preserved clothing and jewelry may take on special significance because of positive contamination through close contact with the deceased. Jewelry is also strongly valued as a powerful mnemonic (Belk, 1991a).

Heirlooms are a special kind of bequest from the dead to the living. In this investigation, we define them as objects given in trust to a younger family member from an older family member of a different generation. Heirlooms differ from cherished possessions in the subjective perception of great age or multigenerational transfer. Great age sometimes trumps concrete significance in conveying value. The following excerpt from our interviews is illustrative:

> *Int:* Ok. Now can you tell me about the history of the ashtrays and the cigarette holder? How long has it been in your family? Are there any special stories or events about it?
>
> *Resp:* Um, there was a story behind it, I forget what it was though. I can't remember it, but probably a hundred years old.
>
> *Int:* Really, it's been in your family for a hundred years.
>
> *Resp:* Un huh. Because my great-grandfather had it, and my grandmother is eighty, and he gave it to her when she was like twenty years old, I forget, it came from Italy so I don't know how he got it, I can't remember the story behind it, I can't remember. (Mary, Female, 20s).

As the excerpt suggests, there may be slippage between objective chronology and perception. Nevertheless, heirlooms allow people to document and remember their ancestors. Heirlooms serve as a link to the ancestors' mythic deeds, granting descendants the ability to archive familial achievements (Belk, 1988; Stone, 1988). They extend the achievements and competencies of celebrated forebears to contemporary family members and they privilege contemporaries through the protective spirit of their ancestors (Belk, 1991a; Price et al., 2000; Tuan, 1976). Heirlooms allow us to extend ourselves through the ownership of the possessions of deceased loved ones (Belk 1988). Through them, people can lay claim to some of their innate skills and accomplishments, as the following excerpt from our data suggests:

Int: Tell me as much about the previous history of these items you can. How long has it been in your family? Are there special stories or events associated with the items?

Resp: As was previously stated, the items were either acquired or presented in the 1800's to members of the family as wedding presents or as a presentation for a family member being associated with guilds or other associations. In all cases, one tends to associate such items with the previous owner and with the three items featured. The first two are most closely associated with my father and his sister, my aunt. (Humphrey, Male, 60s)

Family heirlooms also provide us with a sense of continuity with previous generations (Tobin, 1996). Sometimes cherished possessions received from loved family members are ceded along with information on the object's history (Tobin, 1996). When this occurs, the heirloom becomes inextricably tied to the donor and to the people discussed in associated narratives.

Ritual in Western Consumer Society

Many scholars have confronted the persistence of ritual in contemporary consumer culture (Belk et al., 1989; Bell, 1992; Driver, 1998; Fischer & Gainer, 1993; Grimes, 1995; Kottak, 1983; Moore & Myerhoff, 1977; Rivière, 1995; Rook, 1985; Segalen, 1998; Wallendorf & Arnould, 1991). This work demonstrates that analysis of the distinctive characteristics of customs in particular social structures and temporal periods can provide an enriched theoretical understanding of ritual as a universal human phenomenon. More importantly, contemporary ritual studies have broken free from an overly static and unitary model of ritual grounded in the ethnology of small-scale societies.

Fundamentally, ritual is a way of organizing and assimilating experience (Driver, 1998; Turner, 1967, 1969). It calls on tacit norms and values and links people to them. Ritual is adaptive, however, and is not necessarily enmeshed in a pre-given institutional order (Arnould, Price, & Otnes, 1999). Its seriality provides an effective way for people to communicate with themselves about tacit norms and values and at the same time establish existential truths (Bell, 1992). Ritual conveys order, community, and transformation on human beings (Bell, 1992). In consumer society, ritual makes use of the material that society provides, material that often threatens the efficacy of ritual because of its secular commodity character, but ritual still represents an oppositional force to the logic of the marketplace (Wallendorf & Arnould, 1991). It builds relationships; it is a reversible, ongoing process, that vehicles consumer agency (Cheal, 1989). However, consumer society inflects ritual activity in households in a number of ways to which we now turn our attention.

In summary, this investigation seeks to better understand North American consumers' desire for ritual and to examine how they attempt to satisfy that desire through heirlooms and the development or sustenance of ritual surrounding their cherished possessions. We will make several theoretical points concerning ritual in contemporary North America, illustrated through representative comments from in-depth interviews. We now turn to a discussion of method.

METHOD

We draw on six years of research focused on the origin, meaning, use, and behavioral intentions surrounding cherished and inherited objects. Two specific data sets collected during this larger investigation of consumer rituals and their person–object relationships serve as the database in the present empirical investigation. The first data set was collected between the fall of 1997 and the summer of 1998. Dyadic in-depth interviews were conducted with paired donors and recipients or planned recipients of cherished personal or family items. Informants were interviewed to learn which possessions they considered to be their most cherished, and then to learn of the meanings anchored in those objects. At the end of each interview, we asked what informants planned for the future of each cherished item and, ultimately, informants named a younger family member that they planned to transfer objects to or an individual to whom they had already given a cherished possession. Then, with permission from both parties, we interviewed each respective younger family member to learn of the objects they considered their most cherished and to also learn of their feelings and intentions for the object. This resulted in interviews with 28 informants lasting between 60 minutes and 3 hours from 10 family groups, forming 19 gift exchange dyads.

The second data set was collected between the fall of 1998 and the summer of 2001. Depth interviews with 38 informants within 15 family groups, representing 26 intergenerational dyads comprise this data set. Trained interviewers conducted these interviews in informants' homes; they averaged 50 minutes to 1 hour in length. A small number of telephone interviews was used to contact geographically dispersed family members, as was travel in a number of cases. In about one half the cases, interviewers and informants were blood relations. Semistructured interviews associated with this data set began with a discussion of objects inherited from family members, and included questions about the meanings, uses, and known histories of these objects, including how informants acquired the objects. If informants did not mention future plans for the object we probed to see whether they had future plans and, if so, what these plans might be. We also probed about objects they hoped to inherit, and about whether and what objects they hoped to pass on to younger or future family members.

The interviews were audiotaped and transcribed. Then, the data was organized, analyzed, and stored using qualitative data analysis software. Authors read each transcribed interview, noting specific themes and tensions they felt evident in the data. Axial coding across individual interview transcripts helped to determine shared themes and patterns (Miles & Huberman, 1993). Analysis focused on understanding common and contrasting structures in the informants' emic representations of practices and meanings associated with cherished possessions, and of strategies used to keep objects within the family (Wallendorf & Arnould, 1991). We employed three types of interpretation: analyses focused on an informant, between informants within a family, and between informants across our sample of middle-class Americans (Thompson, 1997).

We incorporated several techniques to ensure the trustworthiness of our results and increase the theoretical generativity of our work (Stewart, 1999; Wallendorf & Belk, 1989). First, to better understand heirloom ritual from the perspective of different family members, we triangulated across informants. Second, trustworthiness was addressed through triangulation across our team of analysts, a team reflecting diversity in gender, research experience, and academic training. Finally, we employed member checks to compare our interpretation with that of the informants. Participants were in substantive agreement with our interpretations.

FINDINGS: THE DESIRE FOR
AND DEVELOPMENT OF FAMILY HEIRLOOM RITUAL

Emerging from the data are two main themes related to family heirlooms. First, we found that informants want to create and to sustain rituals through tangible objects that ultimately are intended to become family heirlooms. Some consumers purchase objects around which to bundle family traditions and rituals. Other informants covet a family possession that has occupied an important role in informal family rituals, hoping to receive that item and intending to pass it forward through the lineage. The second theme that emerges from our data is the latitude that heirloom rituals seem to have, to absorb different ad hoc strategies consumers develop. For example, in some instances, informants visualized a future, mythic, family member that would continue the objects' trajectory through future progeny. Informants spoke of future heirs performing rituals of adoration and reverence with the inherited objects they were planning to pass forward. In other instances, consumers rely on past possession rituals (Rook, 1985) to propel an object forward within the lineage. Finally, they rely on possession rituals in combination with ascribed gender roles to preserve heirlooms for the future. Whatever the strategies that consumers select to mobilize ritual to create and to transfer cherished possessions, they seem to be very effective in using ritual to lock in meaningful cultural categories within the narrow confines of their small communities, their families.

Ritual Desire

As discussed in the introduction, we are struck by the presence of an affective state that might be described as a desire for ritual. Informants' desires reflect an understanding of the role of ritual in broadcasting, enacting, and commemorating tacit values. This affective state seems to translate into a desire for ritual action. This desire is often attached to mundane consumer goods. The following exchange about a tuxedo typifies this situation:

> *Resp2:* No, he wouldn't wear one. They said he had to and your Papa told him he wouldn't go to the wedding. And so when Stacy got married your Mama told him that again and he said if he had to wear one he wouldn't be going to your (Stacy's) wedding.
>
> *Int:* What is wrong with wearing a tux?
>
> *Resp1:* I don't like them, and I've never worn one in my life.
>
> *Resp2:* That black suit he's got hanging in there is so old it's a wonder it's not rottin' off the hanger.
>
> *Int:* How come you've kept it?
>
> *Resp2:* He wants to be baptized in it and buried in that suit.
>
> *Resp1:* If you want to see it, it's way back in that closet. It's a Kirby; it's the only type I used to have is a Kirby. It used to be the best type of suit in the world.
>
> *Int:* How old is it if you had it for Roland's wedding?
>
> *Resp1:* Let's see it must be more than 35 years, I don't know, I bought it downtown at Hooker's. (Married grandparents in their 60s)

Papa's Kirby suit has somehow attracted his desire for ritualized action, realized in relation to three life crises events (baptism, marriage, and burial). The interviewer's mother bemusedly tolerates the desire. Of course, Papa's desire to be buried in the suit forecloses its possibilities for becoming an heirloom!

An excellent illustration of the desire for ritualization surrounding an heirloom object is a ring (introduced in the opening vignette of this chapter) that will pass from grandmother to daughter, and that our informant hopes will later be passed on to her. Amanda echoes the hopes and ritual actions of her grandmother, who plans to pass the ring on to her daughter on her 50th birthday and longs for it to become a family heirloom. Our 22-year-old informant hopes the ring will later be passed on to her. She articulates the belief that she will also pass this ring on to her children. Amanda acknowledges that some may be surprised that she has given such serious thought to the future of this ring at a relatively young age:

> I don't think you'll expect a 22-year-old to already plan out her life minute by minute. I'd pass down the ring to my oldest daughter, assuming I'll get it from my mom. If I have only boys, I'll probably give it to my oldest son's wife. I'll write it in the will, for security, you know, but would give it either on a special occasion, or when I'll be real old. I'll let them know that my grandma and grandpa were in love and that he went to war, and she waited for him, and will ask them to pass it down to the next generation. Hopefully it will be something that will become a family heirloom in the future. (Amanda, Female, age 22)

Sometimes informants are matter-of-fact about their family's desire to develop ritualized intergenerational transfers of heirlooms as in the following exchange:

> *Int:* Could you tell me a little bit about what these objects mean to you? Which, if any you consider special possessions? Would you consider selling or disposing of some other way?

> *Resp:* All these items are family treasures and it is hoped that it will be retained by future generations as part of the historical background of our family therefore they are not for sale. (Humphrey, Male, 60s)

It is notable in Humphrey's comment that family heirlooms have been removed from the commodity sphere (Kopytoff, 1986), a comment echoed in many other interviews.

The following exchange exemplifies the desire for ritual manifest in a purchased product. Some informants do not find it problematic to extract items from the commodity sphere with the intention of injecting them into the sacred domain of heirloom possessions. Betty was asked if she has purchased anything to pass forward to future generations. She replied affirmatively, and said that would be her china and crystal. The informant wistfully accounts for her purchase of china and crystal, quintessentially women's goods in middle-class American consumer culture, in terms of a daughter she might someday have, and a ritualized bequest she might someday undertake. The exchange is noteworthy also because the father already understands and agrees with the ritualized goal to which the purchase is to be put. No further rationalization in terms of the usual grounds of thrift is apparently required. Betty explained,

> Yea. I didn't even have a daughter. The only reason.... Dad said, 'what do you want that for?' I said because maybe I'll have a daughter, and he said 'yeaaaaaa'. (Female, 40s)

Consumers espouse desires to create ritual through new product purchases, through the use of existing objects, or even through meaningful possessions that may have lain dormant for years. Consumers recognize that an inherited object may lie dormant for a generation, but often there is hope that a descendant may replicate ritual use in the future. Consider the following exchange:

> *Resp:* Keep it in the bank.
>
> *Int:* Keep it in the bank?
>
> *Resp:* Yes.
>
> *Int:* So you have never used it?
>
> *Resp:* No, no. It's a man's watch so I can't use it.
>
> *Int:* But no one has ever used it?
>
> *Resp:* Yes. My husband used it a bunch of times after my daddy died. He used it you know when we went out for special occasions. In fact my husband bought the chain.

Subsequently in the interview, when the informant was asked if she can remember getting any objects that she knew right away she would keep in the family, and maybe pass on to children or grandchildren, she replied,

> Oh yeah, the watch. (Mary, Female, 20s)

It might be expected that consumers' ritual longings would become manifest in amorphous and unsatisfied desires for tradition and community leading to simulacra provided by consumer goods and spectacular experiences. What we find instead is that consumers mobilize ritual to create and transfer cherished possessions and to lock in meaningful cultural values within the narrow confines of their small communities. Papa signals the importance of baptism, marriage, and death with his Kirby suit. Amanda's ring captures the ideas of true love, fidelity, and sacrifice. Humphrey's cherished antique silver plate symbolizes family accomplishments and continuity. Likewise, Patty, Mary, and Betty speak to the value they place on intergenerational continuity in same-gender relationships.

Informants hope to transfer both tangible heirlooms, as well as respective lessons, stories, and values tied to the object. Consumers translate their desire for ritual longings into ad hoc strategies through which they exert authoritative agency (Arnould & Price, 2000). Informants also enlist the weight of tradition to achieve authoritative, transformative ritual purpose through plans to duplicate earlier ritualized transfers. As Patty explains, this ring is to be transferred on the 50th birthday of the recipient, her daughter, Patty:

> I'll probably gather the entire family together, show them pictures of Jeff, their late father and grandfather, and tell them about the impor-

tance of the ring to me.... I'll tell her [Amanda] that I want her to pass it down to one of her daughters when she reaches the age of 50, and therefore making it somewhat of a tradition. (Female, age 45)

As consumers try to create ritual around family heirlooms, they seek to identify younger family members who may be interested in receiving, caring for, and later transferring the cherished item. In some cases, people find that there is no appropriate target for their cherished possessions, and they retain what they feel is their right to liquidate them. In other words, if potential targets do not seem likely to engage in ritual use of the object, heirloom caretakers reserve the option to return heirlooms to the commodity sphere. Thus, thwarted desire for ritualization may lead to liquidation.

This is illustrated in the following exchange as Luke discusses his extensive coin collection, acknowledging as an aside "the monetary value behind them is quite high":

> On the coin collection, I will probably give that to my daughter. I have tried to get one of my grandchildren interested in it, but out of the four, none of them so far have showed any interest. I may go ahead, after I have finished my complete inventory, and just sell the whole blasted thing!... The main thing is that I did want to keep it in the family, within the family members, but if no one is interested, well, then I might as well get some benefit for myself. (Male, age 76)

Luke still hopes that he can excite one of his family members with his coin collection, but he wants more than someone who will hold the collection and remember him by it, because he seems convinced that his daughter would do this. Instead, he wants someone who will get involved in the collection and *continue* his coin collecting ritual. This is paramount, for Luke wants to acquire a type of symbolic immortality so he will be able to "live on" through the continued use and building of his coin collection. Baring some promise that the value of continuing his works will transfer, Luke plans to liquidate the collection, and return it to the sphere of marketplace values (Kopytoff, 1986). As a default option, Luke feels that at least if he sells his coin collection, he will be able to find a buyer who will keep his prized collection alive.

Ritual Development

Some discussions of ritual continue to be informed by a Durkheimian vision of the conservative role of ritual in social contexts marked by "mechanical solidarity," while others have advanced the idea that ritual traditions may be creative inventions in modern societies (Moore & Myerhoff, 1977; Rivière, 1995; Rook, 1985; Segalen, 1998; Wallendorf & Arnould, 1991). We emphasize that consumers creatively combine elements of rituals they attribute to prior generations with particularities that mark the inflection of their individual experience. Contemporary consumer rituals are often an elective *bricolage* of new and borrowed elements. Their hallmark is behavioral latitude, a number of conventional narratives wrapped around a relatively small inventory of objects and set of uses. By connecting new events to preceding ones, heirloom rituals are incorporated into a stream of precedents so they are recognized as growing out of tradition and experience. Through a partial insistence on the preexisting and authentic, ritual suggests its contents are beyond question, and authoritative (Arnould & Price, 2000). The ring discussed by the 22-year-old informant quoted earlier illustrates this phenomenon. Amanda hopes to duplicate the disposition rituals surrounding previous familial transfers of the ring.

Storytelling

Even more so than other things (Kopytoff, 1986), people invest inherited objects with narrative. Storytelling figures prominently in the creation of family rituals. Rituals are reenacted with cherished possessions serving as the adhesive to which the family history, values, and beliefs adhere. Cherished items contain a visible, tangible veneer, but more importantly, they also contain intangible elements, including stories of the item's origin, and the values and beliefs the item represents. For example, the informant in the following excerpt explicitly links an inherited object to moral lessons:

> *Int:* Do you have any fond memories of these objects?

> *Resp:* Oh God yes, oodles and oodles of stories but I remember my mother making me read certain parts of the book, I really hated it. She wouldn't let me eat supper until I had read the story and was able to tell her about it. See, she was a real religious kinda person but every story was a lesson well learned. (Male, age 79, married)

In our data, storytelling, especially that containing origin stories, emerges as a strategic means for moving objects from the status of cherished possession to family heirloom. Informants often repeatedly recite the object's history to its future caretaker hoping he or she will learn the object's history and be able to pass the story forward in the lineage:

> Well, actually the children and I were talking about that last night. I have a gold watch that my Grandmother and Grandfather gave me when I was about fifteen that is ... it was my great-aunt's watch and it's actually engraved from her Mother to her. And, it's engraved and was given to her in 1901.... With "To: Nell, From: Mom, 1901. That was my Grandmother's sister and the fact that they entrusted it to me at the age of fifteen is very

special.... It was during a visit. As a matter of fact I think they gave it to me
when Fred and Carmen (brother and sister-in-law) were getting married
and they brought it with them. (Beth, Female, age 42)

Although she remembered telling her adolescent daughter, age 15, the story many
times, she had no idea her son, age 13, was also familiar with it. Absent a narrative
framing and behavioral reenactment, it is unlikely that the ritual surrounding this
watch will take hold. Beth's enthusiasm in explaining how surprised she was to
learn that her son also knew the story of her great aunt's watch was clearly visible:

She (daughter) and I were both surprised last night because she knew
about the watch and she didn't think that David (her brother) did. But,
he knew all about it. He told her the whole story last night.... He knew
the story exactly. He knew. In our house things are very important. I
mean, there are pieces Mother has given, she's given us that we really
cherish. (Beth, Female, age 42)

In addition to storytelling, people select ritual behaviors from a repertory of
those they recognize, but the ritual employment of an object is negotiated differently from generation to generation. Three special ritualized behaviors seem to
structure informants' interaction with inherited objects: use, display, and preservation. In addition to storytelling, these three behaviors give heirloom possessions
their authoritative force (Arnould & Price, 2000). As informants discuss the biography of family heirlooms, they also provide numerous illustrations.

Use

Possession use refers to a small set of devotional acts directed toward cherished possessions. We catalogue a number of the different applications. One is the
replication of use by current custodians consistent with its postulated usage by prior
generations. Inherited collections, which embody the idea of repetition, exemplify
this category of devotional acts frustrated in Luke's case (mentioned earlier).
Humphrey, also mentioned earlier, has a stamp collection he intends to pass on:

Int: Can you ever remember acquiring an object where you knew at that
time you would like to pass it on to future generations?

Resp: The stamps. Yes. It is family tradition to pass on precious items
inherited from previous generations to future generations who it is
hoped will pass them on to their children. (Male, 60s)

A second usage is an invented ritual use, such as the ring which we discussed in an
earlier section on ritual desire that informants plan to pass from mother to daughter
on the daughter's 50th birthday.

The third type of usage is the decision that the item should be preserved for usage by special persons or on special occasions. In this situation, special possessions may symbolize an acquired role within the family, with the object becoming a sort of token of office. Our data contained examples of new roles acquired when an heirloom is received. The following example illustrates this situation. The great aunt under discussion has taken on the role of family historian, with her curatorial role of archiving family possessions (McCracken, 1988). She is said to help keep the family "alive." The great aunt has become the "heart" of the family. Notice the "life sustaining" metaphor used by the informant in her discussion:

> My great aunt holds on to everything. She's become the bearer of the family treasures and with this stuff I am very interested. We have a very close family. My Aunt is very interested in keeping these things. She is like the heart of the family. She has kept all of the memory alive through her. (Cheryl, Female, age 53)

Display

When not preserved for usage, special objects may be displayed as narrative props, as a vessel for a tale that speaks to the values and beliefs to which family members are urged to adhere. Sometimes the display evokes a tale that is honorific and commemorative of ancestors' achievements, as in this account of an imagined display:

> The other thing I got of my grandfather's, um, a leather fishing tackle box. Inside it has all different types of rods, not rods, but reels, fishing reels and hand made fishing flies, that are made out of incredible feathers and pretty jeweled reels and stuff. I'm not a fisherman, but I know that it was very important to my grandfather who was an avid fishermen um, a lot of fly fishing, and these I heard are extremely valuable, some of them. I would never sell them. I would like to maybe make a display case with some of the flies in it, you know, in a room, like a family room or something, and have that to pass on to my kids, just because I know that my great-grandfather and father were fishermen. I'm going to definitely keep that. (Garth, Male, 20s)

Sometimes the item displayed evokes a moral value, such as the importance of marriage, a (warm) hearth, and home:

> Yes, definitely. Also with the wedding we received a gift from my husband's aunt and uncle. It was special because it came with a little story behind it. It was a silver chaffing dish that you would use to serve some kind of hot food to keep it warm or whatever. The chaffing dish had been given by the same aunt when she was real little to her parents on their 25th wedding anniversary, which just happened to be June 21st, which was the same date that we got married and at this time the grand-

parents had passed away. It has been in the family for a long time and also given as a wedding or anniversary gift.

And sometimes an elaborate moral tale is initiated through display, thus socializing the younger family members to the values depicted in the story whenever it is retold. An example of a tale of fidelity, love, courage, and overcoming obstacles is associated with the ring introduced at the beginning of this chapter:

> This ring was given to me by Jeff, my husband. He went off to fight in World War II. He left for nine very long months. Our only communication was a few letters every now and then. Anyhow, when he came home and I saw him for the first time, I was so incredibly happy. It was a joyous reunion. That's when he gave me this ring. I have it here now. Its a 14 carat-gold sapphire and diamond ring. It has 8 marquee-shaped sapphires surrounding 9 diamonds. There is also a diamond on each side of the ring. He bought it in Germany the first month he was there. He used most of the money he had. He told me that it was the most beautiful thing he saw and he immediately thought of me. The following eight months or so he kept the ring with him, and told his best friend that if anything, God forbid, happened to him, that he was to make sure that the ring got passed on to me. (Mrs. Thompson, Female, 72)

Display of the ritual object invites repeated storytelling about the object and tempts family members to recite its lessons as informants did for us.

In the following performance, the informant tells the story surrounding one of her most cherished possessions. It is the tacit religious meanings in the cross watch that persuade the informant's mother to allow her to wear the cross watch received from her boyfriend. Other items, however, contained tacit secular meanings. As this story has been told over the years the family's religious values are subtly reinforced, as well as those concerning the institution of marriage, and parental respect. Iris rarely wears the cross watch, because she is afraid she might lose it:

> A gold cross with a watch; a watch cross that he gave me in 1942, the year we met. And all these years I've kept it.... It's from our first meeting. He was leaving at the time he gave me this. We had known each other for about a month, I guess. Then he left.... He also sent me three Angora sweaters and some gloves. Beautiful sweaters. But I couldn't wear them, because my Mother felt that I didn't know him well enough and that he shouldn't have sent me anything that,... that personal. I had to wait until he got back. I guess I didn't wear them until after we got married. He had given me the cross. That was all right. She thought that was all right because she thought it was something holy or something. The sweaters, no. (Iris, Female, age 78)

Eva, Iris' daughter, was also interviewed in this project and cherished the unique piece of jewelry. She looks forward to receiving the treasured piece and intends to pass it forward to her daughter with its history bundled with it.

Preservation

Object ritual may also be carried out through product nurturing or preservation. What informants term restoration or refinishing exemplifies this behavior as in the following excerpt:

> *Int:* Not necessarily the value, how you feel about it.
>
> *Resp:* Oh- very, very deep. I feel like he's part of me there.
>
> *Int:* And has that feeling increased over the years?
>
> *Resp:* Oh, yeah.
>
> *Int:* The longer you hold on to the watch?
>
> *Resp:* Yes. Every once and a while I get it, and don't know how- it's hard to open and shut it, I'm afraid that … in fact I had it all cleaned and everything at Maas Brothers. Remember when Maas Brothers used to be?
>
> *Int:* Un huh.
>
> *Resp:* I paid $150.00, just to have it restored. (Mia, Female, age unclear)

Seeing an older family member repeatedly, carefully, and respectfully care for an item can communicate its importance to a familial audience and help secure its status as an heirloom. In the following vignette, Alfred discusses how he was socialized to the importance of the family grandfather clock while he was growing up, and illustrates how winding the grandfather clock was ritualized. When visiting his grandmother, she recited stories about the clock's history and its links to preceding family members. As a small boy, Alfred felt proud when his grandmother allowed him to wind it, and as others have suggested, participation in preservation activities is one way older consumers choose future recipients of family heirlooms (Cours, Heisley, Wallendorf, & Johnson, 1999; Price et al., 2000). Through preservation and storytelling, Alfred's family has taught him that this clock was a significant family heirloom attesting to the family's status. In doing so, they imparted a sense of responsibility for its preservation and for sustaining the family history bundled with the timepiece:

> The only thing [cherished possession] I can think of is the grandfather clock that was in the dining room that you saw. But I can remember, as a

real small kid, going to my grandmother's house and looking at this clock. She would let me wind it up. You had to be very careful how you handled it because it was soo old. So I really have a connection with that clock. (Alfred, Male, age 60)

A final kind of preservation is holding an heirloom in trust for a future recipient. Our data shows this is one common way family members seek to ensure an item will become an heirloom. Bequeathing a specific item to a specific individual helps to ensure the item's value by its recipient. In establishing a trust, older family members may make cherished possessions sacred (Small, 1999). Stanley illustrates this idea:

When my grandfather died, he left the watch to my mother with the understanding that she would one day give it to me. Because I was young when my grandfather died, my mother felt I was not ready to understand the significance and responsibility that this watch carried. Without my grandfather around, I lost the desire to wind the watch and soon forgot all about it. When I graduated from high school, my mother gave the watch to me as a gift, not from her, but from my grandfather. You know, this was the best gift I think I have ever received; to know that my grandfather thought enough of me to ensure his watch was passed to me. (Male, age 28)

Tensions Between Display and Use

Over time, the behaviors surrounding a cherished object may change, even if the storytelling does not. The informant stresses preservation over use of her dishes:

I was very young at the time, so I don't remember you know, a lot of details, I just remember that on the holidays when all the family got together my grandmother had a big, large dining room table. We would put the lace tablecloth on the table and she would set the table, and with the dishes and the glassware and that's about all I can remember. Um, it was very special to her, she only used it on special occasions and it was a gift from my grandmothers' daughter, which is my mother, so it held a sentimental value.... I really don't use them. They're in my china cabinet and they're just to admire and cherish. I would like to pass them on. I don't know which one of my children would like to have them, but um, we'll see. No one has ever expressed the desire to have them. (Female, 60s)

Later, this woman's daughter was interviewed and referred to these dishes as those she hopes to inherit. Like her mother, she emphasizes preservation, but to a greater degree than her mother she wants to make sure they are displayed so she can tell stories about them. Ritualization changes in emphasis from display and probable narration, to preservation and limited use of the heirloom glasses and dishes. An heirloom object may thus pass from generation to generation with each holder balancing competing motives somewhat differently. The following represents preservation and limited usage privileged over display and narration:

> *Int:* Tell me about how you use this object [grandmother's pocket watch]?
>
> *Resp:* It basically stays in a drawer and I don't take it out very often because I don't want it to get lost. It is just something that I look at from time to time.
>
> *Int:* Are there any special ways that you store this object?
>
> *Resp:* No, I just keep it in my jewelry box in the top drawer of my dresser. (Lori, Female, 20s)

Consumers recognize that even ritualized use of an object may threaten its preservation for future generations. Use represents a risk to preservation, for example, as when heirloom china is brought out on family feast days. After a lengthy discussion of how she nurtures and displays her heirloom crystal, an older woman reveals the tension between ritual preservation for use and preservation for display and storytelling:

> At times I do use them, special times. Not all times. I use them on holidays but I am careful. I get nervous when everyone touches them, but it's nice to use them. They are beautiful, better then crystal you get today. (Dorothy, Female, age 75)

Too-careful preservation threatens the evocative, narrative potential of cherished objects because an item locked away cannot trigger the spontaneous, ritual retelling of the family tradition that the object represents. Conversely, display and telling stories needlessly risks preservation if the story falls on deaf ears, such as a family member whose personal experiences do not resonate with the traditions embedded in the object. Thus, ritual use varies with how individuals negotiate boundaries between conflicting ritual actions.

The following gives some sense of behavioral latitude and the tensions between preservation for the ritual usage of inherited objects just discussed and preservation for display and narrative. The informant wants to sacralize her grandmother's chairs. The elect may touch them, discuss them, see them, but their use will be constrained. In the course of two generations, the chairs have moved from a furniture store window to a domestic altar (Belk et al., 1989). It also shows the picking and choosing, the *bricolage* amongst available traditions of use:

> *Resp:* The chairs, my mom will rarely use, they are just kinda hidden back in her room, you know, they are not able to, where a lot of people

could see them. And I think I would have them, like my grandmother did, my mamaw, she had them in a small section of the room, you know, a separate little sitting area. I might do something like that maybe, to where they can, I just think they are so pretty and maybe you could section off part of the room in some way.

Int: You wouldn't let anyone sit in them?

Resp: I don't know, maybe a special person (laughs)

Int: Would you keep them to yourself, or what do you think?

Resp: I don't know, I kinda want them to be seen, I want people to know that they were my mamaw's and that, you know, they have been my mom's and then mine.

Int: But you really wouldn't want them to be used?

Resp: No, no, no. (Lisa, Female, age 31)

The Latitudes of Ritual Development

Ritual helps to define as authoritative certain ways of understanding one's culture. It serves to specify what is of special significance in that social group. It draws attention to certain relationships and activities, while at the same time deflecting attention from others. In addition to designated ritual repertoires codified by tradition, often preserved in textual sources and presided over by trained experts, research has begun to recognize people can and do ritualize multiple activities to varying degrees. Work has looked at ritual in sports (Goethals, 1981; MacAloon, 1984; Segalen, 1994), organizations (Bourdieu, 1977; Davis-Floyd, 1994), spectacles (Geertz, 1973), and politics (Kertzer, 1988), but has devoted relatively little time to ritualization within families. In the small ritualizations associated with inherited, cherished possessions, we find people reach back into the past for the meanings of things. The past they reach back to, or perhaps the way they reach back to it, corresponds to the virtual, mythic, "subjunctive" past, which Schechner (1996) and Turner (1967) referred to as a source of ritual meanings generally. The following excerpt exemplifies the way heirlooms facilitate this way of remembering:

Int: Are there any objects you would like to inherit from another family member?

Resp: A mahogany wood dining room table. This has a lot of meaning to me because it belonged to my grandfather who I was close to and who is now deceased. This table was made for my grandfather by a close friend of his. The table was made sometime in the 1930's to be put in a new house my grandfather was building for himself and his family. When I was little, we would go to my grandparent's house for lunch every Sunday. The whole family would sit at this table and enjoy good food and conversation. We also celebrated many of my grandparents' wedding anniversaries sitting around this table. This object is a special possession of its current owner, my mother because it is a reminder of her parents, who are now both deceased. (Ewing, Male, 20s)

The categorical glosses "every," "whole," and "many" are indicative of the mythical nature of the past Ewing describes.

This is a past of the world "as if," steeped in ambiguity and nostalgia (Gillis, 1996). It is a past consumers recreate to serve their needs for the future. One woman reflects on her china in this vein, imagining its meaning to her ascendant relatives and what might happen to it "if." The china signifies family unity, a unity inscribed in the past, but the informant is able to connect it only vaguely to any particular event.

Int: Are there any objects you could think of that you would like to inherit from an older family member? Any object that you could think of? Maybe from your mother or grandmother?

Resp: … Probably my mother's china that she inherited from her grandmother. They'd mean a lot, because, whenever you're passing anything along, they really have a lot of meaning. There's fine china, you know some glasses, with my grandmother's initials on it. They kind of just, to me, mean family, unity. How we all still get along after all these years. Well my mother inherited the china from her grandmother, I believe, well her grandmother inherited from her mother. I think that's how the little train went, and that's about it. I just know that they're always in the china cabinet and they don't get used. They mean a lot to my mother. She obviously has a lot of meaning for the china. She told me they were in her grandmother's china cabinet and I know the significance with the glasses. Especially cause they have the initial on it, D, the initial for Davis, which is my grandmother's last name. And I just know they are very special to her, because every time we move and I help pack, she makes sure, she wants me to be careful and not to break them. If they were to break you know, I … they probably would be irreplaceable and she'd be upset about it. I mean you may be able to find something like that but it's just not the same once it's given to you. (Bertha, Female, 60s)

The following passage again illustrates the way consumers use ritual props to link to a mythic, subjunctive past. Here, the subjunctive quality of the past is symbolized by the use of the gloss "every." It is questionable if "every" one in this town set their watch by his grandfathers' clock. The example does, however, illustrate the very important role this clock plays in his family and in their perception of the history of the town:

> The clock was the town's timepiece for Troy, Ohio. Before nineteen hundred ... my great uncle, would go to Columbus, and set his pocket watch and then go back to Troy and set this clock. He was a jeweler. He had it in the front window and everybody else in town would come by and set their watches, by this clock, the official clock. (Alfred, Male, age 60)

Constructing Descent Groups

Strategies employing gender roles inform the development of heirloom ritual. In connecting to objects, people spontaneously provide evidence of gender-appropriate subject–object relationships, but also seem to be thinking in terms of implicit rules about inheritance. Alfred's grandfather clock is a case in point. It is interesting to note how resolute he is about his responsibility to pass this cherished possession on through the male family line. Although Alfred's story suggests he feels obligated to see that this clock and its biography are passed on to succeeding generations of his family, it was not until his son "finally" had a son that this informant felt confident of the clock's future. This quote is especially interesting because Alfred has two older daughters, who could have inherited the clock. However, gender informs the passage of this clock through Alfred's family line:

> And then I'm the last [male family member], and then I finally had a son, and he now has a son. And that clock has to go through that family, because it has been in the family for about a hundred and fifty years. (Male, age 60)

Implicit in a number of the interview excerpts, such as Alfred's comments, is the idea that one authoritative effect of the ritualization of heirlooms is the construction of descent groups. The following story tells us women are the guardians of the kin group, and the Bible is the sign of this stewardship. The Bible is passed down through the female line. It reveals that four generations is considered a deep genealogy. We learn the family tree is not yet up to date, suggesting some neglect of the kin-keeping role, and when the tree is brought up to date, this will provide symbolic completion of the current guardian's work. It also tells us this cherished, inherited possession is believed to be a more powerful social force than the bureaucratic forces of the State. The family Bible anchors the plot of this story:

> I know my mother gave me the family Bible when I got married because it goes to the first daughter, so it went to me. It will then be passed down to my daughter, Barbara. It has the family tree in it. I got the Bible because I was the only daughter, yeah. But my brother has things too, and most of the stuff my mother still has. She said that she was going to

write down who gets what things so we wouldn't all argue and fight over them.... The Bible, I always remember it being in the family. My grandparents, and then my mother, was the oldest daughter so she got it, and then I got it, and I will pass it to my oldest daughter. So it's at least four generations right now.... I have an interesting story about the Bible. Years and years ago I'd say, when I was a teenager, we're going back at least 50 years, my mother's sister needed to prove how old she was to Social Security and she had no proof. I mean we're talking older than my mother, so we're talking she was born before the 1900s, so her birth was recorded in this Bible and they took the whole Bible down to Social Security and that was all the proof that Social Security needed. Because that Bible is so old, and it has all of the births and deaths and marriages. So it is used as a legal register. I might try to give it to my daughter when I get it caught up to date. Yes, that's one of the things I would like to do when I retire, take the time to get that caught up to date. I have to record my grandchildren in it. (Charlotte, Female, 50s)

More typical of our data is the following exchange that illustrates the active ritualization process through which cherished possessions are used to construct an emotional community of kin linked through descent. The informant provides a detailed post hoc accounting of a set of behaviors involving her rings. The objects are embedded in a web of ritual gift giving that provides them with some of their symbolic charge (Price et al., 2000). The informant also engages in an act of verbal *bricolage* that symbolically charges birthdays and kin and birth order relationships in the family with significance. The behaviors are anointed with the sanctified aura of "tradition" as well:

Resp: Okay, one heirloom I inherited from my grandmother, is a ring. A heart shaped ring [that] has rubies and diamonds in it. Another heirloom I got, was from my mother that was a ring I got for my sixteenth birthday. That contains diamonds and sapphires. Actually, both of the rings I got for my sixteenth birthday.... My grandmother had bought this ring when she was living. And she always said that when I turned sixteen she was gonna give it to me. Okay, my grandmother passed away, therefore, my mother kept the rings for me. And as my grandmother wished, she gave it to me on my sixteenth birthday.... The ring that my mother gave me, was one that she purchased for me for my sweet sixteen, well when I turned sixteen. And the reason why she, I guess, gave one, gave a ring to me is because I am her only daughter and I am the youngest child. The story goes the same for my grandmother. I am her only granddaughter and I am her youngest grandchild. So, I think that's why it was passed along.... I plan on passing them on. I'm gonna pass on the ring my grandmother gave me to my grandchild. The ring my mother gave me to my daughter, my child. I am gonna try to keep that traditional. You know, granddaughter from grandmother, I mean daughter from mother. (Mary, Female, 20s)

People use inherited objects to imagine descent groups that are often temporally shallow and narrow in terms of kin affiliation. Our data suggests a thin and narrow social group is no barrier to ritualization. The ritualization of inherited special possessions projects the "subjunctive" past, the past "as if" and as it "should be," from the present into a project-to-be in the future, with the passing forward of the cherished item (Schechner, 1996). Typically, as in the last example, the mythological horizon evoked in the rituals surrounding inherited objects includes a future descendent. Often, then, a heroic figure who will preserve the family and continue the ritual use of the inherited objects is evoked, but one who exists in the future, not the past. Consider the following two examples:

Int: Do you plan to pass these objects forward to future generations? If so, what are your ideas about who should receive this object and when they should receive them?

Resp: If I have a daughter, I would like them to go to her, the rings and probably the pictures and then if I have a son with no daughter and he gets married and he would take it.

Int: You would give your son's fiancée your rings?

Resp: Probably after they got married, if I liked her. Heh, heh, heh, heh, heh. I would have to care about her like my Mamaw cared about my Mom. ...It really all depends on how my relationship is with my daughter-in-law. If I have as close a relationship as my Mom did, then things, not the rings, the rings would still go to my daughter, but you know some of the other things that we have would have to be considered who it goes to. (Lisa, Female, age 31)

The following also is illustrative:

It was given to me, basically, because of my relationship with my grandmother, before she passed away and because I was the first born in my family, the first born girl.... I definitely want to pass it on in the future. I want to give it to my first born, just as I had it. If I don't have any children, of course I will pass it to my sister Marcie's kid's, because it was her Grandmother also. (Cheryle, Female, age 53)

Thus, in many cases, it seems the small-scale ritualized behaviors associated with inherited cherished possessions and directed toward a mythologized future kinsperson aims to constitute a descent system, a shallow, bilateral system appropriate to American household organization. In this system, women often are constituted in their kin-keeping role, or in the role of provisional heirs who may one day treasure the special possessions people wish to project forward into the future.

CONCLUSION

Our study of the rituals consumers construct around inherited, cherished possessions throws into relief a number of underappreciated phenomena. First, individuals evoke a desire for ritual that enables them to link their own lived experience to imagined communities past and future, and to anchor their behavior in cultural continuities. Informants of varying ages and both genders evince this desire, one that attaches itself to an array of cherished possessions, notably heirlooms.

Consumer goods, the ubiquitous material of consumer culture, is a natural scaffold from which to build family rituals. Through repeated display, use, and storytelling, certain objects are imbued with meanings particular to the family. The small number of heirloom objects culled from the many objects the average consumer has at his or her disposal are selected for ritual attention because of the density of symbolic meanings so embedded. Even when informants cannot articulate what heirlooms have meant to their ancestors, they invoke their strong symbolic meanings. These items typically have the power to evoke nostalgic "affective experiential knowledge" (Belk, 1991a, p. 29), or represent continuity in the face of life's merciless discontinuities (Holak & Havlena, 1992).

Jewelry, for example, is a common heirloom item. Its choice is surely due in great measure to positive contamination gained through repeated close body contact with previous owners. Jewelry is often thought to be part of the extended self of its original owners, and because its acquisition is often linked to other life transitions, is apt to be dense with narrative associations. Through ownership and ritualized display, preservation, and use, contemporary family members are able to incorporate previous owners' strengths and achievements and add their own. With its strong mnemonic power, jewelry can provide surviving family members with a sense of comfort in the face of their loss, as well as a sense of continuity in the midst of change. The financial value inherent in much jewelry also attests to the status of family members. All of these characteristics make jewelry a likely medium for the development and sustenance of heirloom rituals.

Consumers' ritual longings are not amorphous. They are translated into a modest number of actions that enlist tradition while providing scope for personal agency. They are stored, displayed, sometimes restored, and protected from destruction. At the same time, and against this first set of practices, they are repeatedly used in calendrical and life transition rituals as people recognize that without repeated use, meaning is diluted. Finally, consumers concerned about family legacy, family tradition, and family values tell stories about heirlooms and their imagined past and future.

We have some evidence that our informants' strategies of ritualization serve them fairly well. These small rituals persist. They preserve the family's cultural uniqueness, a sense of tradition, and status, and also provide scope for individual action. Small rituals fit into consumer culture, and yet they oppose the mass commodity logic of the marketplace. Small rituals are a means of preserving and producing decommodified material culture and meanings (Wallendorf & Arnould, 1991). Through inheritance rituals, consumers create, reinforce, and negotiate power in household relationships, and assert the little traditions of the household and family against those provided by consumer culture. Ritualization enables people to solidify cultural categories for action and interpretation, and thereby create temporary orders of truth and reality.

Classic accounts of American kinship and the American household are virtually silent on the subject of ritual actions related to inheritance. By contrast, our research identifies cherished possessions that carry meanings particular to individual family groups. Our data is rich in informants' presumptions that mythical future heirs will provide symbolic immortality to the living through their subsequent actions. Ritualization among families draws meaning from, and serves to strengthen, the relationships and roles of family members. Through inheritance rituals, informants speak and act in a subjunctive mode; that is, in ways that privilege a future molded in tradition. Their behavior suggests they believe that traditions, even those constructed today, can endure indefinitely. Theories that announce the end of tradition in postmodernity need to take into account this temporal framing of family traditions.

As Cheal (1989), and participants in the French anti-utilitarian movement MAUSS have discussed (e.g., Caillé, 1994; Godbout, 2000), and our data strongly support, in contemporary ritual and in gift giving generally, the consumer is "no longer an isolated monad in a world without pity" (Nicholas, 1996, p. 87). Instead, the choices made in ritual consumer behavior suppose enlivened, participatory social relationships. Ritual does not mold people. Through ritual, people fashion and mold their world. Ritual is a tool for social and cultural jockeying; it is a performative medium that negotiates authority for and in relationships.

REFERENCES

Arnould, E. J., & Price, L. (2000). Authenticating acts and authoritative performances: Questing for self and community. In S. Ratneshwar, D. Mick, & C. Huffman (Eds.), *The why of consumption: Contemporary perspectives on consumer motives, goals, and desires* (pp. 140–163). New York: Routledge & Kegan Paul.

Arnold, E. J., Price, L., & Otnes, C. (1999, February). Making (consumption) magic: A study of white water river rafting. *Journal of Contemporary Ethnography, 28*(1), 33–68.

Belk, R. (1988). Possessions and the extended self. *Journal of Consumer Research, 15* (September); 139–168.

Belk, R. (1991a). The ineluctable mysteries of possessions. *Journal of Social Behavior and Personality, 6*(6), 17–55.

Belk, R. (1991b). Possessions and the sense of past. In *Highways and buyways* (pp. 114–130). Provo, UT: Association for Consumer Research.

Belk, R., Wallendorf, M., & Sherry, J., Jr. (1989). The sacred and the profane in consumer behavior: Theodicy on the Odyssey. *Journal of Consumer Research, 16*(1), 1–38.

Bell, C. (1992). *Ritual theory, ritual practice.* New York: Oxford University Press.

Bell, C. (1997). *Ritual: Perspective and dimensions.* New York: Oxford University Press.

Bourdieu, P. (1984). *Distinction: A social critique of the judgment of taste* (R. Nice, Trans.). Cambridge, England: Cambridge University Press.

Bourdieu, P. (1977). *Outline of a theory of practice* (R. Nice, Trans.). Cambridge, England: Cambridge University Press.

Caillé, A. (1994). *Don, Intérêt Et Désintéressement: Bourdieu, Mauss, Platon et Quelques Autres.* Paris: La Revue de M.A.U.S.S.

Cheal, D. (1989). The postmodern origin of ritual. *Journal for the Theory of Social Behavior, 18*(3), 269–290.

Cours, D., Heisley, D., Wallendorf, M., & Johnson, D. (1999). It's all in the family, but I want it. In E. J. Arnould & L. M. Scott (Eds.), *Advances in Consumer Research, 26,* 253–259.

Csikszentmihalyi, M., & Rochberg-Halton, E. (1981). *The meaning of things: Domestic symbols and the self.* New York: Cambridge University Press.

Davis-Floyd, R. (1994). The ritual of hospital birth in America. In J. P. Spradley & D. W. McCurdy (Eds.), *Conformity and conflict: Readings in cultural anthropology* (8th ed., pp. 323–340). New York: Harper-Collins.

Douglas, M., & Isherwood, B. (1979). *The world of goods.* New York: Basic Books.

Driver, T. (1998). *Liberating rites.* Boulder, CO: Westview Press.

Fischer, E., & Gainer, B. (1993). Baby showers: A rite of passage in transition. In K. Corfman & J. Lynch (Eds.), *Advances in Consumer Research, 20,* 320–324.

George, G. H. & Nelson, M. A. (1982). Man's infinite concern: Graveyards as fetishes. In R. B. Bowne (Ed.), *Objects of Special Devotion: Fetishism in Popular Culture* (pp. 136–150). Bowling Green, OH: Bowling Green University Popular Press.

Gillis, J. (1996). *A world of their own making.* New York: Basic Books.

Geertz, C. (1973). Deep play: Notes on the Balinese cockfight. In *The interpretation of cultures* (pp. 417–426). New York: Basic Books.

Godbout, J. (2000). *Le Don, La Dette et l'Identité: Homo Donator Vs. Homo Œconomicus.* Paris: La Revue de M.A.U.S.S.

Goethals, G. (1981). Ritual: Ceremony and super-Sunday. In *The TV ritual: Worship at the video altar* (pp. 5–16). Boston: Beacon.

Grimes, R. (1995). *Readings in Ritual Studies.* Columbia, SC: University of South Carolina Press.

Holak, S., & Havlena, W. (1992). Nostalgia: An exploratory study of themes and emotions in the nostalgic experience. In F. Kardes & M. Sujan (Eds.), *Advances in Consumer Research, 19,* 253–259.

Hollingshead, B. (1949). *Elmtown's Youth: The Impact of Social Classes on Adolescents.* New York: Wiley.

Holt, D. (1998). Does cultural capital structure American consumption? *Journal of Consumer Research, 25*(June), 1–25.

Hurd, J. (1985). Sex differences in mate choice among the "Nebraska" Amish of Central Pennsylvania. *Ethology and Sociobiology, 6,* 49–57.

Kamptner, L. (1989). Personal possessions and their meanings in old age. *The social psychology of aging, 17*(6), 493–514.

Kaufmann, J. C. (1980). Learning from the Fotomat. *American Scholar, 49,* 244–246.

Katriel, T. & Farrel, T. (1991). January Scrapbooks as cultural texts: An American art of memory. *Text and Performance Quarterly, 11,* 1–17.

Kertzer, D. (1988). The power of rites. In *Ritual, politics, and power* (pp. 1–14). New Haven, CT: Yale University Press.

Komarovsky, M., & Waller, W. (1945). Studies of the family. *American Journal of Sociology, 50*(May), 443–451.

Kopytoff, I. (1986). The cultural biography of things: Commoditization as process. In A. Appadurai (Ed.), *The social life of things: Commodities in cultural perspective* (pp. 64–91). New York: Cambridge University Press.

Kottak, C. (1983). Ritual's at McDonald's. In M. Fishwick (Ed.), *Ronald revisited* (pp. 52–58). Bowling Green, OH: Bowling Green Popular Press.

Lavely, W. (1992). Family division and mobility in North China. *Society for Comparative Study of Society and History, 10,* 439–463.

MacAloon, J. (1984). Olympic games and the theory of spectacle in modern societies. In *Rite, drama, festival, spectacle: Rehearsals toward a theory of cultural performance* (pp. 241–259). Philadelphia: Institute for the Study of Human Issues.

McCracken, G. (1988). Lois Roget: A curatorial consumer. In *Culture and consumption: New approaches to the symbolic character of consumer goods and activities* (pp. 44–53). Bloomington, IN: Indiana University Press.

Mead, M. (1948). *And keep your powder dry: An anthropologist looks at America.* New York: W. Morrow & Co.

Mick, D., Burroughs, J., Hetzel, P., & Brannen, M. (1999). A global review of semiotic consumer research: Progress Problems and Prospects. Working paper. Madison: University of Wisconsin-Madison, School of Business.

Miles, M., & Huberman, A. (1993). *Qualitative data analysis: A sourcebook of new methods* (2nd ed.). Newbury Park, CA: Sage.

Moore, S., & Myerhoff, B. (1977). *Secular ritual.* Amsterdam: Van Gorcum.

Myerhoff, B. (1996). Death in due time: Construction of self and culture in ritual drama. In R. Grimes (Ed.), *Readings in ritual studies* (pp. 393–412). Upper Saddle Hall, NJ: Prentice-Hall.

Nicholas, G. (1996). *Du Don Rituel au Sacrifice Suprême.* Paris: Editions La Découverte/M.A.U.S.S.

Olsen, B. (1995). Brand loyalty and consumption patterns: The lineage factor. In J. Sherry, Jr. (Ed.), *Contemporary marketing and consumer behavior: An anthropological sourcebook* (pp. 245–281). Thousand Oaks, CA: Sage.

Parsons, T. (1943). The kinship system of the contemporary United States. *American Anthropologist*, n.s., *45*, 22–38.

Price, L., Arnould, E., & Curasi, C. (2000). Older consumers' disposition of special possessions. *Journal of Consumer Research, 27*(2), 179–201.

Rivière, C. (1995). *Les Rites Profanes*. Paris: Presses Universitaires de France.

Rook, D. (1985). The ritual dimension of consumer behavior. *Journal of Consumer Research, 12*(December), 251–264.

Schechner, R. (1996). Restoration of behavior. In R. Grimes (Ed.), *Readings in ritual studies* (pp. 441–458). Upper Saddle River, NJ: Prentice-Hall.

Schneider, D. (1980). *American kinship: A cultural account* (2nd ed.). Chicago: University of Chicago Press.

Schneider, D. (1973). *Class differences and sex roles in American kinship and family structure*. Englewood Cliffs, NJ: Prentice-Hall.

Segalen, M. (1994). *Les Enfants d'Achille et de Nike*. Paris: Métaillé.

Segalen, M. (1998). *Rites et Rituels Contemporains*. Paris: Editions Nathans.

Small, L. (1999). Sacred space (Tremenos) and heirlooms (Sacra) serve a totemic function within the homes of elder Americans. *Journal of Religion, Disability & Health, 3*(1), 99–114.

Stewart, A. (1999). *The ethnographer's method*. Thousand Oaks, CA: Sage.

Stone, E. (1988). *Black sheep and kissing cousins: How our family stories shape us*. New York: Viking Penguin.

Stones from Bones. (2002). *The Economist*, August 24, p. 49.

Sussman, M., Cates, J., & Smith, D. (1970). *The family and inheritance*. New York: Russell Sage Foundation.

Thompson, C. (1997). Interpreting consumers: A hermeneutical framework for deriving marketing insights from the texts of consumers' consumption stories. *Journal of Marketing Research, 34*(November), 438–455.

Tobin, S. (1996). Cherished possessions: The meaning of things. *Generations: Journal of the American Society on Aging, 20*(Fall), 46–48.

Tuan, Y. (1976). Geopiety: A theme in man's attachment to nature and to place. In D. Lowenthal & M. J. Bowden (Eds.), *Geographices of the mind: Essays in historical geography* (pp. 111–339). New York: Oxford University Press.

Turner, V. (1967). *The forest of symbols: Aspects of Nbembu ritual*. Ithica, NY: Cornell University Press.

Turner, V. (1969). *The ritual process: Structure and anti-structure*. Chicago: Aldine.

Unruh, D. (1983). Death and personal history: Strategies of identity preservation. *Social Problems, 30*(3), 340–351.

Wallendorf, M., & Arnould, E. (1988). "My favorite things": A cross-cultural inquiry into object attachment, possessiveness, and social linkage. *Journal of Consumer Research, 14*(March), 531–547.

Wallendorf, M., & Arnould, E. (1991). We gather together: The consumption rituals of Thanksgiving day. *Journal of Consumer Research, 19*(June), 13–31.

Wallendorf, M., & Belk, R. (1989). Assessing Trustworthiness in Naturalistic Consumer Research. In E. Hirschman (Ed.), *Interpretive consumer research* (pp. 69–84). Provo, UT: Association for Consumer Research.

Warner, W. (1959). *The living and the dead: A study of the symbolic life of Americans.* New Haven, CT: Yale University Press.

Wilhelm, M. (1997). Inheritance, steady-state consumption inequality and the lifetime earnings process. *The Manchester School, 65*(4), 466–476.

Zelinsky, W. (1976). Unearthly delights: Cemetery names and the map of the changing American afterworld. In D. Lowenthal & M. J. Bowden (Eds.), *Geographies of the mind: Essays in historical geography* (pp. 171–195). New York: Oxford University Press.

Part V

Pushing the Boundary of Ritual

12

Moving on to Something Else: The Social Relations of Women During Separation

Jean-Sébastien Marcoux
HEC Montreal

The literature on the sociology of the family shows that since the 1960s-1970s the hegemony of marriage and of the nuclear family in many Western societies has been challenged. Other forms of conjugal relationships, such as common law relationships or cohabitation, are important in countries such as Canada, Britain, and France. Single-person households, single-parent families, couples without children, and same-gender relationships are also increasingly common. As Segalen (2000) noted, these new forms of domestic relationships are not new in themselves. What is new is the change in the ideological values associated with them, that is, the fact that such relationships are no longer perceived as deviant. What emerges as socially significant, therefore, are the "new" ways of thinking about domestic relationships. New norms of domestic life and intimacy (deSingly, 1996, 2000; Giddens, 1992; Jamieson, 1998) have arisen that relate to love, sexuality, and the balancing of personal autonomy and freedom with life as part of a couple. These new norms are related to changes in women's status. They are also linked to new attitudes regarding women's sexuality, new means of birth control, and changes in divorce legislation. It is important to note here that there is a growing awareness that relationships do not necessarily last forever. As Segalen (2000, p. 131) put it, "*au couple fusionnel se substitut le couple éphémère*" (transient couple relationships take the place of permanent ones). In other words, divorce and separation have moved into the realm of the ways in which people think about domestic, family, or intimate relationships. How do people cope with changes in relationships? Do changes in relations coincide with changes of places? How does mobility intervene in a separation process? More importantly, is this a gendered process? These are questions that need to be investigated.

WOMEN, SEPARATION, AND MOBILITY

This chapter focuses on women who move on their own in the course of a separation; this move is one that sociologists often describe as difficult. DeSingly (1993) argued that in France women often move out of the conjugal relationship into hardship, and even poverty. In Britain, McCarthy and Simpson (1991) described the postseparation trajectory as a "game of snakes and ladders" for women. Within Canada, the site of the present research, governmental authorities and housing advocacy groups recognize that women looking for an apartment are often victims of sexual discrimination.[1] This is especially true as regards single women with children, women from visible minorities, and women receiving social assistance (O'Hanley, 2002; Société d'habitation du Québec, 2000). Moving on one's own also entails the risk of a loss of status, a loss of position, and housing declassification (Gilroy, 1994). In Montreal, the average income of divorced women is $23,908 (as opposed to $32,314 for divorced men), $20,570 for separated women (as opposed to $32,349 for separated men), and $24,151 for single mothers (as opposed to $45,546 for single fathers)(Statistics Canada, 1997). Women's "financial effort" is greater:[2] Acceding to housing autonomy after a separation is also often more expensive.

Social class and financial condition help to determine whether separation will be a difficult experience. In fact, men may also suffer precarious life conditions after a separation. Having said that, the problematisation of women's experience is motivated by a weak understanding of the gendering of displacement. The idea that moving on one's own may be emancipatory, or at least that it may occur as part of women's emancipation, emerges in recent novels by women, such as Anne Tyler's (1996) *Ladder of Years* or Nancy Huston's (1994) *La Virevolte*. It also resonates in the middleclass ideal of autonomy and the desire to have a successful separation—just as one would try to have a successful marriage (deSingly, 1993). Is this an idealized or fictionalized account? At the very least, this view contrasts with the stereotype of the woman who goes to pieces when faced with a move. This stereotype can be seen in the psychological literature on the pathogenic and disruptive effects of moving emerging in the 1960s-1970s, in which women appear to be more vulnerable than men to mobility, and, indeed, to every kind of change (Butler, McAllister, & Kaiser, 1973; Guibaud, 1979; McCollum, 1990; Millet, Pon, Guibaud, & Auriol, 1980; Vereecken 1964; Weissmann & Paykel, 1972). An aetiology and a psychopathology of displacement identify women as a population at risk of ex-

---

[1]Researchers such as Weisman (1992) go as far as suggesting that housing design that is insensitive to women's realities is often inadequate, not to say discriminating.

[2]For instance, 41% of the women living in the Montreal region (as opposed to 13% of the men) devote more than 30% of their income to housing expenses (Statistics Canada, 1996).

periencing a range of problems associated with moving, from neighborhood pathology to "relocation blues," "postmove blues," "moving day blues," nostalgia, homesickness, homelessness, depression, home mourning, and so forth. The representation of feminine vulnerability lying behind such an essentialist discourse can be found as far back as Aristotle's *Economics* (Foucault, 1984, p. 229). It is also found in 19th-century works on biology, such as those by Geddes (Laqueur, 1990, p. 6; emphasis added), who holds that men are more active, energetic, eager, and passionate than women who, for their part, are passive, conservative, sluggish, and *stable*.

Understanding the Ritualization of Mobility

The present chapter tries to understand women's agency, namely the active role that women play when moving in the course of a separation. This discussion is particularly interested in how women cope with broader social constraint, how they live under the pressure of larger factors they cannot control (e.g., gender inequalities, access to housing and social exclusion), and how they do so through small manipulations of their material environment. The goal is to emphasize how an event such as a separation, which is often constrained, sometimes even violently so, can be invested with the meanings of a ritual and appropriated as such. Drawing on the anthropology of rites of passage (Turner, 1969; van Gennep, 1909) and on the literature on the ritualization of mobility (McCracken, 1988; Petiteau, 1995; Rautenberg, 1989), this chapter explores how such moves are often constructed as opportunities to effect a life transition, to redefine oneself and to order one's life and relationships. The material culture approach inspired by the work of Miller (1987) on the anthropology of consumption can be useful for understanding this transition. The contributions of Belk (1988, 1992) and Mehta and Belk (1991) are also relevant in this regard because they allow for the examination of how such a transition may be imbued with something of a "sacred" character. Belk (1992) examined how migrations may be invested with a quasi-sacred character and how possessions—those possessions that people take with them and they use to recreate their sense of home and their sense of self—may play a "key ritualistic" role. Although Belk's work is based on Mormon migrations in the United States during the 19th century and Indian migrations during the 20th century, his emphasis on "transitional objects" (Winnicott, 1953) as extensions of the self is still highly topical (Parkin, 1999). The analysis of objects in transitory situations is even more interesting in the light of recent works on domesticity (Buchli & Lucas, 2000; Miller, 2001) that emphasize how the home environment provides subjects with an intimate structure, or a "second skin," in which they may exist as a subject. In this respect, it is worth revisiting Belk's consideration of the quasi-sacredness of mobility and extend it to the study of more mundane forms of mobility such as the short, critical moves occurring in the course of a separation. Before proceeding further, however, it is important to give some consideration to the methodology and the general context of the research undertaken for this analysis.

An Ethnographic Approach

This reflection is part of a broader study of the experience of mobility through the process of house moving in North America. It is grounded in ethnographic field-work that took place between September 1997 and July 1999 in Montreal. The ethnographic approach relies on a prolonged immersion in the phenomenon under study and a strict collaboration with informants. Ethnographers do not work "on" the people, but "with them" (Amit, 2000; Wolcott, 1999). In trying to grasp a phenomenon like the dissolution of a household, informants were accompanied throughout the process of their move and assisted in their move: from the preparation of the move through the move per se to the settlement in the new home. Data were collected among some 30 households, through participant observation and interviews. Informants were recruited via real estate agents, social housing authorities, personal contacts, and by word of mouth. The present chapter focuses on women between ages 25 and 44 who move on their own in the course of a separation, or who are in the process of coming to terms with a separation. Most come from the middle class. None were married; all lived in common law relationships. While taking care not to introduce any biases into the study, for the sake of clarity more attention is devoted to certain representative informants.

Most of the informants are women. This may be explained by the fact that women are more often in charge of the move (Desjeux, Monjaret, & Taponier, 1998; Kaplan & Glenn, 1978), or at least more involved in the "hidden" parts of the move, such as its preparation, the house cleaning, and so on. Caring for the family's "equilibrium" is also often a woman's responsibility. This is illustrated by the numerous articles published in magazines like *Parents*, *Children Today*, or *Chatelaine*, during the 1970s–1980s, which advise women on how to ease the move for their families (Harris, 1989; Light & Hass, 1983; Smardo, 1987; Weinstein, 1971). As far as could be observed, the concerns of women who move on their own are no different from those of persons living in stable relationships who move. Their task, however, is probably more difficult. Interestingly, they were more inclined to talk about their experience than men. Because an important element of the transition process analyzed here is the ability to exert one's control over a situation that seems to be getting out of control, taking part in the research probably helped them cope with the crisis by externalizing their fear, anxiety, and anguish.

A central bias in interpretation comes from the fact that what is presented here is a male view of women's reality, a view that is necessarily only partial. One of its limitations is that it does not account for men's experience. Despite these drawbacks, this chapter sheds new light on a common feature of separation, on the gendering of mobility and its ritualization. It reveals how women deal with transitional situations through material culture, and how they assert their agency in such situations.

MOVING ON, ONE STEP AT A TIME

During my fieldwork, I encountered several women who moved on their own in the course of a separation. One was a 37-year-old single woman named Regina who worked in the health sector[3] and whom I met through a real estate agent. She was then living alone in her mother's house, which was left vacant when the latter was institutionalized. Regina had been living in her mother's house since she separated from her partner 3 years earlier. After 3 years, the house was sold. Regina purchased her own condominium within the same area, close to her mother's institution, in case "something happened." People like Regina who get separated or divorced are among the more mobile in Canada (Ram, Shin, & Pouliot, 1994), especially when they are about 40 years old. This is important considering that in the province of Quebec, for instance, the number of marriages celebrated dropped from 49,695 to 23,963 between 1971 and 1996. During the same period of time, the length of marriages became shorter and the number of divorces grew from nearly 5,000 to 18,078 (reaching 48%), but the number of people living in common law relationships increased substantially (Bureau de la statistique du Québec, 1999). Statistics, however, do not account for the progressive dimension of separation. Regina did not separate overnight. She did it progressively, one step at a time. She recalled the first time she left her apartment and moved in with her partner, Thierry, at his own place. After living with him for nearly 2 years, she realized there was no room for her in his home. She could not find an exclusive escape space at "Thierry's place." She felt strangled there. In March, when her relationship with her partner was disrupted, when it was "rocked 'n rolled" as she put it, she had a telephone line put in at her mother's house, as if paving the way for her departure. In May, she moved her furniture into her mother's house. But she herself only moved in November. She moved into her mother's house because it appeared to be practical at that time. It saved her the rent. It gave her some time to move out of Thierry's place and try to move on.

When reflecting on those years she spent in her mother's house, Regina confessed that she always felt in transit. In fact, she never really settled. She did not unpack the boxes of dishes she brought from her partner's house. She simply used her mother's dishes, that had remained in the house. She did not even attempt to appropriate the place as her own. She hung her photographs on the hooks that were there, at the same place where frames had been hung for years, with their forms and contours left on the wall. She simply occupied the place. Still, she considered this

---

[3]In order to protect the anonymity of the respondents, the names have been changed.

move as an opportunity, at last, to recover from her separation, and to come to terms with it and to succeed in it.

Full Ashtrays and Other Details of a Couple's Life

Like Regina, most of my informants separated gradually, by going through different stages. Beatrice, a 41-year-old teacher who is the mother of two children, had been cohabiting with her partner for 2 years and had thought about leaving him for 6 months before actually doing it. She first considered separating after one year of cohabitation, but she gave up her project, as she explained, because she thought that it would probably be better for her children if she remained with their father. She finally decided to leave when realizing that her relationship was not going anywhere, and that she was in charge of everything. However, she had to stay with him under the same roof for 6 months, until she could find her own apartment. She conceded that this had been difficult.

As was common among the informants, Beatrice's and Regina's personal biographies are punctuated by several changes of residence that are themselves punctuated by changes in relationships. A relationship may not be going anywhere, as Beatrice put it. It may have had its day. Things may have changed, as Regina explained. Gigi, a 40-year-old woman, recalls when she left her boyfriend: "We stayed one year together. One year and a half, and at some point, it didn't work. So I left, but I was pregnant with my son. So I went to stay at some friends, to take time to find something else, to rent a flat, to settle again." Middle-class women, like the ones mentioned here, consider separating when the life of the couple does not meet its promises, when they are looking for something else through someone else. The partner, the man, is often depicted as irresponsible, as in the case of Beatrice. He is presented as weakly involved, as Caroline (age 24) put it. Mrs. Blackburn, a 41-year-old woman, preferred to live apart from her boyfriend of 2 years and "see him during the week ends." Others, like Mira, a 49-year-old woman, never lived with their partner. Mira explained that she never stayed with the father of her daughter, adding, "Some people do not bother you if you don't live with them.... Details like full ashtrays become embarrassing at some point."

These women believe in autonomy, and in the mastering of their own fate. In Giddens' (1992) line of thought, their relationships appear to have no other *raison d'être* over and above their own appreciation. They seem to be governed by what deSingly (1996) called a logic of choice, by the freedom to choose a partner. If deSingly's position is pushed to its logical extreme, then a separation does not even mean a rupture. When the partner is not perceived as complementing one's self project, a separation may well be considered. People, however, may have to endure a detrimental situation for weeks, months, even years, before "making a move" in the literal and metaphorical senses. Unlike Regina, they may be forced to live in the same place because of a lack of resources or support outside the home.[4] They may have to remain with their partner even though the separation procedure is initiated, and despite the stress, the tensions, and the common eruption in violence.

Succeeding in One's Separation

Beatrice tried to leave on several occasions, but all her attempts to find an apartment failed. She was handicapped by bad references from her landlord and was discriminated against for having children. She was at last able to relocate on the same street, only 250 meters away. Beatrice remained in the area for the sake of her children: to ensure that her children had some "emotional stability" as she put it. She explained her choice by referring to her attachment to the neighborhood: She knew the neighbors and she felt confident there. By moving in the same area, her children could remain in the same day care. She could also remain close to her job. She knew that she could come back quickly from work if an accident happened to her children. Beatrice and her partner also made residential arrangements. As one consultant in mediation interviewed told me, in some instances of shared custody, people try to remain close by, allowing the children to visit both parents, and to remain in the same school. They may also duplicate their children's world through the arrangement of toys and furniture (Wexler, 1998). In other words, they remain related to each other, relationships keep on mattering, despite the separation. A feeling of autonomy, thus, is not always irreconcilable with maintaining some links with the former partner, although he is conspicuously absent at the time of the move, or is denied any presence, as we will see when discussing the sacrifice of "abject objects."

Far from being manifestations of a failed separation, making residential arrangements, remaining "friends" with the former partner, and continuing to assert one's parental authority help measure the "success" of one's separation (deSingly, 1993). Actually, the women concerned remain where relationships work, among significant people like the friends and relatives who may be expected to provide moral support as well as practical forms of help. They also remain where they can work as members of relationships, whether for their children, or for their parents in need. Paradoxically, they even tend to reinforce the obligations that may contribute to their exploitation as women. In contrast to Tyler's or Huston's depictions of women leaving "everything" behind, they remain within a web of obligations, which helps them cope with the move and gives them a sense of who they are and what they count for. This is particularly important in a crisis context such as this, at the crux of a transition, during a period of uncertainty when familiar landmarks may be lacking. Hence, in the middle-class realm, a separation is construed as suc-

---

[4]Social housing, "transition houses," and "short term solutions" are also important (Front d'action populaire en réaménagement urbain, 2000).

cessful because of the "mental," or metaphorical, transition it allows, not because of the physical distance covered. The move itself, however, remains important as a way of making a separation concrete.

EMANCIPATION IN MOTION?

After 2 years of living with her boyfriend, Caroline, a 24-year-old woman working as a horticulturist, decided to take an apartment with a girlfriend on the grounds that her boyfriend was irresponsible and did not do anything at home. A few days after this announcement, Caroline's boyfriend started to clear out his things and move to his mother's home. Caroline did not intend to provoke such a rupture, but she confessed that she knew it would happen. She moved on purpose!

Caroline is younger than Beatrice, Regina, Mrs. Blackburn, and the other informants. She is entering adult life and this is the first time she has lived with a boyfriend, although he is not her first partner. The major difference probably concerns the extent to which Caroline and her boyfriend were a "couple". The relationship with a "boyfriend" is less formal than that involving a common law spouse, which has legal resonance without legal status.

Actually, Caroline's attitude is reminiscent of that of Shell, the main protagonist of *The Favorite Game* (1963), a novel written by the Montreal poet Leonard Cohen. This novel depicts a Jewish woman who considers her marriage to be a failure, and attempts to shake her husband up by moving on her own. When she realizes that this does not affect him, she takes a lover, hoping to provoke a reaction on his part. She leaves him when she realizes how little he cares for her. Without going as far as Shell, Caroline used the move to renegotiate the terms of her relationship and to provoke some changes in her intimate life. A few weeks after her move, Caroline and her boyfriend came back together, but on a different basis. He was now living at his mother's place. As she explained, she could see him as much as before. The difference was that she would see him whenever she wanted.

The Violence Contained in a Move

Beneath her appearance of an actor in full control, Caroline moved out herself because she could not claim any right over the joint home. As she could not throw her partner out, Caroline was compelled to move in order to take control of her relationship. In her case, the compulsion to move exerted itself subtly. In other cases, it may be far more brutal. Sandra, a 41-year-old single mother, was separated 9 years earlier from a violent partner. She was literally "thrown away" from her place as she explained. She talked about the 9 years following her separation as a come-down. She experienced housing declassification and found herself confined to social housing since then. Sandra's case gives credence to the traditional feminist critique that holds that home is often a space of confinement for women (Duncan, 1981, 1996) or an oppressive space (Madigan & Munro, 1999; Munro & Madigan, 1993). This critique opens up a broader discussion of issues of privacy and privatization. Such issues are based on the notion deeply embedded in North American and British political theories of freedom and sovereignty that home is the place where people can do what they want. Privacy is a concept that patterns and legitimizes the exclusion of outsiders (Chapman & Hockey, 1999). As Duncan (1996) argued, such a construction of home is also employed to construct, control, discipline, confine, exclude, and suppress gender and sexual differences, as well as to preserve traditional patriarchal and heterosexist power structures.

It is worth extending the feminist critique in order to consider the extent to which the compulsion to move may be affected by issues of gender. Caroline could not "throw" her boyfriend out. Sandra could not resist being "thrown out." Regina could not claim any right over "Thierry's place." What varies here is the degree of violence—physical and symbolic (Bourdieu, 1998)—underlying the separation, and then the move. To some extent, a certain degree of violence is always present in such a move. This fact tends to support Parkin's (1999) argument that from a philosophical point of view, it is impossible to draw a distinction between voluntary and forcible movements as elements of both are always involved. In this respect, Beatrice's move can be considered to have been constrained. She could have kept the apartment she shared with her partner, but only at a high cost. Remaining in place on her own would have entailed accepting a significant increase of expenses. To take McCarthy and Simpson's (1991) formula, the apartment would have been a poisoned chalice for her; staying put would have been a "Pyrrhic victory." In other words, Beatrice, no less than other women, was obliged to leave in order to move on. Her case is not singular. In practice, women move more often than men in cases of divorce because of financial hardship (Wexler, 1998). They move more although, in principle, they keep the dwelling more often when children are involved.[5]

Despite the difficulties they encountered when separating and the fact that they were often compelled to move and to face social constraints beyond their control as a result, the middle-class women rarely talked about their move as an act of resignation, or rendition. A move in the course of a separation may be concomitant to the loss of power. At the same time, within the context of middle-class values and financial means, it may provide people with their only room for maneuver. If movement is a polythetic category of experience (Rapport & Dawson, 1998), it possesses no *sui generis* effect. In other words, there is no absolute association between movement and disempowerment, or stability and imprisonment. Moving can be violent, and at the same time liberating.

---

[5]In the province of Quebec, the parent in charge of custody (usually the mother) is usually granted a right to remain in place. In 1998, in the cases of divorce, mothers obtain custody for 68% of the children, fathers 14%, whereas 17% of the children live in shared custody (Duchesne, 2001).

Metaphors of the Fresh Start

The middle-class women interviewed often described their move as liberating, as a way of escaping the pressure of a constraining relationship or of the sediments of that relationship condensed in a place. They described it as a "fresh start," a means of "starting all over again," or as an opportunity for "changing their skin." Such sentiments are consistent with Charbonneau's (1998) work on women's separation. She noted that the move, or the succession of moves, following a separation are often motivated by no particular logic, but rather by the feeling that a change would be preferable to the present situation. The move is intended to put an end to an unbearable situation. This is striking in the case of Sandra, who was forced to move because of violence, and who talked about her move as a "liberation." Beatrice, for her part, considered her move to be a positive event, an occasion to start over again at last, perhaps with someone else. Just like Beatrice, Regina saw her move as a "positive event" because it corresponded to her needs, to the way in which she wished to live at that period of her life. She wanted, as she put it, to effect a certain "withdrawal," to find refuge in a place that would reflect her. She wanted to "recover" from her separation. Regina conceded that living alone was not an end in itself, and she would consider moving into a new place if she were to meet somebody else.

These women differ from the image depicted in sentimental literature, that of the inconsolable woman who forever awaits the return of her Prince Charming. Far from fearing life on their own, or even worse, failing to achieve emotional autonomy, these women consider moving into a new place with someone else as part of building up a relationship. Accepting the idea of moving in with someone else becomes a sign of their willingness to give a potential partner a chance.

The construction of the move as a fresh start is not the product of rationalization, delusion, or alienation. What people strive to assert is a sense of agency, understood in the sense of Buchli (1999) as the creative manipulations of individuals, and their appropriation of constraints. This is not to say that moving is empowering—not in any simple sense. Financial autonomy is strongly related to the capacity to succeed in moving; and, here again, class is important. Nor should the heavy emotional charge attached to such a move be underestimated. Sandra experienced violence, Beatrice went through a hard time, and Caroline likewise admitted how difficult her decision had been. The difficulties that these women went through when moving out from a relationship, or the negative aspects of the separation, should not be underestimated. The downward trend toward poverty that may result from the move, as well as the diminished self-esteem and guilt feelings that may result from the failure of the relationship make the experience a difficult one. However, it is precisely because moving in such circumstances is emotionally charged, because it is difficult, not to say violent, that the symbolic dimension of the move needs to be taken into consideration.

"I USUALLY CHANGE BEDS WHEN I MOVE": ASSERTING AGENCY THROUGH THE MINUTIAE OF LIFE

When discussing the new place she would create after her move, Caroline used to talk about making a place where she could cultivate as many plants as she wanted. Plants, for her, are almost a *raison d'être*. To take up Gilroy's (1994) metaphor, her case subverts the story of Cinderella, who can only attain her castle after being chosen by her prince. Caroline, in contrast, wanted to create the home of her dreams and choose the partner who would fit into it. Her case brings to the forefront the role of possessions: the things one takes with one. Just like Caroline, Regina moved with what she described as her "mobile roots": pieces of furniture inherited from her grandmothers, family heirlooms, and so forth; and objects she used to relate herself to her family, more particularly her female relatives. For Beatrice, those "mobile roots" are "the pink laurels" that have accompanied her for some 10 years, which she dragged along with her through her successive moves and that survived the trauma of the separation—those "loyal" laurels. Otherwise, mobile roots are objectified by the childhood desk or the gifts of friends, objects that provide a sense of the past (Belk, 1992) when facing the uncertainty of the future.

Recent works in material culture reveal how mobile possessions are used in the cases of migrant peoples or refugees to reobjectify oneself into a new place (Parkin, 1999), and to create a new sense of place. Mobile possessions provide a sense of continuity during transition periods (Bih, 1992; McCollum, 1990; Mehta & Belk, 1991; Schouten, 1991). Possessions are more important in most of the cases of the tenants described here—they are all that remains after the separation. In this context, they also easily become a bone of contention. Research in France and Britain shows that the dwelling is an important object of emotional and financial investment, and as such it becomes an object of calculation, dispute, and struggle (McCarthy & Simpson, 1991; Mermet & Buisson, 1988). Similarly, possessions that are not necessarily valued, either financially or sentimentally (McAlexander, Schouten & Roberts, 1993), such as measuring cups, pots, and plates (Marcoux, 2001), not to mention the chainsaw, BBQ, Nintendo station, and so on, may become important objects of contention.[6]

Separation and Its Objects of Contention

A separation will be experienced as particularly difficult when it is accompanied by dispossession. Sandra, who was introduced earlier, was left alone without anything but the "burden" of the children after her separation. She considered herself

---

[6]The legal press reports many cases of people involved in a divorce procedure taking a claim in court: Droit de la famille 1482 (1991), *RDF* 639; *Ibid.* 1965 (1994) *R.D.F.* 293; *Ibid.* 2497 (1996) *R.D.F.* 768.

dispossessed of most of her wealth, repeating she had been "skinned" by her former partner. In principle, the *Loi sur le patrimoine familial* in Quebec aims at favoring an equitable division of the family's patrimony between spouses in the case of a divorce. Women like Sandra who live in common law relationships, however, are not protected in any sense. They may need to resettle, reequip themselves, find a new kitchen table and new appliances, which increases the costs of the separation. This is where the expression "starting from scratch" takes its full meaning. In some of the cases observed, friends and relatives help resettle the person who moves. The move, in fact, provides a good opportunity to measure the extent of one's support, and to reactivate support networks.

The social context of crisis in which a separation takes place is embedded in a material matrix to the point where it can be hazardous to try to extract the separation crisis from the material one. Not only does a crisis arise over the objects, it also acquires acuteness in their division. Problems and tensions often arise over who may keep what. What is mine? What used to be his, but is now mine? What reflects me, what does not? McAlexander et al. (1993) reported that in cases of divorce, important communication takes place in the destruction of special possessions, the repossession of special gifts, the heated battle of meaningless objects, or the methodical division of shared furnishing. What happens with the household's possessions will depend on who owns them and who brought them in the first place.

Most of the young people I met (between ages 18 and 30) who combined their possessions when moving in together remained aware of what "belonged" to whom in case of a separation. There can only be speculation on what would really happen if a separation occurred. Still, in accordance with deSingly's work, this shows that a concern for autonomy may prevail in the very formation of the couple. Objects may be snatched, as in the case of Sandra. They may be divided as a result of compromises or agreement. Possessions may also be exchanged with the partner. One takes the collection of CDs built up over the years, the other one takes over the collection of photographs. Objects may also be given back as "payments" (Simpson, 1997), in order to disconnect oneself from the past (Kleine, Kleine, & Allen, 1995), and "erase" obligations of reciprocity (Mauss, 1923–1924) that could persist in the future. The gifts offered during the relationship are returned to the former partner in a form of disavowal. A box full of books, "bits and pieces," and mementos given here and there during the relationship is sent back. It is not abandoned randomly. It is sent back in order to clearly mark the gesture. Here, the reciprocation of the gift is a "strategic" gesture (Sherry, 1983) intended to reverse the process of relationship creation. It becomes a tangible, ostensible, symbol of dissolution, a way of clearly signaling the end of a relationship in a farewell goodbye (Ruth, Otnes, & Brunel, 1999). If it is the thought that counts, pain, rage, and disdain may be the prevailing ones.

Abject Objects that Are Left Behind

The separation is also often accompanied by the disposal of possessions (McAlexander, 1991), not to say a form of purification of the self, enacted through the purification of the material world. It has been argued elsewhere that the sorting of possessions on the occasion of a move is mostly governed by a symbolic logic of order (Marcoux, 2001). Sorting things lies, at least partly, in the sorting out of relationships that get materialized between individuals through things, because things embody relationships and the history of relationships. From this perspective, sorting one's things is like sorting one's relationships. This logic is exacerbated when objects associated with the disgraced partner move from intimacy to enmity, becoming as such what is called "abject objects" that are particularly targeted.

For example, Julie, a 27-year-old informant, described with a tone of vengeance how she tore up all the photographs of her ex-boyfriend when she moved. In the same vein, Beatrice got rid of her bed when she moved. She admitted that she usually moved house when she changed partners and that she changed beds when she moved house because the bed was the symbol of the relationship for her. Since the end of a relationship was far from being the end of her "womanhood" as she put it, she preferred to change beds. This informant explained that she liked life as part of a couple, but that she would simply be unable to sleep with somebody else in the same bed. Her case is a reminder of the commonplace image of women who cut their hair on the occasion of a separation, or who change hairstyles to emphasize life transitions (McAlexander & Schouten, 1989) and more generally of the ways in which body changes accompany identity transformations (Schouten, 1991).

The reasons for separating need to be taken into consideration. Finding one's partner in one's bed with someone else may require a very particular form of "purification." Cleaning or washing the bed may not be sufficient because the bed is stained; it is polluted in Douglas' (1966) sense. Getting rid of those objects associated with the partner and the partner's body, like the bed, may also be necessary. The women interviewed, however, did not get rid of everything that was associated with the former partner. A photograph may be kept in a box, out of sight, at least for a while. A piece of furniture may be perceived as valuable, comfortable, or useful, provided it is used in a different context (i.e., in the living room or in a guestroom). In other cases, the presence of the partner's belongings may be endured long after his departure, as if they were the partner himself, until he "decides" to clear the place at his convenience. These objects that assert themselves painfully become harassing. It is only after they are recuperated that the place can finally be "purified," by being rearranged or painted. Until then, there is the feeling that the space is still shared; there is a feeling of intrusion and of a violation of intimacy.

A parallel could be established here with Garvey's (2001) observations of small acts of refurbishment among working-class women in Norway. Just as Garvey compared those small acts of reordering to major works of refurbishment, the sacrificial destruction of small objects (as opposed to the larger instance of the move) involves the most intimate and personal feelings. Objects such as the bed, the linen, and the former partner's clothes are particularly associated with the body, sexuality, and intimacy. They bear in themselves the traces of the relationship, the imprint of the "ex" partner, the marks or the "smell" of his body, and are treated as if they contained in themselves the relationship. As a matter of fact, the senses play a central role in the constitution of memory, as demonstrated by Howes' (1988) work in Melanesia. It is not the case that these objects are discarded because they do not matter, but rather the contrary. They are strongly, closely related to the person. Possessions, therefore, may be treated as extensions of the body, while presenting the advantage of reversible mortification. Their sacrifice is not only intended to purify the body along the same lines of the purification of the place, however, it is also intended to act as a metaphorical change of skin, to set the stage for the fresh start and help prepare oneself physically and spiritually—or at least morally—for the journey to come. They provide a means for trying to assert a sense of agency when facing adversity.

A MOVE WITH SOMETHING OF A "SACRED" CHARACTER

The move that occurs in the course of a separation is often constrained, sometimes violently so. It can only seldom be considered voluntary because the crisis context may affect a person's appreciation of a situation. Nonetheless, such a move can be analyzed as a transition ritual in anthropological terms; the passage from one statutory position to another that is often physically enacted and performed through the transition from one place to another (Turner, 1969; van Gennep, 1909). The ethnographic evidence presented here reveals that this move revolves around the three stages that commonly characterize transition rituals: the preliminal, the liminal (or liminoid), and postliminal stages.

In Turner's (1969) words, the first stage entails a symbolic behavior leading to the detachment of the individual from a certain position in a given social structure, from a set of cultural characteristics, or from both. The preliminal stage may begin with the instance of the couple's separation, although the very beginning of a separation is not always clear. People may change their minds, reconcile, even come back together after sleeping in separate rooms for a while. As such, it may be difficult to try to formally distinguish the first stage from the second, liminal stage, an in-between stage during which people defy classificatory schemes.

There is no clear status attached to people during the liminal period. People may still live together, without considering themselves to be a couple. They may live under the same roof, in separate rooms. Or they may be physically separated while their possessions remain in the same place, recalling the uncertainty of the situation. At this stage, the characteristics of the "passenger" are ambiguous (McAlexander et. al. 1993; Turner, 1969); she crosses a cultural domain that has few, or none, of the attributes of the state left or of the state to come. People are sep-arated, but they keep on sharing a place, a key, kitchen utensils, and other objects of daily life, and they still have access to the other's most intimate possessions. The move itself does not so much initiate a transition as it aims to put an end to such a period of uncertainty—of interlude. It gives separation a concreteness. It marks the separation. As such, the day of the move figures as a temporal threshold that is particularly difficult to pass through (McCollum, 1990): Beatrice was extremely anxious on the eve of her moving day, when thinking about meeting her ex-partner, and dividing the things that remained. She was accompanied by a few friends and relatives who came to give her a hand and support her. Similarly, Mrs. Blackburn was accompanied by many of her friends.

Inasmuch as the move is appropriated as a closure, it requires a form of "mourning"; there is a certain loss of a part of the self and a certain loss of identity. It is, however, a transition that may be imbued with a quasi-sacred character. Here the discussion follows Belk (1992), who held that sacredness may be useful as a secular concept for understanding how a journey may be transformed into a rite of passage, and how possessions may play key ritualistic roles in it. Belk's position may be considered akin to that of Moore and Myerhoff's (1977) attempt to go be-yond Durkheim's opposition between the sacred and the profane by showing that one is often contained in the other. In contrast to the situation described by Belk, these people did not, could not, or refused to move far. Still, they experienced a rupture with the past as is evident in the transformation of their intimate environ-ment. This comes through in the remarks made by Beatrice, who changed beds when putting an end to a relationship. It is indeed at the level of minutiae that the transition or passage can be fully appreciated and that ritualization takes place. In-deed, possessions have the power to symbolize change, and give change an exis-tence. This does not imply that a new wholeness and completeness emerges from the time of the move, allowing for a rebirth. As one person who commented on this chapter remarked, gaps and missing spaces where possessions used to be mani-fested themselves after her parents' separation: "We no longer had a washing ma-chine. The breadboard had gone to my father. The dinner service was at Dad's. The everyday stoneware at my mum's." These gaps in the reformulation of the home serve as painful reminders of the old shell and it takes time for them to be filled.

Once Bitten Twice Shy

The women in this ethnography did not describe their move as a ritual per se. Nor did they consider their move as sacred in a religious sense. Anthropologists know too well that the people they work with do not necessarily use anthropological cat-egories. People, however, do talk about "changing skin," "starting again," "starting over," or "turning over a new leaf," which are all metaphors and clichés that clearly convey the acts of mourning, transition, and rebirth that lie at the basis of transition rituals and provide this move with an emancipatory character. In practice, achieving the separation, consummating the transition and reaching the postliminal stage (Turner, 1969) may require many attempts, transitory arrangements, and false starts—numerous moves in the end. The separation is a process that recalls a journey with its preparation and its associated hesitancy and hedging. It is a process that is at least thought about and performed progressively, one step at a time, if it is undertaken at all. It takes time to effect the transition, as seen in the first section of this chapter. It may require first "getting out of there," trying to sort things out, and only later finding a new place. Actually, most of the women still related to their separations, although these had occurred some 2 to 9 years before. They were still in the process of rupturing, of coming to terms with the past relationship.

Despite all the discourse about a fresh start, people never start all over again. Past relationships leave marks in memory. They leave corporeal traces and incorporated impressions in the form of memories of caresses or violence, ways of ordering objects, and ways of folding clothes that the body does not forget. The move is rather used to redefine the boundaries between the self, the body, and the external world, or the contours of one's "shell." Some informants talked about creating a place in which to recover before moving on to something else, with someone else. It was important for them to first let time pass, to delay thinking about a relationship until later, "to learn first to live alone without expecting anybody at night". They were often careful not to expose themselves in the sense of making themselves vulnerable again. They were afraid of going through the same kind of experience when and if they considered starting a relationship with someone else.

Not all the women I met, however, expressed a desire to settle with someone else. Some aimed at creating a place "free of men" (i.e., a safe and secure space), especially when they had suffered from violent relationships in the past as Sandra did. "Once bitten twice shy" as she put it. I was often told that the desire to remain alone manifested itself more strongly when the separation occurred later on in life. I was also told that there is a "fear" among women over age 40 of becoming "invisible" in the eyes of men. This raises the issue of gender inequality again, taking it into the realm of the social construction of the body in time, along the life cycle. More research is needed here, which is beyond the scope of this chapter.

Still, in a *Bourdieusian* fashion (Bourdieu, 1998), it can be argued that the assessment of the definition of possibilities and of the "hopes" placed in the move will be greatly determined by subjective conditions such as gender, body, class, and age, which will be constructed as objective conditions. In fact, the younger middle-class women interviewed appeared to have more confidence in their ability to effect a transition, and to use the move in order to do so. They try new places, and by the same token new relationships, in tiny doses, little by little, because relationships are constructed in a particular place. A place may suit them for the moment. It may be temporary. It may not be the perfect place. It may not suit them entirely. However, it may at least be satisfying for a while.

THE TRANSFORMATIVE POWER OF A MOVE

A conception of womanhood that is threatened by moving and mobility, by every kind of change, characterizes a part of the 1960s–1970s psychological literature interested in the pathogenic and disruptive effects of moving. Whereas this representation of the vulnerable woman does not appear for the first time in the 1960s–1970s, it is reinforced by the medical discourse of this period, when new forms of domestic relationships like single-parent families and "reconstituted families" are still conceived of as "dysfunctional," "pathological," or "deviant." This is no coincidence. In the medical literature of the period, the family's equilibrium is strongly associated with the stability of the home, which is itself a woman's moral duty. Dutiful wives are expected to follow ambitious husbands in their successive moves (Seidenberg, 1975).

In the social and historical context studied, the post-1970s era, moving on one's own may have become a symbol of emancipation for middle-class women. It is strongly associated with a concept of autonomy. It is also associated with or nourished by the idea or the hope of a new start, although its outcome is difficult to predict, and things do not always follow the course expected (Charbonneau, 1998). For example, 2 years after the completion of the fieldwork, a follow-up was conducted with Beatrice. She was still in the same apartment, on her own with her two children. Since her separation, she had had a few love affairs, but nothing serious in her own words. Her plans of settling with somebody else had not materialized. She had come to resign herself more or less to remaining alone. Beatrice did not recognize herself when reading this chapter. She contained that the situation depicted pertained to the past, to whom she had been in the past, almost another person. Still, she talked about her move with pride. She insisted on saying that it had not been easy. But because of that, because she was through with it, she contended that she had become more confident in herself. This event changed her as she put it. The move transformed her.

The idea that women may be vulnerable to mobility may be founded, but not in any essentialist sense. A discussion about woman's vulnerability to mobility, would have to recognize that in a context like a divorce or a separation, women are not necessarily in *position de force*. The difficulty of the move, however, does not alter people's capacity to give meaning to their actions, but rather the opposite. The crisis exacerbates the need for meaningfulness, and a certain ritualization epitomized in the small manipulations of intimate possessions becomes the more important when the separation is imposed or comes to impose itself. Women facing a separation often have to cope with disadvantageous social constraints. They live under the pressure of larger factors they cannot control, such as gender inequalities and discrimination. These women rarely command the housing resources available to them. Their best, and perhaps their only, means to engage the material world is through the use of what Buchli (1999) called "objects and spaces created by socially dominant others" (p. 6).

A woman may move out in the hope of escaping an unhappy relationship, in an attempt to control her own life and home, or to try to sort out a relationship. She may move hoping to gain access not only to a "room," but to a home of one's own to take up Virginia Woolf's (1929) well-known phrase. Having one's own home, one's own lease, one's name on the doorbell, on the electricity or telephone account may become particularly important. Similarly, retrieving one's maiden name in the course of a separation may take on a particular importance in forming or reforming one's identity. A separation may produce deep feelings of guilt and diminished self-esteem. It may also help to put an end to a relationship that is not fulfilling, the success of one's separation becoming a source of valorization.

Hence, just as much as Buchli (1999, p. 6) showed that "spatial logics can be radically subverted—absolutely and discontinuously—by the most ephemeral manipulations of material culture," the people I met in the course of this ethnography attempt to assert their sense of agency in motion despite a limited or illusory freedom to maneuver. In analogy to Foucault's (1975) small gestures or "micro-physics," small moves become an attempt to assert one's presence and identity. For want of the opportunity to exercise power, they become attempts to assert one's agency.

ACKNOWLEDGMENTS

I would like to thank the Social Sciences and Humanities Research Council of Canada for its financial support. This article has also benefitted from the reading, the insights and the contributions of authors who are too numerous to be cited. Two persons however, must be particularly mentioned: Daniel Miller and Lucy Norris for their comments and critiques of the preliminary versions of this chapter. In addition, I wish to thank Christianne Dubreuil, for her advice on legal issues; and the anonymous reviewers of this chapter. Most of all, I wish to thank my informants for sharing their experiences with me.

REFERENCES

Amit, V. (2000). *Constructing the field: Ethnographic fieldwork in the contemporary world.* London: Routledge & Kegan Paul.

Belk, R. (1988). Possessions and the extended self. *Journal of Consumer Research, 15,* 139–168.

Belk, R. (1992). Moving possessions: An analysis based on personal documents from the 1847–1869 Mormon migration. *Journal of Consumer Research, 19,* 339–361.

Bih, H. (1992). The meaning of objects in environmental transitions: Experiences of Chinese students in the United States. *Journal of Environmental Psychology, 12,* 135–147.

Bourdieu, P. (1998). *La domination masculine*. Paris: Seuil.

Buchli, V. (1999). *The archeology of socialism*. Berg: Oxford.

Buchli, V., & Lucas, G. (2000). Children, gender and the material culture of domestic abandonment in the late 20th Century. In J. Sofaer-Derevenski (Ed.), *Children and material culture* (pp. 131–138). London: Routledge & Kegan Paul.

Bureau de la Statistique du Québec (1999). *Un portrait statistique des familles et des enfants au Québec*. Ste. Foy: Gouvernement du Québec.

Butler, E., McAllister, R., & Kaiser, E. (1973). The effects of voluntary and involuntary residential mobility on females and males. *Journal of Marriage and the Family, 35*, 219–227.

Chapman, T., & Hockey, J. (1999). The ideal home as it is imagined and as it is lived. In T. Chapman & J. Hockey (Eds.), *Ideal homes?* (pp. 1–13). London: Routledge & Kegan Paul.

Charbonneau, J. (1998). Trajectoires sociales et stratégies individuelles en contexte d'incertitude. In Y. Grafmeyer & F. Dansereau (Eds.), *Trajectoires familiales et espaces de vie en milieu urbain* (pp. 395–413). Lyon: Presses Universitaires de Lyon.

Cohen, L. (1963). *The favorite game*. Toronto: McClelland & Stewart.

deSingly, F. (1993). *Sociologie de la famille contemporaine*. Paris: Nathan.

deSingly, F. (1996). *Le soi, le couple et la famille*. Paris: Nathan.

deSingly, F. (2000). *Libres ensemble: L'individualisme dans la vie de couple*. Paris: Nathan.

Desjeux, D., Monjaret, A., & Taponier, S. (1998). *Quand les Français déménagent*. Paris: PUF.

Douglas, M. (1966). *Purity and danger*. London: Routledge & Kegan Paul.

Duchesne, L. (2001). *La situation démographique au Québec*. Québec: Institut de la Statistique du Québec.

Duncan, J. (1981). From container of women to status symbol: The impact of social structure on the meaning of house. In J. Duncan (Ed.), *Housing and identity* (pp. 36–59). London: Croom Helm.

Duncan, N. (1996). Renegotiating gender and sexuality in public and private spaces. In N. Duncan (Ed.), *Body space* (pp. 127–145). London: Routledge & Kegan Paul.

Foucault, M. (1975). *Surveiller et punir*. Paris: Gallimard.

Foucault, M. (1984). *Histoire de la sexualité: L'usage des plaisirs*. Paris: Gallimard.

Front d'action populaire en réaménagement urbain (2000, January). *Logement au Québec: Femmes et pauvreté*.

Garvey, P. (2001). Organized disorder: Moving furniture in Norwegian homes. In D. Miller (Ed.), *Home possessions* (pp. 47–68). Berg: Oxford.

Giddens, A. (1992). *The transformation of intimacy: Sexuality, love and eroticism in modern societies*. Cambridge, England: Polity Press.

Gilroy, R. (1994). An agenda for action. Issues of choice, freedom and control. In R. Gilroy & R. Woods (Eds.), *Housing women* (pp. 260–269). London: Routledge & Kegan Paul.

Guibaud, J. M. (1979). *Déménager: Contribution à la psychopathologie du déménagement*. Unpublished doctoral dissertation, Toulouse; Université Paul-Sabatier.

Harris, R. (1989). Moving. How to help your family adjust. *Chatelaine, 62,* 146.

Howes, D. (1988). On the odor of the soul: Spatial representation and olfactory classification in Eastern and Western Melanesia. *Anthropologica, 144,* 84–113.

Huston, N. (1994). *La Virevolte.* Nimes: Actes Sud.

Jamieson, L. (1998). *Intimacy: Personal relationships in modern societies.* Cambridge, England: Polity Press.

Kaplan, M. F., & Glenn, A. (1978). Women and the stress of moving: A self-help approach. *Social Caseworks, 59,* 434–436.

Kleine, S., Kleine, R., & Allen, C. (1995). How is a possession "me" or "not me"? Characterizing types and an antecedent of material possession attachment. *Journal of Consumer Research, 22,* 327–343.

Laqueur, T. (1990). *Making sex: Body and gender from the Greeks to Freud.* London: Harvard University Press.

Light, P., & Hass, E. (1983, June). Moving day. Here's advice on helping your family adjust to their new home. *Parents Magazine,* 124, 126, 127, 128, 131.

Madigan, R., & Munro, M. (1999). "The more we are together." Domestic space, gender and privacy. In T. Chapman & J. Hockey (Eds.), *Ideal homes?* (pp. 61–71). London: Routledge & Kegan Paul.

Marcoux, J. S. (2001). The refurbishment of memory. In D. Miller (Ed.), *Home possessions* (pp. 69–86). Berg: Oxford.

Mauss, M. (1923–1924). Essai sur le don. *L'Année sociologique, 2,* 145–284.

McAlexander, J. (1991). Divorce, the disposition of the relationship, and everything. In R. Holman & M. Solomon (Eds.), *Advances in Consumer Research, 18,* 43–48. Provo, UT: Association for Consumer Research.

McAlexander, J., & Schouten, J. (1989). Hair style changes as transition markers. *Sociology and Social Research, 74,* 58–62.

McAlexander, J., Schouten, J., & Roberts, S. (1993). Consumer behavior and divorce. In J. Costa & R. Belk (Eds.), *Research in Consumer Behavior, 6,* 153–184. Greenwich, CT: JAI Press.

McCarthy, P., & Simpson, B. (1991). *Issues in post-divorce housing.* London: Routledge & Kegan Paul.

McCollum, A. (1990). *The trauma of moving: Psychological issues for women.* Newbury Park, CA: Sage.

McCracken, G. (1988). *Culture and consumption.* Bloomington: Indiana University Press.

Mehta, R., & Belk, R. (1991). Artifacts, identity and transition: Favorite possessions of Indians and Indian immigrants to the United States. *Journal of Consumer Research, 17,* 398–411.

Mermet, J., & Buisson, M. (1988). Pratiques sociales de l'habitat et dynamiques de la divorcialité. In C. Bonvalet & P. Merlin (Eds.), *Transformation de la famille et habitat* (pp. 83–93). Paris: PUF.

Miller, D. (1987). *Material culture and mass consumption.* Oxford, England: Blackwell.

Miller, D. (Ed.). (2001). *Home possessions.* Berg: Oxford.

Millet, L., Pon, J., Guibaud, J., & Auriol, G. (1980). Déménager. Réactions psychopathologiques aux changements d'habitation. *Annales Médico-psychologiques, 138,* 212–221.

Moore, S., & Myerhoff, B. (Eds.). (1977). *Secular rituals.* Amsterdam: Van Gorcum.

Munro, M., & Madigan, R. (1993). Privacy in the private sphere. *Housing Studies, 8*, 29–45.

O'Hanley, S. (2002). No kids, please. *Montreal Hour, 10*, 8.

Parkin, D. (1999). Mementoes as transitional objects in human displacement. *Journal of Material Culture, 4*, 303–320.

Petiteau, J. (1995). *Déménager, emménager dans l'ancien et le nouveau monde.* Toulouse: Certop, plan urbain.

Ram, B., Shin, Y., & Pouliot, M. (1994). *Canadians on the move. Catalogue no 96–309-XPE.* Ottawa: Statistics Canada and Prentice-Hall Canada.

Rapport, N., & Dawson, A. (1998). *Migrants of identity.* Berg: Oxford.

Rautenberg, M. (1989). Déménagement et culture domestique. *Terrain, 12*, 54–66.

Ruth, J., Otnes, C., & Brunel, F. (1999). Gift receipt and the reformulation of interpersonal relationships. *Journal of Consumer Research, 25*, 385–402.

Schouten, J. (1991). Selves in transition: Symbolic consumption in personal rites of passage and identity reconstruction. *Journal of Consumer Research, 17*, 412–425.

Segalen, M. (2000). *Sociologie de la famille* (5th ed.). Paris: Armand Colin.

Seidenberg, R. (1975). Moving on to what? *MH, 59*, 7–11.

Sherry, J., Jr. (1983). Gift giving in anthropological perspective. *Journal of Consumer Research, 10*, 157–168.

Simpson, B. (1997). On gifts, payments and disputes: Divorce and changing family structure in contemporary Britain. *Journal of the Royal Anthropological Institute, 3*, 731–745.

Smardo, F. (1987). Helping children adjust to moving. *Children Today, May*, 10–13.

Société d'habitation du Québec (2000). *Les femmes et le logement.* Montreal: Gouvernement du Québec.

Statistics Canada. (1996). *Census data.* Ottawa: Statistics Canada.

Statistics Canada. (1997). *Survey of income finance, 1997.* Ottawa: Income Statistics Division.

Turner, V. (1969). *The ritual process: Structure and antistructure.* London: Routledge & Kegan Paul.

Tyler, A. (1996). *Ladder of years.* Croydon: Bookmark.

van Gennep, A. (1909). *Les rites de passage.* Paris: Émile Nourry.

Vereecken, J. (1964). Sur quelques cas de dépression du déménagement. *Encéphale, 53*, 614–626.

Weinstein, G. (1971). Moving made easy. Here's how one mother prepared her youngsters to make the big change from city to suburb living. *Parents Magazine, 46*, 70, 71, 100, 101.

Weisman, L. (1992). *Discrimination by design.* Urbana: University of Illinois Press.

Weissmann, M., & Paykel, E. (1972). Moving and depression in women. *Society, 9*, 24–28.

Wexler, M. (1998). Une vie dans deux foyers: Les enfants en garde partagée. In Y. Grafmeyer & F. Dansereau (Eds.), *Trajectoires familiales et espaces de vie en milieu urbain* (pp. 355–370). Lyon: Presses Universitaires de Lyon.

Winnicott, D. (1953). Transitional objects and transitional phenomena. *International Journal of Psychoanalysis, 34*, 89–97.

Wolcott, H. (1999). *Ethnography: A way of seeing.* London: Alta Mira Press.

Woolf, V. (1929). *A room of one's own.* New York: Fountain Press.

13

Sacred Iconography in Secular Space: Altars, Alters, and Alterity at the Burning Man Project

John F. Sherry, Jr. and Robert V. Kozinets
Northwestern University

Historically and etymologically, altars harness and liberate some of the most potent forces of consumer behavior that late capitalism has struggled to marketize and commodify: sacred and profane, gift giving and sacrifice, utterance and ineffability, immanence and transcendence, public and private, self and other, material and ethereal, agency and community, order and chaos. As mediating vehicles between realms of experience, altars invite the exploration of antinomies, and encourage the probing of relationships. As metaphoric high places of supplication, altars comprise both a metaphysical fulcrum and catechetical crucible, on and within which materiality is transmuted into quintessence. Altars are the sites of creative destruction and destructive creation. Altars reify what people deify, and deify what people reify.

In this chapter, we describe and theorize altars at Burning Man. Burning Man, or the Burning Man Project, is a weeklong festal gathering that takes place every year in the desolate Black Rock Desert of central Nevada, which is one of the most lifeless places on earth. From the Black Rock Desert—a barren Pleistocene lake bed, engulfed in alkali dust—arises Black Rock City, a techno-shamanic city of art, Blake's Golgonooza. It is a place of imagination built to disappear in a blazing no-when of immediacy. It is a love offering to the world wherein process trumps product and evanescence proves essential. In Burning Man's temporary community, diversity is *de rigueur*, everyday life is an incessant series of celebratory moments, spectacle is continuously created in universal performance rather than passive observation, and otherness is the common bond among residents.

The event began in 1985 when two friends, accompanied that year by a group of friends and range of attracted onlookers, decided to burn an 8-foot wooden effigy of a man on San Francisco's Baker Beach. The psychic energy released by the burning of the man was an epiphany for its originators. Holding the event every year, they found that it attracted more people and more attention, and so felt a need to elongate and elaborate the stature of the effigy in return. By 2001, the event attracted over 25,000 people to a gigantic celebration climaxing in the Hollywood-effects style torching of a 50-foot effigy. Our chapter is based upon our ethnographic fieldwork at Burning Man in 1999 and 2000. As we will describe, altars are central in many ways to Burning Man. Altars are perhaps best recognized as the ground of alterity, the celebratory loci of otherness (Taussig, 1993). Burning Man is an experiment in temporary community that celebrates the practice of radical self-expression. This practice is reflected on the individual level in the discovery and release of the alter (ego). Participants work actively to allow their second (and third and ...) selves to emerge, and perform this emergence for others to appreciate. As unfamiliar or unacknowledged aspects of the self unfold, and each participant individuates in the presence of a community of emergent selves, apostasy becomes the order of the day. Avatars meander on the playa, the demarcated desert surface that serves as Burning Man's central staging ground. Acolytes thus commune with their extended, multiphrenic selves, with each others' rapidly individuating selves, and with those geomantic and cosmological forces that all those many selves see fit to summon to the table. We can conceive of the altars at Burning Man as the staging grounds for the event's reenchantment of the worlds, both inner and outer, of its participants. The quotidian self is sacrificed on the altar, allowing more authentic, immediate selves to arise. Communitas emerges in turn, as alters mime and riff throughout the week.

In addition, because Burning Man's organizers tightly control the event, and forbid (through a local police force called the Rangers) any commerce or commercial activities, people must abandon the marketized consumer behaviors of their everyday lives (see Kozinets, 2002). Instead, they embrace apotheosis as their acknowledged goal. Acolytes offer their selves to each other upon a variety of natural, communal, and self-constructed altars. Alterity in this temporary autonomous zone (Bey, 1994) is the lived experience, enjoined and engendered by the community. It is manifest in gifts and offerings, sacred sacrifices emplaced within and on altars.

A NOTE ON RESEARCH
AND REPRESENTATION

We alert the reader to our enterprise with some specific admonitions. While our account emerges from several years of ethnographic and netnographic inquiry, during which time we made extensive use of participant observation and interview, this chapter arises from the photographic and videographic records we made of our field experience. This chapter is essentially a photoessay, and the text may be regarded as an extended caption. Denser descriptive accounts of our fieldwork are available elsewhere (Kozinets, 2002, 2003; Kozinets & Sherry, in press a, in press b; Sherry, 2003), and, in these sources, we provide more global and nuanced interpretations of the Burning Man Project. These works also provide the detailed emic perspectives, rich informant quotes, and reflective descriptive fieldnote passages and analysis that are hallmarks of ethnography. They are absent from this visual enterprise because they speak of a form of representation that is currently not our intent.

Here, hopefully, the images will bear the brunt of evocation, giving the reader a feel for the spiritual ethos that pervades Black Rock City. We offer our own interpretation of these images, an etic one informed by emic perspectives, but couched in language evocative enough to complement the images (Sherry, 2000; Sherry & Schouten, 2002). It is one of a "layering of seeings" (Schechner, 1985, p. 297) we are putting down to capture the complexity of the event, and we hope readers will be moved to consult our other works. Our present effort resembles the practice of ritual criticism (Grimes, 1990), and shapes not only our own ongoing engagement with the Burning Man Project, but also that of a host of other secular ritualists involved with the event, to whom our interpretations are widely disseminated over the Internet.

Our ephemeral fieldsite, whose closest ethnographic analog may be the biannual Australian ConFest (St. John, 2001), is created by people from all over the world, but has a distinctive West Coast presence. Residents of Black Rock City are predominantly White, relatively affluent and well educated, and range in age generally from their twenties through eighties. Gender is balanced, and often publicly negotiated in performance. Residents of this heterotopia truck everything necessary for creating and sustaining an enclave of radical self-expression—building materials, porta-potties, generators, electronics, art and craft components, groceries, and dwelling structures—into the middle of the desert. There they build a community that prohibits vending, encourages a gift economy, and demands that everyone participate in the creation of a temporary autonomous zone (Bey, 1994). Residents live in villages of theme camps, giving the city a sense of subcultural variation. Through thousands of local acts of individual performance and collectively orchestrated erections of mega-installations of art, a communitas emerges among residents that functions as a critique of their real-world everyday lives. This communitas is enhanced by altered consciousness borne of deprivation, ecstatic drumming and dancing, drug use, authentic interpersonal encounters, and countless other means. The event culminates in a postmodern potlatch of conflagration, the burning of a week's aesthetic production and the dismantling of the entire city, reminding each resident of the primacy of creativity over that which is created.

Much of the activity at Black Rock City is geared toward shifting residents' lived experience away from materialism per se, and toward materiality. Residents come to question their relationship with the material world, speculate on the essential essence of things, and explore the cybernetic self. Active production rather than passive consumption is the order of the week; participation is exalted, whereas spectating is demonized. Because agency is inseparable from stuff, the strategic use of consumer behavior in a nonmarket setting—particularly the interplay of sacred and profane (Belk, Wallendorf, & Sherry, 1989)—is an attractive research opportunity. The numinous dimension of consumption is perhaps nowhere more apparent than in the ubiquitous presence of altars throughout Black Rock City. We capture something of that presence in the images and words that follow.

ANALYZING ALTARS

Of the many ways of characterizing the altars of Black Rock City, we have chosen three interpenetrating aspects to organize the discussion: structure, process, and magnitude. Every altar partakes of these aspects, but none of these aspects is irreducibly nonproblematic in any of the altars. The altars are perversely polysemous, resisting any master reading in their local particularities. Charles Simic's poem "The Altar" (2001) might profitably be read in this regard. Altars harbor animal, mineral, plant, food, human, deity, demon, and technology icons. Often these icons share space on the same altars. Some altars have an archaic feel, others a retro feel, and still others a futuristic feel. Again the same altar may reference multiple temporal eras. Some altars are stationary, and others are mobile. Sometimes environmental affordances prompt the raising of an altar; sometimes the environment is made to conform to the demands of an altar. Where some altars resemble completed installations, others are being installed continuously. Some altars are attended, others self-serve. Devotional activity is organized at some altars and spontaneous at others. Altars sport attitude from reverent to blasphemous, from arcane to popular. Any of these dimensions might be unpacked at great length. For the purposes of our essay, we confine ourselves to just a few diagnostic aspects we find compelling.

Structure

The structure of our altars can be described along dimensions that appear in Fig. 13.1 to be continua, but that are best understood as dialectical relations. One dimension is represented by the poles of Ritual and Ceremony. Recall that these poles are simply representational conceits, and they actually exist compressed in intimate tension. Ritual carries primarily a religious valence, whereas ceremony is predominantly aesthetic in nature. The distinction is a traditional one, the former indicating some agentic orientation to a transcendent power, the latter more an attitude toward immanence shaped largely through secular performance. The second dimension unfolds along the line between the poles of Personal and Communal. Again, this unfolding occurs in the dynamic association of these conceits. The for-

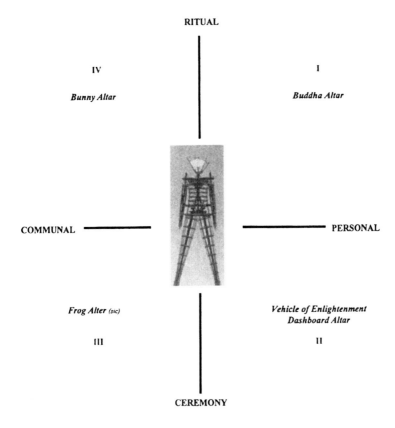

RITUAL

IV

Bunny Altar

I

Buddha Altar

COMMUNAL ————   ———— PERSONAL

Frog Alter (sic)

III

*Vehicle of Enlightenment
Dashboard Altar*

II

CEREMONY

Fig. 13.1.   Structure.

mer denotes a private experience, the latter a public one. The tension here exists
between the harboring and the sharing of experience. By doing some representational violence to dialectical distinctions, we are able to characterize the altars of
Black Rock City by quadrant, recognizing all the while that drift occurs across
quadrants, and that the intersection of the axes exerts an irresistible pull on the altars toward the source of greatest semiotic intensity: the center. The center of
alterity in Black Rock City is the Man, a 40- to 50-foot stylized effigy constructed
of wood and neon, and placed on a raised platform at the very heart of Burning
Man's city. Each altar is the physical manifestation of the metaphysical and symbolic force in play in its quadrant.

Of the types of altar characteristic of Quadrant I, simple shrines devoted to
the Buddha are perhaps the most common (Fig. 13.2). Such shrines are most often
located in relatively domestic space, in the interior of theme camps and off the
heavily traveled circuits of the playa and esplanade. For the event, the desert is

Fig. 13.2.   Buddha altar.

carved into streets, with a main promenade circling the Man, and lesser roads spreading concentrically outward, with intersecting roads like the spokes of a wheel. These altars typically contain the sacred icon, along with incense sticks or votive candles, as well as flowers. Often they may have straw mats laid out before them. The altars are also rarely elevated very far off the ground. These altars afford the opportunity for meditation and introspection, usually conducted by solitary individuals. Occasionally, passersby too busy for an extended visit may *wai* or *namaste* the icon as they move through the area. Such walk-by ritual bowing becomes a species of gestural performance remarked on by observers. These altars appeal not only to the Eastern mysticism of their tenders, but also to the New Age sensibility of many unchurched seekers. The chthonic grounding of these altars suits the "tread lightly" ecophilosophy of Black Rock City residents.

Quadrant II—type altars are epitomized by the Vehicle of Enlightenment, an art-car whose dashboard contains an altar comprising an intriguing collage of sacred and profane icons. (Fig. 13.3). The outer body of the entire car is completely encrusted in tchotchkes, both sacral and kitsch. A veritable bibelot-mobile of multicultural detritus, the vehicle sports adhesions from talismans to toys, and CDs to seashells. Its riotous, cornucopic display of material culture draws onlookers close, to ponder the meanings of the montage. Inside the car, the dashboard provides a fortuitous affordance that invites the installation of an altar. This mobile altar effectively grounds the driver, providing connection and integration not only with here and there in a metaphysical sense, but also with home and away in political/domestic economy kind of sense. The driver is able to carry the hestial into the

Fig. 13.3.   Vehicle of enlightenment altar.

hermetic. The sacra reflect the vehicle's theme. Sitting behind the steering wheel and looking beyond the images of Felix the Cat, Mickey Mouse, and a host of amulets and aliens, the driver is able to contemplate some principal icons uniting the worlds. Coral and dice, a Catholic nun, a man in the moon, Confucius, Buddha, and Gumby reside above the instrument panel. Above the glove compartment, the Blessed Virgin bears a rock guitar, and Lord Gautama, sitting zazen, works a laptop computer. A rubber duckie, a scale model of the Vehicle of Enlightenment, crystals, flowers, several Felix decals, and numerous medallions adorn this shelf. The visor is festooned with rosaries and amulets. Looking beyond this altar, through the windshield, the driver contemplates a kindred congeries on the hood. As a liminoid phenomenon itself, the car is a profoundly appropriate vehicle for altaric mediation between worlds.

The Alter (sic) of the Mystical Frog of the Playa—the literal misspelling seeming to be an emic declaration of the function of altars—is an exemplar of the type of altar described in Quadrant III (Fig. 13.4). Erected to the Frog Goddess, the votive altar allows communicants to write projective fantasies on a piece of parchment to be publicly read and burned at 4:30 each afternoon. Acolytes stress the ceremonial nature of the devotional practice, and the apposite interplay of themes of permanence and impermanence in the ceremony. Projected dreams need not be religious in nature, merely expressive of self. The altar rests in a covered shrine fronted by an enormous frog head. The altar consists of a laptop writing desk ringed with frog figurines and stocked with writing implements. Leaf-shaped mats lay before the altar, parchment and bowls to the side, and a tall columnar frog idol to the rear. Offertory bowls abut this idol. The entire altar rests on a large carpet

Fig. 13.4.   Mystical frog altar.

whose back corners are arrayed with small frog figurines, as well as a lantern and drum. Although frogs abound here like a biblical plague, it is useful to recall that the frog symbolizes genesis and reproduction. The frog is a lunar symbol and a favorite of magicians. Its humanoid features make it an apt symbol of psychological transformation (Beidermann, 1992). A sign stands before the shrine, instructing the uninitiated in the rite. This altar permits both personal and communal expression, but serves primarily as a public vehicle of performance and display.

Altars in the provenance of Quadrant IV are perhaps best represented by the Bunny altar (Fig. 13. 5). The rabbit is a common cross-cultural lunar symbol, whose polysemous accretions across time and space include vigilance, fertility, lust, purity, rebirth, and humanity; it figures in both Christian and Buddhist legend, in the latter instance as a salvific symbol of self-sacrifice. Rabbit is also a trickster figure in aboriginal American mythology (Biederman, 1992; Radin, 1987) and in American cartoon tradition. Occasionally in American advertising, all these meanings may coalesce in a single rabbit. The Bunny altar originated in the form of a childhood gift, a 2½-foot bronze-colored wooden figurine that remained precious enough to its owner to be retained by her well into her twenties. She brought the bunny to Black Rock City as a mere decoration, but the statue was sacralized on site. The bunny was elevated to the status of deity. Residents believe that an offering made at the Bunny altar results in the miraculous reception of drugs, and leg-

Fig. 13.5.   Bunny altar.

end assigns a 100% effectiveness rating to the transaction. Publicity over Radio Free Burning Man stimulates pilgrimage to the site of the altar, much as broadcast sightings of the Blessed Virgin in oil stains or tree trunks accomplish back in the "real" world. Pilgrims from all over Black Rock City gather at this votive altar, making offerings, telling stories to one another, and creating a spectacle for the unbelievers to enjoy. Again, a synthetic New Age collage of sacra—Mexican votive candles, extraterrestrial head, marabou vestment, flowers—marks this altar as a hybrid gathering of ideologies.

The site of greatest semiotic intensity, the center of the diagram on which all quadrants of the figure converge, is the Man (Fig. 13.6). Semiotic center is both a nexus and a vortex. The Man personifies and objectifies, as well as synergizes, the other altars represented in the sample. The Man is a projective vehicle nonpareil at individual, social, and cultural levels of discourse. The Man is all things to all people: art and icon, beacon and lodestar, sin eater and Trojan horse, Christ and Lucifer, matter and essence, puppet and master, hestial fire and hermetic fire. The Man is the mystery of transubstantiation offered up for edification and debate. The Man is the Anti-"The Man," the apotheosis of radical self-expression couched in a nurturing community whose totalizing dictum (ablaze in postirony) is simply "perform, don't conform; produce, don't consume." Presiding over a short eternity of cultural hybridity and cultural transvestism, a frenzy of self-effacement and self-discovery, and a hope of transfusing the balance of the year's experience (whether lived online or in real life) with a numinous essence believed evacuated

Fig. 13.6.   The Man.

by late capitalism, the Man bestrides Black Rock City like a colossus of roads not often taken. This altar is a polysemous paradox. The Man's erection is supervised by firefighters. The man bears a memorial plaque dedicated to fallen firefighters. Firefighters have secreted a smoke alarm in the Man's crotch as an inside joke. Firefighters ignite and tend the burn. (Insofar as there may be a touch of arsony in all our souls, what better guardians of the flame can be imagined?) The Man is a paraprimitive, technoshamanic manifestation. The erection has grown over time from inches to stories, its devotees from tens to thousands.

Process

Altars represent both a physical and metaphysical construction project whose dynamics are endlessly fascinating. No matter what kind of projective field an altar comprises (rejuvenation, personal identity, ancestor shrine, sanctuary, fetish focus, transmigration portal, eschatological challenge, etc.) the material altar requires manipulation. Altars must be tended. A gathering of things, of relics, of memories, of heirlooms and memorabilia, must occupy the acolyte. Acolytes are bricoleurs, culling, combing, and configuring sacra into appropriate presentations. This activity is both intentional and unconscious; sometimes the doing supercedes the thinking. The conversion of collections to heterotopias may well be more an organic than a technical process, and consequently may defy articulation. The Diderot unities that obtain between sacra on the altar are both strategic and emergent. The collectings and arrangings, the mantlings and dismantlings, the takings and leavings are all integral to the integration of sacred and profane realms of experience (Chester, 2000; McMann, 1998; Turner, 1999). Altars are animate and must be cultivated.

Many of these altaristic impulses are at play in Black Rock City. Bricolage, and its resulting collage or montage manifestation, is most readily apparent in the gift-giving and sacrifice behaviors associated with the simplest, most ubiquitous altars of the Burning Man Project (Fig. 13.7). These take-and-leave altars invite communicants to receive sacra from the altar and replace them with something of personal significance. Such altars range from nominal nourishment tables, a secular inversion of Thai spirit house etiquette that encourages the taking of food and

Fig. 13.7.   Take-and-leave altars.

leaving of a benediction, to elaborate installations of public sacra offered in exchange for private sacra. The playa is dotted with makeshift altars holding mendicant bowls encouraging pilgrims to leave something as they take something. In sacralizing the circulation of gifts and marking the nobility of sacrifice, these altars also shape the processual dynamics of creation in the service of wildly variegated and emergent works of art.

A wedding altar erected in Black Rock City is a striking example of the dynamism and centrality of some of the altars at Burning Man (Fig. 13.8). The wedding altar reposes in a self-described "chick camp" dominated by female touches. It is designed for use in a Burning Man wedding, a cognate ritual seen by its participants (devoted attendees over the last 4 years who had met at the event) as a more highly personalized accompaniment to the traditional wedding ritual they recently

Fig. 13.8.   Wedding altar.

performed in the "real world" outside Black Rock City. The alternate wedding, scripted by the partners themselves, involves what they call "a central altar." The altar is positioned on a thin, tall table covered with faux leopard spot-patterned fur on which is placed a variety of sacraments. A child's purple pail and a half-empty teddy bear-shaped jar of branded animal crackers (Low Fat!) suggests the import of childhood and playfulness to the event, and the unimportance of allegedly profane brands to the sacred practice. The crackers also serve as an offering to human passers-by. A long thin red candle is painted with gold Chinese swirls and characters and positioned upright in a matching red-painted metal container. Its presence suggests exoticism, Eastern mysticism, and also the temporariness and the delicate fires of passion. A matching leopard skin case joins the teddy bear and African motif table to invoke elements of animalism, primitivism, and wildness. The matching ensemble in soft leopard skin also gives a distinctly feminine touch to the altar, indicating that its decoration is ritually akin to the more elaborate and deliberate body decoration of female fashion and of domestic decorative sensibilities. Set next to the table is a tall arched shelf, covered in matching leopard fur. Nestled in one of the shelves is a large female doll, dressed in a flowing chartreuse dress, a twirling southern pixie caught and frozen in flight. The entire altar is intended to be suffused in different colors of cloth in order to evoke "the colors of the different chakras" as revealed to communicants through their New Age studies. Various small bowls are arrayed on the table. The bride's friends have created several "little staffs," each holding a candle, a bowl, and bearing "the symbols of the elements on them," again as revealed through their New Age studies. The staffs are set up in a circle around the altar table. During the ceremony, the participants traverse the circle, taking each of the elements from the bowls on the periphery and bringing them to the center to be burned. The ceremony is described as an elaborate ritual for "creating a sacred space" for the "central exchange" of more spiritually meaningful wedding vows.

As with the wedding altar's blend of African Art Deco primitivism, branded cookie kitch, childhood nostalgia, and New Age sophistry, some altars exist primarily as a kind of syncretic melange, with no intentionally unifying theme pursued by the builder, nor any necessary relationship obtaining between the sacra on display. Here, free rein is given to the projective impulses of creator and communicant. For example, on a folding camp stool, perched atop a profane work surface, arises an altar whose focal icon, a Buddha, sits under a bo tree fashioned from brain coral (Fig. 13.9). The icon is bracketed fore and aft by vegetation (branches and cactus leaf), and rests amidst an improvised alms bowl and offertory gifts of ointments, beer, and food. Lashed to a leg of the altar, bound (and bondage is an apt conceit) by red ribbon, a naked Barbie® doll, head cocked in rapt attention to the idol, gives every appearance of ascending the mountain toward enlightenment. The altar's creator has cobbled the tableau together from elements at hand. He refers to Barbie® as "the Goddess," and emphasizes the sexual nature of her aura. He burns incense and makes food offerings at the altar, and gives sacra away to com-

Fig. 13.9.   Syncretic altar.

municants who admire particular pieces. He keeps an altar everywhere he goes (i.e., home, office, car, motel, etc.) because it "grounds" and "centers" him.

The Man epitomizes the kind of barn-raising, quilting bee ethos that encourages community to emerge from individual labor and private aspiration (Fig. 13.10). The icon is built in sections by teams of volunteers in off-site locations prior to the burn, and assembled, finished, and erected in the desert. Wood scraps from the construction are recycled into other art projects and edifices on the playa, such that the tangibilized aura of the Man is dispersed throughout Black Rock City. The altar's base is erected on-site from hay bales whose form and function are integral to the burn. Over the course of the week, communicants visit the site of the rising altar, to check its progress, banter with its builders and each other, and ponder changes in themselves that are mirrored by the icon's change of phase. The material construction is preceded by a year of contemplation, much of it brokered over

Fig. 13.10.   Raising The Man.

the Internet in chat rooms devoted to harnessing the energy released in the previous year's burn. In these contemplative conversations, veterans and novices alike plan not only for the personal transformation they hope will occur via their physical participation, but also for how they might sustain the spirit of the Burning Man Project in their everyday lives when they return to the world. The altar is the focus of a time- and space-binding experience. The sacrifices communicants make in attending the burn are offered in the hope that one day process will trump product, that the urgency and immediacy of temporariness will suffuse the mundane, and that self-expression will be elevated to a life project.

Magnitude

Far from the buzz of activity arising from the center of the playa, in an almost empty quarter of the desert, sits a solitary simple altar, visited in all likelihood more often by accident than by intention (Fig. 13.11). It is a small lawn table encrusted with seashells, themselves adorned with eyes that give the impression of the mollusks being vigilant, as if watching approaching pilgrims. The altar bears the inscribed message "Be of Good Cheer," whose polysemous import the communicant is invited to ponder. Is it biblical reassurance or exhortation crying out in the desert? Is it evolutionary teleology winking from the former lake bed? A *memento mori* reminding people that isolation is both inescapable and ennobling? Is it all of these? Or, is it none of these? The effort exerted by the wanderer to reach the altar and divine a reading—a labor-value measure of sacrifice—is repaid with the benediction. To a large extent, epiphany is its own reward, and demands no human mediation.

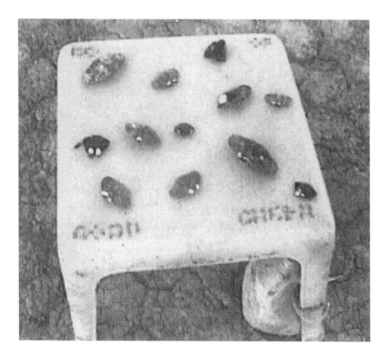

Fig. 13.11.   Seashell altar.

The Secret Dakini Oracle altar is grander in design and execution (Fig. 13.12). Set deep in an encampment in Black Rock City, flanked by banners bearing Buddhist and Hindu images, the altar fronts a tented sanctuary, where pilgrims are able to escape the sun, rest awhile, meditate, and consult adepts of divination. The shrine is reminiscent of remote hill top Dakini temples of ancient India. A Dakini (literally a "Sky Dancer") is a spirit (as well as an archetype and embodiment) of feminine energy, wisdom, and intuition, a tantric agent of self-transformation. The altar exhibits a minimalist aesthetic of empty space and natural sacra, mediated by the augur's book. The table is set to invite gnostic exploration, which is undertaken either with a guide or as a solitary journey. At one corner of the altar, a recumbent cat, disarticulated and surrounded by shells and candles, appears to ponder the codex and divination deck. The cat is a prominent player in homeopathic magic and occult practice, a force to conjure with. Mythologically, the cat is perhaps identified most closely with the god Bast, a lunar symbol of fertility, sexuality, and joy. Its invisible midsection also recalls the Cheshire cat, reminding beholders of their having moved behind the looking glass, darkly. In another corner, tissues and gift packaging, aromatic oil and ersatz currency, and votive light and veils grace the altar. Plant life brackets all these artifacts. A number of experience worlds is integrated on the altar; these worlds are traversed through the medium of the gift, via sacrifice and exchange.

Fig. 13.12.   Secret Dakini oracle altar.

The Man itself is grander still than either the seashell or Dakini altar. The effigy stands atop a 30-foot pedestal designed to resemble a Mayan altar, and that functions as a pyre to ensure the complete consummation of the holocaust the Man becomes. Not only is the 50-foot Man a fiery vessel in its own right—packed as it is with neon lights and pyrotechnic payloads—but also it is animated, engineered to raise its flaming arms as if in exultation, victory, or even ascension. The Man is communally built, assembled, attended, ignited, and celebrated. The entire altar site is encircled with boundary stones in the form of lights embedded in the ground. Further, the surrounding playa is staked out with pillars on which are mounted mirrors and lasers whose beams are directed to form the shape of the man (transecting communicants on the ground), such that the symbol is visible from the sky above. The Man is oriented to an avenue of mega-installations in such a way as to form the apex or pinnacle of artistic process. The entire population of Black Rock City—some 25,000 souls—turns out for the conflagration, cheering, chanting, singing, drumming, and praying as the Man is engulfed in flame. The alchemical mantra spoken so often in conversation at Black Rock City—"What did you bring to burn?"—achieves its transcendental purpose at this moment, as celebrants answer this question in their hearts.

The altar of greatest magnitude at "the burn" would have to be the desert itself. Baudrillard (1988, pp. 71, 121) referred to the desert as a "sublime form that banishes all sociality," a "suspended eternity," whose "definition is absolute" and whose frontier is "initiatory;" for him, the desert is "void of all meanings." The residents of Black Rock City inscribe meaning into this liminoid surface through their offertory rites. As Crace (1998) made so poignantly evident in his mystical novel, the desert has long served as a sacred site of personal transfiguration and social transformation. The entire culture of Black Rock City, from artifact to ideology, is dedicated to immolation. The ordeal that must be suffered in arriving at and surviving in the desert, the shedding of former lives and forging of new personae, the constant circulation of gifts, the exaltation of artistic process in creation and destruction, and the ever-present consummation of fire all serve to keep the practice of sacrifice uppermost in resident's lives. The very etymology of immolation—a sprinkling of holy grits—inscribes itself on the body of every participant, as the alkalai dust of the desert works itself deep into pores, scalps, membranes, and orifices, not to mention clothing and other possessions. The reverential "leave no trace" dwelling ethic enforced by residents protects against the burn scars and pollution the desert must inevitably suffer as a consequence of such commerce, and is often couched in ecotheistic language. The universal greeting, extended even to "newbies" (i.e., "Welcome Home"), paints the desert in religious tones, religion being etymologically a binding back to the source. Every aspect of everyday life, from walking to sitting, cooking to eating, and bathing to sleeping, reminds residents of their literal grounding in the desert. A technoaesthetic installation of revolving mirrors permits individuals to absorb a panoptic view of the desert that contains them, a kind of tethered spaceship

earth experience that fills participants with a sense of indwelling even as they inhabit the site.

CONCLUSIONS

Fire festivals are common across time and cultures, and are generally linked to a liturgical calendar grounded in nature. It is difficult not to read the Burning Man
Project against its own ideological grain, and link its Labor Day week timing to the
ethos of the event, a manifestation of synchronicity rather than coincidence. Four
*P*s seem to animate these festivals: purification, productivity, protection, and pro-
pitiation. Further, (giant) human effigies are often burned at these festivals.
Whether interpreted as a ritual reenactment of a dying god, or as a sublimated survival of the days of human sacrifice (Frazer, 1974), some kind of exorcism appears
to be at work. The holocaust features as a species of scapegoat. The sacrifice af-
fords personal and communal (if not cosmological) renewal to those willing to participate in its consummation.

    If an *axis mundi* can be said to exist in Black Rock City, it passes through the
Man. This altar is cosmogonic in so far as it encodes symbolism of world creating
and integration of time. As both the highest point and sacred center of the temporary community, it has geomantic properties as well. The Man is venerated by residents as an aspect of their "nostalgia for paradise" (Eliade, 1958, p. 385), a kind of
prelapsarian, tribal vision of utopia returning humans to a sacred source. The Man
is at once a sentinel and a portal, permitting communicants to cross over to the
realm of exalted experience. The Man stands as a kind of cosmic koan, a public
proposal whose resolution lies in the pondering of human sacrifice.

    Even acknowledging explicitly the playful interpenetration of pastiche and
parody occurring across the altars of Black Rock City, the sacralization of the secular in the celebration of alterity is unmistakable. Collectively, the altars are manifestations of what might be called the comedy of the commons, the essence of
Burning Man. Comedic techniques of satire, irony, and caricature are everywhere
at play in Black Rock City (Koestler, 1949). Authentic comic activity involves sacrifice and feast, debate and passion; it is a "triumph over mortality" via faith in "rebirth, restoration and salvation" (Sypher, 1956, p. 37). The essence of comedy is
"religious and ribald, knowing and defiant, social and freakishly individual"
(Langer, 1953, p. 331). The mythos of comedy involves reversal of social standards and a rebellion against the status quo; the disruption of order always recalls a
utopia (Frye, 1957, p. 171). The carnivalesque ethos of the Burning Man Project is
evident (Bahktin, 1988). Each of the residents of Black Rock City becomes a sacred clown.

    In their workaday lives, back in the world, communicants largely employ an
orientation to the cosmos Tambiah (1990) called "causality": a principally cogni-

tive, distanced, neutral, and analytic posture. In Black Rock City, as sacred clowns, they display an orientation he called "participation": a principally affective, holistic, configurational grasp of a mythic landscape (Tambiah, 1990). Residents transform the desert into sacred geography through sympathetic immediacy, performative speech acts, and ritual, which are enacted to exorcise the enervating, entropic, alienating effects of mundane experience (Tambiah, 1990, p. 107). The altar is the foundational locus of relationships of contiguity, contact, existential immediacy, and shared affinities (Tambiah, 1990, p. 106) that characterize the Burning Man Project at large. The altar in its sheer physicality is an artifact possessed of reflexive power, allowing communicants to reconstitute experience, to offer their gifts of being and presence (Richardson, 2001). The altar is a microcosm of the event.

REFERENCES

Bahktin, M. (1988). *Rabelais and his world*. Bloomington, IN: Indiana University Press.

Baudrillard, J. (1988). *America*. New York: Verso.

Belk, R., Wallendorf, M., & Sherry, J. F., Jr. (1989). The sacred and profane in consumer behavior: Theodicy on the Odyssey. *Journal of Consumer Research, 16*(1), 1–38.

Bey, H. (1994). *Immediatism*. Edinburgh Scotland: AK Press.

Biedermann, H. (1992). *Dictionary of symbolism: Cultural icons and the meaning behind them*. New York: Meridian.

Chester, L. (2000). *Holy personal: Looking for small private places of worship*. Bloomington, IN: Indiana University Press.

Crace, J. (1998). *Quarantine*. New York: Picador.

Eliade, M. (1958). *Patterns in comparative religion*. New York: Meridian.

Frazer. J. (1974). *The golden bough*. New York: Macmillan.

Frye, N. (1957). *The anatomy of criticism*. Princeton, NJ: Princeton University Press.

Grimes, R. (1990). *Ritual criticism: Case studies in its practice, essays on its theory*. Columbia, SC: University of South Carolina Press.

Koestler, A. (1949). *Insight and outlook*. New York: Macmillan.

Kozinets, R. V. (2002). Can consumers escape the market? Emancipatory illuminations from Burning Man. *Journal of Consumer Research, 29*(1), 20–38.

Kozinets, R. V. (2003). The moment of infinite fire. In S. Brown & J. F. Sherry, Jr. (Eds.), *Time, space, and the market: Retroscapes rising*. New York: M. E. Sharpe.

Kozinets, R. V., & Sherry, J. F., Jr. (in press-a). Dancing on Common Ground. In G. St. John (Ed.), *Rave ascension: Youth, technoculture and religion*. London: Berg.

Kozinets, R. V., & Sherry, J. F., Jr. (in press-b). You will be filled with Other: Constructing (con)temporary community at Burning Man. In L. Gilmore & M. Van Proyen (Eds.), *Afterburn: A research anthology*. New York: Routledge & Kegan Paul.

Langer, S. (1953). *Feeling and form*. New York: Scribner's.

Long, C. (2001). *Spiritual merchandise: Religion, magic and commerce*. Knoxville, TN: University of Tennessee Press.

McMann, J. (1998). *Altars and icons: Sacred spaces in everyday life*. San Francisco: Chronicle Books.

Radin, P. (1987). *The trickster: A study in American Indian mythology*. New York: Schocken.

Richardson, M. (2001). The gift of presence: The act of leaving artifacts at shrines, memorials and other tragedies. In P. Adams, S. Hoelscher, & K. Till (Eds.), *Textures of place: Exploring humanist geographies* (pp. 257–272). Minneapolis, MN: University of Minnesota Press.

Schechner, R. (1985). *Between theatre and anthropology*. Philadelphia: University of Pennsylvania Press.

Sherry, J. F., Jr. (2003). Bespectacled and bespoken: The view from throne zone and five o'clock and head. In S. Brown & J. F. Sherry, Jr. (Eds.), *Time, space, and the market: Retroscapes rising* (pp. 19–34). New York: M. E. Sharpe.

Sherry, J. F., Jr. (2000). Place, technology and representation. *Journal of Consumer Research, 27*(2), 273–278.

Sherry, J. F., Jr., & Schouten, J. (2002). A role for poetry in consumer research. *Journal of Consumer Research, 29*(2), pp. 218–234.

Simic, C. (2001). The altar. In *Night picnic* (p. 25). New York: Harcourt Brace

St. John, G. (2001). Alternative cultural heteropia and the liminoid body: Beyond Turner at ConFest. *Australian Journal of Anthropology, 12*(1), 47–66.

Sypher, W. (1956). The meanings of comedy. In R. Corrigan (Ed.), *Comedy: Meaning and form* (pp. 18–60). Scranton, PA: Chandler.

Taussig, M. (1993). *Mimesis and alterity: A particular history of the senses*. New York: Routledge & Kegan Paul.

Turner, K. (1999). *Beautiful necessity: The art and meaning of women's altars*. New York: Thames & Hudson.

Tambiah, S. (1990). *Magic, science, religion, and the scope of rationality*. New York: Cambridge University Press.

Part VI

Afterword

14

Interesting Stuff:
A Commentary on *Contemporary Consumption Rituals*

Dennis W. Rook
University of Southern California

I read the chapters included in this collection with atypical enthusiasm. In selecting which one to read next, I sometimes felt like I was looking at a 2-pound Godiva
chocolate sampler. Am I in the mood for binge drinking rituals, or for public disrobement in the streets of New Orleans? Or perhaps a baby shower? This was fun,
and it made for several intellectually stimulating days. When I finished reading all
the chapters, I came to the following conclusions.

RITUALS ARE RIVETING

When I completed my reading, my omnibus reaction was "Wow, what an interesting assemblage of material." This reaction is similar to the feelings I experienced
frequently 20 years ago, when I began working on my dissertation about ritualized
consumption under Sidney Levy's guidance. The literature was vast, and spanned
the anthropological, sociological, and psychological fields; it also extended far
back in time. Ultimately, I discovered that rituals were riveting phenomena, both in
their own right, and certainly in comparison to the more narrowly circumscribed
information-processing experiments that dominated the consumer research field
at the time.

Looking back, it seems odd how frequently I had to defend the relevance of rituals to skeptical scholars. Reading this volume leaves no doubt about the significant
social, psychological, and cultural impact of consumption rituals on people's lives,
all over the world. The marketplace significance of rituals is also striking. Consumers' participation in holiday, event-driven, familial, religious, workplace, and
transition rituals trigger huge expenditures with predictable regularity. But, what
would the economy be like without such extensive involvements in ritual-related

315

consumption? In addition to such obvious and broad sources of significance, it is hard to imagine a more truly interesting perspective for studying consumption behavior. Scanning across the diverse studies here, one appreciates the juicy behavioral ingredients that constitute the recipes of these rituals: *communitas*, cathexis, catharsis, uncertainty, anxiety, liminality, numenescence, lots of shopping, voracious consumption, and occasional nudity. All of this stimulates the following thoughts about ritual behavior generally, and specifically the contributions of the chapters herein.

RITUALS ARE ALIVE

A theme that runs across all the chapters in this collection is the organic and dynamic nature of rituals. As enduring products of human endeavor, rituals arise in the cultural stew, and grow, elaborate, mutate, petrify, and endure or fade away. This aspect of ritual behavior has long intrigued me, and reminds me of a somewhat traumatic event that occurred during my doctoral studies at Northwestern. Seeing her work cited in several chapters triggered my memory of an occasion when I met Mary Douglas to discuss the evolutionary nature of rituals, and to see if she might consider being on my dissertation committee. Her office was across the street from Kellogg's buildings, and after making an appointment, I entered it with anxious enthusiasm. Things did not go very well. I raised an issue that troubled me in some of the social science literature on ritual. Specifically, more than a few scholars concluded that the ritual pool was drying up, and rituals were disappearing from postmodern, secular societies. I thought this was pretty much nonsense, and explained my perspective. Unfortunately, Professor Douglas seemed to agree with the rituals-in-retreat thinking, and suggested all the good ones were dying or dead. I countered with, "What about Super Bowl Sunday?," and she pretty much dismissed me, and declined to serve on my committee.

Undoubtedly, some rituals were dying in 1981. Memorial Day, for example, had evolved (or devolved) from the sacred role that Lloyd Warner depicted in *The Living and the Dead*, to its contemporary start-of-the-summer holiday function. Time provided increasing distance from the tragedies of war, and community parades and large-scale ceremonies have gradually decreased. Yet, the Memorial Day holiday today still ceremonially commemorates veterans' deaths, but layers onto it a more immediate and upbeat agenda about barbeque parties, summer shopping, and home improvement projects. Similarly, modern science and technology have made ancient nature-control rituals (e.g., dance ceremonies and sacrificial offerings) seem a somewhat silly attempt to induce rain. Cloud seeding is generally more effective. Yet, as these articles vividly demonstrate, rituals evolve today perhaps more frequently than ever, and like marketplace products, some eventually fail, and others arise in their place. The ritual studies in this volume falsify the notion that rituals are receding from the scene.

The majority of these studies investigate classic *rites de passage*: weddings, births, marriage dissolution, and death. Together they demonstrate the dynamic, evolutionary aspects of ritual, which contrasts with the view that rituals are unchanging in practice and meaning. We learn, for example, how the content of Turkish marriage dowries has expanded from needlework to items that reflect the country's economic development and urbanized cultural direction (Sandıkcı & İlhan). Some higher status urban women do not even bother with learning how to sew, but simply outsource production of the traditional dowry artifacts, which allows them to concentrate on newer and more important dowry items such as household appliances, consumer electronics, and real estate. The evolution of wedding rituals is also vividly illustrated in the chapter on the complicated cross-cultural negotiations that arise when two individuals from different cultures decide to get married, which is an increasing global phenomenon (Nelson & Deshpande, chap. 7). Some might view variation in a ritual's artifactual and scripted content as indicators of its deterioration. I believe a more compelling perspective interprets such changes as signs of its resilience, adaptability, and vitality.

The chapters also illustrate how totally new rituals emerge within cultural substrata, renewing the ritual pool. Chapter 13 by Sherry and Kozinets on the Burning Man Project takes us to ground zero of this bizarre, amorphous, neo-pagan, individualistic annual desert celebration. The lack of modern plumbing facilities makes this ritual unappealing to me, but the article documents its increasing popularity. It also suggests an uptick in pagan practices. Several years ago, the World Council of Churches allowed pagan workshops for the first time, and these sessions were by far the best attended, which caused the council's governing body to rule against further pagan participation. Although it is less perfectly new than the Burning Man Project, Mardi Gras celebrations have in recent years added new ritual elements, particularly public disrobement, as Shrum (chap. 3) describes and interprets. Like products, rituals can enter the cultural marketplace as entirely new, or as new-and-improved offerings. Staying with a market metaphor, one chapter in particular points to how studying ritual behavior leads to the identification of new ritual development opportunities. In sharp contrast to the highly developed portfolio of wedding-related rituals, individuals are far more on their own when it comes to marital separation and divorce, as Marcoux's study (chap. 12) reveals.

"RITUAL" IS A BIG HOUSE

Several authors note or imply the lack of common agreement about the definition and domain of "ritual." Some suggest that it should only apply to large-scale, public, highly ceremonial events, not to either everyday or individualistic activities. The chapters herein, taken together, constitute an argument for a broad conceptualization of ritual behavior. Some do focus on large-scale annual rituals such as

Mardi Gras and the Burning Man Project. Others examine classic *rites de passage*, whereas still others investigate rituals that materialize within the immediate family in dowry preparation, heirloom transfer, spousal separation, and small-group drinking rituals. As Curasi, Arnould, and Price (chap. 11) suggested, a single definition of "ritual" is unlikely to accommodate all the behavioral variation that ritual performance involves. Historically, *rites de passage* are ritual's prototypic form, but as cognitive studies have discovered, any particular manifestation of a category is likely to exhibit only a relatively small number of its prototypic features. Still, as these chapters demonstrate, rituals do tend to have similar structural and content similarities, which appear in their artifactual content, behavioral roles and scripting, and relevant audience. And there is almost always the aspect of transition, whether the ritual occurs in public or private space, or on a large or smaller scale. This notwithstanding, there are abundant opportunities for conceptual progress. Interesting future work might profit from investigating the fuzzy borders between habitual and ritualized behaviors. Another issue that has received little attention is the situation in which a ritual has become stiffly formal and "ritualistic," which is typically indicative of its deterioration.

RITUALS CAN BE A DRAG

A few years ago I was sitting around a hotel pool bar in Bali, and business was slow. I began chatting with the bartender's assistant, a young man who was eager to talk about the cruise industry. Indonesians constitute a large percentage of cruise ship employees, and their employment provides an opportunity for working-class individuals to save enough money over a 2- or 3-year stint to return to Indonesia with seed money for college, a business start-up, or more frivolous consumption. This guy had a plan: He was trying to get to Miami, and needed about $1,000 U.S. The cruise line he had contacted would guarantee him an employment contract, and put him to work immediately, but he was financially responsible for getting to Miami. The problem, as he put it, were "all these damn rituals." As soon as he had saved up some money, a relative would solicit a donation for an upcoming cremation, tooth filing ceremony, or other ritual occasion. The Balinese culture is ritually intensive, so donation requests were frequent, and the young man was despairing about his chances of ever working on a cruise ship.

This theme appears in several chapters. Ruth's (chap. 9) study of gift exchange rituals in the workplace is to the point. This relatively new secular ritual seems to have a life of its own, and materialized in various forms: office holiday gift exchanges, employee birthday celebrations, secretary's week, retirement parties, and so on. The growth of these rituals has occurred despite their many annoying aspects. Who wants to buy something for someone you may not even like? Who wants to risk offending the boss, or disappointing a colleague? And who has enough time for all the shopping required? Even sacred rituals such as weddings generate more than a little grumbling about their expense, planning, and negotiation requirements, which increase when they involve cross-cultural participants (Nelson & Desphande, chap. 7). Seemingly sweet little baby showers induce all sorts of front and back stage anxieties and oppressive expectations, as Wooten and Wood (chap. 10) illustrate.

I guess it would be naïve to expect uniform sentiment about behavior systems that are so complex, involving, and extended. After all, many rituals transit the basic cultural dialectics: sacred–profane, insider–outsider, nature–civilization, boy/girl–man/woman, and others. How could the resulting tension not generate waves of ambivalence? And as the editors of this collection brought to our attention several years ago, ambivalence is interesting too.

Author Index

Note: *n* indicates footnote, *t* indicates table

A

Acitelli, L., 182, *209*
Alden, D., 214, *234*
Alexander, V. S., 64*n*
Allen, C., 280, *288*
Allen, V., 219, *233, 235*
Amit, V., 272, *286*
Andersen, H. C., 101, *120*
Anderson, D. A., 71*n*, 73*n*
Anderson, R., 125, *148*
Andsager, J., 17, *19*
Arat, Z., 153, *174*
Armitage, S. H., 72*n*
Arnold, S., 99, 117, *121*, 206, *209*
Arnould, E. J, xx, *xxv*, 100, 118, *120, 122*, 150, 159, 165, 167, *176, 177, 178, 261*, 238, 239, 240, 241, 243, 246, 247, 248, 249, 252, 258, 261, *264*
Auriol, G., 270, *289*
Austin, E., 17, *19*

B

Bahktin, M., 309, *310*
Bailey, M., 74*n*
Baker, M., 194, *209*
Banarjee, K., 150, 151, 155, *174*
Banks, S., 214, 215, 224, 227, 231, *234*
Banner-Haley, C. P. T., 75*n*
Baradar, M., 79*n*

Baraka, I. A., 65*n*, 69*n*, 70*n*
Barber, E., 125, 144, *148*
Barker, D., 127, *147*
Bator, R., 185, 192, 201, 203, *209*
Baudrillard, J., 308, *310*
Baxter, L., 200, *208*
Beck, U., 149, *174*
Belk, R., xx, *xxv*, 112, 120, *120*, 126, 129, *147*, 150, 159, 164, 167, *175*, 181, 191, 194, 197, 199, 202, 203, *208, 209*, 214, 220, 224, 226, 227, 233, *234*, 238, 239, 240, 241, 243, 254, 260, *262, 264*, 271, 279, 283, *286, 288*, 294, *310*
Bell, C., 125, 126, 147, *147*, 239, 241, *262*
Beltramini, R., xxi, *xxv*, 181, *209*
Bennett, W., 87, *97*
Berger, J., 87, *97*, 100, *120*
Berry, J., 132, *147*
Bettelheim, B., 102, *120*
Bey, H., 292, 293, *310*
Beyer, J., 181, 183, 195, 197, 205, *211*
Bhopal, K., 150, 155, *175*
Biedermann, H., 298, *310*
Bih, H., 279, *287*
Billig, M., 151, *175*
Birkhauser-Oeri, S., 102, *120*
Blau, P., 128, 145, *147*
Blumberg, H., 219, *234*
Boas, F., 42, *57*

321

Subject Index

Note: *f* indicates figure, *t* indicates table

Rite, Ritual → Routine
- definitions
- ritual
  - parts (How)
  - why (Driver)
  - examples of expression
- codify vs other ritual

- Change agent (pg. 44)

advanced
beauty
"I should have
Stopped that as"

LaVergne, TN USA
21 January 2010
170795LV00007B/40/P

9 780805 847796